Database Systems Engineering

Database Systems Engineering

Nick Ryan
Dan Smith

INTERNATIONAL THOMSON COMPUTER PRESS

I(T)P   An International Thomson Publishing Company

London • Bonn • Boston • Johannesburg • Madrid • Melbourne • Mexico City • New York • Paris
Singapore • Tokyo • Toronto • Albany, NY • Belmont, CA • Cincinnati, OH • Detroit, MI

Database Systems Engineering

I(T)P   A division of International Thomson Publishing Inc.
         The ITP logo is a trademark under licence

British Library Cataloguing-in-Publication Data
A catalogue record for this book is available from the British Library

First printed 1995

Commissioning Editor: Samantha Whittaker

Made in Logotechnics CPC Ltd., Sheffield

Printed in the UK by Cambridge University Press

ISBN   1-85032-115-9

International Thomson Computer Press
Berkshire House
High Holborn
London WC1V 7AA
UK

International Thomson Computer Press
20 Park Plaza
14th Floor
Boston MA 02116
USA

Imprints of International Thomson Publishing

CONTENTS

PREFACE

Effective data- and knowledge-based systems must firstly be designed to capture the complex semantics and behaviour of advanced applications in engineering, geographical, embedded and real-time applications, and in the rapidly expanding multimedia systems area. Secondly, these systems must offer adequate performance and reliability to support what are often mission-critical applications. Thirdly, in order to construct working systems that take advantage of advanced systems architectures a grasp of the fundamental techniques and algorithms is needed.

The approach here is to show how straightforward techniques for logical and physical design can be used to reason about the many complex issues and trade-offs involved in designing and implementing data-intensive systems. This view provides the central theme of the book, linking the different sections and unifying the treatments of logical design, physical design and implementation.

The principal themes developed in this book are:

- the description of the core elements of database technology in terms of their principles and implementation techniques;
- the use of parallel and distributed systems;
- the integration of physical and logical design activities;
- the development of data-intensive systems and applications for a wide variety of non-traditional database applications areas.

Organization of the book

The book is divided into four parts:

Part I, which comprises the first two chapters, provides background material which is necessary for a proper appreciation of the topics described in later chapters, outlining the relationships between database management systems, modern hardware and software environments.

Database systems have long been associated with business data processing applications such as stock control and order processing. The benefits of the database approach, including security, reliability and the independence of logical and physical views of data, are well established. There is now considerable interest in extending these benefits to a much wider range of applications. We describe how the requirements of conventional business applications have shaped the capabilities of established DBMSs, before considering the demands of a number of applications areas that are influencing the development of current systems.

Chapter 2 describes the hardware environment within which modern database systems operate. The emphasis of the chapter is on the organization and technology of the storage hierarchy.

Part II is devoted to database design. We describe methods for designing the logical schema, encompassing data, functional and behavioural aspects. These are followed by chapters on physical design and performance evaluation.

In Chapter 3 we first describe the principal abstractions for conceptual data modelling: classification, aggregation and generalization. This is followed by a treatment of Extended Entity Relationship modelling. The third part of the chapter describes data modelling methods, emphasizing structured transformations to achieve successive refinements of an initial model. A brief outline of normalization, used as a model-checking technique, concludes the chapter.

Chapter 4 comprises, first, a description of data-oriented functional modelling using Data Flow Diagrams and the development of large functional models by refinement and levelling. We then describe selected object-oriented methods which are applicable to database design. The final section describes joint functional and data modelling.

Chapter 5 is devoted to a discussion of (event-ordered) behaviour modelling. A discussion of behavioural concepts is followed by a description of techniques for modelling integrity, procedural and timing constraints in data-intensive environments; the focus is on statecharts. Second, methods for developing behavioural models based on statecharts are described. We next describe interaction diagrams and decision tables. The chapter concludes with a discussion of approaches to the integration of behavioural models with data and functional models.

Performance is a vital aspect of most data-intensive applications, but is frequently neglected until late in the design process. In Chapter 6 we describe simple physical design methods derived from an analysis of the fundamental physical characteristics of data-intensive systems and illustrate their use with extensive examples.

In Chapter 7 we describe the principal approaches to performance measurement and estimation, and show how they can be incorporated into the wider design process. Most of the second half of the chapter is devoted to a discussion and analysis of database benchmarks and benchmarking techniques.

Part III is devoted to the software technology on which database management systems are built. The physical design and performance issues discussed in the latter chapters of Part II are determined by the technological constraints and trade-offs discussed in these chapters.

In Chapter 8 we describe the main storage access methods used by conventional DBMSs. These are essentially one-dimensional, providing access to stored data on the basis of a single key. The application of database technology to the management of spatial, scientific and CAD data brings with it the need for efficient access using multi-dimensional search keys. Several suitable methods are described.

Chapter 9 concentrates on the issues, problems and trade-offs encountered in the development of scalable systems capable of representing and manipulating large amounts of procedural and rule-based information. The provision of rules, stored procedures and event triggers is an important feature of many recent database systems. We first discuss Event–Condition–Action rule systems and how they can be used to provide the event-ordered behavioural functionality needed for active database systems. When combined with stored procedures these provide a method of directly incorporating behaviour in a database. In the second part we cover deductive rules and their use in developing large knowledge-based systems. The use of ECA and deductive rules has been the focus of intensive research over the past decade and this work is now being implemented in commercial systems, which are briefly described here.

All database systems must provide mechanisms to ensure that the database remains consistent when it is updated by multiple users. In Chapter 10 we discuss the concept of atomic transactions which, in conventional database applications, are typically of very short duration. The second half of the chapter describes mechanisms for maintaining consistency, concentrating on locking, and a discussion of methods for dealing with the special problems of distributed transactions. This is followed by a discussion of the particular problems encountered with applications such as CAD where individual transactions may last for several hours or more.

In Chapter 11 an outline of the concepts underlying reliability and its scope is followed by a description of conventional log-based recovery, showing the effects of the choice of logging strategy on recovery operations. We focus on the concepts and technology for fault tolerance. The use of large memory in simplifying and reducing the overhead imposed by reliability mechanisms is covered. The next section describes commit protocols, paying particular attention to distributed and long transactions. The final section describes basic shadowing and replication issues, focusing on RAID technology.

Chapter 12 begins with a discussion of techniques used to split complex queries into multiple simple operations. Next we describe methods of implementing these low-level operations. The efficiency of query processing algorithms is crucial to the performance of a DBMS. There may be several different ways in which a complex query can be performed and in the second half of the chapter we concentrate on optimization techniques used to choose an efficient execution plan.

Part IV is devoted to descriptions of the data models, query language and architectures employed in current database management systems.

Chapter 13 provides a summary of the structural and operational aspects of the relational model. The model is presented as an extensible framework in preparation for the material covered in the subsequent chapters.

SQL is now 'intergalactic dataspeak'. In Chapter 14 we describe the syntax and usage of the current standard, SQL 2. This chapter provides a tutorial approach to the language, including an extensive description of embedded programming and Dynamic SQL.

In Chapters 15 and 16 we describe the two main approaches to the development of data management systems capable of supporting the diverse needs of modern applications. Object-oriented systems were developed initially in response to the needs for secure, reliable and persistent storage systems to support applications written using object-oriented programming languages. At the same time, database system developers were examining methods of extending the relational model to cater for a wider range of applications. These chapters provide a discussion of both approaches, emphasizing their similarities and shared objectives.

The rapidly increasing use of parallel machines poses a challenge to the designers and implementors of database management systems. In Chapter 17 we show how parallel systems can be classified and describe the main design choices involved in parallel DBMS, drawing on the literature and the authors' experience. Next we describe the more loosely coupled environment of distributed DBMS, concentrating on conventional distributed applications, and client–server systems and their application in multimedia and engineering applications. The final section describes the principal features of federated database systems.

The annotated bibliography contains a selected list of the principal works treating the material covered in the book, works cited, and important descriptions of systems and prototypes.

Readership

The anticipated readership for this book is:

- advanced students (undergraduate and graduate) taking data and knowledge base management courses;
- practitioners designing and developing data-intensive and multimedia systems;
- software engineers and computer scientists needing an overview of modern data management technology and design methods.

For a first course on database systems we suggest the material in Chapters 1 and 2 to provide a suitable background. For most courses it would be best followed by the data modelling material in Chapter 3 and the first part of Chapter 4, covering Data Flow Diagrams, giving students the basics of conceptual database design. Selected material from Chapter 6, on the physical design, completes an introduction to design issues. For this audience we suggest following the design material with Chapters 13 and 14, to cover the relational model and SQL.

In an advanced course we would explore database functional and behavioural modelling in more depth, using the material from Chapter 5 and the second part of Chapter 4. We firmly believe that an appreciation of database server technology is an essential prerequisite to building high-quality modern database applications and so a substantial portion of our advanced database courses is devoted to the topics covered in Part III. Our suggestion for the final part of an advanced course builds on this foundation by examining extended relational and object-oriented data models, and parallel and distributed architectures.

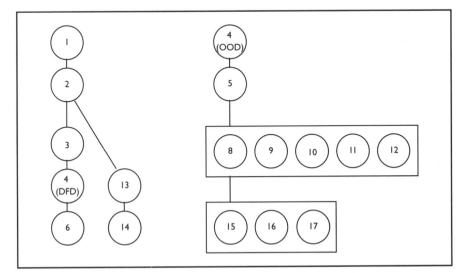

Suggested use of this book for (a) a first course, (b) an advanced course in database systems.

We believe that, for professionals and practitioners, the material covered in Parts II and III provides a concise description of current design and implementation techniques. In particular, the physical design and performance-related discussions of Chapters 6, 7 and 8 draw together relevant material from a number of contexts. This is complemented by the description of data models in Part IV.

Acknowledgements

Many people have helped and encouraged us in writing this book. In particular we would like to acknowledge the help of our colleagues, especially Luke Fitzgerald, Peter Dearnley and Peter Stocker for suggesting improvements, although we retain full responsibility for the faults. We thank our students for their constructive comments on early versions of some chapters. Austin Wade deserves special thanks for his work on the implementation of TPC-C at UEA. Our families have suffered our preoccupation and unavailability; without their tolerance it would not have been possible. Finally, the encouragement of our editor, Sam Whittaker, has been invaluable.

Norwich,
Halloween 1994

Part I

INTRODUCTION

Chapter 1

PRELIMINARIES

We begin by outlining some of the limitations of conventional file-based applications when applied to large organizations and large collections of data. These limitations provide much of the motivation for the database approach to data management which is described in Section 1.2.

The history of database design methods has been one of ever-closer integration between the treatments of static data and dynamic processes. In Section 1.3 we discuss the major influences on the development of modern design methods and provide an introduction to the techniques described in Part II of this book. Section 1.4 describes the facilities provided by typical modern database systems, and the distinctions between centralized and distributed databases are discussed in Section 1.5.

For many years database systems have been used predominantly for a limited range of commercial and administrative applications. The earliest systems were employed as a basis for batch-oriented 'data processing'. In due course this role was extended to cover interactive information systems. Today, information system requirements are becoming increasingly complex with many modern systems being expected to support a much wider range of data types. The final part of the chapter provides an introduction to the requirements of today's increasingly complex information systems and to the widening range of applications of database systems.

1.1   The motivation for database systems

Any complex set of data can serve multiple purposes and may be viewed from many different perspectives. The management tasks of an enterprise might be divided between areas such as personnel, research and development, planning, production, finance and sales. Each of these areas needs to interact with and shares some of its information requirements with one or more of the others.

However, this overlap in departmental requirements is only partial. Each will have a different view of the data and information needs of the organization. Some of this data will need to be shared and some will remain private to the different departments. For example, both personnel and finance departments may need access to information about employees. Both need basic details such as name, address, current job and date of birth, but information about salary and taxation will be treated as confidential with access limited to those responsible for the payroll. Details of a person's employment or training history might be maintained by the personnel department and, although normally less sensitive, are unlikely to be of interest to the pay office.

Similarly, in a hospital, information about a patient's admission, treatment and discharge would be used and updated by a wide range of staff, both administrative and medical. Although both groups need to collaborate at various stages throughout the patient's stay in hospital, their tasks and hence information requirements are quite different. Again, some information such as detailed medical records should only be available to appropriate medical staff. Other information, such as when patients were admitted, which ward they are in, when they are to undergo particular tests or an operation and when they are to be discharged, are needed by both administrative and medical staff.

In both of these cases there is a conflict between the need to share common data and for adequate security measures to limit access to authorized users. Early file-based systems often developed in piecemeal fashion, attempting to solve the information-handling requirements of the different parts of an organization with separate programs and data files. Separation satisfied the security requirement but prevented sharing, with the result that the common data items were often duplicated in several different files.

This duplication, or **data redundancy**, is a major source of problems in file-based systems. Inconsistency is inevitable because common data items are entered and updated separately. Changes are difficult to synchronize because most updates are performed manually. Even when additional programs are written simply to convert data from one storage format to another, there are delays as information is propagated through the separate systems.

Other problems arise from redundant processes. Several programs might perform the same operations on the same or different data files. This leads to considerable duplication of programming effort as each program has to be modified to cope with changes that affect file structures.

Application programs present external models of data and processes to their users. To achieve this they need:

- internal data structures;
- process models including rules governing the behaviour of the objects they manipulate;
- methods for converting between their own internal data structures and external physical storage structures.

Conventional file-based programs, whether they are using simple stream or record I/O or more advanced access methods, must contain descriptions of the stored record structure, available indexes and access methods.

Much of this information is necessarily duplicated through many programs and no single program has complete knowledge of the entire collection of data. Such applications are therefore highly dependent on the structure of their data files. Should it be necessary to add a new field to the records in a file, or to change the physical storage structure so that a different access method can be used, all programs that use the file must be modified before they can continue to read and write records.

Piecemeal development of information systems leads to severe data and system maintenance problems. Development is fragmented and it becomes impossible for anyone to have a clear understanding of the overall information needs of the organization. Keeping track of the interdependencies between data files and the applications that use them becomes increasingly difficult. Without central control of both data and applications and equally, if not more, importantly facilities to support such control, an increasing proportion of effort is devoted to maintaining old code, leaving fewer resources to work on new projects. Eventually something must break.

1.2   The database approach

A **database** is a coherent collection of related data. It represents a model of a particular domain of interest, often called the Universe of Discourse (UoD). The content of the collection is such that it supports those features of the UoD that are relevant to a defined set of purposes such as a suite of applications.

A database is self-describing because the data is held together with descriptions, known as metadata. Metadata descriptions may include simple type and size information, relationships between data items, simple internal constraints such as ranges of permitted values and more complex referential constraints. Although the term database is often used loosely to describe any coherent collection of data, the combination of data and metadata is implied throughout this book.

A **DataBase Management System (DBMS)** is a general-purpose software system that controls shared access to a database, and provides mechanisms that help to ensure the security and integrity of the stored data. The term **Database System (DBS)** is often used to describe the combination of DBMS and database.

The main requirements of a DBMS are to:

- Provide the means to define and construct a database. This includes support for links or relationships between related records, and for the storage of and access to metadata describing the contents of the database. The storage methods used should minimize redundancy in the stored data.
- Provide efficient and reliable shared access to the stored data. Access controls are required to limit read and write operations to authorized users. A transaction control mechanism is needed to maintain database consistency

while maximizing concurrent access. This ensures predictable behaviour when errors occur and when several users attempt to update the same data item.

- Support multiple views of a common data resource to suit the needs of different functional areas and applications. Data within such a view may correspond directly to stored data, or it may be virtual data: data derived from other items by a transformation function such as addition, counting, string concatenation or substring extraction.
- Maximize reliability and availability by provision of efficient backup and recovery systems. These should support normal archiving requirements and enable automated recovery from system failures, while having a minimal impact on normal system performance.
- Reduce the need for application maintenance by supporting a high level of independence between applications and the logical and physical structure of the database.
- Provide high-level tools to simplify application development.

These objectives can be summarized as simplifying both the construction and management of a shared data resource and the development and maintenance of the applications that use it. They have largely been achieved by the current generation of relational DBMSs. However, the increasing range of database applications discussed below in Section 1.6 introduces further requirements which are being addressed by the more recent development of extended relational, object-oriented and deductive database systems.

1.2.1 DBMS architecture

The classic model of database system architecture is known as the **ANSI/X3/SPARC architecture** after the standards committee that proposed it [Tsichritzis and Klug 1978], or more simply as the **three-level** or **three-schema architecture**. Whereas conventional programs interact with the underlying machine through the medium of the operating system, this architecture introduces three levels of abstraction between application programs and the stored data (Figure 1.1). The model was never formally adopted as a standard but it remains a firm basis for many of the above objectives. In particular it emphasizes support for multiple views of a shared data resource and maximizes independence between applications and stored data.

- **External schema, subschema or views**. A database may contain several logical models representing subsets of the database. Each view describes the data used in a single application area so, for example, there might be separate administrative and medical views that cover overlapping parts of the patient data within a much larger hospital database. Each external schema is derived from, and is a subset of, the overall conceptual schema.

- **Conceptual schema**. A single consistent logical model of the complete database. It contains metadata descriptions of all data stored in the database.
- **Internal schema.** This is the physical storage model containing information such as file locations, structures, indexing and access methods.

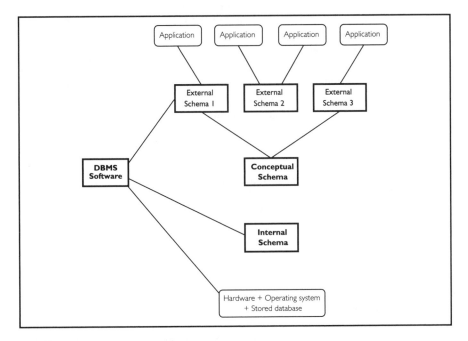

Figure 1.1 Three-level or three-schema DBMS architecture.

The DBMS connects each level of the system to the next and provides translation, or mapping, between the different models. The metadata descriptions of each schema level are stored in the database and used to support the mapping process.

Each application interacts with the DBMS using the data model presented by an external schema. Operations on this schema are translated into operations on the main conceptual schema. These in turn are translated into operations on the internal schema which is used by the DBMS to control interaction with the underlying machine and the physical database.

1.2.2   Data independence

The separation of the applications, the logical model and the physical model minimizes their dependence on each other and makes it possible to change one or other model with a minimum of disruption at other levels.

- **Logical data independence** is achieved by isolating applications from changes in the logical structure of the stored data. It is supported by the separation of external and conceptual levels. Changes to the conceptual schema such as adding a new class of records or adding a new field to an existing record type take place at the conceptual level. Applications that need to access these will use views that include the new data, but the views used by other applications remain unchanged.
- **Physical data independence** is achieved by isolating applications from changes in the organization of physical storage. It is supported by the separation of conceptual and internal levels. The conceptual schema is a logical model that takes no account of the way in which the data is stored. Details of physical storage layout, indexes and access methods are hidden in the internal schema, so a change in physical organization is invisible to the higher-level logical models.

Operating systems provide a limited degree of physical independence for conventional file-based programs by isolating them from the detailed working of the underlying hardware. The history of DBMS has been one of increasing logical and physical independence. Early systems based on the hierarchical and network models achieved limited levels of independence because of the close association between access paths and physical organization.

Relational systems introduced a higher degree of independence by the simple abstraction of modelling all data as equally accessible logical tables. Access paths (relationships) are represented by data values, rather than as part of the physical storage structure. Current systems provide a sufficient level of logical independence to isolate applications from minor changes to the conceptual schema, but there is still room for improvement. Techniques for managing schema evolution remain an important area of research in the more recent forms of database system.

1.3 Database design

During the 1970s and early 1980s, database design was invariably presented in terms of static representations of data. The functional and behavioural requirements of a system influenced data design but were seen primarily as inputs to a separate, only loosely related, process of application design. This separation of data representation (state) and process (behaviour) reflected contemporary approaches to system development, programming languages and data management systems.

Since then, the growth of 'structured' design methods such as SSADM [Ashworth and Goodland 1990] have emphasized a more holistic approach to system design. Such developments were part of a more general trend towards developing interactive information systems and away from the earlier generation of batch-oriented data processing systems.

Simple data modelling methods, notably Chen's Entity-Relationship (ER) model [Chen 1976], have been extended to express a more extensive range of the semantics of objects within the UoD, and to express them more precisely. The semantic data modelling approach [Hammer and McLeod 1981; Hull and King 1987] has had a significant influence on this development. More recently, object-oriented design methods such as those of Booch [1994] or Rumbaugh *et al.* [1991] have also been influential.

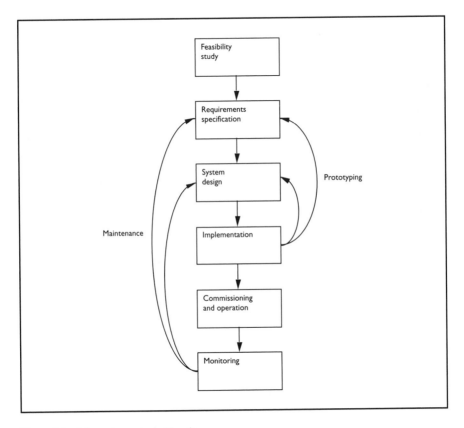

Figure I.2   Information systems lifecycle.

Developments in programming methods and languages, notably the functional and object-oriented paradigms, have influenced the development of new forms of DBMS. Systems based on the functional data model [Shipman 1981] have yet to attract much direct attention beyond the database research community. However, extended relational [Stonebraker *et al.* 1990a] and object-oriented database systems [Atkinson *et al.* 1989] are now in an early phase of commercial development. Despite their different origins and history these approaches share a concern with the management of objects, including both their state and behaviour, rather than simply with static data representation [Cattell 1991a]. These newer forms of DBMS also require more holistic approaches to system design.

In the second part of the book we present an approach to database design, incorporating data, functional and behavioural requirements of the system. This expansion of the scope of conventional database design strategies is essential to cope with the more complex and demanding requirements of modern applications (*see* Section 1.6). These frequently have significant interactions with their environments and need to capture systematically aspects of the application's functional and behavioural semantics.

The process of information systems development typically has six principal phases, a number of which have strong feedback relationships (Figure 1.2). The distinctions between the phases are often not rigid, although successful projects invariably have well-defined milestones and deliverables. In Chapters 3 to 5 we present techniques for data and functional design and methods for integrating them in order to meet the design requirements of modern applications. These chapters are concerned principally with the system design process and, to a lesser extent, with requirements specification. Chapter 6 is devoted to a discussion of physical design methods. Chapter 7 describes performance estimation techniques, emphasizing their importance in applications with significant timing constraints. These activities are related to both the system design and the monitoring phases of information systems development.

The concepts useful in this context fall into three groups: those concerned with the classification of data (entity, relationship), those concerned with activity (function, process and action) and those concerned with behaviour (conditions, constraints).

1.4   DBMS facilities

In this section we describe the main features provided by most modern DBMSs. Early systems needed to support the needs of the database administrator (DBA) and of the programmers responsible for producing applications and writing programs to generate reports. Modern systems must support the needs of a wider variety of users:

- The DBA, whose tasks cover implementing and maintaining both logical and physical designs, controlling access, monitoring performance and tuning physical storage structures, importing and exporting data, backup and recovery.
- Analysts and programmers who require tools to support design and rapid application development as well as conventional report generation.
- End users who require access to highly structured application interfaces developed by programmers and, increasingly, to tools that enable them to develop limited applications and reporting functions themselves.

I.4.I   *System catalogues and data dictionary*

At the core of any database system is a repository of data descriptions, or metadata. All information needed by the DBMS to control the mapping between external, conceptual and internal schemas is stored in a part of the database usually known as the **system catalogues**. In most cases, these catalogues only contain information required for the normal operation of the system.

Data dictionary systems have become established as desirable tools to support the design and documentation of databases. These are often closely integrated with the system catalogues and can be used to generate the database schema at the end of the design process. Although some DBMSs allow a limited amount of documentation to be stored in association with the system catalogues, most data dictionary systems are developed in-house by database users, or supplied by third parties.

I.4.2   *DBA utilities*

Most systems include a range of utility programs to support the implementation and maintenance tasks of the DBA. These include:

- Starting and stopping the system, and controlling user access to a running system.
- Authorization of users and granting of specific permissions, such as the ability to access a particular database.
- Data import and export facilities for bulk loading or unloading of data.
- Backup utilities which are used to dump an entire database to tape or other tertiary storage as an archive and as insurance against major failures.
- Performance monitoring utilities which allow the DBA to examine the load on the system and determine which users or processes may be imposing heavy demands on resources, and the behaviour of the concurrency control and automatic failure recovery mechanisms.

I.4.3   *Data Definition Language (DDL)*

All systems provide some form of data definition language to define and modify logical and physical data structures. Several forms are possible:

- A distinct special-purpose **schema definition language** used together with a schema compiler. Physical and logical definitions may be combined or divided between separate languages and compilers. This was the method used by most of the earlier generation of hierarchical and network model DBMSs.

- A subset of a general-purpose **query language**. This approach is typical of relational systems where data definition and manipulation are both part of a single, typically declarative, language such as SQL.
- An interactive forms-based interface that hides the complexity of the more normal command-based language. Many systems now provide such tools as an alternative means of data definition in addition to the more normal command language.
- An extension to a conventional programming language enabling definition of persistent data objects using essentially the same syntax as that used to declare ordinary, transient, program objects. This method is used in many object management systems where an object-oriented language such as C++ or Smalltalk is extended to include persistent classes and other features such as references to collections of stored objects.

1.4.4 Data Manipulation Language (DML)

Data manipulation languages enable input, retrieval and update operations on stored data. As mentioned in the previous section, the separation of DDL and DML may be artificial. In most relational DBMSs they form part of a single language, most commonly SQL.

DMLs may take one of several forms:

- As part of a declarative query language that may be used for *ad hoc* queries by end-users.
- As an **embedded** language where special-purpose data manipulation statements are embedded within a **host** program written in a conventional programming language.
- A general-purpose programming language may be extended to include data manipulation functions, thus forming a database programming language.
- As a special-purpose database programming language. They may be closely integrated with user-interface construction tools and may extend a declarative query language to provide computational completeness. Such languages are often referred to as **Fourth Generation Languages (4GL)** to distinguish them from conventional, or third generation, programming languages (3GL).
- As an **Application Programming Interface (API)**, typically provided as an add-on library of functions callable from a conventional programming language such as C.

The primary distinction here is between interactive query languages designed to be used by skilled end-users and **database programming languages** used by programmers or, in the case of some 4GLs, by end-users to construct applications. A modern DBMS typically supports both these approaches.

Query languages

One of the most significant results of the development of relational DBMS was the higher level of physical data independence achieved by the introduction of declarative query languages. A procedural language places an obligation on the user to select the most efficient sequence of operations to update or retrieve the required information. This is not possible without a considerable knowledge of both the structure and content of the database. Declarative languages enable this obligation to be transferred to the system which can then apply optimization techniques to determine an efficient way of executing each query.

With many earlier systems, developed before the growth of interactive computing, there was little demand for an interactive query capability. However, changing application requirements and the inevitable delays between identifying a need and the development of a program to address it have made *ad hoc* query facilities an indispensable part of many modern database systems. This in turn has contributed to the emergence of skilled end-users who are not wholly dependent on system development staff for their information needs.

Although a number of other query languages have been developed, the standard language for relational systems is SQL (Structured Query Language). SQL is an ANSI and ISO standard database query language providing both data definition and data manipulation statements. It was developed from a language originally called SEQUEL (Structured English QUEry Language) designed by an IBM research team as part of the experimental relational database project System R [Chamberlin *et al.* 1976]. It was later adopted as the query language for the IBM commercial systems SQL/DS and DB2.

The first ANSI standard for the language, now commonly known as SQL 0, was published in 1986 and adopted the following year. Subsequent revisions, SQL 1 in 1989 and SQL 2 in 1992, have extended the language and the process continues with the next version, SQL 3, which is currently in draft form.

At the time of writing, almost all major commercial systems support SQL 1 and most of these also comply with the SQL 2 standard (ANSI X3.135-1992, ISO/IEC 9075:1992) [ISO 1992]. However, the extent of compliance varies widely as the standards permits entry level, intermediate and full grades of conformance. In addition, commercial systems often include their own non-standard extensions, many of which will need to be modified to comply with the forthcoming SQL 3 standard.

The main features of SQL 2 are discussed in Chapter 14. Here we present two simple examples that illustrate the main features and the declarative form of the language. If information about hospital patients is stored in a logical table named *patient*, details of those patients admitted to a particular ward after a specified date might be retrieved by the following statement:

```
SELECT name, admission_date, condition
FROM patient
WHERE ward_name = 'Nightingale'
AND admission_date > '1994-12-31';
```

The SELECT clause specifies the columns that should appear in the result. These are derived from tables listed in the FROM clause. The WHERE clause indicates the conditions that should be applied to determine whether a row in the source tables should be used in the result. The result is another table, albeit a temporary one, containing the rows and columns specified in the query.

A more complex query involving several tables follows a similar pattern. Given a second table containing summary medical histories of patients which is linked to the patient table using a patient identifier, the above query might be extended to include details of each patient's history:

```
SELECT patient.name, patient.admission_date,
patient.condition,history.date, history.diagnosis,
history.treatment
FROM patient, history
WHERE patient.patient_id = history.patient_id
AND patient.ward_name = 'Nightingale'
AND patient.admission_date > '1994-12-31';
```

Here, the WHERE clause also contains a linkage or join condition that specifies how rows in the two columns should be combined.

In both cases the entire query is expressed in terms of the logical model and the query optimizer determines how best to execute the query. In doing so it will take account of the sizes of the tables, the physical storage methods used and whether indexes exist on any of the columns specified in the WHERE clause.

Query languages are intended to provide interactive access to internal database operations. They are, therefore, computationally incomplete because they do not support any form of flow control such as the conditional branching and looping constructs of conventional programming languages. Consequently they must be combined with other languages if they are to be used to construct complete programs.

Embedded or hosted data manipulation languages

Embedded data manipulation languages extend conventional programming languages by allowing database-specific commands to be included within a host program. Typically there is a small set of instructions to insert, retrieve, update and delete database records. In most cases the program code is preprocessed to translate these special-purpose instructions into conventional function or procedure calls in the host language.

An embedded DML may support **navigational access** where records are retrieved one at a time, perhaps iterating over a collection of records using a loop in the host program. This procedural approach allows other conventional program statements such as conditional branching or function calls to be executed between database operations. As a result, however, it provides a lower level of independence and limits the optimizations that can be applied by the system.

Expressed in pseudo-code, the patient admissions and histories example might be executed as follows:

```
patient.ward = 'Nightingale'
$FIND FIRST patient USING ward
while record found do
    $GET patient
    if patient.admission_date > '1994-12-31' then
        $FIND FIRST history WITHIN patient_history
        while record found do
            $GET history
            print patient.name, patient.admission_date,
                patient.condition, history.date,
                history.diagnosis, history.treatment
            $FIND NEXT history WITHIN patient_history
        end while
    end if
    $FIND NEXT patient USING ward
end while
```

The embedded language statements used here (those beginning with $) are based on the CODASYL DBTG proposal followed by most network model DBMSs. Details of error handling and status checking have been omitted for clarity. Record and field names are derived from the schema definition, which also serves to bind these names to program variables. A similar approach was also taken in most hierarchical system DMLs.

Relational systems almost invariably use **Embedded SQL** which, like the interactive form, is largely declarative and goes beyond data manipulation to support data definition statements. Depending on the environment that the system is expected to work in, Embedded SQL preprocessors may be supplied for a wide range of programming languages, including C, Pascal, FORTRAN, COBOL, Ada, PL/1 and MUMPS. As with the interactive language, the syntax is defined by the SQL standard, allowing developers to select a suitable host language for their problem domain. This avoids the need to learn new data access commands, and eases portability between different DBMSs.

However, because an SQL query returns a set of records, there is a conflict with the single-record-at-a-time processing style of conventional procedural programs. This problem is usually referred to as an impedance mismatch by analogy with problems in linking electronic circuits. As is often the case with electronic circuits, the solution involves additional components. The simplicity of the SQL query is offset by the need to deal with the table rows individually and to copy data between the result table structure and the program variables. These tasks add significantly to the complexity of the embedded language.

Embedded SQL uses a **cursor** which acts as a reference to the current row in the result table. The cursor is first declared together with the query it serves. This is simply a declaration and has no effect on the database. It is also necessary to enclose the declaration of any program variables that must be visible to database operations in an SQL declaration section:

```
EXEC SQL DECLARE pcursor CURSOR FOR
     SELECT  patient.name, patient.admission_date,
             patient.condition, history.date, history.diagnosis,
             history.treatment
     FROM patient, history
     WHERE patient.patient_id = history.patient_id
     AND patient.ward_name = 'Nightingale'
     AND patient.admission_date > '1994-12-31';
...
EXEC SQL BEGIN DECLARE SECTION;
     declare program variables pname, date_admitted,
                               pcondition, hdate, hdiagnosis,
                               htreatment
EXEC SQL END DECLARE SECTION;
```

Opening the cursor instructs the system to execute the query, after which the cursor refers to the first record in the result set. Data values are then copied from the table structure into program variables using the FETCH statement. When no more records are available, the cursor is closed:

```
EXEC SQL OPEN pcursor;
do
     EXEC SQL FETCH pcursor INTO
                          :pname,  :date_admitted, :pcondition,
                          :hdate,  :hdiagnosis,  :htreatment;
     if record found then
         print pname, date_admitted, pcondition,
               hdate, hdiagnosis, htreatment
     endif
while record found
EXEC SQL CLOSE pcursor;
```

The embedded SQL statements are those shown beginning with EXEC SQL. As before, details of error handling and status checking have been omitted for clarity.

In addition to this static form of the language in which query statements are explicitly coded in the program, there is also a dynamic form that allows arbitrary statements to be constructed at program run time. This and other aspects of the language are discussed more extensively in Chapter 14.

Database programming languages

There are several motivations for the development of database programming languages:

- simplifying application development by using a single, internally consistent, language;
- a desire to provide conventional programming languages with the benefits of persistence, transaction management and recovery systems;
- the impedance mismatch problem and the overhead in dealing with it. In the current relational approach complex objects must be assembled by joining data from many different tables. Here, an efficient navigational approach may be more appropriate than the set-oriented methods of relational languages.

One approach to satisfying the first of these is the use of Fourth Generation Languages. These are often extensions to existing query languages that add the necessary programming constructs needed for a computationally complete language. In addition they are usually tightly integrated with user-interface construction tools. This approach is discussed below.

Applications may also be simplified by extending the query language by adding support for the definition of stored procedures, rules and triggers. These are then stored in the database rather than being part of (possibly many) application programs. They are typically used to implement common aspects of a system's behaviour. As with 4GLs, parameter passing, looping and conditional branching are required to support stored procedures.

Triggers are a mechanism for initiating an action in response to an event such as an insert, update or delete on a stored record. The action might perform another database operation such as inserting a record elsewhere, or it may involve operations external to the database such as sending an electronic mail message to a user. Triggers may also be combined with simple rules of the form 'If <condition> then do <action>' in order to allow conditional execution of the required action. Procedures, triggers and rules are discussed in Chapter 9.

Other motivations for the development of database programming languages arise from attempts to extend the benefits of database systems to a wider range of applications. For a number of years two quite distinct approaches have been followed, but with related aims. The first involves extending the functionality of relational systems to improve support for a wider range of data types, including complex objects. The second comes from the object-oriented programming community who have recognized the benefits to be gained by the integration of programming languages with database functionality.

We briefly discuss the requirements of this wider range of applications in Section 1.6 and provide a more detailed discussion of extended relational, object-oriented and other evolving database models in Chapters 15 and 16.

Forms-based queries and Fourth Generation Languages (4GL)

Most modern DBMSs provide a forms-based interface as an alternative to the command-driven query language. Default forms may be generated automatically to match stored records, and in most cases there is also a form editor that can be used to design new forms or customize the default forms.

Forms may be used in a 'Query by Example' mode (QBE) in which the user enters required values to form a result skeleton [Zloof 1981]. The system generates a query based on these values, then retrieves and displays all records matching the skeleton. Other systems generalize this simple idea to work with both default and user-defined forms. A typical example designed for character displays is INGRES/QBF [INGRES 1991a]. Forms may be designed to work with multiple tables either by using a predefined external view, or by specifying the links between tables as a *JoinDef*. Once designed, these forms may be used to retrieve, update or delete records in the attached tables.

This approach is adequate for applications that allow users simply to browse, insert or update stored information. However, when the application must also perform some processing of the retrieved or user-entered data, further programming is required. In some cases this can be achieved by linking Embedded SQL programs with the database forms system, but a more widely used approach is to provide a special-purpose language. These languages are usually referred to as Fourth Generation Languages or 4GLs.

There is no general agreement on what features a 4GL should provide but several common features can be identified amongst the systems to which the label is applied. Typical 4GLs:

- Are self-contained 'high-level' database application building tools. They may include graphical or character-based form editors, program editors, design and documentation tools.
- Support a consistent user-interface style. For character-based displays this usually consists of forms containing editable fields, and a simple menu system. Systems designed for use in graphical user-interface (GUI) environments usually provide a much wider range of interface and control elements.
- Use conventional query language statements (typically SQL) to retrieve and update stored data, and provide additional language elements such as flow control so that they can be used to produce complete programs.
- May employ an 'event-driven' programming style. That is, programs consist of procedures that are executed in response to some event. Events may include key presses associated with menu items, entry to or exit from fields on a form, changing values in fields, and so on.
- May include application generators that can be used to create simple database programs. Where the application is intended simply to browse or update data without any specialized processing requirements, the program code and query language statements can be generated automatically from built-in templates. In some cases the templates can be customized to suit local requirements and

generated programs may be modified by a programmer. Graphical query editors may be used with application generators to enable end-users with little or no programming and query language expertise to develop simple programs.

Because they are designed specifically to support database access, some 4GLs are able to use a greatly simplified syntax to achieve similar results to Embedded SQL. These include automatic binding of database columns to fields on a form and hiding the use of a cursor by simply attaching a block of code to an SQL query.

An increasing emphasis on Management Information Systems (MIS) has meant that whereas users were once satisfied with weekly printed reports, they now require rapid access to up-to-date summary information about the state of their organization. Some 4GLs now provide facilities for displaying information as line graphs, bar or pie charts, while other systems enable data to be loaded directly from the database into spreadsheet programs for further analysis, or into word processors for inclusion in documents.

Generalized graphical capabilities have become more commonplace as 4GLs have moved into GUI environments. In addition to basic charting facilities, many now support the display of images and vector graphics under program control.

The relative accessibility of 4GLs and related tools has led to their promotion as suitable for end-user computing in which moderately skilled end-users develop management support applications for local use, leaving specialist data management and programming staff to concentrate on more critical transaction processing applications. Nevertheless, there are distinct limits to what can be achieved without some programming effort. With the trend towards increasingly powerful 4GLs it is likely that end-users will continue to require considerable support from computing professionals.

Application Programming Interfaces (API)

An API is essentially a library of functions supplied either by the DBMS vendor or by a third party. This approach has generally been ignored by the major vendors of relational DBMSs (except SYBASE). A preprocessor is often used to translate Embedded SQL statements in a host program into calls to a proprietary library but few vendors document this layer of their systems.

The increasing power of desktop machines capable of being used in client–server environments (*see* Section 1.5.1) has reawakened interest in this approach as a means of connecting PC-based applications to remote databases. Microsoft's Open Database Connectivity (ODBC) is perhaps the most well-known example [Microsoft 1994]. It provides a common protocol and interface enabling a program to connect to both local and remote databases from many different vendors. The ODBC interface is based on the X/Open and SQL Access Group CAE SQL draft specification [Newmann 1992]. It includes functions for querying the capabilities of the remote system as well as for constructing, executing and retrieving results from SQL queries.

1.4.5   Report generators

Although report generation facilities have a longer ancestry, most modern systems use similar approaches to those of 4GLs, the major difference being that reports are intended to be read only and, in most cases, to be printed on paper.

Report generators come in two forms. The first provides an interpreted or compiled report programming language tailored towards text formatting instructions. Material is derived from the database using query language statements embedded in the report generation program. This approach is comparable with many programming language based 4GLs.

The second is closer to the application generator form of 4GL, employing graphical editors for interactive report and query design. The report is then generated automatically from the interactively prepared specification. As with application generators, the intention is to enable non programming end-users to produce reports without the help of a programmer. In some cases the report specification can be saved as a program, and edited by a programmer.

1.4.6   CASE tools

In addition to the range of tools and facilities discussed above, some DBMSs provide one or more programs that can be classified as Computer Aided Software Engineering (CASE) tools. These are intended to support and partially automate the various stages of system design and implementation. There is a wide range of software in this category, ranging from low-level tools such as graphical debuggers to project and version management systems.

In the database context, most CASE tools are intended to support high-level design functions. They usually include graphical editors tailored to producing diagrams such as ER models or dataflow diagrams. These diagrams are often linked to data dictionary information stored in a database throughout the design process. Typical output may include diagrams, other documentation and complete schema definitions expressed in a suitable DDL.

Where offered by database vendors, CASE tools are usually supplied as additional options rather than as part of the main DBMS package. Similar systems capable of interfacing with many of the major database products are also available from several specialist third-party software suppliers. Some suites of CASE tools are supplied as complete systems intended to support all stages of one of the more established design methodologies. Examples include *LBMS SSADM Workbench* which provides support for all aspects of SSADM version 4 or *Rational ROSE* which supports Booch's Object-Oriented Design method [Booch 1994; Rational 1993]. Others are aimed at individual design tasks such as ER modelling. Some include reverse engineering facilities that can be used to extract models from existing system implementations.

1.5 Networking and distribution

Early database systems were confined to single large centrally located machines with applications accessed via simple dumb terminals. Mainframe solutions are still employed for very large systems, but for many applications the trend of recent years has been away from centralization towards multiple smaller machines supporting **client–server** and **distributed** systems. These approaches have been made possible by the development of powerful microcomputers and workstations and of inexpensive networking technology.

Local Area Networks (LANs) connect machines within a single site. Most are based on physical interconnection using one of three forms of Ethernet cabling, although several other proprietary connection systems are also used. At larger sites, fibre-optic cables may also be used to provide a high-speed, high-bandwidth, **backbone** connecting many small networks. **Wide Area Networks** (WANs) provide connections between separate sites. They normally use telephone or other telecommunications services to provide the physical medium.

At the simplest level of networking, **peer-to-peer** connection provides a simple file and resource sharing mechanism. Disks, printers and other devices attached to one machine are made available to other machines where they appear to both users and applications as local devices. This approach is suitable for small offices that need only limited file sharing capabilities.

For larger networks, a more structured approach is appropriate. One or more machines may be dedicated to use as **file servers**. These provide the bulk of the filestore for all machines on the network. Again, the remote storage devices can appear indistinguishable from local devices. Such systems are easier to manage because single copies of both software and data can be stored on the servers, rather than being scattered over the network.

Other than the possibility of sharing a single copy of the executable programs, neither of these approaches is suitable for more than the simplest database applications. A physical database stored on a file server and accessed by programs running on the other machines will place a considerable load on the network. Query execution would involve transferring entire files or data tables from the file server to the client machine where the actual selection of records takes place. Ethernet and similar networks have a maximum bandwidth of about 10Mbit/sec (megabits per second), significantly less than can be achieved with a local disk drive. Even with faster network technology, say 100Mbit/sec, a small number of concurrent users performing such bulk transfers would soon swamp the network.

Both of these forms of network are implemented by relatively simple extensions to the operating system to enable access to the remote devices. The remote devices are brought within the scope of the normal I/O model. Similar extensions enable communication between software processes running on separate machines. Typically this is achieved either by providing communication channels that may be treated as normal stream or block I/O devices, or by a remote procedure call mechanism (RPC). This method enables a process running on one machine to pass parameters to, and retrieve returned values from, a second process on the remote machine. These mechanisms may be used to support client–server and distributed database systems by allowing the application and query processing to be divided between machines.

1.5.1 Client–server DBMS

The client–server approach separates the processes that use (the client) and provide (the server) a service. In a database management system the server receives and executes queries and returns results to the client. The client is typically an application program responsible for displaying query results and, more generally, managing the user interface (Figure 1.3).

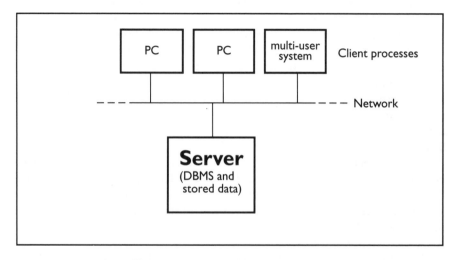

Figure 1.3 Client–server DBMS. A single server machine provides database services for client processes running on PCs or multi-user machines.

Client and server processes may both be run on a single machine, or on separate machines with communication via the network. The main benefit of separation is that the large and complex server processes, which make heavy demands on memory and secondary storage, may be placed on a dedicated machine. Server performance then depends only on the query load and is unaffected by other processes that would also be running on a general-purpose machine.

Similarly, the clients need not compete for resources with the server processes. When both client and server run on the same machine it may be necessary to give the server a higher priority so that it is never preempted by other processes. This will have an adverse affect on the perceived performance of clients and other applications running on the same machine if it is heavily loaded.

Client–server systems maximize performance by distributing processes. In its ideal form, the clients run on individual PCs or small workstations, and thus only compete for network and server resources. Textual queries expressed in a language such as SQL are passed from the client to the server. The server executes the query and returns the result to the client. The network load is low, particularly when compared with a fileserver based system in which a data management process must access remote disk files. With graphical or multimedia data, however, network throughput limitations may constrain performance.

1.5.2   Distributed DBMS (DDBMS)

Many organizations are distributed over more than one site, each with different information processing requirements. Often the majority of transactions performed at one site will involve only locally relevant data, with a relatively small proportion needing to access data that is generated and managed elsewhere. A single centralized system would permit sharing of information between sites, but all operations would depend on the reliability of one system. On the other hand, separate systems at each site would localize the effect of any failure, but would limit the ability to share data with other sites. Distributed DBMSs are intended to address both of these requirements. Here, we outline the main forms of distributed systems; Chapter 17 provides a detailed coverage of the major issues.

Distributed DBMSs are concerned primarily with the distribution of data resources. Two or more machines, each with its own data management software and stored data, cooperate so that their separate databases may be accessed as if they were all parts of a single database (Figure 1.4). Each server manages a subset of a larger logical database.

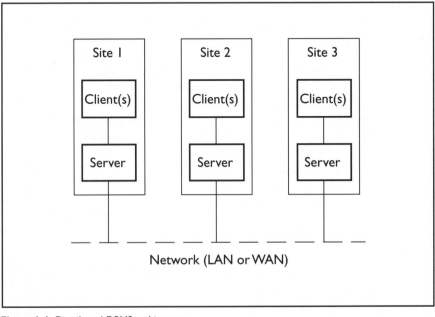

Figure 1.4 Distributed DBMS architecture.

Every site has a complete conventional DBMS and is responsible for maintaining its own local schema and local data. Typically a single site acts as the controller for the distributed system and maintains a master copy of the distributed schema. This schema contains information derived from all local schemas and may be partially or fully replicated at each site. Similarly, data may also be partially or fully replicated.

The main potential benefits of distributed systems are:

- Data may be held where it is most often used.
- Improved performance, because delays in fetching data from a central site are minimized, local databases are smaller and they have a lower transaction load per machine than a single central system.
- The system is only partially dependent on the reliability of a single node. If any one node fails the overall functionality of the system is reduced, but local processing can continue at the other sites. In practice, failure of the controlling node can cause greater problems if the data required at each site is not fully replicated.

Distributed systems vary in their degree of central control. They may be designed to present the outward appearance of a single centralized system while benefiting from the performance and reliability improvements that come from distribution. In this approach the central schema is a true superset of all local schemas and the administrator of the controlling node has the ultimate responsibility for both local and central schemas. The alternative approach, known as a **federated DBMS**, treats each node as an independent system that chooses to export some part of its schema for use by other nodes.

Another important issue that influences the complexity of the distributed system is the degree of homogeneity of the software components. A **homogeneous** distributed system is one in which identical software is used at each node. This is the most straightforward and thus most established form. A **heterogeneous** system is one that links systems from different vendors and, in some cases, with different data models. This is an altogether more complex approach requiring a common interface language and translation software to convert between this and the form required by each distinct system. Federated systems are invariably also heterogeneous.

Heterogeneous systems are becoming increasingly important for two reasons. Firstly, there is a need to integrate separate systems under the umbrella of higher-level information systems. Many organizations have information managed by systems that were originally designed for limited and separate purposes. These independent systems may be controlled by different software products which were selected to suit a particular purpose at a particular time, with no thought for future integration.

Secondly, the increasing range of applications of database systems makes it likely that this variety of DBMS types will continue. At present the emphasis of heterogeneous and federated DDBMSs is on integrating modern relational DBMSs with existing legacy systems based on hierarchical and network data models. In due course this will probably shift towards integrating extended relational and object-oriented systems with other special-purpose data management software.

1.6 Advanced applications

Database systems have long been associated with business and administrative transaction processing applications such as stock control, payroll, automatic teller machines (ATMs) and order processing. The requirements of such applications have played a major part in shaping the facilities offered by current DBMSs. However, it can be argued that because of this close association, the capabilities of current systems have in turn served to limit perceptions of the role of database systems.

The principal characteristics of this traditional range of database applications can be summarized as follows:

- They use a limited range of data types such as integer and real numbers, character strings and dates. These are usually combined to form simple fixed-length records.
- They involve a high volume of relatively simple, short-duration, transactions with an emphasis on throughput.
- They present a snapshot view of the modelled reality and have little concern for its past states.

The development of MIS and other forms of information systems has been similarly constrained. Many simply provide an additional layer on top of a transaction processing system to provide summary views of the state of the system and operational trends. However, the rapid growth in the use of PCs and workstations during the past ten years has brought many other forms of data under the everyday control of computer systems and resulted in users being exposed to a much wider variety of applications.

Although many of these applications and data types do not fit the traditional database models, they are nonetheless equally concerned with the manipulation of valuable information resources. For example, in a medical information system, patient records would be stored in a conventional database as highly structured records of past consultations, diagnoses and treatments, perhaps with limited textual notes attached. Although quite complex, this fails to capture the full content of modern medical records. There is a need to store more extensive notes and other internally structured documents, X-rays, CAT scans and other imagery, and the complex results of laboratory tests. None of these types of data are well served by conventional database systems.

From the administrative perspective, there may be other demands that cannot easily be satisfied by current systems. In addition to a similar requirement to manage complex documentary material, resource and inventory management and planning activities may benefit from graphical displays of the layout of wards, theatres and laboratories. A further development might involve integration of these applications with CAD software so that existing and projected views may be compared. This in turn would benefit from version management capabilities to provide a clear separation between past, present and possibly several projected views.

Almost all applications that handle significant quantities of data could benefit from many of the facilities provided by DBMSs. Effective transaction management, concurrency control and recovery mechanisms are desirable features of any system that allows multiple users to update stored information.

These requirements have resulted in two approaches, initially quite distinct but now widely seen to be converging:

- Extending the capabilities of database and information systems to cover a wider range of activities, many involving data types and operations that are not well catered for by current systems. This path has led to the development of extended and extensible database systems, mostly based on current relational technology.
- Extending the capabilities of modern programming languages to incorporate many of the benefits of database systems. This alternative route has been followed by many researchers whose starting point is in programming language development, particularly object-oriented languages, rather than in database systems.

These two approaches are discussed in Chapters 15 and 16. Here, we provide an indication of the problems associated with certain types of data and of how some of these are being addressed in the new generation of database systems. This is followed by a brief outline of the requirements of several classes of modern applications, some of which may be more suited to implementation by the second of these approaches. These themes will recur throughout the book.

1.6.1 Extending the range of data types

A major limitation of the relational and earlier data models is their limited ability to represent the semantics of complex objects. The simplicity and elegance of the relational model are at once its main strengths and its main weaknesses. By reducing all objects to simple components expressed in table form it benefits from simplicity of structure, but suffers because it must ignore all higher-level semantics of a complex object.

One of the most important features of extensible database systems is the provision of richer, extensible type systems.

Temporal data

Conventional snapshot databases only maintain historical information in off-line archives as part of their normal logging, recovery and archiving mechanisms. None of this information is directly available to applications or *ad hoc* queries. This is a direct result of the normal 'overwrite in place' approach to storage management. As a result, any applications that require access to past states of the stored data must do so by maintaining historical information in addition to normal snapshots.

For example, in a stock control context an MIS user might wish to ask 'How many widgets were in stock last week?' This can be achieved either by storing past values separately from the normal stock data, or by a 'no overwrite' strategy in which all records have additional timestamp information indicating their period of validity and all updates are performed by inserting new records. Decreasing storage costs have made this latter approach viable for some applications. However, its implementation adds complexity to applications and all queries must take account of the presence of the timestamps.

There is an extensive literature on temporal databases and query languages and it remains an active research area. For a detailed coverage of current issues, *see* [Tansel *et al.* 1993]. Several prototype systems allow temporal information such as transaction timestamps to be used without any programming overhead. A query with no temporal qualification can then retrieve the current (snapshot) state, whereas the addition of a suitable qualification restricts the result to the required historical moment or period.

Spatial data

Geographical Information Systems (GISs) have become increasingly important, not only as research tools but also to support planning and management activities in local, regional and national government. Some of their capabilities have also attracted interest in commercial applications ranging from marketing to vehicle scheduling.

Current systems typically store spatial data using a storage-engine optimized for vector or raster data, and any associated non-spatial or 'attribute' data in a conventional DBMS (Figure 1.5). This adds complexity to queries that must access both types of data and makes it difficult to maintain the integrity of relationships between them. The reason for this separation is simply that current database systems do not provide adequate performance because they lack suitable storage structures and access methods for spatial data.

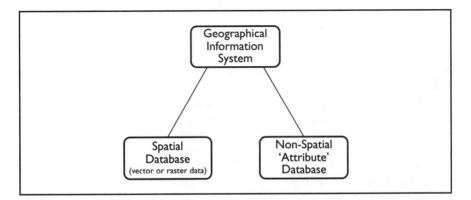

Figure 1.5 The typical Geographical Information System (GIS) architecture enforces a clear separation between spatial and non-spatial data.

The addition of new built-in data types, user-defined data types and, in some cases, access methods are features of many recent experimental DBMSs, and similar facilities have begun to appear in major relational systems such as INGRES. With adequate support for spatial types, the artificial division of data in current GISs can be overcome, with additional benefits in reducing the complexity of both GISs and applications.

Large objects: image and multimedia data

Many applications need to manipulate objects that are considerably larger than the simple numeric and character types of conventional systems. Examples include graphical images and multimedia audio and video. Current database systems are largely designed to handle records with a maximum size of only a few kilobytes whereas these large objects may occupy many megabytes.

Until recently it has only been possible to deal with large objects either by storing only references to external files or by splitting the object across many records. As a first step towards more effective ways of dealing with large objects, several commercial DBMSs now provide support for Binary Large Objects (BLOBs). These are arbitrarily sized and often must be handled differently from small objects. However, like small objects they are treated as atomic (indivisible) units. This means that, even if the object has an internal structure, it is invisible to the database system which can only support storage and retrieval of complete BLOBs. It is not possible to retrieve or update a component part such as a single frame or a brief sequence in the middle of several megabytes of video.

Large objects are not a satisfactory solution for any but the simplest of applications. Retrieving an entire video sequence just to view a single image or a short sequence imposes a unnecessarily heavy load on the network and other parts of the system. As with the spatial information discussed above, the solution lies in a mechanism for defining new data types; such facilities exist in many prototypes and are beginning to appear in commercial systems.

1.6.2   Applications

Here we discuss several application areas that have not been well served by conventional database systems. The first two, document management and CAD, both deal with complex structured objects that require quite different storage structures from those suited to tabular data. They also have access patterns that are better served by navigational rather than set-oriented querying methods.

In both of these cases there are strong arguments for claiming that these characteristics make them better suited to solutions based on object-oriented programming methods and persistent object stores. However, the third area, Computer Integrated Manufacturing (CIM), introduces the need for information sharing and cooperation between conventional MIS and a variety of specialized applications. Here, whichever architecture is used for the individual components, the need for cooperation will be paramount.

Document production and management

Document production and management systems rarely make use of conventional database systems. Instead they rely on a variety of software, including modern word processors, desktop publishing packages, hyperdocument systems and inverted index based text retrieval systems.

Of course, it is possible to define a schema for managing documents in a relational database system, but the text must be arbitrarily divided at the lowest level into small units that will fit within the limitations on record length. Decomposing a document into individual words stored one per record maximizes flexibility but imposes a massive overhead on retrieval and reassembly of text. The unit of storage must inevitably be somewhat larger. Conventional systems are poorly suited to handling variable-sized fields and records or to maintaining links between parts of fields. It is therefore difficult to divide text into meaningful units such as paragraphs or sentences or to maintain cross-references at the level of an individual word or phrase. The alternative of storing text in external files and only maintaining references to these files in the database is hardly acceptable because it would lose all benefits of query capabilities, security and transaction management on the text.

Similar problems apply to the storage of any graphical elements in a document. The only possibilities for bitmap graphics are again arbitrary subdivision or external storage. Vector representations are more straightforward and may be stored as collections of points, lines and polygons, but again complexity and the overhead it imposes on retrieval and reassembly would prove a major limitation.

Inevitably applications that manage such data would suffer from poor performance and it would be difficult to achieve compatibility with widely used non-database software such as word processors, electronic mail, hyperdocument systems and graphics editors.

Computer Aided Design (CAD) systems

CAD systems are often regarded as sophisticated drawing packages, although many also provide a considerable degree of automation and may be tightly or loosely coupled with a wide variety of testing and analytical tools.

The basic need to store drawing objects and their properties calls for the ability to combine simple objects into ever more complex, often hierarchical, structures. Although it is possible to model the properties of components, the lists of connections between them and any constraints on their layout using a relational approach, such structures are often better served by a system that supports navigational queries. As with GIS, some CAD systems allow additional information stored in an external relational database to be attached to the internally managed CAD objects.

Electronic CAD applications may be concerned with several different levels of abstraction in circuit design, the layout of discrete components on a printed circuit board, or the design of VLSI devices. They usually incorporate automated placement of components and interconnections.

Mechanical CAD systems need to support simulation techniques such as finite element analysis. This is used for detailed examination of stresses on mechanical components under projected load conditions. Simulation techniques are also used in electronic CAD systems. Electronic circuit simulation enables many aspects of the electrical behaviour of a circuit design to be tested without the need to produce a physical prototype. In both cases, expensive prototyping need only be undertaken after simulation tests have proved the basic integrity of the design.

Simulation experiments require high performance that cannot be achieved simply by running queries against a database. Typically this will involve downloading the relevant parts of the design to the workstation and performing the tests on a model held largely in local memory. Similarly, mechanical and architectural applications often use rendering software to enable visualization of the finished appearance of a design. Many of these techniques employ time-consuming processor-intensive operations that must be performed in memory.

The need to move large sections of a design between the data store and memory is found in many aspects of CAD operation. It requires careful transaction management to deal with cases where several designers may be working on different, but overlapping, aspects of a design. A related requirement of most CAD applications is the need for versioning methods to support design evolution.

Computer Integrated Manufacturing (CIM)

Computer Aided Manufacturing (CAM) and process control systems include a variety of embedded and real-time applications for controlling robots and machine tools, and monitoring sensors. As with other applications discussed here, many of these need to manage complex forms of data and there are benefits in bringing together all of the machinery in a production system under central control. However, many modern industries require rapid design and development cycles and responsive production schedules. Computer Integrated Manufacturing (CIM) systems are a response to this need by enabling these systems to share data and interact with other, traditionally quite separate, applications.

Requirements may include interfacing manufacturing systems with CAD applications so that designs may be transferred directly to the machine tools for prototyping and production. The machines need to be supplied with materials so that a well-integrated manufacturing system will also need to communicate with robot delivery systems and more conventional warehousing applications including inventory, stock control and materials ordering. At this level of integration, MISs may also provide information on the current state of production systems (Figure 1.6). The combination of distinct functional areas with limited information sharing makes CIM a suitable target for a federated database approach.

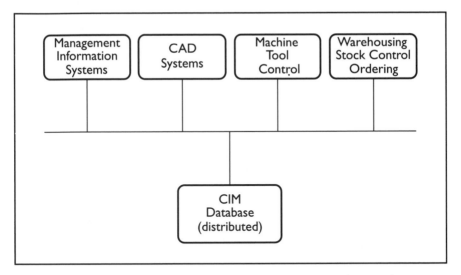

Figure 1.6 Computer Integrated Manufacturing (CIM) systems link together design workstations, production machinery and conventional database applications in MIS and warehousing.

1.7   Summary

Database management systems have been highly developed and optimized to suit a limited range of applications. They provide a number of benefits over systems developed using conventional programming languages and data files. These benefits include declarative query languages, a high degree of logical and physical data independence, transaction management, concurrency control, recovery mechanisms and access control.

Application developers may use conventional languages, together with an embedded query language, to access stored data. They may also choose from several forms of rapid application development systems tailored specifically to database applications, ranging from simple forms-based systems to 4GLs.

Although often labelled as 'conventional business systems', modern information systems have a much wider scope. They are increasingly required to deal with much more than simple numeric and character data. There is a growing demand to extend their coverage to support a wider range of data types and provide effective ways of managing large and internally complex objects. Amongst these are complex documents, spatial coordinates, graphical imagery and multimedia video and audio data. This demand has led to the development of extended and extensible DBMSs.

A second parallel trend has been the extension of programming languages to provide many of the benefits of conventional database systems. This approach is intended to simplify the development of applications that manage complex data, to provide ways of developing safer and more reliable programs and to reduce the effort required for program development through software reuse.

Chapter 2

STORAGE SYSTEMS

In this chapter we turn our attention to the physical characteristics of data storage systems. The material presented here is intended to provide a background for the more detailed coverage of physical system issues in later parts of the book. In particular, we discuss physical database design in Chapter 6, performance measurement and estimation in Chapter 7 and file storage structures in Chapter 8.

Here, we first describe the characteristics of the major types of physical storage media ranging from high-speed but volatile main memory to the slow but highly stable magnetic tape. This is followed by an introduction to the role of the operating system in providing an access model for data files stored on disk.

2.1 The storage hierarchy

The essential characteristics of the storage hierarchy are a number of storage devices, each lower level of which is slower and also usually cheaper and more stable (Figure 2.1). As a result the installed storage capacity of a system usually increases, often by several orders of magnitude, at each lower level of the hierarchy.

At the top of the hierarchy are the **primary storage devices** or main memory which is directly accessible by the processor. This is used to hold active executing programs and data that is being processed. As soon as a program terminates, its memory becomes available for use by other processes.

Secondary storage is composed of peripheral devices such as magnetic and, to a much lesser extent, optical disks. The main role of secondary devices is to provide stable storage where software and data can be held ready for direct use by the operating system and applications. Magnetic disks are also used as virtual memory or swap space for processes and data that either are too big to fit in the physical (primary) memory, or must be temporarily swapped out to disk to enable other processes to run.

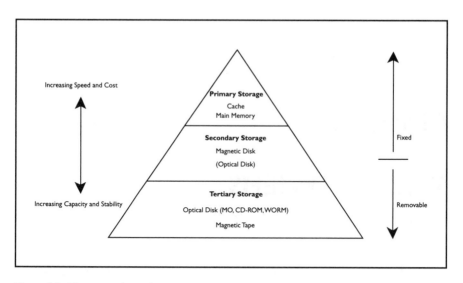

Figure 2.1 The storage hierarchy.

Tertiary storage is primarily used for archival purposes and has usually been provided by magnetic tape devices. Data held on tertiary devices is not directly loaded and saved by application programs. Instead, operating system utilities are used to move data between tertiary and secondary stores as required.

For many years the combination of relatively small amounts of main memory, disks (either fixed or removable) and tape has been universal, but the combination of hardware developments and increased demands from a wider variety of applications is resulting in a wider variety of configurations. For example, the advent of optical disks has blurred the distinction between secondary and tertiary storage because, unlike most other devices, they can be used in both roles.

In balancing the requirements for the different types of storage there are considerable trade-offs involving cost, speed and capacity. Main memory and most magnetic disks are fixed media; their capacity can only be increased by adding further devices.[1] Tape and optical disks, although slower, are relatively inexpensive because they use removable media. Once the read/write devices are installed, storage capacity may be expanded simply by purchasing further tapes or disks. Against this must be weighed the extended access time when the required tape or disk must be located and mounted on the device.

In early multi-user systems with limited secondary storage, user requirements often greatly exceeded the available disk space. It was common practice to limit the number of concurrent users and temporarily allocate each a limited amount of disk space into which their files were copied from tertiary store. This allocation lasted

---

1 Removable magnetic disks and low capacity floppy disks are available but are usually only of interest in specialized applications and small PC systems. Indeed, the floppy disk is steadily being replaced by CD-ROM as a software distribution medium for small computer systems.

only for the duration of a session and any updates were copied to the tertiary store when they logged out.

As secondary storage device costs have decreased and their sizes increased, these limitations have largely been overcome. At most installations the majority of files are now held 'on-line' on secondary devices. Most tertiary storage is now used to hold backup copies of the secondary store to enable recovery from system failures.

Nevertheless, there remains a class of applications with very large data requirements where the volume of data does not justify the cost of secondary storage. In many of these the frequency of access to individual items is low, but the overall access frequency is high. Examples include storage of historical information such as individual medical or taxation records. In other cases the volume of data increases at such a rate that it is only feasible to store it on a removable tertiary medium. A typical example would be an application that seeks to provide access to an ever growing body of satellite imagery.

Tape robots are often used for these types of application. These machines select and load tape cartridges under the control of the operating system without operator intervention. Files are transferred between tertiary and secondary storage on demand Optical devices are becoming increasingly important as somewhat faster tertiary storage. Again, robot machines can provide automatic selection and loading of disks from large libraries.

2.1.1   Granularity

A major distinction between primary and other storage devices lies in their access **granularity**; in other words, the size of the smallest unit of data that may be transferred to and from the device. Main memory is normally organized as a single linear address space in which each addressable unit (a **word**, typically 32 or 64 bits wide) may be accessed directly and equally rapidly by the processor. Compared with the purely electronic switching of main memory, delays in moving the mechanical components of secondary and tertiary storage devices dominate their access times.

The relatively slow access times of these devices would prevent adequate performance if their contents were addressable at the byte or word level. Instead, they are organized as **block-oriented** devices in which data is stored in fixed-size blocks. The operating system transfers these blocks between the device and main memory buffers where they can be accessed directly by the processor. Access to tertiary devices may use larger block sizes than those for secondary storage, reflecting their slower access times.

These differences in granularity have a major impact on the way in which data held on the various types of device is structured, and hence manipulated, by applications. Many conventional data structures designed for use in main memory, such as those based on trees and lists, can only be used in a modified form on block devices. Different algorithms must be used to address data held on these devices and there can be benefits in locating related data close to each other. These topics are addressed in Chapter 8.

In the following sections we outline the main characteristics of the more important types of storage device at each level of the hierarchy: main memory, magnetic and optical disks and magnetic tape.

2.1.2   Main memory

Main memory access is fast, typically measured in tens of nanoseconds, but it is volatile and the contents are lost if there is a power interruption. Within the broad category of main memory there may be a hierarchy of memory types employing different forms of electronic storage devices. Most main memory consists of the relatively low-cost dynamic memory. High-speed cache memory using more expensive static devices may be used to overcome differences between the access speed of the main memory and the I/O speed of the processor(s). While there may be several tens or hundreds of megabytes of main memory, cache sizes are more typically measured in hundreds of kilobytes.

Decreasing memory costs have made large main memory systems possible. Of course, the meaning of large is both relative and changeable. Five years ago systems with a few tens of megabytes of main memory were considered large. Current large systems might have several hundred megabytes and within a few years multiprocessor systems with gigabytes of main memory may be relatively commonplace. Nevertheless, these figures remain small compared to potential secondary and tertiary storage capacities.

The general increase in main memory sizes is paralleled by an increasing complexity and hence size of both software and data. Graphical user interfaces, multimedia and graphical data all lead to larger process sizes, as well as needing higher processor and storage performance than earlier character-based applications. To maintain adequate performance the need to swap processes out to disk must be minimized, so memory must expand to accommodate these demands.

Another effect of increasing main memory size has been to open the possibility of keeping large parts of a database active in main memory rather than on secondary storage devices. Rather than simply increasing the amount of memory used to buffer disk blocks, this approach benefits by using data structures that are more appropriate to in-memory processing. The volatility of conventional memory would appear to make this a risky proposition but, by providing some stable memory using battery-backed power supplies, significant performance gains are possible. This is discussed further in Chapter 11.

2.1.3   Magnetic disk

Magnetic disks are the main form of secondary storage device. Access speeds are approximately three orders of magnitude slower than main memory and are typically measured in tens of milliseconds. However, disks are inherently stable and well suited to providing persistent storage for databases. Unlike magnetic tape, disks are random access devices; in other words, it is equally easy to access data stored anywhere on the disk surface.

The following discussion concentrates on the description of small, non-removable disks that have become commonplace in small to medium-sized computer systems. Chapter 6 contains further details of some of the parameters needed for modelling disk drive performance. These relatively inexpensive sealed unit disks, derived from technology originally developed for workstations and microcomputers, have largely replaced the high-performance fixed-head and removable disk systems for most applications. Specialized high-performance disk units are now largely confined to mainframe installations. The major differences are in cost, physical size, capacity and performance. However, the performance gap is narrowing and similar operational principles apply to all forms of disk.

Data is stored in concentric **tracks** on the disk surfaces. Each track contains a linear sequence of bits, but it is divided logically into fixed-size blocks or sectors (Figure 2.2). These are usually of 0.5 kilobyte, although larger sizes up to 4 kilobytes are also used. Addressing information (track number, block number, and so on) together with empty data blocks are recorded when the disk is first formatted or initialized. When in use, checksums for error detection and correction are recorded with each data block. The address and error-handling information are used only by the disk controller. To the operating system, the disk appears simply as a linear array of individually addressable data blocks.

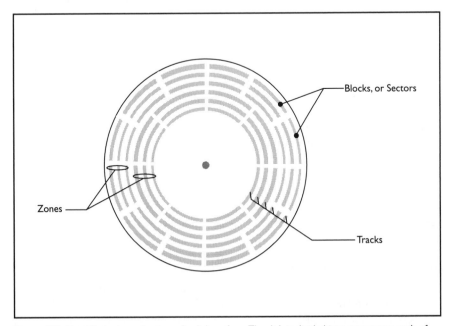

Figure 2.2 Simplified schematic view of a disk surface. The disk is divided into two zones, each of three tracks. The tracks in the outer zone contain twelve sectors, while those in the inner zone have eight.

To maximize capacity the longer outer tracks may contain more blocks than the shorter inner ones. This ensures that the recording density, typically measured in bits per inch, is kept near the optimal level. The disk surface may be divided into several concentric **zones** within which each track has the same number of sectors.

In the conventional movable head-disk the head assembly can position the read/write heads over any required track under software control (Figure 2.3). The disk rotates at several thousand r.p.m. so there is a brief delay, or **latency**, between the positioning of the head assembly over the selected track and the required block passing beneath the heads (8.3 ms on average for a disk rotating at 3600 r.p.m.).

Most disk units have between two and twelve **platters**, each of which has two recording surfaces, thus at any one head position two tracks on each platter are available for reading or writing. These groups of tracks are often referred to as a **cylinder**. Rapid switching between surfaces is achieved by switching heads electrically, but in practice a brief settling period is also required for fine adjustment of the head alignment.

The access time for any data block is the sum of the **seek time** in which the heads are moved to the required track, the latency and the **block transfer time** in which the data is transferred between disk surface and memory. The seek time includes components of acceleration, constant speed motion, deceleration and a settling period. Very short seeks are dominated by the settling time and very long seeks by the constant speed phase. For a typical modern 3.5 inch disk, the seek time may vary from about one millisecond for adjacent tracks to 20 ms for the full width (3000 or more tracks) of the disk surface.

Sequential read and write operations may cross track boundaries. After reading or writing the final block on one track, it may not be possible for the heads to move to the next and settle in time to continue with the first block. Track **skewing** avoids the need to wait for a near complete revolution before the operation can continue. The start of each track is offset by one or more sectors from its predecessor to allow time for head movement and settling.

Fixed-head disks are sometimes used in large mainframe installations. These have a separate read/write head for each track, unlike the more common movable- head disk in which a single head moves over the disk surface. The main benefit of fixed heads is that there is no mechanical delay in moving the heads. Switching between tracks is performed electronically, giving a uniform seek time across the entire surface. The disadvantages lie in their very much higher cost and the limitations on track spacing, and hence their capacity, due to the need to accommodate a large head assembly.

The block transfer time depends on the number of blocks per track and the rotational speed of the disk. It is much smaller than either the seek time or latency, typically a small fraction of a millisecond. Data transfer performance is more often specified as a transfer rate. For example, the DEC DSP3000L series 3.5 inch drives have between 59 and 119 sectors per track, each of 512 bytes. At 5400 r.p.m. this gives a media transfer rate between disk surface and local controller ranging from 2.7 to 5.5 megabytes per second [DEC 1993]. These figures are typical of the current installed range of small inexpensive devices, but 7200 r.p.m. disks are becoming

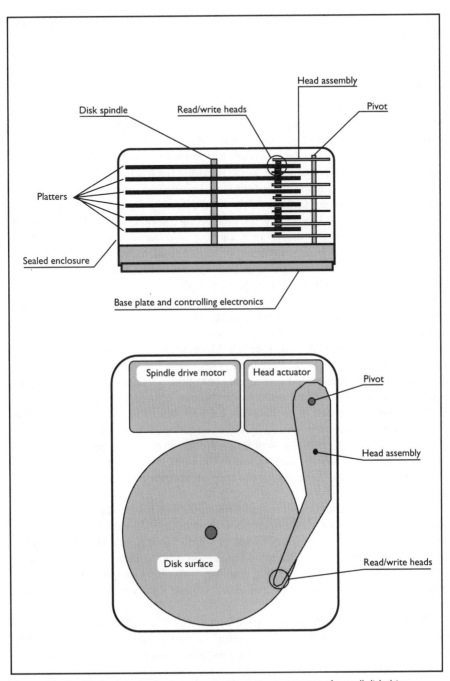

Figure 2.3 Simplified schematic diagrams showing the main components of a small disk drive.
To move the heads across the disk surface, the head actuator rotates the head assembly
arm about the pivot.

increasingly common and have correspondingly higher transfer rates. Some of the higher performance devices used in mainframe and large minicomputer installations achieve transfer rates in the 10–20 megabytes per second range.

Caching

The effective transfer rate for read access may be improved by buffering. Most modern disk drives are equipped with several hundred kilobytes of cache memory which is normally used to store whole tracks. Whenever a read request is received for a block that is not in the cache a normal seek and read is performed but, instead of stopping at the end of the requested block, the entire track is transferred to the cache.

Subsequent reads on the same track can be satisfied directly from the cache, irrespective of the current location of the head assembly. Data is transferred to the host machine at the full speed of the bus connecting computer and disks. Apart from increasing the apparent transfer rate, caching also reduces the need for head movements. If one process is performing sequential reads with intervening delays for processing, other processes might issue access requests that force head movements before the next sequential block is requested. If the required block is in the cache, there is no need for the heads to return to the original track. Disk head movements are also reduced by intelligent controllers that rearrange the order of requests so that they may be serviced in the most efficient manner.

Caching is not limited to disk drives. Modern disk controller hardware often contains cache memory or the operating system may maintain a software cache in conventional main memory. In practice, only one of these is normally used as multiple caches may negate some of the performance benefits of a single cache.

So far, our discussion of caching has been limited to read operations. Similar performance benefits can be gained by buffering disk writes, but only at the expense of potential reliability problems. Writes that are still in the cache and have not been copied to stable disk storage may be lost in the event of a system failure. This may make it difficult to determine the state of the system at the point of failure and hence institute effective recovery.

The ability to guarantee that critical write operations have updated a reliable and stable storage device is essential to the correct operation of most database systems and their recovery processes (*see* Chapter 11). Writes to transaction logs containing details of all changes made to the stored data must avoid volatile cache memory and be flushed directly to disk. Transaction logs may be a major bottleneck and improvements in their write performance can provide significant performance gains for the entire system.

One possible approach is to provide a backup (usually battery) power supply for the cache on the disk controller. By ensuring that the cache memory is non-volatile the state of the cache can be preserved across failure and recovery in other parts of the system. After recovery, suitable controller software can then ensure that all writes still in the cache are flushed to the stable magnetic disk before normal processing continues. Similar benefits may also be gained from the solid state disks discussed later in this section.

Increasing disk performance

As with electronic memory devices, disk storage capacities and relative costs continue to improve. The figures quoted above are representative of small sealed unit disk drives at the time of writing, but storage densities have been increasing by between 1.6 and 1.8 times *per annum* [Ruemmler and Wilkes 1994]. Much of this gain comes from increased recording density, both in linear bits per inch and in reduced track width. Similar capacities can therefore be achieved with smaller diameter disks. Increased linear density and higher rotational speeds contribute to higher transfer rates. Smaller devices require less power and are subject to less mechanical stress, and lighter head assemblies combined with reduced track widths lead to reduced stepping times.

Currently, 3.5 inch disks capable of storing several gigabytes are available at a cost equivalent to a few tens of megabytes of dynamic memory devices. The older 8 inch devices have largely disappeared and 5.25 inch disks may be destined for a similar fate. Assuming that this trend continues, 2.5 inch drives with capacities of a gigabyte or more should be widely available by 1996 and 1.3 inch drives should reach similar figures by about 1998. Although the main use for these smaller sizes is currently in portable laptop or notebook-sized machines, it is likely that increased capacity will lead to the development of **disk array** subsystems that will fit in the space occupied by a single 5.25 or 3.5 inch disk.

Despite rapid improvements in capacity that keep pace with or even exceed those of processor performance, the rate of increase in disk performance is less spectacular at about 1.1 times *per annum* [Ruemmler and Wilkes 1994]. This increasing gap between processor and disk performance represents a major challenge to both hardware and software designers. This is, however, not a new problem and it has long provided a major incentive for research into ways of improving I/O performance.

Apart from advances in large main memory systems, attempts to overcome this performance gap include disk arrays in which contiguous logical blocks are distributed over several physical disk drives. The separate disk units can perform read and write operations in parallel. Seek times are not improved, but a disk array can appear as a single disk with an apparently increased recording density. The increased number of blocks per logical track gives better performance for small, tightly clustered, and longer, sequential, accesses but does little for those applications involving large numbers of small accesses with intervening seeks.

Several disk array configurations are used, some of which are intended to increase disk system reliability rather than performance. The various configurations, including those known as RAID (Redundant Arrays of Inexpensive Disks) levels, are described in detail in Chapter 11.

Effective recording density can also be increased by data compression techniques. These can only be of use in increasing disk throughput, rather than effective capacity, if the encoding and decoding processes can be performed very rapidly. Most software-based methods fail in this respect. Only marginal improvements can be achieved across a broad range of file types because general-purpose encoding techniques rarely achieve more than a 2:1 compression ratio. More complex encoding schemes designed for specific forms of data may save much more storage space, but take longer to process than transferring uncompressed data to and from the disk.

However, hardware compression equipment may be used to good effect in specialized applications, particularly with multimedia video and audio data. The problem with video data is that the normal transfer rate of uncompressed video may be inadequate to support the required display speed and resolution. Hardware implementations of suitable compression schemes can both reduce the data volume to manageable levels and ensure adequate effective transfer rates.

Solid state disks

Another approach to the problem of disk performance is the solid state disk. These systems provide very fast access. They are not real disks but are in fact large arrays of semiconductor memory devices with a controller and interface that allows them to be connected in place of a conventional disk. They exhibit a constant access speed unaffected by seek times or latency, and can transfer data in both directions at the maximum speed of the data bus connecting computer to disks.

These systems usually contain a battery power supply to guard against short-term power failures, and backup magnetic disks that mirror the data stored in the memory devices. Updates to the data stored in the memory devices are copied asynchronously to the magnetic disks. Capacities range from tens to a few hundred megabytes, roughly reflecting the available range of primary storage.

The main use of solid state disks is in applications designed for use with conventional disk systems but which require much more rapid access to some of their data. They are suited to situations where heavy access to a relatively small amount of data leads to a significant I/O bottleneck, the volume of reads is too large for main memory buffering, or writes are too critical to system reliability to risk the volatility of conventional main memory. Effectively, they provide similar benefits to those obtained by using non-volatile controller caches.

Solid state disks are fast when compared with magnetic disks but cannot compete directly with main memory performance. The reasons are twofold; firstly, the I/O bus transfer rate is usually much lower than that of the internal bus connecting processor and memory. Secondly, because the device is a simple plug-in replacement for a conventional disk, the data must be stored in block form. Main memory systems can employ data structures suitable for direct manipulation by the processor and inevitably there must be a translation between the two forms whenever data is moved between primary and secondary storage.

2.1.4   Optical media

There are a number of optical storage devices on the market. In general they offer access times somewhat slower than conventional magnetic disks and a storage capacity of several hundred megabytes or more per disk. The different technologies include **Magneto-Optical (MO)** which combines both magnetic and optical storage methods, and the purely optical **Write Once Read Many (WORM)** and **CD-ROM**. We describe CD-ROM in more detail below, but other forms of optical storage have similar characteristics. For a discussion of the general principles of optical storage media, *see* [Udell 1993].

CD-ROM was introduced as an inexpensive read-only medium using mechanisms based on consumer audio devices. It is more robust than conventional magnetic media and appears to be extremely durable, although it is too early to be certain of this. CD-ROM is increasingly becoming the medium of choice for distribution of large software, data and documentation sets, both for PCs and larger systems. In this role it is steadily replacing floppy disks and magnetic tape cartridges.

Material distributed on CD-ROM is used in one of two ways. Firstly, disks may be used purely for distribution with their contents copied to normal (magnetic disk) secondary storage before being used. Alternatively they may be used as a read-only secondary store with software and data loaded directly from the disk. The latter approach is widely used in PC multimedia applications, but is also suitable for access to large documentation sets and other reference material. This is only possible for applications where the slower access time does not impose an unacceptable delay on the application and where the sustained transfer rate is appropriate.

Recorded disks are normally produced by large-scale industrial techniques. However, the introduction of relatively cheap recorders, coupled to the popularity of disk readers, suggests that CD-ROM may become an important optical recording medium over the next few years. Writeable CD-ROM drives are becoming widespread in PC installations and are increasingly employed as a layer of tertiary random access storage in multimedia information systems and other applications where large volumes of (mostly read-only or infrequently updated) data must be stored. While the other optical media may dominate specialized, data-intensive, applications, the writeable CD-ROM provides an inexpensive medium for tertiary (archival) storage and small-scale information and software publishing.

Each CD-ROM disk holds a maximum of 680Mb. Data is organized as 2048-byte blocks in a continuous spiral rather than the concentric tracks of a magnetic disk. Instead of an alternating magnetic field recorded on the disk surface, data bits are represented by small pits burned into a thin metal layer encased within the transparent plastic body of the disk. When reading, light from a small laser is directed onto the disk surface by a system of lenses and mirrors. The reflected light is detected and converted into an electronic data stream. Writeable CD devices employ a second, higher powered, laser to burn pits in the recording surface.

Average access times are typically in the range 150–300 ms. The slow seek speed when compared to a magnetic disk is due to the relatively high mass of the lens assembly which cannot be moved as quickly as magnetic heads.

Sustained data transfer rates depend on the speed of rotation of the disk. Usually these are a multiple of about 150 kilobytes per second, the rate achieved at the rotational speed of an audio CD. Typical inexpensive single disk devices provide two to four times this rate, and more expensive devices with multiple disk magazines four or more times this rate. As with magnetic disks, caches may be provided to buffer frequently used blocks and enable burst transfer rates of 2.5–5 megabytes per second.

MO and WORM devices have capacities ranging from 128Mb on 3.5 inch MO disks to two gigabytes or more on 5.25 inch disks. Their performance is usually somewhat better than that of CD-ROM with maximum access times below 100ms and media transfer rates of one gigabyte per second or more. These performance figures are steadily improving as the technology matures.

The larger capacity WORM and MO devices are increasingly employed as tertiary storage where larger capacities are required. Very large storage systems are possible using robot devices with a small number of read/write mechanisms. A much larger number of disks is held in a storage rack from which single disks can be selected and loaded in a few seconds.

Recent research into multi-layer optical media indicates that storage densities of up to ten times current values can be achieved. Approaches include using shorter wavelength laser light to reduce the size of pits, and encoding information in the depth of the pits rather than simply in their presence or absence. Such disks will be incompatible with current readers as they require more elaborate optical and electronic decoding systems. However, this research indicates that the recording density and capacity of optical media is likely to continue to increase at a similar rate to those of magnetic media.

2.1.5 Magnetic tape

Magnetic tape is widely used as an archival medium. Its high capacity, portability (for off-site storage) and relatively low cost make it the preferred choice for most sites. The overriding disadvantage for applications other than archiving and backup is that access is sequential. Tape is a linear medium and all reading and writing must begin at the start of the tape and continue until completed. Sequential devices are only suitable for applications where a large and continuous body of data must be read or written at one time and slow access can be tolerated.

The standard medium for many years was the 9-track tape. These large open reels of half-inch tape are being steadily replaced by more compact media. The QIC (Quarter Inch Cartridge) formats became popular as a software distribution and archival medium during the late 1980s, particularly for workstations and more powerful PC-based systems. Their capacity ranges from the early 60-megabyte tapes to one or more gigabytes. Proprietary formats such as Digital's DC50 cartridge provide similar capacity and performance in non-standard packages.

Quarter-inch tape cartridges are no longer adequate to provide backup for modern disk drives with capacities measured in gigabytes. These demands are now being satisfied by small cartridge systems with a capacity of up to 8 gigabytes on either 8 mm or 4 mm tape. The cartridge formats are based on standard 8 mm video and 4 mm DAT (Digital Audio Tape).

Access times for tape devices are variable. If the tape is not mounted on the device, allowance must be made for locating and loading the required tape. Robot devices typically take less than ten seconds to mount a tape but in a manual system, where intervention by operators is needed, the task may take several minutes. Once mounted, the seek times for all types of tape device are measured in tens of seconds or minutes rather than fractions of a second. They depend entirely on how far along the tape the required data is located. Once the data block is found, transfer speeds of 0.2–1.0Mb/sec are typical for the current generation of tape drives.

2.1.6   Peripheral buses

Storage devices are normally connected to host machines by some form of serial or parallel bus. The widely used SCSI (Small Computer System Interface) bus may be used to connect many types of peripheral including magnetic and optical disk and magnetic tape devices (Figure 2.4). The host controller is a general-purpose bus control device that maps data and commands between the host computer and the bus. Each disk unit or other peripheral contains its own local controlling electronics responsible for translating commands from the host system, controlling caches, and receiving and transmitting blocks of data from and to the host. Several disk units may be attached to a common bus that links them to a controlling device on the host. Other, often proprietary, buses may follow a similar pattern, or may provide more complete disk control electronics on the host controller with correspondingly simpler electronics on the individual peripherals.

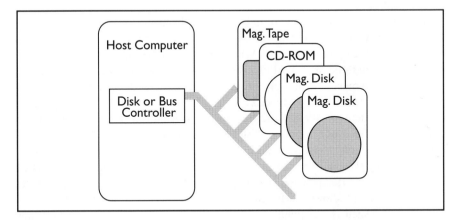

Figure 2.4 A single bus (for example, SCSI) may be used to connect several peripheral storage devices.

The SCSI bus transfer rate is between 5 and 20 megabytes per second depending on bus width (8/16 bit) and transfer mode (synchronous or asynchronous). The proprietary buses used by some manufacturers typically provide similar performance. Given that current magnetic disk systems achieve media transfer rates covering a comparable range, these bus transfer rates are likely to limit throughput when several devices on the bus attempt simultaneous transfers. A future development of the SCSI standard is expected to double potential transfer rates by using a 32-bit bus width. However, it is likely that faster serial transmission standards using similar technology to that used for network connections will evolve over the next few years to cope with these limitations.

2.2 File organization and management

One of the roles of an operating system is to provide a coherent I/O model for use by application programs. Here we are concerned with that part of the I/O model that describes disk access. Disks are random access block devices. Any block may be accessed given an address that locates its position on the disk surface. Files are organized as named collections of blocks that may occupy contiguous locations or be scattered over the disk surface. In either case the operating system maintains a list of the blocks that make up each file.

The use of contiguous sequences of blocks is preferred because it minimizes the need for relatively slow disk head movements when accessing a file. However, this is not always possible as blocks must be reused when a file has been deleted or truncated. When there is insufficient contiguous space to write a new file or extend an existing one, the file must be stored as several sequences of blocks at different locations on the disk. This is known as fragmentation, and in severe cases can degrade disk performance. In time it may become necessary to reorganize the files to occupy contiguous locations.

Data is always transferred to and from disk in fixed-size blocks, thus a read operation always involves copying one or more blocks from disk into memory buffers maintained by the operating system. Whole blocks must be copied even if only a few bytes of data are to be read. Writing also takes place in whole blocks. To update an existing block, it must first be copied from disk into a buffer then, once modified, the entire block is copied back to the disk.

All I/O models provide an interface to this mechanism. Perhaps the simplest model uses buffered I/O to present disk files as sequences of bytes. The description here is based on the UNIX `stdio` library, but similar operations are supported by most operating systems. The model effectively hides the underlying block structure from the program. It supports sequential read and write operations on single bytes or larger units and allows the file to be treated identically to other sequential I/O stream devices such as a terminal or printer. It is also possible to access directly any arbitrarily sized sequence of bytes by specifying its offset from the start of the file. The basic file operations are:

Open a file in **read**, **write**, **update** or **append** mode. In read mode, if the file exists the operating system prepares a buffer and copies the first block from the disk. In write mode an empty buffer is prepared and a new file is created by reserving disk space and recording details such as the identity of the owner and time of creation. In both cases a pointer is set to the start of the memory buffer to indicate the current insertion or extraction point.

In update mode data can be both read from and written to the same preexisting file. The file is opened as for read mode, but subsequent operations can include both read and write (modify). In append mode data is written starting at the end of an existing file. The final block of the file is located and copied into a buffer. The insertion pointer is then set to point at the first byte after the end of the current contents.

Read one or more bytes. Data is copied from the buffer to a location determined by the program. As each byte is copied, the extraction pointer is incremented to indicate where the next sequential read will start. If the pointer is moved beyond the last byte in the buffer, the next block is fetched from the disk and the pointer reset to the start of the buffer.

Write one or more bytes. Data is copied from a location determined by the program into the buffer. As each byte is copied, the insertion pointer is incremented to indicate where the next sequential write will start. If the pointer is moved beyond the last byte in the buffer, the buffer is written to disk and the pointer reset to the start of the buffer. If the file was opened in update mode, the next block is fetched into the buffer ready for reading or modifying.

Seek an arbitrary byte. An offset from the start of the file is specified in bytes. The operating system calculates which block is required and fetches it into the buffer. The pointer is then set to indicate the required byte.

Close the file. For a file that was opened in read mode, the buffer is released. In write and append mode, the buffer is written to disk (flushed) before being released.

For many purposes, sequential reading and writing are quite adequate. Any more complex access methods can be constructed on top of this simple base. The ability to read and write an arbitrary number of bytes makes it possible to manipulate larger units, and the seek function enables any such unit to be addressed within a file. Together these can be used to implement block I/O in terms of arbitrarily sized logical blocks which can provide the basis for the access methods discussed in Chapter 8. Other operating systems may provide a much more extensive I/O model with several different access methods supported directly at this low level.

Within a file, data is usually stored in **records**. These may be of fixed or variable length. Records are subdivided into one or more **fields** containing individual data values. Fields may also be of fixed or variable length, and there may be a variable number of fields per record. Each record normally represents an instance of an entity type and the fields contain the attribute values. All records in a file are usually of the same type and the file represents a set of occurrences of the type. However, **mixed files** in which different record types are clustered together may also be used. This approach enables related entity occurrences that are frequently accessed together to be clustered so that disk accesses can be minimized.

The basic operations that can be performed on a file are insertion of new records, and retrieval, modification and deletion of existing records. The file **organizations** and **access methods** described in Chapter 8 have different performance characteristics for each of these operations, making them more or less suitable for particular applications and access patterns. Here, file organization refers to the structure of the file as stored on disk or when transferred to memory buffers, whereas access methods are the software techniques and algorithms used to manipulate the records in the file. A file has a single organization, but may be accessed by several different methods. The file organization determines which access methods can be used.

In order to operate on a single record, that record must be distinguishable from all others. One field, or a sequence of fields, is designated as the primary key of the file and must contain a unique value in each record. Records may often be stored so they can be retrieved in (usually ascending) order of their **primary key** values. This is not always the case; sometimes they may be stored in order of some other field(s). For example, a file of information on people may use a unique identification number as the primary key, but may be ordered on the person's name. The field, or sequence of fields, that determines the retrieval order is known as the **ordering key** or **sort key**.

	PatientId	Name	AdmissionDate	Condition
(a)	1234567890	Jones	12-Aug-1994	Angina
	1	11	29	40

(b)   1234567890‡Jones‡12-Aug-1994‡Angina¶

(c)   PatientId:1234567890‡Name:Jones‡AdmissionDate:12-Aug-1994‡Condition:Angina¶

Field terminator ‡   *Record terminator* ¶

Figure 2.5 (a) Fixed-length record and fields. The fixed offset to the start of each field is shown below. (b) Variable-length record and fields using field and record separator or terminator characters. (c) Field name and value pairs may be used to implement a variable number of fields per record.

The simplest file organizations use fixed-length records each with the same number of fixed-length fields. The location of the start of any record in a file, and of any field within a record, can be calculated from the known record and field lengths and they may be updated by overwriting existing values (Figure 2.5a). Location is not so straightforward when variable-length records or fields are used. In these cases special field and record terminator characters are usually employed so that the start and end of each record or field can be detected when reading the file (Figure 2.5b). Updates frequently cannot be achieved by overwriting as they may increase the length of a record. Instead, the old record must be deleted and the new version inserted at a different location, usually the end of the file.

Many other record and field structures are possible. When each record contains a variable number of fields, the presence of a particular field can be indicated by various methods including tagging. Here, both the name and value of a field are recorded together (Figure 2.5c). Various combinations of these methods may be found together. For example, the records in Figure 2.5 could be stored using fixed-length fields for PatientId and AdmissionDate and variable-length fields with terminators for Name and Condition.

2.2.1   Pages

The block size used by an operating system for disk storage and transfers between disk and memory is chosen as a compromise to suit a general mix of applications. In data-intensive applications it is often more efficient to transfer data in larger units. These larger logical blocks are known as **pages**. They are of fixed size, usually 2–32Kb, and are equivalent to a whole number of physical disk blocks. In many database systems each page contains a small amount of administrative information such as a page identifier, and record and free space pointers, but most of the space is available for data.

```
(a)
┌─────────────────────────────────────────────────┐
│ Page  1   Record  1   Record  2   Record  3      │
└─────────────────────────────────────────────────┘

┌─────────────────────────────────────────────────┐
│ Page  2   Record  4   Record  5   Record  6      │
└─────────────────────────────────────────────────┘


(b)
┌──────────────────────────────────────────────────────────────┐
│ Page  1   Record  1   Record  2   Record  3   Record  4   ptr │
└──────────────────────────────────────────────────────────────┘

┌──────────────────────────────────────────────────────────────┐
│ Page  2   4  (cont)   Record  6   Record  7   Record  8   ptr │
└──────────────────────────────────────────────────────────────┘
```

Figure 2.6 Unspanned and spanned records. (a) Unspanned fixed-length records. Unused space in each page is shown shaded. (b) Variable-length spanned records. When pages are not contiguous, a pointer field indicates the page where the incomplete record continues.

Many database systems use only fixed-length records and the page header typically indicates which of the available record slots contain current records. However, variable-length records may also be accommodated by including the offset of the start of each record in the page header. In either case the page structure is normally organized to ensure that records do not cross page boundaries. Such records are said to be **unspanned** (Figure 2.6a).

Spanned records that cross page boundaries may be used with some applications (Figure 2.6b), but are rarely used by conventional database systems. They frequently employ a pointer field to indicate the page on which an incomplete record is continued. This avoids the necessity to continue a record in the immediately following block.

In an unspanned organization each page usually contains one or more complete records. While this limits the maximum size of any record to the space available in a single page and usually results in some wasted space, it prevents inefficiencies arising from reads and writes crossing block boundaries and causing multiple disk I/O operations. Pages need not be filled to capacity, indeed with many file organizations pages are initially only partially filled. The available slots are then used to insert records in key or other order and to delay the need to allocate new pages as new records are added.

2.2.2 Database files and operating systems

Many DBMSs use the native file system abstraction provided by the operating system for data storage. This has the benefit of simplicity and eases portability between different operating systems and hardware configurations. For example, INGRES uses a separate directory for each database with system catalogues, data tables and indexes managed as distinct files. The contents of the directory and the internal organization of individual files are controlled by the DBMS. The database may be partitioned for storage on more than one disk, or disk partition, to overcome space limitations or improve performance. In such cases a separate directory is used on each device for the single database.

Another approach, used by systems ranging from the PC-based Access to Oracle, employs a single or small number of large files per database. Although still reliant on the I/O mechanisms provided by the operating system, this gives the DBMS greater control over the internal organization of the database. For example, different types of records that are frequently accessed together and might otherwise be stored in separate files can more easily be clustered to minimize disk seeks.

In the case of specialized database machines, or systems where the DBMS, operating system and hardware are provided by a single supplier, there is much more scope for optimization of disk access. Here, the operating system often provides direct support for access methods used by the DBMS.

A further possibility that may be used where the operating system permits is raw disk I/O in which one or more disk partitions are dedicated to the sole use of the DBMS. Typically this is used for circumstances where there is a benefit to be gained from careful I/O tuning as, for example, in the option to store the INGRES log file on a raw partition. The logging system is a potential bottleneck in any high-activity environment and some gains can be made by using highly optimized access methods.

2.3 Summary

In this chapter we have described the main characteristics of a range of data storage devices, ranging from on-chip cache memory to magnetic tape; we have emphasized the characteristics of magnetic disks because these are the principal type of storage device for almost all database systems. The memory hierarchy is frequently seen in terms of devices, but is actually determined by the way a particular system organizes its data (typically into in-use, active and archival sets) and maps this organization onto suitable devices. We have also described the essential concepts for mapping logical records onto physical storage media, as background to the more detailed discussions of these issues in later chapters.

Part II

DATABASE DESIGN

Chapter 3

DATA MODELLING

In this chapter we describe the data modelling process, which covers the later phases of requirements analysis and the development of the database logical model (Figure 3.1). We first examine data modelling abstractions and the role of conceptual data modelling in information systems development. The Extended Entity Relationship (EER) model, described in the second part of the chapter, is the most widely used framework for data modelling. The third part of the chapter describes methods for refining an initial model using a set of consistency-preserving transformations to achieve a good design that avoids a number of undesirable characteristics and, for relational databases, results in normalized relations. The final section contains a description of the normal forms and their characteristics.

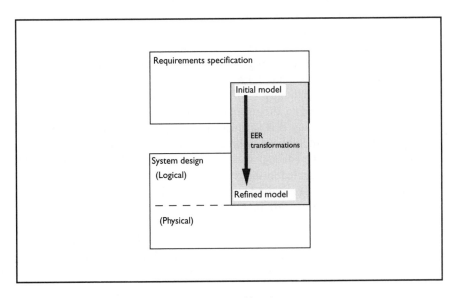

Figure 3.1 EER modelling in the information systems lifecycle.

The starting point in this view of data modelling is a very high-level view of the principal data objects of interest. The initial model is refined in a series of increasingly detailed intermediate models into a final form which can be directly translated into the data definition language of the target DBMS (or into suitable record and class definitions for a persistent programming language and other types of data store).

3.1 Data modelling concepts

There is a small number of concepts that underlie data modelling and between them provide a comprehensive means of describing the structure of a domain of interest, the Universe of Discourse (UoD).

3.1.1 Identity

A database is an abstract model of some UoD; as such it attempts to model the features of the UoD that are important for some set of purposes (typically an application or suite of applications) while ignoring detail that is irrelevant. What is irrelevant detail for one set of purposes may be the primary focus of another; for example, a ward-based inventory might record a number of 'Phase I Resuscitation Kits', whereas a medical stores inventory might record quantities of defibrillators, oxygen masks, and so on.

The UoD can be regarded as a collection of related things of interest, which can be aggregated into classes. Attributes describe the properties of interest of the class. If the modelling has been done at an appropriate level it follows that a pair of instances of a class which have identical values must be indistinguishable in the model, even if they are physically distinct. For example, several copies of a book in a bookshop are identical (the information required is the description of the book and the number of copies in stock) but for a librarian the distinction between individual copies is important (as a loan must involve a particular instance of a book).

This notion is captured in the relational model by the requirement that every tuple must have a unique key. It is adequate for strong entities, but causes problems for weak, or dependent, entities whose identification is dependent on their relationship with another (strong) entity [Teorey *et al.* 1986]. In this case the dependent entity is represented in the relational model with a composite key, built from the key of the 'parent' entity and one or more attributes of the dependent entity. Relationships between entities are more generally represented by the use of foreign keys.

A significant disadvantage of this value-based scheme of identity is that it entails expensive key maintenance operations when the value of a key is changed (for example, a customer's name changes). Additionally where there is no obvious natural key the application designer must resort to artificially generated values, which are difficult to maintain.[1]

The advantages of object identifiers (OIDs) in this role is that they provide a system-maintained unique value for every entity and the need for an application to generate its own unique identifiers is avoided.

3.1.2   Classification

Classification is the act of dividing objects into groups which have common properties. An instance is allocated to a class (is-a relationship) for example, Pauline is-a doctor. The classification process may be based on:

- Classical view. This view attempts to define classes in terms of a (small) set of necessary and sufficient conditions that unequivocally define the members of the class.
- Probabilistic view. Classes are defined as groups defined in terms of the overall similarity of individuals in terms of a large set of attributes.
- Archetype view. A 'typical' or 'characteristic' member of the class is described and an individual is assigned to a class on the basis of its similarity to the archetype.

In classical theory classes are distinguished from each other by the presence or absence of certain attributes. In some cases classification is easily done (for example, hospital in-patient, medical practitioner) where there are well-defined classificatory attributes. Nevertheless these often have some ill-defined cases (how long does a patient have to be in hospital to qualify as an in-patient? – the hospital and insurance company can have different views; what medical qualifications are recognized? – countries have differing requirements). The classical approach works adequately for many classes, but in many cases class membership is much less easy to define.

Much of the modern impetus for probabilistic classification has come from the biological sciences, where the application of classical classification techniques failed to produce biologically meaningful classes; the classic work is in this area [Sneath and Sokal 1973]. The outcome of numerous attempts to define 'natural' classifications in many subject domains has led to a widespread conclusion that natural classes do not exist. Any domain (UoD) can be classified in numerous ways, depending on the viewpoint and purpose of the classifier.

From a database design perspective this means that we can only hope to define a classification that supports the intended uses of the database.

---

1   For example, if new identifiers are generated as a function of a value which is updated after each identifier is generated, then access to that value will be a bottleneck in a conventional relational system, as it is locked until the end of the transaction.

3.1.3   Aggregation

Aggregation allows a new class to be defined in terms of a collection of other classes. Each component of the aggregation is a part of the aggregation class (PART-OF relationship). For instance, a clinical department might be defined as an aggregation consisting of a director, an administrative team, a number of medical teams and one or more ward teams. At a further level of detail a ward team might be seen as an aggregation consisting of a ward sister or charge nurse, several staff nurses, a number of nursing auxiliaries and a ward clerk.

3.1.4   Generalization

The generalization abstraction provides the means of defining generic classes, or supertypes, given a collection of classes sharing common elements. It is similar to classification, except that the instances are classes and not individuals for example, a surgeon IS-A person. The application of generalization provides designers with a means of refining the class hierarchy.

From a database designer's point of view there are two important coverage criteria for generalizations:

- **Partial or total coverage**. This criterion distinguishes generalizations where the subclasses completely cover the extent of the superclass and those where they do not.
- **Exclusive or overlapping subclass membership**. The distinction in this case is between generalizations where an instance may belong to a single subclass and those where it may be a member of several subclasses.

This gives four possible types of generalization:

1. **Total and exclusive**. The class of medical specialists is made up of cardiologists, gerontologists, neurologists, and so on (Figure 3.2a). A doctor can only be a specialist in one discipline, but a particular doctor's specialism may change over time (for example, a psychiatrist may undertake extra training to become a psychogeriatric specialist).
2. **Partial and exclusive**. Cars, vans and ambulances are types of vehicle of interest to a hospital transport manager (Figure 3.2b). There are many other types of vehicle (bicycle, truck, and so on) which do not form part of the hospital UoD; the coverage is exclusive since a vehicle can only be of one type.
3. **Partial and overlapping**. A hospital employee may hold public office, be a registered student or be a staff representative (Figure 3.2c). A particular person may have none, one or many of these roles.

4. **Total and overlapping**. A qualified nurse may be a practitioner, researcher or manager (Figure 3.2d). An individual nurse falls into at least one, and possibly several, of these categories.

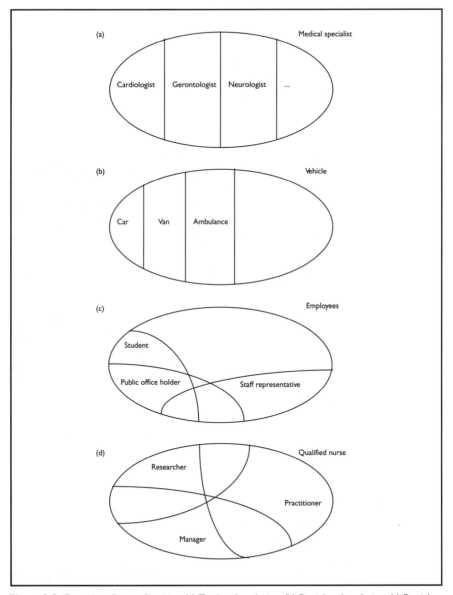

Figure 3.2 Examples of generalizations: (a) Total and exclusive, (b) Partial and exclusive, (c) Partial and overlapping, (d) Total and overlapping.

3.1.5 Relationships between classes

The abstractions we have described so far only allow certain structural relationships between classes. For a model to have sufficient expressive power to be useful it must also provide mechanisms to express arbitrary relationships between classes. These mechanisms can be categorized in two ways:

1. **Cardinality**. Specifies whether participation in a relationship is mandatory or optional and the number of participating instances of each class. This information is most readily captured by the concepts of minimum cardinality (MIN-CARD) and maximum cardinality (MAX-CARD).

    - A MIN-CARD of 0 indicates optional participation in the relationship, that is, there are instances in the optional class that do not participate. For instance, not all employees drive vehicles, so the relationship between employee and vehicle is optional on the employee side.
    - A MIN-CARD of 1 shows a mandatory participation in the relationship. If we assume that every vehicle must have a driver who is an employee the relationship between vehicle and employee is mandatory on the vehicle side.
    - A MAX-CARD of 1 indicates that the relationship involves only a single instance of that class.[2] Thus, an employee may only drive one vehicle at a time.
    - A MAX-CARD greater than 1 allows several instances to participate in the relationship. For instance, a vehicle may have several drivers at a given time. The number of max-card is usually not fixed but may be in certain cases. For example, if an occupational therapist cannot be allocated more than three wards to work with, the maximum cardinality of this relationship is fixed at 3.

2. **Degree**. Specifies the number of classes participating in a relationship. A relationship may be unary, binary or n-ary.

    - A unary relationship involves only members of a single class (for example, an employee is managed by another employee).
    - A binary relationship involves two classes. The examples above are all binary relationships, involving vehicles and employees or wards and occupational therapists.
    - N-ary relationships involve more than two classes, although there are very few that involve more than three classes. For example, the consultation relationship, involving a doctor, a patient and a room, is ternary.

---

2 A MAX-CARD of 0 is irrelevant, since it implies no relationship between the classes.

3.2   EER modelling

The basic notation for Entity-Relationship modelling was introduced by Chen [Chen 1976]; several extensions, to provide greater expressiveness, were proposed. This extended model is systematically described in [Teorey *et al.* 1986]. The EER model is based on entities, attributes and relationships. We describe each in more detail before considering the model as a whole.

3.2.1   Entity

An entity (strictly an entity type) is 'a thing which can be physically defined' [Chen 1976], but it may also be abstract (for example, job). In a text description of requirements or of the UoD, entities typically appear as nouns. It is sometimes useful to categorize entities:

- strong – have internally derived unique identifiers;
- weak – the unique identifier is derived from some 'parent' entity and the weak entity will cease to exist if its parent is removed.

Entities may be simple entities or they may be recognized as generalizations, either overlapping or exclusive. The distinction between overlapping and exclusive generalizations raises important implementation issues for any implementation, although the distinction is less important for conceptual modelling.

In the model a simple entity is represented diagramatically by a rectangle; a weak entity is commonly shown by a double rectangle.

Because of the importance of the different types of generalization in the later phases of the design process we prefer to use quite distinct notation for these two types of generalization. Our preferred notation is a large rectangle containing smaller rectangles for a non-overlapping generalization and a rectangle with arrows pointing to it from other rectangles to show an overlapping generalization.

3.2.2   Attribute

Attributes list all the properties of interest of an entity and can usually be identified as qualities of an entity in a text description. The attributes contain all the extensional information in a database; they can be divided into:

- **identifiers**, which uniquely distinguish entity instances (the key in a relational context);
- **descriptors**, which describe properties of the entity.

Whatever the target system it is necessary to be able to identify every instance uniquely, since otherwise a reference to, or operation on, an instance cannot adequately identify its target. For instance, given indistinguishable instances of the entity CHAIR and applying the operations:

```
Paint(chair, black)
ApplyLogo(chair)
```

it is not possible to determine whether or not the two operations are applied to the same chair or to different chairs.

All entities of a given type have common attributes; these may be:

- **simple** (for example, age) or composite (for example, address),
- **single valued** (for example, age) or multivalued (for example, skills),
- **base** (for example, date of birth) or derived (for example, age).

Simple attributes are represented by a short line with an open circle; identifiers have a filled circle. Composite attributes are shown by an oval.

3.2.3   Relationship

A relationship is defined as 'an association among entities' [Chen 1976] and is typically expressed in verbs or verb phrases. The model allows relationships of any degree and cardinality to be shown.

Cardinality can be most easily represented as a pair (min-card, max-card). This notation allows precise cardinalities, or limits, to be shown if they are known, which is not possible with alternative representations.

The degree of a relationship is shown by lines connecting the relationship to one or more entities.

A unary or binary relationship is represented by a diamond and a ternary relationship by a triangle. In EER modelling there are many representations of relationships and no well-defined standards, although all the alternative notations are similar and present no real problems of interpretation.

3.2.4   Adequacy of the model

The ER, and subsequently the EER, model has achieved very widespread currency and is used in a large number of design methods.

The model is sufficiently expressive to capture the salient structural relationships needed to construct database schemas. The model is minimal, with the exception of composite attributes, since no concept can be represented in terms of the others. Composite attributes can be represented in terms of collections of relationships and attributes, but are a useful mechanism for representing conceptually simple items that have a complex structure (for example, address).

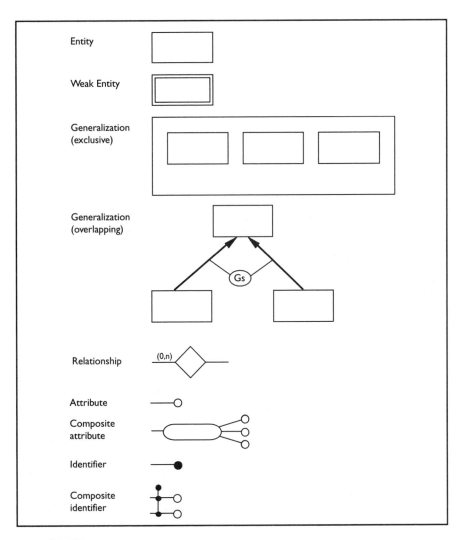

Figure 3.3 EER notation.

Entities, attributes and relationships are not given – an object may take on a number of roles in different contexts (for example, a city can be an entity or an attribute). Individual designers will produce different solutions to the same problem as a result of differing perceptions of the problem and previous experience. It should be seen as a normal result of any moderately flexible design approach and as such is a strength of the approach, not a weakness.

A high degree of correspondence can be seen between EER modelling and object-oriented approaches to data modelling. The differences between the approaches lie in the more detailed stages of the design, where the architecture of the target system influences the design.

In use the model has proved sufficiently flexible to represent a wide variety of situations and can readily be supported by CASE tools. In the next section we describe its systematic use for database design applications.

3.3   Data modelling methods

The process of constructing a schema is best approached as a series of iterative refinements. In this section we present an iterative approach to database design, based on that described by Batini and his colleagues [Batini *et al.* 1992]. A number of other useful approaches have been defined, of which that of Teorey [Teorey 1993] contains many useful observations, but is nevertheless essentially a linear approach. The analysis of many system development projects, our own experience and current folk wisdom strongly suggest that an iterative approach to software design, especially when coupled to the use of prototypes, is more likely to lead to good designs than other approaches. This is particularly true for the types of complex application domains discussed in Chapter 1.

The refinement of any design occurs along two axes:

1. Refinement resulting from a greater understanding of the problem domain (UoD).
2. Refinement resulting from incorporating more detail into the design.

In any complex design it is essential to have a disciplined approach to the refinement of the design. This can be achieved by the application of:

- **refinement primitives** – a set of transformations that can be repeatedly applied to an initial schema to produce a final schema. The rigorous application of a suitable set of primitives will result in reliable transformations of the schema that do not introduce internal inconsistencies, although the correspondence with the UoD is the designer's responsibility. We can distinguish two sets of primitives: top-down and bottom-up.
- **design strategy** – restricts the use of different types of refinement primitives in a design. This can result in a pure top-down strategy, where there is a consistent movement from general (abstract) to specific (concrete) concepts, a pure bottom-up strategy, which is the converse, or an intermediate strategy.

These refinement primitives and design strategies can be combined to produce design methods suited to particular organizations and application domains.

Schema refinement

Any consistent schema transformation must:

- provide a mapping between names in the starting schema and those in the resulting schema,

- maintain all the logical connections defined for the starting schema in the resulting schema.

It is possible to define a set of top-down refinement primitives that can be applied to produce consistent refinements of an initial high-level, abstract starting schema to derive a final detailed schema. The definition and application of bottom-up primitives is more problematic, as their use introduces new concepts into the schema and these new concepts may have effects on other parts of the schema. Nevertheless, for practical applications, their use is essential because they provide a disciplined way of incorporating the designer's increased understanding of the UoD into the design.

Top-down primitives

The set of top-down refinements has seven[3] primitives, shown graphically in Figure 3.4. These primitives allow the full range of top-down refinements. Each operates on a single element of the starting schema and is free of side-effects.

T1. An entity is decomposed into two entities with a relationship between them. For example, a hospital (physical view) can be refined into a number of buildings, each of which may contain one or more clinics (Figure 3.5a).

T2. An entity is refined into a generalization. For example, a medical team can be refined to a collection of doctors, nurses, clerks, and so on (Figure 3.5b).

T3. An entity is refined to a collection of uncorrelated entities. For example, a scan entity is refined to an ultrasound scan entity and a CAT scan entity (Figure 3.5c).

T4. A relationship is refined to two parallel relationships. For example, an admission is refined to be either a planned admission or an emergency admission (Figure 3.5d).

T5. A relationship is refined into two relationships and an entity. For example, a planned admission may be refined into a waiting-for relationship, an intended treatment entity and a planned consultant relationship (Figure 3.5e).

T6. An entity or relationship is refined by introducing attributes. For example, the entity person is refined to have a name, date of birth and sex (Figure 3.5f).

T7. An attribute is refined to a composite attribute or a collection of attributes. For example, a name attribute can be refined to a composite attribute comprising forename, surname (family name) and known as (alias) (Figure 3.5g).

---

3   Batini *et al.* propose an additional primitive (their T7): composite attribute development. We exclude it from our primitives because it can be expressed in terms of attribute development (T6) followed by attribute refinement (T7).

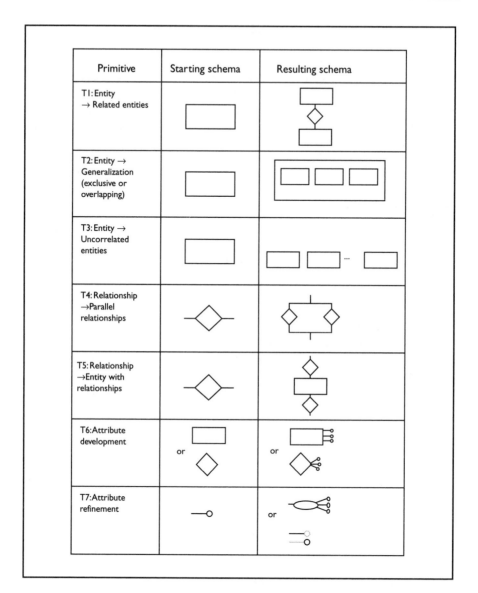

Figure 3.4 Top-down primitives (after [Batini *et al.* 1992]).

Bottom-up primitives

Bottom-up transformations add new concepts to the design, or modify existing concepts. There are three main occasions when bottom-up primitives are needed in the design process:

1. When new features of interest are discovered. This is the case of refinement resulting from greater understanding of the UoD.

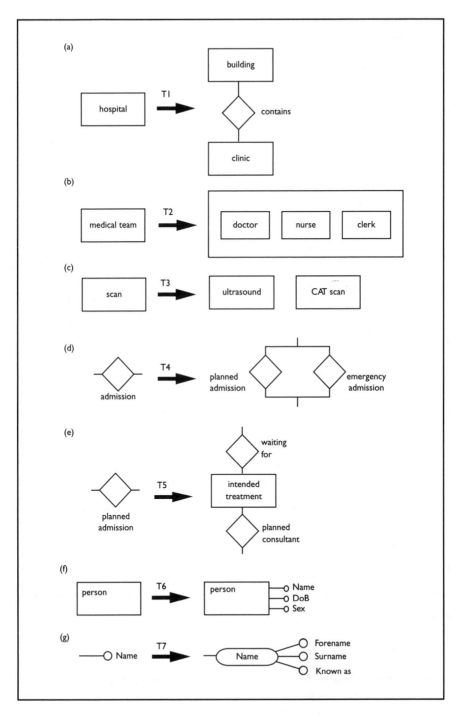

Figure 3.5 Examples of top-down refinements.

2. When two or more partial schemas (views) are merged in the process of view integration, that is creating a global schema by amalgamating a number of partial schemas.
3. When a schema is being reverse engineered from an existing implementation.

A set of five bottom-up primitives is minimal (that is no primitive can be expressed in terms of the others) and provides all the transformations necessary to generate any schema from a collection of attributes or entities. Arguably the most important use of design methods based on bottom-up transformations is the reverse engineering of designs from existing implementations.

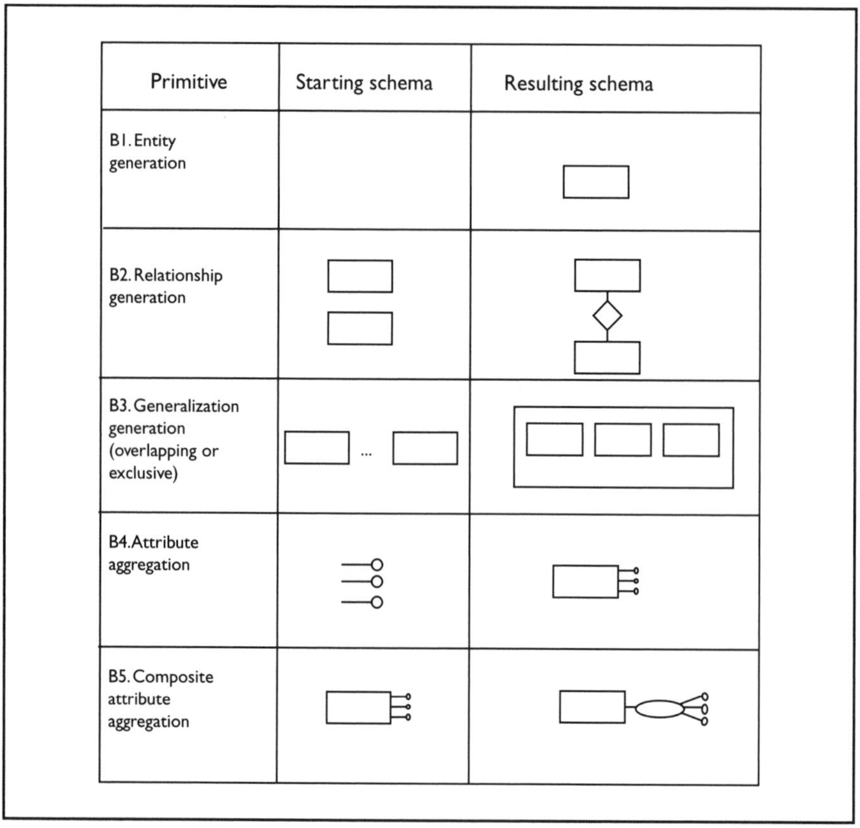

Primitive	Starting schema	Resulting schema
B1. Entity generation		
B2. Relationship generation		
B3. Generalization generation (overlapping or exclusive)		
B4. Attribute aggregation		
B5. Composite attribute aggregation		

Figure 3.6 Bottom-up primitives (after [Batini *et al.* 1993]).

The primitives are:

B1. Generates a new entity. For example, if it is realized that sites are of interest in modelling health care facilities, we have to introduce a new entity to represent this concept (Figure 3.7a).

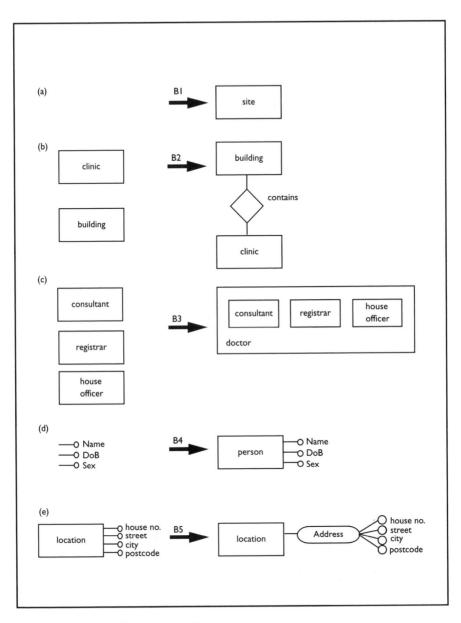

Figure 3.7 Examples of bottom-up primitives.

B2. Generates a new relationship between two entities. For example, a clinic may have a relationship to one or more buildings (Figure 3.7b).

B3. Generates a generalization from a collection of entities. For example, the staff called consultant, registrar and house officer can be covered by the generalization doctor (Figure 3.7c).

B4. Aggregates attributes which are formed into a entity (either new or existing). For example, a person entity may be created from a collection of attributes concerned with general information about a person. This is closely related to T5 (Figure 3.7d).

B5. Generates a composite attribute from a collection of previously defined attributes. For example, given a patient entity with attributes house number, street, city and postcode we can create a composite attribute address (Figure 3.7e).

3.3.1   Design strategies

It is possible to identify several useful design strategies, given the two sets of primitives that we have described.

Top-down strategy

A pure top-down strategy starts from an initial very high-level view of the design domain and applies successive refinements to the concepts in that schema until a fully elaborated final schema is obtained. The principal merit of the approach is that each concept can be refined without reference to others. The main drawback is that the designer must have a comprehensive high-level overview of the design requirements at the start of the process, which can be difficult or impossible for large and complex designs.

Bottom-up strategy

The bottom-up design strategy starts by identifying attributes from the application domain and proceeds to add more abstract concepts to the schema. The advantage of the approach is that it allows the designers to concentrate their attentions on a small fragment of the problem. The principal disadvantage is that the schema may need to be repeatedly restructured to accommodate increased understanding of the higher-level concepts that are discovered. In practice we believe that bottom-up approaches are only likely to be optimal for reverse engineering projects.

Inside-out strategy

The inside-out strategy is a variant of the bottom-up strategy. Here we start with the most accessible part of the design, and identify and refine a key concept into a small group of entities, their relationships and attributes. From this core the design spreads to discover adjacent concepts and thus diffuses outwards until the limits of the application domain are reached. The strategy preserves the disciplined use of transformations, but loses the different levels of abstraction.

Mixed strategy

Large and complex application domains are difficult to manage without partitioning the design in some way. The mixed strategy achieves this by starting with a skeleton schema containing the principal entities and their most important relationships. This schema can be partitioned and each partition refined separately, using a top-down strategy. In the final phase of the strategy the schema fragments are integrated using a bottom-up approach (view integration) and guided by the skeleton schema produced at the start of the process. The strategy is best suited to large projects and works well if the designer of the skeleton schema has a good grasp of the overall structure of the application domain. If the skeleton schema has significant design flaws these can be difficult to correct in the view integration stage.

3.3.2   Design guidelines

In addition to a well-defined design strategy a series of pragmatic guidelines is desirable to guide the designer and avoid unproductive effort.

Guidelines for classification:

- Entities should contain descriptive information. If an object is represented only by its identifier it should be treated as an attribute.
- Classify multivalued attributes as entities in a relational design. Making attributes single valued simplifies later design by avoiding non-first normal form entities.
- Attributes should directly describe the entity.
- Avoid composite identifiers.

An entity with a composite identifier whose elements are all identifiers of other objects should be defined as a weak entity or a relationship. Entities with identifiers that are partially composed of identifiers of other entities may often be redefined as multiple new entities with relationships between them.

If the composite identifier is easily identifiable in the UoD, it should be kept.

Decomposing generalization hierarchies

The decomposition of generalizations is a common problem that occurs in the later stages of a relational design, arising from the constraint that all data in a relational system is stored in flat tables – although decomposition is not always necessary. These issues are discussed further in Chapter 13.

There are two principal options available to a designer when decomposing generalization hierarchies:

1. Put the identifier and attributes applying to all subtypes in the supertype entity. This results in a single (large) table that will have null values for

inapplicable attributes (Figure 3.8). This option is generally preferred in applications where the dominant query load relates to the supertype or to several subtypes simultaneously.

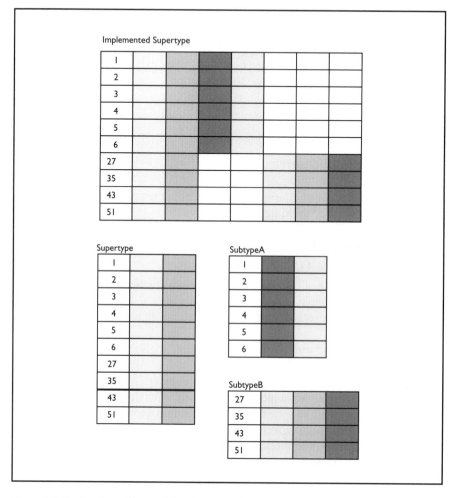

Figure 3.8 Posting the attributes of the subtypes to the supertype.

2. Put the supertype identifier into the subtypes, together with the attributes specific to each subtype. The result of this is that there is a table for each subtype with additional attributes which are common to all the subtypes (Figure 3.9). This option is generally preferable where the majority of queries refer to a single subtype.

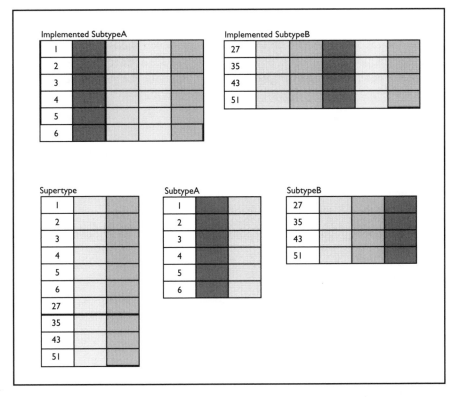

Figure 3.9 Posting the supertype's attributes to the subtypes.

Ternary relationships

Ternary relationships cannot be represented by several binary relationships. They can be identified most easily as relationships that involve three identifiers and therefore cannot be decomposed. One of the most common examples of a ternary relationship is a meeting that involves two parties (for example, radiologist and patient) and a location (for example, X-ray room).

3.4 Normalization

Normalization was developed as a formal technique for defining relations with certain desirable characteristics. Many of the principles underlying normal forms are in fact desirable for any logical design.

The aim of normalization is to produce a set of relations that contain minimum redundancy, so that any change to the values stored in the database can be achieved with the fewest possible update operations. The motivation for this is that updating large numbers of values in response to a single change is generally inefficient and error-prone. Storing only the smallest number of values necessary to represent the semantics of the database minimizes the storage required.

Normalization is a bottom-up design technique, which makes it difficult to use in large designs. For this reason it has been largely superseded by the top-down approaches described earlier in this chapter. The technique can still be useful in some circumstances:

- as a different method of checking the properties of a design arrived at through EER modelling;
- as a technique for reverse engineering a design from an existing undocumented implementation.

We present the normal forms in order, motivating them through the discussion of update anomalies. A more formal treatment of the topic can be found in [Ullman 1988]; the classic informal treatment of normalization through update anomalies is [Date 1994].

A normalized schema has a minimal redundancy, which requires that the value of no attribute of a database instance is replicated except where tuples are linked by foreign keys (the inclusion of the key of one relation in another).

We also require that a normalized schema:

- does not lose any information present in the unnormalized schema;
- does not include spurious information when the original schema is reconstructed;
- preserves dependencies present in the original schema.

When used as a design checking technique, normalization can be performed manually:

1. Identify the key (simple or composite) of each relation.
2. Identify any foreign keys in a relation.
3. Check that the other attributes in the relation are determined by the relation's key.
4. Create a new relation comprising any attributes not determined by the relation's key.
5. Repeat steps 2–5 for every relation.

Functional dependence

The normal forms are based around the notion of **functional dependence**. Given a relation R with (possibly composite) attributes A and B, if each value of A has a single value of B associated with it, $R_A \rightarrow R_B$; that is, R_B functionally depends on R_B. Alternatively, we can say that R_A functionally determines R_B. Functional dependence can be represented by rectangles representing attributes and a heavy arrow showing dependence, shown in Figure 3.10.

For example, there is a functional dependency between ward and building, since every ward is only located in a single building: $R_{ward} \rightarrow R_{building}$. This is illustrated in Figure 3.11.

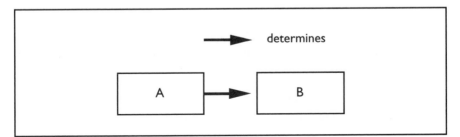

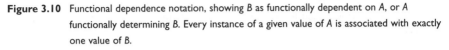

Figure 3.10   Functional dependence notation, showing *B* as functionally dependent on *A*, or *A* functionally determining *B*. Every instance of a given value of *A* is associated with exactly one value of *B*.

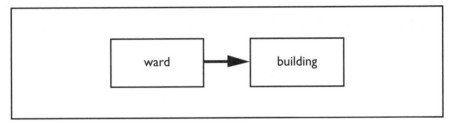

Figure 3.11   Functional dependence between ward and building.

We define a **primary key** as an attribute (which may be composite) that uniquely identifies tuples in a relation; a **candidate key** is an attribute that may be used to uniquely identify tuples, although it may not be selected as the primary key. This is discussed further in Chapter 13.

First Normal Form

First Normal Form (1NF) is the starting point for relational systems. A relation is in 1NF if it contains atomic values only. This eliminates any structure with attributes that are collections, repeating groups or other complex structures. The term Non-First Normal Form (NF2 or NFNF) is often used to describe tuples containing nested or repeating groups that do not comply with these requirements.

Consider the following relation (shown in Figure 3.12) which *inter alia* records details of appointments between doctors and patients:

OneNF (Patient, DateOfBirth, <u>Doctor</u>, PhoneNo, <u>DateTime</u>, Duration)

The compound key is chosen to reflect the fact that a doctor cannot have two simultaneous appointments. A similar observation applies to patients, so the Patient and DateTime attributes are also a candidate key.

There are several problems with this structure:

- We cannot represent a doctor who does not currently have an appointment with a patient.
- Similarly, we cannot represent a patient who does not currently have an appointment with a doctor.
- Information such as the patient's date of birth and the doctor's phone number is stored redundantly. This requires considerable care when inserting new records and updating existing records to ensure that all instances retain the correct values.
- If we delete the last remaining record containing details of a patient or a doctor, then all record of that patient or doctor is lost.

The real problem is that this relation contains information relating to several distinct entities which need to be separated. This is the essence of the normalization process.

OneNF

Patient	DateOfBirth	Doctor	PhoneNo	DateTime	Duration
Williams	1972-01-12	Cameron	1234	1994-08-10 10:00	10
Garcia	1981-03-18	Cameron	1234	1994-08-10 10:10	15
Fisher	1950-10-22	Finlay	2345	1994-08-10 10:50	10
Waldon	1942-06-01	Kildare	3456	1994-08-10 10:20	10
Fisher	1950-10-22	Finlay	2345	1994-09-12 11:10	20
Williams	1972-01-12	Finlay	2345	1994-08-17 10:00	10
Fisher	1950-10-22	Kildare	3456	1994-10-14 10:30	15
Garcia	1981-03-18	Kildare	3456	1994-09-24 10:40	10
Williams	1972-01-12	Cameron	1234	1994-08-24 11:30	20

Figure 3.12 Relation OneNF.

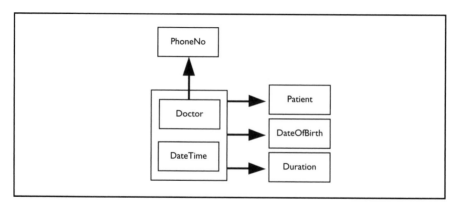

Figure 3.13 Functional dependencies for OneNF.

Figure 3.13 shows the functional dependencies in the OneNF relation. From this diagram it is clear that although the patient's name and date of birth and the duration of the appointment are dependent on the key, the doctor's phone number depends on only part of the key.

Second Normal Form

A relation is in 2NF if it is in 1NF and every non-key attribute is fully dependent on the primary key. Second Normal Form (2NF) is only of passing interest as an intermediate step towards higher normal forms.

The partial dependency of phone number on doctor in the OneNF relation indicates that the relation is not in 2NF. The first refinement is to separate information about doctors and their phone numbers from information about patients and appointments. This gives two tables (shown in Figure 3.14), both of which are in 2NF:

> Doctor (<u>Doctor</u>, PhoneNo)
> TwoNF (Patient, DateOfBirth, <u>Doctor</u>, <u>DateTime</u>, Duration)

TwoNF

Patient	DateOfBirth	Doctor	DateTime	Duration
Williams	1972-01-12	Cameron	1994-08-10 10:00	10
Garcia	1981-03-18	Cameron	1994-08-10 10:10	15
Fisher	1950-10-22	Finlay	1994-08-10 10:50	10
Waldon	1942-06-01	Kildare	1994-08-10 10:20	10
Fisher	1950-10-22	Finlay	1994-09-12 11:10	20
Williams	1972-01-12	Finlay	1994-08-17 10:00	10
Fisher	1950-10-22	Kildare	1994-10-14 10:30	15
Garcia	1981-03-18	Kildare	1994-09-24 10:40	10
Williams	1972-01-12	Cameron	1994-08-24 11:30	20

Doctor

Doctor	PhoneNo
Cameron	1234
Finlay	2345
Kildare	3456

Figure 3.14   Relations TwoNF and Doctor.

In this case we have the following anomalies:

- Deleting a record from TwoNF may lose patient details.
- Any changes to the patient details may involve changing multiple occurrences, because this information is still stored redundantly.

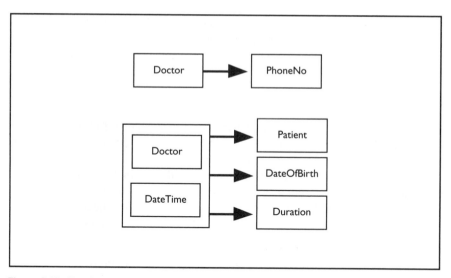

Figure 3.15 Functional dependencies for TwoNF and Doctor.

Third Normal Form

A relation is in Third Normal Form (3NF) if it is in 2NF and all the non-key attributes (that is, attributes that are not part of the primary key) are:

- mutually independent,
- functionally dependent on the primary key.

This means that a relation in 3NF consists of the primary key and a set (possibly empty) of independent non-key attributes. The transition from 2NF to 3NF is concerned with removing any dependencies between non-key attributes.

In the relation TwoNF there is, for example, no dependency between Patient and Duration. However, Patient and DateOfBirth are not mutually independent, so the relation is not in 3NF. While it is true that each value of the key has a single associated value of the date of birth, there is a further dependency not shown in Figure 3.15. This is a **transitive dependency** linking DateOfBirth indirectly to the key, through its dependency on the patient's name (Figure 3.16).

The solution to this problem again comes from splitting the relation to remove those parts that are not directly dependent on the key. In this case, we remove the DateOfBirth attribute from TwoNF and create a new relation, Patient, holding the patient details. All three relations are now in 3NF:

    Doctor (Doctor, PhoneNo)
    Patient (Patient, DateOfBirth)
    ThreeNF (Doctor, Patient, DateTime, Duration)

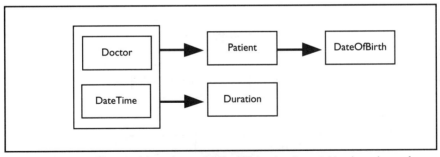

Figure 3.16   Revised functional dependencies for TwoNF showing the transitive dependency of DateOfBirth on the key, via Patient.

Three NF

Patient	Doctor	DateTime	Duration
Williams	Cameron	1994-08-10 10:00	10
Garcia	Cameron	1994-08-10 10:10	15
Fisher	Finlay	1994-08-10 10:50	10
Waldon	Kildare	1994-08-10 10:20	10
Fisher	Finlay	1994-09-12 11:10	20
Williams	Finlay	1994-08-17 10:00	10
Fisher	Kildare	1994-10-14 10:30	15
Garcia	Kildare	1994-09-24 10:40	10
Williams	Cameron	1994-08-24 11:30	20

Patient

Patient	DateOfBirth
Williams	1972-01-12
Garcia	1981-03-18
Fisher	1950-10-22
Waldon	1942-06-01

Doctor

Doctor	PhoneNo
Cameron	1234
Finlay	2345
Kildare	3456

Figure 3.17   Relations ThreeNF, Patient and Doctor.

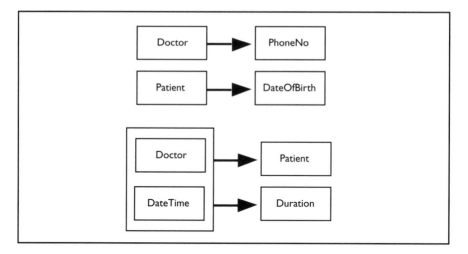

Figure 3.18 Functional dependencies for ThreeNF, Patient and Doctor.

Boyce–Codd Normal Form

BCNF is a stronger, but conceptually simpler, expression of 3NF. It was introduced to overcome possible anomalies in 3NF relations. It is, however, much simpler to apply as a means of checking an existing model developed by other methods.

The rule states that a relation is in BCNF if every determinant is a candidate key.

The procedure for checking a design is simply to examine the functional dependencies within each relation. If all non-key attributes depend upon only the complete key, the relation is in BCNF. In our example, the three final relations all comply with the BCNF rule.

For most purposes 3NF, or preferably BCNF, is considered to be sufficient to minimize problems arising from update, insertion and deletion anomalies.

Fourth Normal Form

Fourth Normal Form is concerned with dependencies between the elements of compound keys, specifically, those composed of three or more attributes. Here, a relation may be in 3NF or BCNF yet still exhibit undesirable internal dependencies.

Consider a different example in which we record the information that a doctor works on one or more wards and treats one or more conditions. In other words, the doctor works on a set of wards and treats a set of conditions. We assume that these are general wards on which a range of conditions may be treated. This leads to redundancy because we have to record multiple instances of a doctor working on the same ward, and multiple instances of a doctor treating the same condition (Figure 3.19).

In order to deal with this redundancy we introduce the concept of **multivalued dependencies** (**MVD**) [Fagin 1979]. A multivalued dependency is a functional dependency where the dependency may be to a set and not just a single value. The decomposition which allows for these dependencies is also shown in Figure 3.19.

DWC

Doctor	Ward	Condition
Finlay	George III	Depression
Finlay	George III	Angina
Finlay	Victoria	Depression
Finlay	Victoria	Angina
Kildare	George III	Delusion
Kildare	George III	Depression
Kildare	Victoria	Delusion
Kildare	Victoria	Depression

DC

Doctor	Condition
Finlay	Depression
Finlay	Angina
Kildare	Delusion
Kildare	Depression

DW

Doctor	Ward
Finlay	Victoria
Kildare	Victoria
Finlay	George III
Kildare	George III

Figure 3.19 The relation DWC and its decomposition into DC and DW.

Fifth Normal Form

There exist some relations which cannot be decomposed into two higher normal form relations by means of projections in the way we have shown so far in this section. It is possible to decompose these into three (or more) relations which can be reconstructed by means of a three-way (or more) join.

This normal form is not of practical significance for our purposes and the interested reader is referred to [Fagin 1979] or [Ullman 1988] for a full description.

3.5 Summary

In this chapter we have presented the concepts fundamental to data modelling: classification, aggregation and generalization. We next described how these concepts are represented in the EER model and discussed its adequacy for general data modelling purposes. The third section of the chapter describes strategies for using EER modelling constructs and transformations in a disciplined manner to achieve good data designs. The last section provides an overview of normalization for relational structures.

Exercise

Design the data schema for the scenario described below, which is based on the adult care needs of Social Services Departments in England and Wales.

The Social Services Department of Dunwich Metropolitan Borough Council is installing a new Care Management System in its Adult Services Division to try to improve the management and administration of its services by directly supporting Care Managers, Team Leaders and Divisional Managers in their work. Nobody in the Division has much experience of using this sort of system.

The Division's clients include people with a variety of physical disabilities (from accidents, illness and so on), severe learning difficulties and many frail elderly people. For management and planning purposes, each person is categorized as belonging to a particular client group (for example, young physically disabled, elderly mentally infirm). Each person has a record containing their name, address, data of birth, sex, client group, care manager, services received and a brief description of their problems and needs. The present manual records do not contain financial information. The new records must contain all the information in the current records and also show how each service received by a person is being paid for.

At any given time the Division has approximately 3500 people receiving some sort of assistance; the principal services available are:

- domiciliary care (help with cleaning, shopping and so on),
- day care (taking clients to a social centre for the day),
- lunch and social clubs,
- an incontinence laundry service,
- sheltered workshops and adult training centres,
- residential homes and hostels,
- nursing homes,
- counselling.

The client's record must show which services are being received, their weekly costs and who is making what contributions towards the costs.

These services are provided in one of two ways:

- by block contracts with other agencies (mostly voluntary organizations or other sections of the Social Services Department),

- by individual contracts with other agencies.

The block contracts specify that the Division will pay a fixed sum for a certain amount of service (for example, a contract might be made with an independent service provider to supply 25 day care places for a year for 62,000 sceattas[4] – the cost to the Division is the same whether or not the places are filled). Individual contracts are made where no block contracts exist – in these cases payment is made on the basis of the actual service provided.

The system must contain information on:

- the location, type and cost of a particular service,
- details of the service provider (organization, contact person, address and so on),
- what sort of contract exists for the service.

Details of block contracts are also needed:

- the type and quantity of service in the contract,
- the provider,
- the current use of the service,
- the total use of the service for the year.

The cost of the services provided to a client may be met in a number of ways, by contributions from:

- the Division's own budget,
- the Health Authority,
- the Independent Living Foundation (ILF),
- the client's own resources.

In the case of contributions from the ILF it may take several months before payments are made; in this case the Division will meet the initial costs from its own budget and be reimbursed later.

Most services are funded from more than one of these sources; the amounts paid from each source are dependent on the client's circumstances.

The Division employs three teams of Care Managers; each team covers a particular district of the borough. A team consists of between four and six Care Managers and a Team Leader.

The job of the Care Managers is to assess the needs of each client and then to arrange a 'package' of services which meet those needs as far as possible. The needs of a client are likely to change over time (for example, a client may need intensive domiciliary help for a few weeks after an operation, but little after that).

---

4   The sceatta is the currency in use in Dunwich.

Care Managers must be able to find out:

- what services are available (examine only),
- the cost of a service (examine only),
- who among their existing clients receives which services (examine and modify),
- how the costs are being met (examine and modify),
- the full details of a particular client (examine and modify).

The principal constraints on the Care Managers are that:

- the team shall not overspend its annual budget,
- the quantity of each service available is finite (for example, a residential home has only a fixed number of beds).

Team Leaders must be able to examine (but not modify):

- full details of clients of Care Managers in their team,
- the use being made of particular services (individually and overall, for example, to find out how many people are attending lunch clubs and how many are attending a particular club – broken down by client group),
- details of what has been spent and what future commitments have been made on the Team's budget.

Divisional Managers need to review the overall patterns of service provision; to do this they must be able to see:

- which client groups are receiving which services,
- which districts in the borough they come from,
- what are the costs,
- what contracts the Division has,
- the details of block contracts,
- how many clients there are in each client group, their average age and what district they live in.

The Divisional Managers should not see any details that would enable them to identify individual clients.

Divisional Managers negotiate block contracts and update the list of available services; they must therefore be able to modify all the data concerning contracts and available services.

Chapter 4

FUNCTIONAL MODELLING

In this chapter we concentrate on approaches to developing the parts of a functional or processing schema that are relevant to database design. Functional analysis concentrates on the transformational aspects of the system. In the first part of the chapter we take a similar approach to that in Chapter 3, describing firstly the concepts, secondly approaches to functional analysis using Data Flow Diagrams and thirdly strategies for joint functional and data modelling. The second part of the chapter describes some object-oriented techniques and shows how they are integrated into an overall method, using Booch's Object-Oriented Design as an example. In our presentation of object-oriented methods we emphasize the importance of responsibilities and contracts as abstractions for functional schema design.

4.1 Functional modelling concepts

Functional analysis is the process of identifying the activities that take place within the Universe of Discourse (UoD) that are of interest to us. The result of a functional analysis is a functional schema, a description of the activities of interest in the UoD. Given that our focus is on data-intensive systems, the activities of most interest are those that generate and transform data.

There are two areas of particular concern from a database designer's perspective:

- Ensuring that there is a match between the data and functional schemas, that is, the database contains all the items needed by the processes of interest and there are processes that operate on all the stored data.
- Determining the rules and constraints that govern the permitted modifications and constraints that should be applied to the database. This activity typically entails determining the enterprise rules and procedures as they affect the data.

The emphasis on the second area only arises with more modern database systems, which implement database procedures, methods or integrity checks (other than the most elementary); otherwise it forms part of the application design.

The concepts useful in this context are those concerned with the classification of activities: function, process and action.

Function

The overall characterization of an area of activity. A function can be viewed as a declarative specification of one of the (tactical) goals of an organization or as a description of what the organization does. For example, a function of a warehouse is to receive goods; a hospital may have a function to provide day surgery for minor orthopaedic operations.

Process

The mechanisms by which the function is achieved. A procedure typically has a set of rules specifying under what conditions it should be used, exception conditions, and so on. There is frequently a defined order (or partial order) among the procedures; the ordering criteria may be those of normal sequence or may be necessary prerequisites. For example, the procedures involved in providing day surgery for minor orthopaedic procedures may involve, for a particular patient:

- appointments scheduling,
- admissions procedure,
- preoperative procedure,
- one or more surgical procedures,
- post-operative procedure,
- discharge procedure,
- follow-up procedure.

Action

An action is a step in a procedure. In an office-based context this might be filling in a form, or a manufacturing stage in an industrial environment. Many actions can be further decomposed; the level of detail required will depend on the aims of the modelling. Actions frequently have strong pre- and postconditions, but in many procedures the sequence of actions can be weakly ordered or unordered. For example, the actions in a day surgery admissions procedure might be:

- verify patient's identity,
- obtain outline social history,
- obtain history of recent medical conditions and medication,
- check food and fluid intake in the previous 24 hours,

- verify the surgical procedure to be performed,
- check transport arrangements for discharge.

These actions have no strict ordering and all but the second are necessary preconditions for the surgery to be carried out.

4.2   Data Flow Diagrams

Data Flow Diagrams (DFDs) have been widely used since the late 1970s as a technique for describing processes and their interactions with stored data, resulting in a high-level program specification. The technique is based around a top-down decomposition of the system being studied and uses four concepts: process, flow, data store and interface (frequently called a source or sink). The first three concepts describe the components of the system and the last concept describes the external objects that interact with the system. Every instance of a concept in a DFD must be named; the names convey the semantics of the process.

The process of modelling using DFDs conventionally starts with a very high-level diagram, the context diagram, which contains the external interfaces and the principal dynamic concepts (functions) of the system. The context diagram is then refined to show more detail (processes); refinement stops when a further refinement would describe algorithms or program-level procedures (actions or details of an action). The technique uses the term process to describe any data transformation activity (creation, destruction, modification) in the system. Each DFD process is numbered to indicate its place in the refinement hierarchy. In the rest of this section we use the term process in this wider sense.

It is important to remember that DFDs do not show flows of control, but flows of data. Often it is helpful to conceptualize a DFD as a series of conveyors, which move data about between processes within the system. This makes it easy to recognize if the activity has slipped into modelling flows of control rather than flows of data.

There are four concepts used in DFDs:

Process. A process generates, destroys or transforms data. It is shown as a soft rectangle.

Data store. Any place in the system where data is stored, either permanently or temporarily, is shown as a data store. Its diagrammatic representation is an open rectangle. Data stored permanently usually represents the result or record of work performed by the system; temporary data stores are typically queues waiting for service by a process.

Flow. Processes are connected by flows, which show the movement of data between processes.

Interface. An interface is an object external to the system which either generates data for the system's processes to transform, or consumes data transformed by the system. An interface is represented diagramatically by a double square.

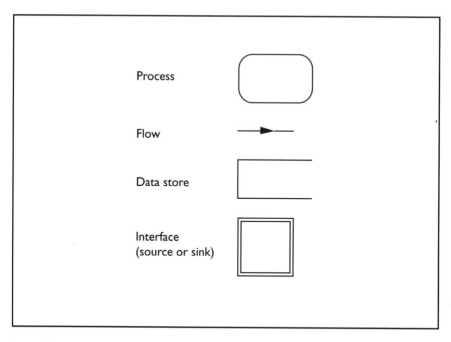

Figure 4.1 Data Flow Diagram symbols.

Functional analysis primitives

Functional modelling with DFDs is normally a top-down process involving a series of iterative refinements (Figure 4.2). At each refinement step the existing logical connections of the refined concept must be maintained.

We can identify a useful set of seven refinement primitives for DFD modelling:

T1. Process decomposition with intermediate data flow. Here the refinement recognizes that a single process can be decomposed into two separate processes linked by a flow. For example, the process of discharge planning is broken into the separate processes of assessing the patient's capabilities and preparing a care plan on the basis of the assessment (Figure 4.3a).

T2. Process decomposition with intermediate data store. In this case a process is recognized as being composed of two lower-level processes linked by an intermediate data store. For example, a discharge referral can be refined into the processes of preparing a discharge summary and sending a referral (Figure 4.3b).

T3. Process decomposition without connections. A process is recognized as being composed of two separate, disconnected processes. For example, an initial patient interview may be decomposed into two processes of making the relevant social and medical enquiries (Figure 4.3c).

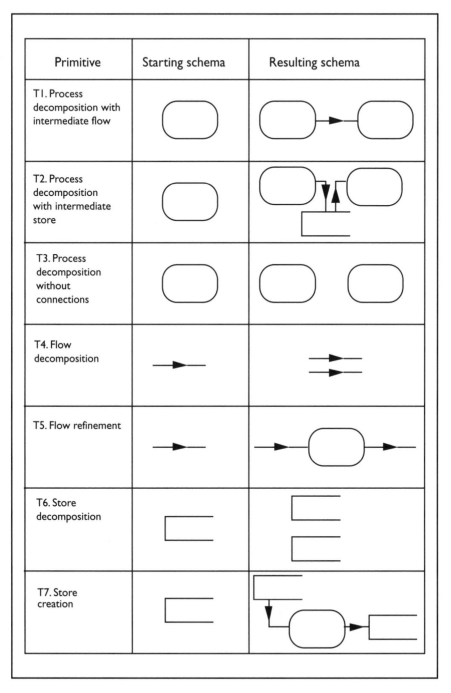

Figure 4.2 Top-down DFD primitives (after [Batini et al. 1993]).

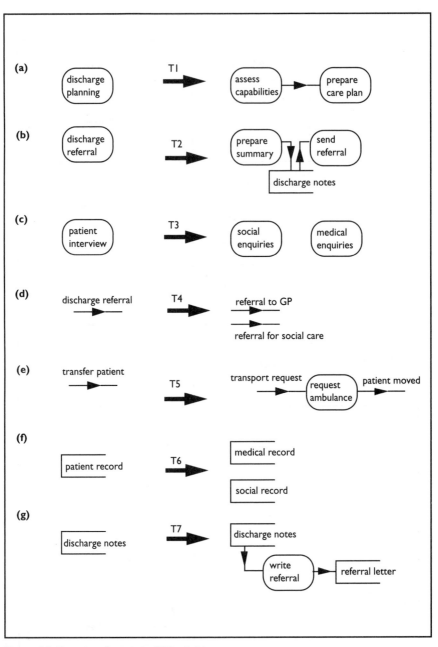

Figure 4.3 Examples of top-down DFD primitives.

T4. Flow decomposition. A data flow is seen to comprise two separate data flows. For example, a discharge referral can be refined to either a general practitioner referral or a social care referral (Figure 4.3d).

T5. Flow refinement. This transformation is applied when it is recognized that a data flow undergoes some transformation along its length. For example, a transfer of a patient can be refined into a transport request to obtain an ambulance in which the patient is moved (Figure 4.3e).

T6. Store decomposition. Here a store is split into two subsets, each relating to different flows or interfaces. For example, a patient's record can be refined into a patient's social record and medical record (Figure 4.3f).

T7. Store creation. A transformation which is applied when it is recognized that a data store can be divided into two subsets and that there is a mapping between them. For example, the discharge notes data store is divided to transform the initial discharge notes into a referral letter (Figure 4.3g).

Data flow model development

Most accounts of functional modelling describe a top-down approach, particularly for DFD modelling, although mixed and inside-out strategies are also viable [Batini *et al.* 1992]. The refinement of the functional schema is not formally defined, but should cease when further refinement would describe the structure of the computer processes (as opposed to the organization's processes). The application of any transformation should maintain the logical external connections of the original schema.

Top-down strategy

The majority of DFD transformations are process decompositions (T1, T2, T3); each decomposition should be designed to produce sub-processes that have the greatest degree of independence. This type of approach is described in detail in most structured systems analysis texts, for example [DeMarco 1978; Weaver 1993].

Inside-out strategy

The starting point for an inside-out strategy applied to functional design is to proceed from the interfaces (sources or sinks), following the flows through the system. This approach is often productive in applications where there are existing complex and overlapping paper-based systems which are to be replaced.

Mixed strategy

The mixed strategy starts from a skeleton schema which is split into several sub-schemas. Each sub-schema is refined using a top-down approach and the final schema is constructed by integrating the sub-schemas, guided by the skeleton schema.

External schemas

In order to describe the structure of the data in a data store or needed by a process we can introduce the concept of an external schema. An external schema is effectively a database view, that is, a description of the data seen from the perspective of a particular process, user or application.

An external schema for a DFD is a fragment of an EER diagram which is associated with a process or data store. This is shown by associating a DFD concept with an EER fragment, enclosed by a hexagon, via an arrow linking the two; the notation is shown in Figure 4.4.

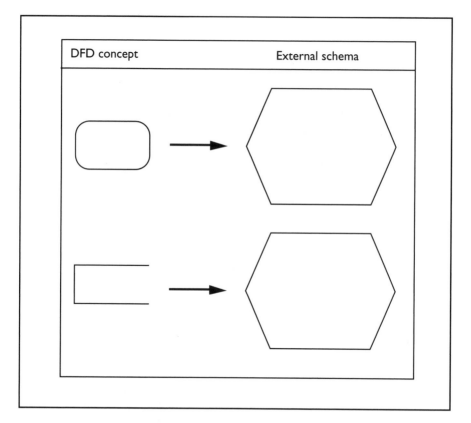

Figure 4.4 External schema notation.

The EER fragment associated with a DFD concept should be a self-contained diagram, showing the data required by that process. It does not have to be fully refined, but reflects the refinement appropriate to the level of detail being modelled.

In principle it is possible to start from a functional schema, associate the necessary external schemas with the functional concepts and then integrate all the separate external schemas to form the global data schema. For any but the simplest schema this is unworkable, because of the unmanageably large number of views and the complexity of the schema changes resulting from the bottom-up approach.

External schemas are best used as a means of checking the completeness of the data schema and guiding its refinement. In this role the external schemas provide an important bridge between the data schema and the functional schema, since they identify data that must be in the database and help ensure that processes exist which use each item in the database.

The use of external schemas can be illustrated by the day surgery example:

- Data used by a process. For example, the request ambulance process uses data identifying the patient to be transported, the origin and destination of the journey and when the patient is to be moved.
- Description of a data store. For example, a medical record used in the admissions process may consist of a patient's identifying details, medical condition and the doctor responsible for treating that patient.

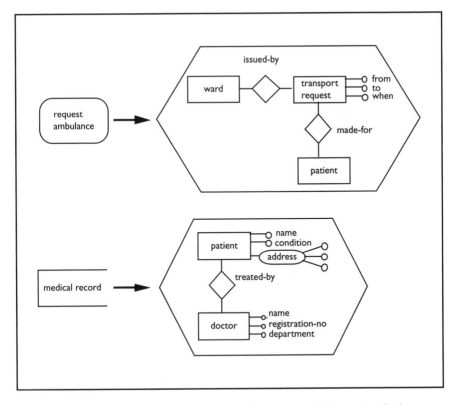

Figure 4.5 Examples of external schemas: (a) data used by a process, (b) description of a data store.

4.3   Joint functional and data modelling

In the preceding sections we have shown how top-down iterative approaches can be applied to the development of data schemas and to the development of functional schemas. Here we describe two methods that utilize the data and functional schemas to obtain a series of mutual refinements. The first method is based on the top-down or mixed approach, and the second on the inside-out approach.

The aims of both methods are to ensure that the processes in the functional schema have all the necessary data and that the entities in the data schema are all maintained by suitable processes.

Top-down or mixed approach

The steps in joint functional and data modelling based on a top-down or mixed approach are:

1. Design a skeleton functional schema. This identifies the principal interactions with external entities and thus defines the scope of the system.
2. Design a skeleton data schema. Identify the principal entities and relationships of the system. As a general guide, a skeleton schema should fit onto a single sheet of paper.
3. Split the skeleton schemas into sub-schemas (for large or complex designs only). The skeleton schemas should be split along the same lines so that the functional and data sub-schemas are aligned.
4. Refine each (sub-)schema. The top-down primitives are applied to refine each schema to the next level of detail. In general the refinement should occur evenly over the whole schema, so that no part of a schema is substantially more refined than another.
5. Completeness check. This step involves constructing external schemas to link fragments of the functional schema with their counterparts in the data schema. The purpose of this step is to check the functional schema to ensure that every concept in the data schema is referenced and to check the data schema against the functional schema to ensure that there exist processes for the creation, deletion and modification of every entity in the data schema that needs these operations.
6. Repeat steps 4 and 5 until the schemas are fully refined.
7. Integrate the sub-schemas (for large or complex designs only).

Inside-out approach

The steps for joint functional and data modelling based on an inside-out approach are:

1. Start from a source or sink and identify the processes connected to it. This gives a small portion of the data schema, refined to a high degree of detail.
2. Develop the corresponding fragment of data schema.

3. Expand the scope of the functional schema to encompass the adjacent parts of the system.
4. Repeat Steps 2 and 3 until the system boundary is reached.

4.4   Object-oriented analysis and design methods

Numerous object-oriented analysis and design (OOAD) methods have been proposed, mostly since 1988. This work can be broadly classified according to whether OOAD is seen as an evolutionary step from conventional structured methods or as a revolutionary development. The developments of structured methods that we have described provide equivalent concepts and expressive power to the methods proposed by evolutionary OOAD writers such as Rumbaugh [Rumbaugh *et al.* 1991]. In this section we concentrate on some of the more 'revolutionary' aspects of OOAD which may provide good alternatives to the data flow approaches described earlier in this chapter.

The major focus of many OOAD writers has been towards specifying functional and behavioural characteristics of objects. Often the attributes are regarded as solely part of the internal implementation of an object to be considered at a detailed design stage and it is seen as sufficient to define the object's external interface.

It is frequently suggested, following Wirfs-Brock [Wirfs-Brock *et al.* 1990], that classes should be identified and grouped according to responsibilities. The Wirfs-Brock approach emphasizes that classes act as servers, providing services to others, and are also clients, requesting and consuming services. Servers and clients participating in any behaviour have responsibilities for different aspects. The focus is on defining these responsibilities and specifying contracts for the interactions between clients and servers. These contracts define an object's interface.

The aim of object-oriented analysis (OOA) is to produce a description of the UoD in terms of a set of interacting objects with well-defined external behaviours and attributes (the internal details and their implementation belong to a later phase). In our view the significant advance made by OOAD writers that is relevant to database designers is the notion of contracted responsibilities, since this allows a clear specification of the functions of an object or class. As part of the implementation phase these specifications can be mapped into procedures, either in the database or as part of the application code.

In the rest of this section we describe some of the techniques of OOAD and show how they are used in Booch's OOD method, selected as a representative and popular 'revolutionary' approach.

Object-oriented analysis and design techniques

Here we briefly summarize several object-oriented techniques that may be considered when constructing the functional schema for a database application. First we discuss the classic OOA technique, although we do not recommend it for any but the smallest problems. Next we sketch the Use-Case, Object Behaviour Analysis and Class

Diagram techniques. These are generally applicable to successively more detailed stages of the analysis and design process.

Classical object-oriented analysis

The classical object-oriented analysis approach is similar to the classical structured approaches. At its simplest it is to:

- identify nouns in the problem domain (often a requirements specification) and make them into objects;
- use the verbs applicable to each noun to determine the message interface (function);
- use the adjectives as the basis for the definition of an object's logical properties (behaviour).

This simple approach assumes that a good description of the system exists and also has a strong bias towards tangible objects. The failure of this approach to identify conceptual objects and its reliance on a complete requirements specification or similar documentation makes it unsuitable for large or complex systems, although it may have a part to play in the early stages of their development.

Use-Case Analysis

Use-Case Analysis, developed by Jacobson [Jacobson *et al.* 1992], is another technique that focuses on system behaviour examined through prototypical examples. It relies on series of storyboards (similar to those used in television and advertising) which depict scenarios. The design team uses these for walkthroughs which identify the participating objects, their responsibilities and relationships.

It is most often used as part of the high-level analysis of the UoD, although it can also be useful in recording informal procedures in interviews with domain experts and practitioners.

Object Behaviour Analysis

An interesting approach is proposed by Rubin and Goldberg [Rubin and Goldberg 1992] in their Object Behaviour Analysis (OBA), using an approach influenced by Function Point Analysis [Dreger 1989]. They focus on identifying the functions performed by the system, which they term its behaviour.

The heart of the method lies in the identification of the **initiators** and **participants** in any behaviour. Significant participants are identified as objects and are assigned clearly defined responsibilities corresponding to their roles in the system's behaviour. Roles are identified by examination of prototypical situations, describing idealized behaviours (often obtained by interviewing domain experts). The behaviour and its participants are captured in a tabular **script**.

The principal elements of an OBA script are:

- **Initiator**. The actor (person, object) responsible for starting the action (for example, doctor's secretary).
- **Action**. A description of the action (for example, record case notes).
- **Participant**. Other actor(s) involved in the action (for example, doctor).
- **Service**. The specification of what the participant must provide for the action to be successful, expressed declaratively (for example, provide case notes).

The format of a script is shown in Figure 4.6.

Script Name	*Take Case Notes*		
Author	Rosemary		
Version	1.0		
Precondition	Patient file exists		
Postcondition	Modified file		
Trace	Record Insertion		
Initiator	**Action**	**Participant**	**Service**
Doctor	Make case note	Dictation machine	Make recording
Secretary	Find case file	Filing cabinet	Search
Secretary	Record case note	Doctor	Write note
Secretary	Replace file	Filing cabinet	Search

Figure 4.6 Example OBA script.

A script also contains information such as the name of the behaviour, how it was derived, its relationships to other aspects of the system, and so on; a number of annotations for script cells are also provided. Rubin and Goldberg present a full description of their approach, with a worked example based on making modifications to a spreadsheet.

Class diagrams

Class diagrams are an important part of Booch's OOD method, forming the core of the data and functional definition of the method. They are used to provide:

- Assignment of operations and services to classes,
- Relationships to other classes (including inheritance),
- Attribute definitions.

The notation for class diagrams is shown in Figure 4.7. The class itself is shown as a 'cloud' which contains the class name, its public attributes and operations. A class's relationships to other classes are shown by connecting lines. Abstract classes are shown by the letter 'A' in an inverted triangle; the inverted triangle is used for all adornments (that is, useful secondary information about a concept).

Associations are represented by a plain line, labelled with the relationship name and, optionally, its cardinality.

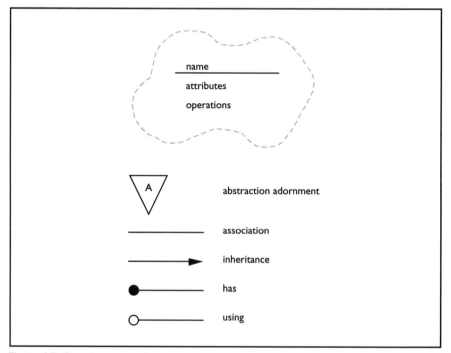

Figure 4.7 Class diagram notation.

Inheritance is denoted by an arrowed line, with the arrow at the superclass end. Generally the subclass is assumed to inherit the attributes and behaviour of the superclass and multiple inheritance is allowed. Inheritance is almost always tree-structured; cyclic inheritance is not allowed. Overloaded names (that is, names representing more than one implementation of an attribute or method) refer to the instance of the name at the lowest point in the hierarchy; overloading from multiple inheritance hierarchies is resolved using implementation-specific rules. Booch suggests that these semantics are in fact determined by the programming language to be used in the implementation. Since it is usually better to decouple analysis and logical design from implementation decisions we prefer that the semantics of the diagrams are defined independently of the implementation language.

The 'has' arrow is used to define aggregations (that is, 'part-of' relationships); the blob is placed at the aggregate end of the relationship. The relationship does not imply physical containment; cyclic and reflexive aggregations are allowed.

The 'using' relationship links servers to their clients; the client end is shown with an open circle.

From the database designer's perspective class diagrams provide a data schema representation comprising a simple list of visible attributes, with mechanisms for showing aggregation and specialization. The other features of the technique address the functional schema, showing a richer set of relationships than can be represented by DFDs.

Booch's OOD method

Booch's OOD method [Booch 1994] is derived from his earlier work on Ada design. It uses a very wide range of tools and techniques, ranging from informal lists to a variety of formal diagramming techniques, and has very few definite steps, preferring instead a series of iterations, incrementally refining aspects of the design in an approach similar to Boehm's spiral model [Boehm 1986]. Good software design usually requires innovation and creativity which is fostered by a loosely structured environment. This seeming lack of structure and reliance on *ad hoc* tactical decisions conflicts with the well-defined structure needed to develop large systems. Booch reconciles this conflict by distinguishing between the micro and the macro-level of development. His macro-level is a well-defined, disciplined series of procedures and milestones that represents normal good project management practice. Project management and other macro-level issues are outside the scope of this book and the interested reader should consult Booch and suitable texts on project management (for example, [DeMarco 1982; Abdel-Hamid and Madnick 1991]).

The choice of technique at the micro level is mostly tactical, depending on the problem at hand. However, four principal steps can be identified in each iteration:

1. Identify classes and objects

The aim is to discover the important concepts in the UoD and map them to classes and objects; in the early stages these can often be identified as tangible objects. The boundaries of the system are defined in the initial phases; later this activity shifts its focus from identifying concepts in the problem domain to inventing abstractions that form part of the solution. The main deliverable is a data dictionary which is developed to contain a specification of every element of the system; its principal benefits are:

- to record a common consistent vocabulary for the system,
- to act as a learning resource for new team members,
- to provide a unified global view of the system design as it evolves.

2. Identify semantics of classes and objects

This phase is concerned with identifying the behaviour and attributes of the objects and classes identified in the previous stage of the cycle. The data dictionary is refined to include the responsibilities of each object or class. Interaction diagrams (described in Chapter 5) and object diagrams (similar to the class diagrams described above) are used to represent the objects' responsibilities and relationships. Booch recommends that object specifications be captured as soon as possible, using programming language constructs such as C++ header files, or database stored procedures. The interfaces for the provision of common services and responsibilities should be defined at a project level rather than on a class-by-class-basis, in order to achieve consistency.

3. Identify relationships between classes and objects

This step defines the relationships between objects and classes, defining aggregations and inheritance hierarchies; it also formalizes the allocation of responsibilities and concerns from the previous step. The result of this step is expressed in class diagrams, object diagrams and module diagrams[1]. The focus of this step is on the identification of relationships in the early phases. As the analysis and design proceeds the relationships are refined using a top-down approach, constraints are added, redundant relationships eliminated and the whole set of relationships is checked for compliance with the scenarios examined earlier in the cycle. In the later phases this step is concerned mostly with the grouping of classes and objects to ensure a good modularization of the application. The quality of the result can be assessed in terms of cohesion, coupling and completeness.

4. Implement classes and objects

The implementation step in the cycle is concerned with achieving a satisfactory representation of the functional behaviour defined in earlier steps of the cycle. The insights from the implementation in each cycle are fed into the next iteration of the design process. In the analysis phases the implementation step typically delivers class specifications, which may be documented by class diagrams, showing their static semantics. Dynamic behaviour can be represented by using statecharts and interaction diagrams (described in Chapter 5). As the design progresses the products of this step are realized as executable code.

4.5 Summary

In this chapter we first described the basic techniques for functional modelling using data flow diagrams and second, the use of object-oriented methods for designing the functional schema.

The data flow approach has concentrated on the transformation of data by processes and we have described iterative methods for integrating the development of the data and functional schemas. The combination of this type of transformational approach, coupled with the development of a data schema, is sufficient for the majority of conventional database applications.

---

1   Module diagrams are concerned with the allocation of objects and classes to program modules as part of the physical design of the system and are not discussed further here.

Our discussion of object-oriented techniques has emphasized the notion of responsibilities and contracts to partition the functional schema between the elements of the system. We believe that techniques based on this approach can provide significant benefits in the design of modern distributed systems.

Exercise

Use the techniques described in this chapter to model the steps involved in making an appointment to see a physician (general practitioner).

Chapter 5

BEHAVIOUR MODELLING

5.1 Introduction

The preceding two chapters have described data modelling and functional modelling. However, these approaches cannot represent many of the dynamic and behavioural requirements of advanced applications, so we also need techniques for specifically modelling the time-dependent behaviour of systems: our concern here is with techniques for representing the dynamic behaviour of the system required by its users.

The whole area of dynamic modelling is underdeveloped. Harel's observation that: 'The literature on software and systems engineering is almost unanimous in recognizing the existence of a major problem in the specification and design of large reactive systems' [Harel 1987] is still broadly true. Some progress has been made in developing methods of representing the dynamic behaviour of large systems, although none have been generally adopted for the specification of database behaviour. The reasons for this may be summarized as the immaturity of reactive database systems technology and the consequent lack of importance of behavioural specification.

Historically, concern with the specification and description of time-dependent system behaviour has been confined to traditional real-time control systems, ranging in complexity from washing machine programmers[1] to power station control systems. These applications are generally characterized as needing to respond to events in a controlled and timely fashion, but without a need to store or manage any appreciable amount of data. The approaches and techniques developed for these applications must be modified and extended in places to fit well into data-intensive applications domains.

---

1   Although many people would strenuously dispute the notion that a modern washing machine is simple!

The conventional view of the database is that it is a static object operated on by processes. This characterization is not adequate for modern DBMSs which have the capability to respond actively to external events through the provision of rules, triggers and stored procedures (discussed in Chapter 9). In order to accommodate the design needs of database applications with important time-dependent aspects we need design methods which can adequately capture the temporal aspects of modern applications.

In this chapter we describe a pragmatically oriented view of dynamic behaviour specification. A more abstract approach to capturing the temporal aspects of database behaviour, based on Montague's intensional logic, has been developed by Clifford and Warren [Clifford and Warren 1983; Clifford 1990]. Our approach is based around the use of statecharts, supplemented by interaction diagrams and decision tables. The refinement of statecharts through the use of structured transformations is treated in a similar way to that of EER and DFD diagrams. We associate fragments of the behavioural schema with concepts in the data schema and the functional schema through the use of external schema diagrams.

In this chapter we first outline the conceptual basis for behavioural modelling. Second, we describe the representation of behaviour using statechart notation and outline methods for developing behavioural models using statecharts. We then describe interaction diagrams, concentrating on their use for capturing ordered sequences of interactions, and decision tables. The final part of the chapter describes the integration of behavioural schemas with data and functional schemas.

5.2   Behavioural modelling concepts

The fundamental concepts for behaviour are that a system reacts to some external stimuli by exhibiting some behaviour. The system's behaviour persists until either it satisfies some termination conditions or further stimuli cause it to engage in different behaviour. The focus of our concern here can be viewed as an extension of the concepts related to function (described in Chapter 4) with the addition of concepts of duration and temporal constraints.

A simplified external view of the system is that it responds to some stimulus (event) which causes a reaction. The reaction will eventually cease and the system will become quiescent unless it is interrupted by further stimuli. More detailed views see the system as composed of subsystems, each of which may respond to stimuli generated by other subsystems as well as to external stimuli.

This view sees stimuli (events) as instantaneous and response (**behaviour**) as having measurable duration. In describing stimuli as instantaneous we are defining them as being of too short a duration to be of interest in the Universe of Discourse (UoD); that is, their existence is of interest but their internal structure is not.

5.2.1 State

The **state** of a system represents the current result of its cumulative behaviour. A state has measurable duration and is composed of a number of actions. The duration of a state may be unbounded (for example, a scanner in standby mode) or well defined (for example, a scanner is activated for a bounded period).

A state is composed of a sequence of activities. This sequence may be a repeated series, for example a heating system which turns the heater on and then repeatedly measures the temperature every five minutes until the specified temperature is reached.

5.2.2 Transition

A **transition** is the movement between one state and another within the system; it is assumed to be instantaneous. A transition is caused by a combination of the notification of an event and the fulfilment of various conditions; alternatively a transition can be described as being triggered by an event and the satisfaction of a set of conditions. The presence of events and conditions is optional. In some cases a transition between states is mandatory and is unaffected by any external factor (for example, a critical section of a program may be uninterruptible – except by catastrophic system failure).

5.2.3 Event

An **event** is an action external to the system (or subsystem) which causes the system (or subsystem) to move from one state to another. For the purposes of this discussion we assume that an event is instantaneous – strictly we are only concerned with the notification of an event and not the underlying process that caused the event.

5.2.4 Activity

An **activity** is an atomic component of a state; it may be refined so that at a greater level of detail it is seen as a state itself.

5.2.5 Action

An **action** is the response of a system to an event. It is the triggering of a behavioural sequence (that is, a collection of transitions) in response to an event. The action taken in response to an event may depend on the state of the system at the time the event was notified.

Triggers

The completion of an event may cause a succeeding event to commence, that is, one event triggers another. For example, the completion of an operative procedure triggers a post-operative procedure.

In other cases the completion of an event does not trigger another, but places an item on a queue or in a store for subsequent processing. For example, when an admission procedure is completed the admission record is stored until it is required for the discharge procedure.

This distinction between events that trigger others and those that do not allows us to represent active (that is, event) and passive (for example, queue) objects. If we do not allow this distinction, we find that objects such as stores and queues must be represented as active objects. In practice this means that we are not satisfied with a world in which things can *only* be modelled as objects that respond to messages. (This does not imply anything about the suitability of a pure message-passing abstraction in other areas of systems building.)

In our example, the lack of a passive modelling abstraction would lead to the store of completed admissions records being represented as an admissions record server, feeding the discharge procedure. We have a strong preference for representing active behaviour as a property of the object executing it. In the case of our example we might model the discharge procedure as having an operation to fetch an admissions record, or alternatively we could introduce an admissions record fetching agent between the discharge procedure and the admissions record store. The choice should be dependent on the desired semantics of the application and not on artificial restrictions of the processing model.

5.2.6   Condition

A condition is a constraint which may be specified to be true before, during or after a behavioural episode or may govern its duration. These may be:

Preconditions

A **precondition** is a condition that must be true before an action can be triggered in response to an event. For example, a precondition for an X-ray machine might be that the treatment room door must be locked before the machine can be operated.

Postconditions

A **postcondition** is a condition that must be true when a system makes a transition out of a state. For example, after a new X-ray machine is installed the radiographers must complete a training course before the machine is brought into service.

Normal sequence

It is frequently difficult to distinguish between mandatory preconditions and postconditions and the **normal sequence** of activities in a procedure. In any case it is important to be able to represent the normal sequence of events, while also showing necessary conditions for an event to occur.

To model event sequences that do not have strict preconditions or postconditions we must introduce the concept of the normal sequence of behaviour. When coupled with preconditions and postconditions, this determines an ordering or partial ordering of states, as well as showing their usual sequence of occurrence.

In our example of a day surgery, a surgical procedure has the preoperative procedure as a precondition. However, although the acquisition of a patient's personal details procedure is normally performed before the preoperative procedure it is not a precondition of it and is only a necessary prerequisite of the discharge procedure.

Constraints

A **constraint** specifies certain limits or restrictions which the event must respect if it is to complete successfully. For example, a blood analyser must be kept at a temperature between 5°C and 20°C.

Timing constraints

An increasing number of applications have a requirement that one action has a temporal dependency on another. The majority of conventional commercial applications have no significant time dependencies between the components of the application, so the modelling of temporal constraints has received relatively little attention until recently.

A temporal dependency may be:

- a minimum or maximum time between the start or completion of two distinct events (for example, pethidine injections must be at least four hours apart; successive video frames must be transmitted at no greater than 1/25 second intervals);
- a statistical timing constraint (for example, 90% of requests will be completed in under 2 seconds);
- a specified minimum or maximum duration for an event (for example, a blood chemistry profile must be performed within four hours; a sample must be cultured for at least 24 hours).

5.3   Dynamic modelling using statecharts

Statecharts have been developed from State Diagrams by Harel [Harel 1987]. Harel's intention was to develop a graphical formalism that is capable of representing the event-ordered behaviour of large systems.

The problem being addressed is that of representing the behaviour of reactive (that is, event-driven) systems in a rigorous framework. The starting points are states, conditions and events. A system, given some conditions, responds to an event by taking some action that causes a transition from the initial state to another; this transition may trigger other actions.

5.3.1 Statechart notation

The elements of statechart notation are shown in Figure 5.1 and are described below. The set of elements we describe is not minimal (that is, some elements can be expressed in terms of others), since it contains some that are useful conveniences rather than fundamental concepts of statecharts.

State

A state is the primary unit for encapsulating behaviour and represents the current behavioural snapshot of an element of the system. It is represented by a soft rectangle. A state has a name and an optional list of actions which must be performed (for example, on entering or exiting the state) and constraints (for example, that the state must not last more than two seconds).

Transition

A transition is the change from one state to another; it is represented by an arrow. The arrow is labelled with the name of the event that causes the transition. Any condition that restricts the transition is shown in parentheses as an annotation to the arrow.

A transition arrow connected to or from a superstate applies to all its substates. If the transition only applies to one of the substates the transition arrow can point directly to that substate.

Default state

In many cases it is desirable to identify a default state to which the system will return if no other state or substate is specified The default state is indicated by a curved arrow with a blob. The convenience of this notation is that it permits us to specify a state the system will be in, unless it is in another defined state in response to specified events. For example, it is useful in modelling an ambulance service to specify that an ambulance crew is in a standby state unless they are performing other duties (for example, called out); we do not have to model explicitly the return to the standby state at the end of a callout or other activity.

Superstate

Superstates are used to represent either exclusive generalizations of substates or aggregations of substates. A superstate is represented by a series of soft rectangles within a large rectangle.

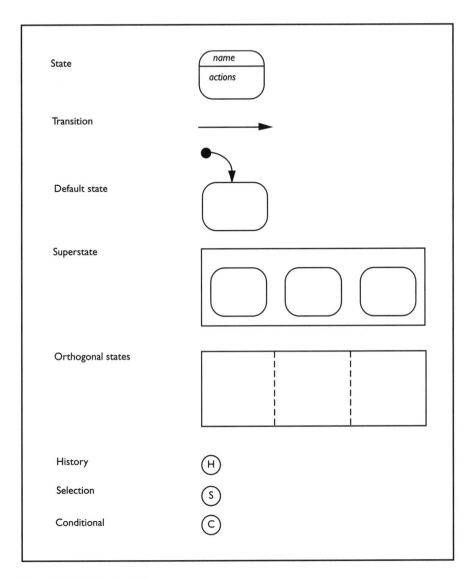

Figure 5.1 Statechart notation.

A superstate that represents a generalization has the semantics that entry into the superstate implies entry into a single one of its substates (that is, it has the semantics of XOR); the substate entered depends on the values of the associated conditions.

In the case of an aggregation the substates are connected, as they represent the internal states of a higher-level behaviour. Here, entry into the superstate will normally lead directly to one of the substates that represents the first step in a sequence.

Orthogonal state

Orthogonal state represents the case where a transition activates several of its substates; it is represented by a rectangle divided with dashed lines. Each division of the rectangle may contain several substates. One state is activated from each orthogonal group of substates of an orthogonal state (that is, it has the semantics of and). The most common use for this is where an event causes several procedures to start. Each of these procedures has its own set of states and events.

For instance, a transition to the alarm state of a heart monitor may enter the audible alarm state, the visual alarm state and the remote alarm state. The behaviour in each of these states will depend on the type of event generating the alarm.

Orthogonal states are not necessary for the model's completeness and can be modelled by a collection of independent states; for this reason they are sometimes excluded from the model (for example, in [Booch 1994]). We follow Booch in preferring to model orthogonal states as a collection of independent states and do not discuss them further; the interested reader is referred to Harel's [1987] description of them.

History

History in this context means returning to the most recently accessed substate of a superstate. For instance, an audible monitoring function on a heart monitor may be activated or deactivated by repeated pushes of a button. In this case the starting point on entry to the monitor's audible monitoring function is always the most recently accessed state (activated or deactivated).

Conditional and Selection

In charts where there are a number of possible substates of a superstate, one of which is selected on the basis of either a choice or a condition, it may be convenient to reduce the number of arrows by using either the selection or condition connectives. They are a useful way of reducing the visual complexity of the diagram and do not represent new concepts.

5.3.2   Statechart primitives

We can define sets of primitive transformations for statecharts in a similar fashion to those we have defined for EER and DFD models. The transformations described here are not rigorous, but are useful groupings for top-down and bottom-up refinement of statecharts (Figure 5.2).

Top-down primitives

   T1. A state is refined into separate states with a transition. For example, a call for an emergency ambulance to attend an accident can be refined into the ambulance travelling to the accident and attending to the accident victims (Figure 5.3a).

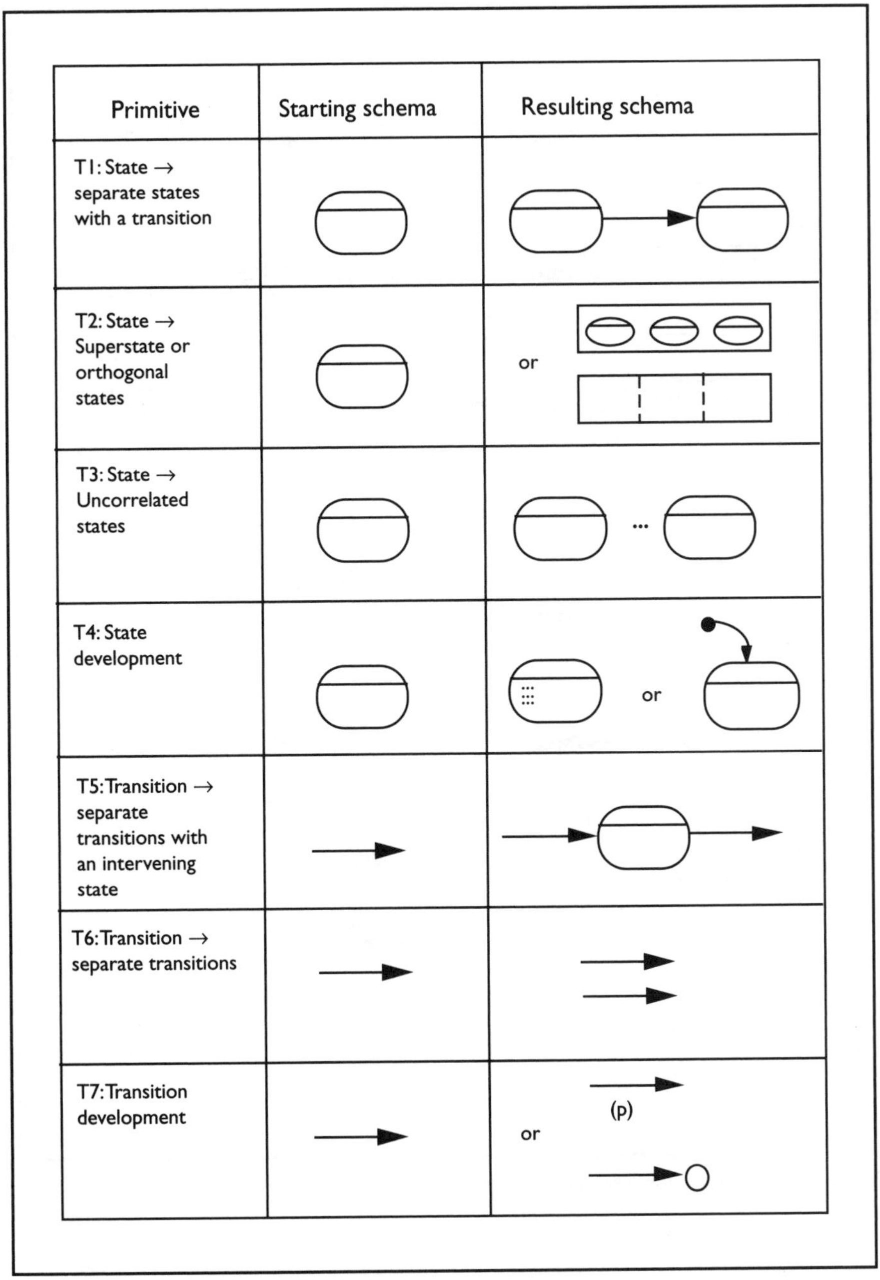
Primitive
Starting schema
Resulting schema
T1: State → separate states with a transition
T2: State → Superstate or orthogonal states
or
T3: State → Uncorrelated states
...
T4: State development
or
T5: Transition → separate transitions with an intervening state
T6: Transition → separate transitions
T7: Transition development
or
(p)

Figure 5.2 Top-down primitives for statecharts.

T2. A state is refined into a superstate or set of orthogonal states which contain a number of separate states. For example, the state of AMBULANCE UNAVAILABLE may be refined to become the separate states of ambulance

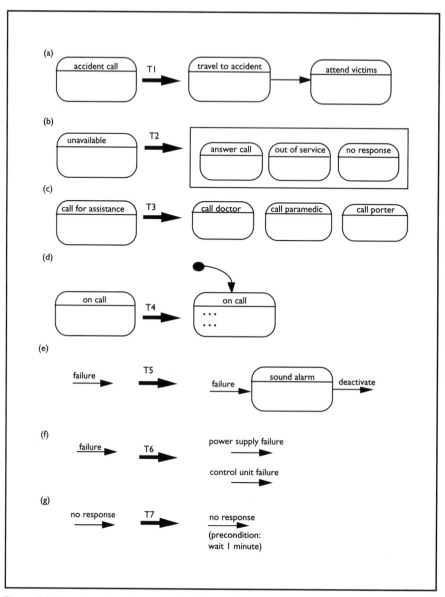

Figure 5.3 Examples of top-down primitives for statecharts.

answering call, ambulance out of service or ambulance crew not responding to request (Figure 5.3b).

T3. A state is refined into a series of uncorrelated states. For example, a CALL FOR ASSISTANCE state can be refined to call a doctor, call a paramedic or call a porter (Figure 5.3c).

T4. A state is populated with actions (shown as ... in Figure 5.3d) or is identified as a default state. For example, the default state for an ambulance crew is identified as being on call (Figure 5.3d).

T5. A transition is refined to two transitions with an intervening state. This refinement results from a recognition that a transition entails passing through a state. For example, the transition of an X-ray machine from WORKING to FAILED can be recognized to have an intermediate state of sounding an alarm (Figure 5.3e).

T6. A transition is refined into several separate transitions. For example, a FAILURE transition can be refined to be either a power supply failure or a control unit failure (Figure 5.3f).

T7. A transition is developed so that it acquires conditions or a connective. For example, a transition to a COMMUNICATIONS FAILURE state is triggered when there is no acknowledgement of a message within 1 minute (Figure 5.3g).

5.4 Interaction diagrams

Interaction diagrams provide a means of describing the prototypical behaviour and interactions between a collection of object (or entity) instances over time. None of the techniques described so far carry an explicit notion of time-ordered behaviour; this capability is important in the specification and design of many modern application domains. The specification of time-ordered behaviour has also become more relevant to database design as vendors have implemented rules and stored procedures in their products, facilitating the construction of more complex database applications. The use of interaction diagrams is particularly appropriate for describing procedures, protocols and other structured sequences of actions.

The basics

Here we present the basics of the technique, following [Booch 1994]. Booch's treatment is a synthesis based on Rumbaugh's event trace diagrams [Rumbaugh *et al.* 1991] and the interaction diagrams described in [Jacobson *et al.* 1992]. The basic notation is shown in Figure 5.4.

In an interaction diagram the sequence of events is shown by their vertical ordering, so that the earliest events are always at the top of the diagram. The duration of an instance can be shown by the extent of its rectangle. This implies that an instance is created when the rectangle is opened and is never modified after the rectangle is closed. This does not imply that an instance may not continue to be a valuable source of information, but once it has been closed it does not have any further direct role in the system's external behaviour. Thus, once a consultation is finished it will not be modified again, although it may be referred to subsequently.

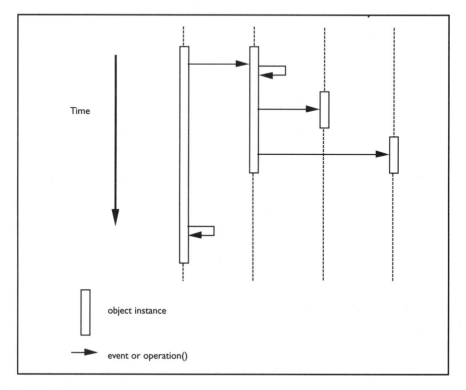

Figure 5.4 Notation for interaction diagrams.

The arrows in an interaction diagram indicate an interaction between instances; this may be an event, an operation or the passing of a message which has no behaviour observable within the system. The distinction between event and operation is frequently one of perspective, but an event is generally seen as instantaneous (typically a signal to which the receiving instance must respond) while an operation has a duration and is likely to be decomposable into a sequence of actions or operations at a finer level of detail. In general we are more concerned with representing the events that must be recorded or that drive the externally visible processes of the system. The arrow turned back on itself represents an event or operation that involves only a single instance – any other participants are external to the system.

The technique can be applied to show how messages are passed between object instances and how they respond to events. The example in Figure 5.5 shows this for a fragment of a log of ambulance activity.

The events shown in Figure 5.5 are that the ambulance is signed on at the start of the shift; at some later time it is called out to an accident. At the scene of the accident the ambulance crew make an initial assessment and provide emergency treatment to the victim. They then load the victim into the ambulance and transport him or her to hospital. During the journey they send their expected time of arrival (ETA) which is recorded in the log. On arrival at the hospital they report their arrival and inform the Accident and Emergency (A&E) team of the details of the accident. Finally the ambulance returns to standby mode.

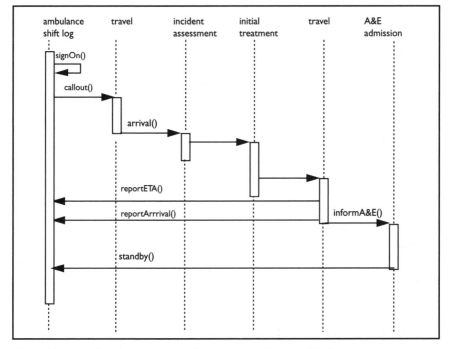

Figure 5.5 Interaction diagram showing a fragment of an ambulance shift log.

As a second example we illustrate how this basic notation can be also be used to describe a simple procedure, or protocol, in Figure 5.6. The diagram does not attempt to show all the possible courses of events, but describes the normal sequence which is followed for the majority of cases.

This example shows a procedure for investigating cases of suspected anaemia. The sequence starts with a consultation record in which details of a patient's problems are recorded; then a referral is made for a blood sample to be taken at the hospital. At the hospital the patient's details are recorded and the sample taken. The sample is divided into parts for various tests. The test results are then reported back and included in the consultation record. This is slightly artificial, since each result is shown as being separately reported, whereas in practice the results are all reported together. Using the results of the tests the physician formulates and records a treatment plan. The final event in the consultation is to make a further appointment with the patient.

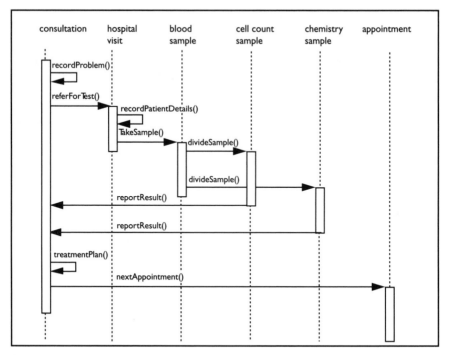

Figure 5.6 Example of an interaction diagram for investigating cases of suspected anaemia.

Elaboration

The basic notation for interaction diagrams lacks a number of desirable features:

- It contains no method of conveying a message to several entities.
- There is no notation for optionality.
- It is not possible to represent an event or precondition which may originate in one of a number of places.

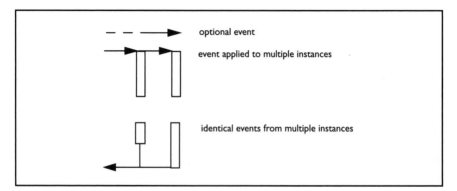

Figure 5.7 Extensions to interaction diagram notation.

In order to increase the expressiveness of the technique we can extend it, using a number of additions to the basic notation, shown in Figure 5.7.

The extra richness of the extensions to the basic notation allow us to represent more complex situations, shown in an elaborated version of the ambulance scenario from Figure 5.5. This is illustrated in Figure 5.8.

The use of optionality allows us to represent additional likely outcomes of a callout to an accident: the victim is given emergency treatment and then loaded into the ambulance to be transported to hospital; or the victim is taken straight to hospital; or the callout is a false alarm and the ambulance returns to standby mode.

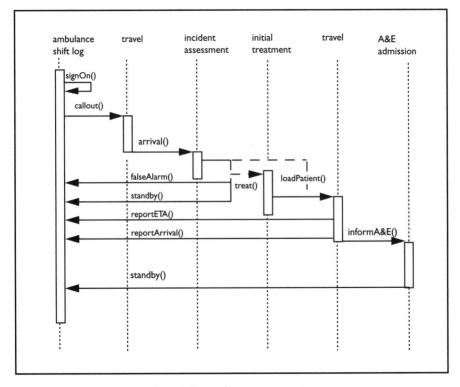

Figure 5.8 Interaction diagram for ambulance callout using extensions.

The extra features also help in describing the second example; a view of a more detailed version of this example now shows that the referral for a blood test is optional. If a blood test is specified the blood sample is divided into three; the different sizes of the sample instances (cell count, chemistry and viral samples) indicate the differing lengths of time they take to process. The results are reported back and incorporated into the consultation instance. The dashed line at the end of the reportResults() arrow shows its optionality, which is the complement of the optionality of referForTest(). The use of a single arrow (for divideSample() and report Results()) simplifies the diagram and shows a single operation affecting many instances, an event being composed of actions from several instances and in this case being the results gathered and reported as a group. The final feature of the example is that we have shown the specialization of the nextAppointment() operation into urgent and normal appointments, depending on whether the results of the test are exceptional. This could be further elaborated to show more detail of the constraints and conditions by adding an annotation similar to that used for constraints in statecharts.

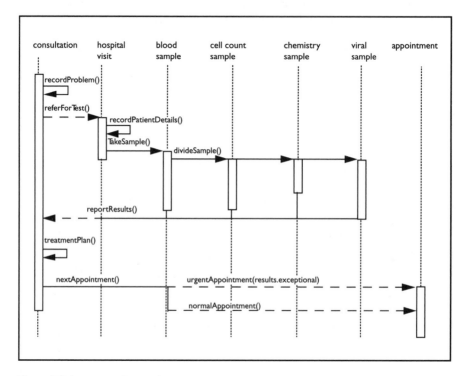

Figure 5.9 Interaction diagram for suspected anaemia using extensions.

5.5   Decision tables

Many systems have a number of conditions and several combinations of actions that may be invoked in response to some combination of conditions. The easiest way to represent many of these situations is through a decision table. A **decision table** consists of a grid with a list of all the conditions of interest labelling the rows of the top portion of the table. Each combination of possible states is a condition of the system and the response is an action; in combination the condition and action are termed a rule in decision table terminology. The lower part of the table contains a row for each action that may be invoked in response to a condition. For each combination of conditions the required actions are marked. This exhaustively enumerates the states and the desired response to each. The basic form of a decision table is shown in Figure 5.10.

	R1	R2	R3	R4	R5	R6	R7	R8
C1	Y	Y	Y	Y	N	N	N	N
C1	Y	Y	N	N	Y	Y	N	N
C1	Y	N	Y	N	Y	N	Y	N
A1	I	I	I			I	I	
A2	I		I				I	I
A3		I	I	I		I	I	

Figure 5.10 Decision table.

The use of the technique can be shown by the description of a simple evaluation procedure for assessing the actions that might be taken to safeguard the financial well-being of a frail elderly person, shown in Figure 5.11. This simplified example uses three conditions: whether a person suffers from confusion, whether somebody has been appointed to look after the person's affairs if he or she becomes incapable and whether the person is a property owner. Depending on these conditions a series of actions can be prescribed, in this case to apply for the person's affairs to be managed by the Court of Protection, to contact the person's attorney and to check the person's eligibility for welfare benefits.

	R1	R2	R3	R4	R5	R6	R7	R8
Confused	Y	Y	Y	Y	N	N	N	N
Enduring power of attorney granted	Y	Y	N	N	Y	Y	N	N
Property owner	Y	N	Y	N	Y	N	Y	N
Apply to Court of Protection			I	I				
Contact attorney	I	I			I	I		
Check welfare benefits eligibility		I		I		I		I

Figure 5.11 Decision table example.

For systems with a moderate number of possible states the technique is simple, can be checked for completeness and is easily read and understood by users. However, if there are n conditions, each of which is binary, then there will be $2n$ columns in the table. This combinatorial explosion of states makes the technique unsuitable for specifying the behaviour of systems with a large number of possible states.

5.6   Behaviour in information systems specification

The notations we have presented above contain many useful notions for capturing interesting system behaviour, but have not been as fully developed as techniques for specifying the data or functional schemas. There is scope for substantial further work in this area.

Since not all objects of interest to the database designer have significant event-ordered behaviour we recommend that behavioural fragments are associated with such objects, typically DFD processes, through external schemas. The use of external schemas to link fragments of the data schema, the functional schema and the behavioural schema is illustrated in Figure 5.12.

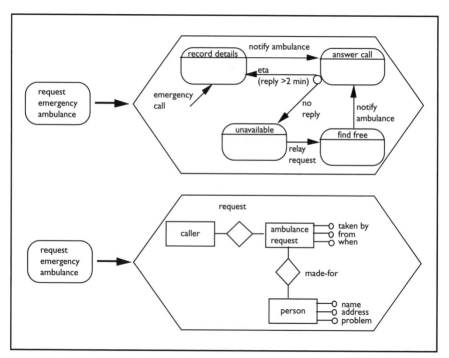

Figure 5.12   Examples of external schemas.

The first fragment of Figure 5.12 shows the schematic behaviour for an emergency ambulance request. The receipt of an emergency call triggers the record details state, which unconditionally triggers the notify ambulance transition when it completes. The receipt of an emergency call puts the ambulance into an answer call state. If no reply, giving an expected time of arrival, is generated within two minutes the unavailable state is entered. This state simply posts a notice of that ambulance's unavailability and triggers the transition to the find free ambulance state. The cycle is broken when a reply is received from an ambulance that it is responding and giving its expected time of arrival.

The second fragment associates a fragment of EER diagram with the request emergency ambulance process. The presentation of these together gives a more comprehensive visual description of the features of interest than can be achieved otherwise.

The choice of meaningful names is important in conveying meaning to anybody reading the diagrams. The database designer must consider the technical, cultural and linguistic background of the audience if the intended meaning of the design is to be conveyed. It is also important to be consistent in the use of the chosen names and terminology. In large projects this may frequently entail the explicit definition and maintenance of suitably limited vocabularies.

5.7   Summary

In this chapter we have described a number of methods for describing a system's external behaviour; other methods are described in [Davis 1988; Booch 1994; Coad and Yourdon 1991a; Coad and Yourdon 1991b]. Davis also provides a series of useful comparisons between methods.

The event-ordered behaviour of a complex system can be described using statecharts; the notation allows for the progressive refinement of a behavioural schema using a top-down approach. We believe that the technique as presented by Harel permits too much detail to be shown in a single level. Consequently we have emphasized and developed the hierarchical aspects of the technique here. Statecharts are capable of representing many interesting aspects of behaviour, but untrained users often find them difficult to understand [Hutt 1994].

Interaction diagrams are useful for capturing event generation and message passing between instances, explicitly incorporating the passage of time. The technique is well suited to describing the structured sequences of behaviour that can often be found in procedures and protocols.

Decision-intensive parts of an application can be represented by decision tables, showing the combinations of actions to be invoked in response to a particular set of conditions; decision trees provide a diagrammatic method of representing the same information. Decision tables have the advantage of being readily translatable into the type of rules and stored procedures found in many commercial database systems.

Many interesting aspects of system behaviour can be captured using these methods, although the techniques for specifying behavioural schemas are not as well developed as those for data and functional schemas.

Exercises

1. Take an example (for example, telephone answering machine) or description (for example, Therac-25 in [Leveson and Turner 1993]) of a machine and attempt to produce a series of statecharts describing its behaviour.

2. Take an example of a human-based system (for example, order processing, university degree course requirements) and attempt the same exercise. Pay particular attention to the preconditions and postconditions associated with the states of the system.

Chapter 6

PHYSICAL DESIGN

6.1 Introduction

Performance is a vital aspect of most data-intensive applications, but is frequently neglected until late in the design process. In this chapter we describe simple physical design methods derived from an analysis of the major characteristics of data-intensive systems.

Physical design cannot be completed until the logical design has been finalized, but preliminary versions of the database physical design can be developed concurrently with the logical design, using additional information derived from successive refinements of the logical design to develop increasingly complete versions of the physical design. In many large projects such concurrent approaches are being extensively used to reduce the overall development time.

Many of the decisions and trade-offs that have to be made during physical design are dependent on the file structures used for a particular application; these are discussed in Chapter 8.

6.2 Workload estimation

A reasonable workload estimate is essential for the physical design although a precise analysis of the workload is often impossible, as the detailed usage of the finished system cannot be accurately predicted. The starting points of the workload analysis are:

- the definitions and frequencies of the principal transactions,
- the distributions of the attributes used in search criteria,
- the expected modification patterns.

Frequently the actual workload will depend on how well the system meets the users' stated objectives and what extra tasks (if any) the completed system can perform that help users in their work.

Transaction characteristics

There are a number of important parameters of a transaction workload that are needed for the physical design process.

1. Determining the specification of the principal transactions, including required response time and other constraints.
2. Determining the expected frequency of each of the principal transactions.
3. Determining the approximate composition of any background workload.
4. Likely future developments affecting the database.

It is frequently convenient to express the transactions in a suitable declarative language (typically SQL or a related language) or as a high-level navigational specification for transactions that cannot easily be expressed in purely declarative terms. Each transaction must be analysed to determine the number and type of accesses it makes.

The access patterns of interest can be summarized in a number of broad categories:

1. Single record access.
2. Access to a group of records of the same type that meet some criterion.
3. Sequential access to every record of a type (or a large fraction of a type).
4. Frequency and pattern of insertions (for example are all insertions random or appended in some predefined pattern such as date order).
5. Deletion frequency and pattern.
6. Update frequency and pattern.

The actual frequency of each type of transaction is often difficult to determine, but for the design process their relative frequency is more important (unless the actual frequencies are very different from the estimates).

Data characteristics

It is important to know the approximate number and size of records returned from the database by any query. This is a function of the selectivity of the search criteria and the distribution of values in the database. Thus it is important to know approximately how large a group of records will satisfy the search criteria of each transaction, how many records will be updated by a transaction, and so on. The steps required to discover this information are:

1. Analyse the distributions of values for each attribute used in a search.
2. For each search criterion used in the principal transactions, estimate the average and largest (worst case) number of records that meet that criterion.

It must be borne in mind that the values used in the criteria will not be uniformly distributed (that is, some values will be favoured above others) and that the distribution of favoured values is usually skewed.

The third principal requirement is for a characterization of the data to be included in the database:

1. An estimate of the cardinality of each record type (that is, tuples in a relation or members of a class).
2. An estimate of the future growth pattern of each record type.
3. The ageing pattern for each record type (for example, how long must paid invoice records be kept on-line, how long before a completed drawing can be moved to tertiary storage).

Note that secondary indexes should be counted as tables containing duplicated data (the index keys) for the physical design process – this is discussed fully in Chapter 8.

6.3   Estimating access times

For the majority of database systems performance is dominated by I/O costs, which form the principal focus of this section; other costs are described in less detail.

CPU usage

For most purposes the performance of conventional database structures is dominated by I/O costs. We only include a brief outline of processing costs since these are rarely critical for database design and they are thoroughly covered in other texts (for example, [Harel 1992]; [Aho *et al.* 1974]).

In the case of memory-based and object-oriented systems which make extensive use of methods and procedures to implement data access operations the CPU costs of operations must also be taken into account. The performance of these is determined by algorithmic analysis.

Given:

t_p time to evaluate a predicate for a record,

l_q qualification length (that is, number of predicates in the expression).

The upper bound for a single record (where every predicate must be evaluated before the result of the expression can be determined) is $t_p . l_q$ and for N records it is $N . t_p . l_q$ In a machine with P processors, assuming that there is a uniform distribution of records between processors, the upper bound will be $(N . t_p . l_q)/P$.

In current systems a range of between 15 ns – 90 μs is appropriate for the value of t_p, depending on the type of object being compared (character, integer and so on), CPU speed and the efficiency of the implementation.

Disk access time

Here we describe the cost structure of a disk access. We provide this at a reasonable level of detail, since the costs can vary significantly between disks, depending on a number of physical characteristics; the balance of costs is changing with the evolution of disk technology. The cost of a disk access is made up of a number of components.

For many purposes we can simply regard a disk as a linear sequence of logical blocks. In a simple model we assume that the cost of reading any single block is a full disk access (seek, rotational delay and transfer time). Access to a group of logically contiguous blocks costs a full disk access for the first block, followed by transfer time only for subsequent blocks.

Seek time

Seek time is the time taken to move the disk arm from its present position to the next required position. Simple models typically use an average seek time, which is often adequate. If all seeks are independent the average seek distance will be one third of the maximum. Disk drive manufacturers may quote average seek times in a number of ways, for example, the time for a seek over one third of the maximum distance, one third of the maximum seek time.

A more sophisticated view may be needed for modelling demanding applications. In this case a seek can be decomposed into four component parts:

- Speedup – the disk controller accelerates the disk arm until it reaches half the seek distance or a fixed maximum velocity.
- Coast – the movement at maximum velocity for long seeks.
- Slowdown – the disk controller decelerates the disk arm until it is positioned approximately above the desired track.
- Settle – the controller adjusts the disk arm to its final position.

The structure of seek times is dependent on the seek distance and extrapolation of the performance of short seek distances cannot readily be determined from seeks over a long distance.

- The shortest seeks (2–4 cylinders) are dominated by the settle time of 1–3 ms.
- The major component of short seeks, of between 200–400 cylinders, is the speedup time; settle time is the secondary component. The time taken by a short seek is proportional to the square root of the distance.
- Long seeks are dominated by the coast component, so their times are approximately proportional to distance with a constant overhead for the other phases.

The time to switch heads from one track to another is currently in the range 0.1–1.5 ms. As track densities increase the alignment differences between tracks in the same cylinder become more important and the head switch time increases and approximates to the settle time.

Rotational delay

Rotational delay is the time between the head settling and the required sector coming under the head. On average it is the time for the disk to complete half a rotation. The most common rotation speeds are 3600, 5400 and 7200 r.p.m. The average rotational delay times for these speeds are 8.33, 5.56 and 4.17 ms respectively.

It is common for disks to be laid out so that a track switch positions the head just ahead of the next logical block, thereby eliminating most of the rotational delay for a track switch.

Transfer time

Transfer time is the time taken to actually read the data. The transfer rate is usually quoted in Mb/sec. The transfer of a page from disk to memory is affected by a number of factors:

1. Disk transfer rate;
2. Disk controller throughput (important when a controller is responsible for several disks);
3. Bus performance (and contention) in transferring data from the controller to memory.

Typical modern disks have transfer rates of 2–20Mb/sec, but an actual transfer rate that is lower than the maximum may be imposed by the host system bus.

Data allocation between disks

In a system with multiple disks the designer must attempt to partition the data over the disks so that the load is evenly balanced over all the disks.

Every updating transaction must record sufficient information there to allow for recovery and rollback procedures (described in Chapter 11). In normal operation the database log file is a write-only file where new records are always appended to the end. It is almost always beneficial to allocate a separate disk to the log file because the disk arm will remain positioned over the right track, avoiding the need for a seek when writing to the log. In many UNIX-based systems it is recommended that the log disk is configured as a raw device, giving the DBMS full control over it. For small installations and sites in a distributed system with few update transactions it may be uneconomic to assign a separate disk for the log. In small systems the log disk is also frequently used for checkpoints, journal files, and so on.

The access pattern for the DBMS software and related files is different from other parts of the database system, so these files are frequently kept on a separate disk. The DBMS vendor's installation manuals usually provide suggested configurations for a number of types of database system usage.

The major issue to be addressed in allocating secondary storage is to partition the data efficiently among the available disks; for this we must estimate the I/O load on each table or other unit of data to be stored. In order to estimate this I/O load we ideally need to know:

- The ratio of reads to writes;
- The distribution of accesses between records (skew);
- The stability of the access pattern (particularly for the most frequently accessed records);
- The proportion of accesses that will be satisfied from pages cached in the buffer pool.

It is possible to approximate much of this information using a model built on the concepts of size, 'heat' and 'temperature'.

Size	is measured in bytes.
Heat	is defined as the number of accesses to a database object (table, page, record).
Temperature	is the size divided by the heat.

This gives us a uniform measure for calculating the I/O load and a simple, often effective, strategy is to estimate the temperature of each table and then to distribute tables over disks so as to obtain an even temperature.

An important refinement of this approach comes when we recognize that accesses are not evenly distributed over a table. In this case the procedure is to approximate the skewed accesses by using a suitable distribution (for example, Poisson) to estimate the heat of the individual pages and take into account the effect of the buffer pool (in reducing I/Os for the hottest pages) and differentiating between read and write accesses (modified pages must have log records written and the data is eventually written back to disk).

Data allocation to pages

Most database systems allow the database administrator to vary the amount of space left free on each page (the fill factor). The aim of leaving free space is to allow additional records to be inserted without having to have a partial reorganization of the table (allocating overflow pages or splitting groups of pages).

The amount of free space that it is desirable to leave depends on the balance between reads, inserts and deletes:

- Read-only tables are best packed full, since this minimizes the number of pages that are retrieved.
- Tables with many insertions into their middle should be initially allocated with a high proportion of free space, since this delays reorganizations caused by pages overflowing.

- Inserts at the extremes of a key range (for example, a monotonically increasing series of order numbers) do not benefit from a low fill factor within the page, but will benefit from the table being allocated a block of unused space sufficient to accommodate the initial growth before space can be reclaimed from deletions.

For most file organizations a default value of 60–80% full is used and this represents a good compromise for many applications.

Transactions frequently require access to groups of objects of different types. If these can be stored near to each other, either on the same page or on a group of contiguous pages, the I/O cost can be very substantially reduced as less unwanted data is retrieved on behalf of the transaction.

Communications costs

Continuing developments in network technology, involving increases of several orders of magnitude in usable bandwidth, have changed the perception of how computing power and storage can be distributed. However, it is still true that network capacity must be regarded as a scarce resource as the use of network capacity has grown at least as fast as the capacity itself (bigger networks, more services, image and sound transmission, and so on).

The time taken to send a message (command, data or result) over a network depends on:

- Time to prepare the message. This is usually approximated by a constant (since the preparation of a long message is overlapped with its transmission).
- Network latency (that is, the time to establish a connection).
- Effective network bandwidth, usually measured as the sustained throughput (unless there are significant congestion or other transmission delays).
- Time to assemble the message and make it available to the recipient. Typically this can be modelled as a constant and is usually assumed to be the same as the preparation time. This simplification makes transmission and receipt mirrors of each other and simplifies cost calculations.

For a modern parallel processor typical values for these are a start or receive time of 30 μs, network latency of 15 μs and a sustained throughput between any pair of nodes of 80Mb/sec. The first three of these figures are largely dependent on processor speed and the use of dedicated hardware. The values quoted here are estimates for an EDS system prototype using dedicated network processors and ASICs [Wong and Paci 1992]. Conventional Ethernet LANs are rated at 10Mb/sec, although they are very prone to congestion if there are many transmitting nodes and current fibre-optic networks have bandwidths of 100–140Mb/sec.

Charging for a wide area link may be on the basis of connection time, volume of data or flat rate. All methods are in use, depending on the technology of the link and the charging regime of the telecommunications provider. This may affect the design, depending on the optimization criteria being used (that is, minimum time, minimum cost or some trade-off between them).

6.4 Calculating logical I/Os

For the majority of database applications a reasonable first approximation to a good physical design can be obtained from a series of rough calculations. Since these calculations are often part of an iterative refinement we suggest that they are usually best done using a spreadsheet package, which lends itself to the iterative development of a performance estimate. This is particularly useful for building up alternative models of a workload with several important transaction types.

Retrievals

The analysis of the I/O behaviour of a retrieval query starts from a characterization of its access pattern:

- **Single record retrieval** is most efficiently done using a hash organization, which gives constant time access for a single record. An ideal hash organization would result in a single I/O; the size of the departure from this ideal is a function of the number and chaining of overflow buckets. Single record access through a B-tree organization involves traversing the internal levels of the tree from the root and then accessing a single data page. For a single record retrieval access through a secondary index has a very similar cost to that of retrieval through the storage structure.
- **Range retrieval**. The most widely available efficient organization for accessing a group (ordered sequence or range) of records is the B-tree. The cost can be calculated as that of traversing the tree to find the first page and then counting the number of pages that contain records of interest (in key order). Access through a secondary index will involve a traversal of the index and then one I/O for most records retrieved, since there is little chance that the secondary index key will be correlated with the storage key.

  It is worth noting that in an environment with a mix of single record and range accesses to the same table it is generally a better strategy to organize the records for the range access and to provide a secondary index for the single record accesses.
- **Whole table access**. Access to a large group of records or the whole table. As the fraction of records retrieved increases there comes a point when it is likely that every page in the table will be retrieved. At this point it is more efficient to perform a sequential search of the table and ignore any indexes. Query optimizers in relational systems can generally recognize this situation and produce an appropriate query plan.

Similarly, for any access that requires every record in the table there is no benefit from any index and a heap structure will be the most efficient, since records are packed into pages without any structuring overhead. In practical applications these situations are likely to be when a history or transaction file is processed to produce audit trails, management reports, consistency checks, and so on.

The procedure is:

1. For each transaction in the workload, estimate its I/O cost using likely organizations and secondary indexes. Weight the costs by the relative frequency of the transaction.
2. For each candidate organization sum the costs.
3. Select the organization with the lowest costs.

This initial estimate can be refined in a number of ways to produce a more realistic, although still rough, analytical result:

- The upper-level pages of a B-tree structure in active use will tend to remain in memory, since pages are usually discarded from the buffer pool in least recently used (LRU) order. This reduces the costs of B-trees and may lead to them being favoured over hash structures for single record accesses. The logic behind this is that if all the relevant internal pages are in memory and the only I/O is for the data page this will be cheaper than a hash access, which will require more than one I/O on average to fetch the required data page.
- Small tables (typically used for lookup) can be beneficial, particularly if they can reduce the search space of other queries. In a relational system it can often be efficient to implement a series of small index or lookup tables if they are sufficiently frequently used to remain in the buffer pool for the majority of the time. In such an implementation it is highly desirable to hide the extra complexity of queries from users by encapsulating the query in a database procedure. Such small tables are best implemented as heaps if the whole table can be made to fit onto a small number of pages (for example,fewer than five).

  The computational efficiency of complex query processing using either navigational methods or joins and the cost of page faults can play an important part in the overall performance where many transactions make significant use of in-memory structures.

For most applications (especially particularly large and performance-critical ones) it is essential to test the adequacy of the analysis with experiments. Experimental approaches are described in Chapter 7. The experimental results can be used as a basis for refining the analysis and the design can be iteratively refined until a satisfactory organization is achieved.

Updates

Update operations have additional factors that must be taken into account:

- An update of a variable-length record that increases its length may cause a page overflow which will result in at least two logical I/O operations: to write the original and overflow pages – others may be incurred.as a result of updating indexes and so on.
- An insertion into a B-tree may cause a page split. In the worst case the split is propagated to the root, increasing the depth of the B-tree.
- A modification of a field with a secondary index on it will cause an update of an index page as well as the data page being modified.
- A deletion may cause an underflow on a page and the consequent reorganization of a B-tree may decrease its depth in the worst case.

More commonly, commercial B-tree implementations do not attempt to reclaim space from deletions except by releasing pages that become empty. This can lead to poor performance if there are many retrievals of sparsely populated pages. The solution offered by most current systems is to provide utilities that perform in-place reorganizations to reclaim space.

The picture is complicated by the fact that most systems perform delayed writes. When the update is made only the updated values are written to stable storage (in the log). The write of the modified data page is deferred until a checkpoint or until the page is forced from the buffer pool. Since the write is not immediate there is a chance that the page will be updated again before it is written. Multiple updates of a page have the benefit of amortizing the I/O cost over several updates.

There comes a point where the benefit of spreading the cost of a disk write over multiple updates is offset by transactions having to wait before being able to access the page to be updated.

Hot spots

Pages that contain too many frequently updated records become hot spots which limit the performance of the whole system. (Frequently read items do not suffer the same problems, since access to them is shared.)

Part of the database designer's task is to analyse the distribution of updates in order to be able to choose file organizations that minimize the occurrence of hot spots.

The outline procedure for hot spot analysis is:

1. Determine the frequency with which records are updated, using the frequency of update transactions.
2. Determine the distribution of values that are updated, using any available information about the application semantics.
3. Determine the overall frequency with which the most volatile records will be updated and the distribution of these between pages.

4. Any page that has an update frequency of the same order as the transaction residence time (that is, the time the transaction takes in the database server) is likely to be a hot spot and should be analysed further.
5. Organize the application logic so that hot items are locked for the minimum time (that is, they are acquired as late as possible).
6. If the system will allow control over the locking granularity, perform the hot spot analysis using fine-grained locking for the hot spots. In many current commercial systems it is possible to vary the fill factor used in various table organizations – in some cases it is possible to simulate the effect of fine-grained locking by specifying a low fill factor (this is only feasible for small tables as otherwise the extra I/Os caused by the wasted space outweigh the locking benefits).
7. If there are still hot spots, reexamine the basic physical design using different table organizations or distributions to see if a significantly better solution can be found.

For all but the most simply structured problems it is infeasible to attempt an exact solution and a suitable analytic model must be developed. Such models are outside the scope of this book, but see [Leutenegger and Dias 1993] for an example.

6.5   Distributed database design

Design for a system with multiple sites and communications links between them introduces some extra factors. The greatest problem is how to allocate the data among sites to achieve some 'best' configuration. Best is defined in terms of response time or throughput.

We assume a fully connected network of sites, each of which generates a database workload. The tasks of constructing a distributed database design are:

- to produce a series of good local designs,
- to partition the data among sites,
- to minimize the amount of inter-site activity,
- to balance the load evenly.

These last two activities may be contradictory and decisions about trade-offs will have to be made (for example, increased communications costs against better load balancing).

6.5.1   *General considerations*

Partitioning

To allocate fragments of a table to several sites we partition (decluster) it in a combination of two ways:

- horizontally, assigning complete records to sites;
- vertically, assigning fragments of records to sites (together with sufficient identifying information to reconstitute the whole record).

Any combination of vertical and horizontal partitioning may be used, provided that the complete record can be reassembled with a combination of union and join operations. In general the level of fragmentation should be small to moderate, because highly fragmented designs are very sensitive to workload changes.

For example, if we have a health care organization that cares for patients at several sites it is likely that a site will generate most of the queries relating to patients treated there. Therefore it makes sense to partition the patient records by treatment site (horizontal partitioning). Conversely, if one site generates most of the transactions relating to a portion of the patient record (for example, blood transfusion records at an Accident and Emergency site) then it is advisable to partition the patient record vertically to allow for this.

Replication

Data that is frequently accessed from a number of sites is often replicated to increase availability. The trade-offs are:

- cheaper reads, because the transaction is less likely to require access to remote data;
- greater availability in the presence of failures as a result of there being multiple copies;
- the extra cost of updating all the replicated copies;
- the extra storage required by the extra copies.

The best candidates for replication are data fragments that are frequently read and rarely updated (or at least updated at slack times).

6.5.2 Data allocation

There are two basic methods for allocating tables to sites. For simplicity we discuss the strategies in terms of whole tables, although the extensions of these methods to deal with partitioned tables are obvious.

Best fit

In this method there is no replication of tables. The procedure is:

1. Determine the total number of accesses (read and write) to each table from every site.

2. Allocate each table to the site that maximizes the number of local references to that table.

This is a very crude allocation strategy and its results are correspondingly crude. To improve the performance of this method a number of additional factors must be taken into account:

- The simple reference count should be replaced by the aggregate I/O cost.
- The strategy needs a subsequent refinement after the initial allocation to allow for the effect of distributed joins and other operations involving data from several tables or classes.
- The capabilities of the communications links (capacity, cost, and so on) between the sites must be taken into account.

All beneficial sites

This strategy tries to allocate a copy of a table to every site where the benefits of having that data locally available outweigh the costs.

The method proceeds as follows:

1. At each site determine the difference between local and remote access to a table by summing the time required for all the accesses required by that site,
2. Determine the costs of extra remote updates. This is done by considering, for each table, the remote update costs incurred if it is placed at a site (that is generate a matrix of tables and sites populated with the remote update costs).
3. Place a copy of the table at each site where the benefits clearly outweigh the costs.
4. For marginal allocations, where the costs and benefits are approximately equal, the allocation decision should be based on likely future trends (for example, whether there are likely to be more or fewer updates or reads in future).

The performance of the method can be most easily improved by:

- allowing for operations (for example, join) that access several tables,
- allowing for differences in communications links.

6.6   Physical design examples

We give two simple examples, the first showing the calculations for determining file organizations at a single site and the second showing the allocation of tables, using a simple Distributed Best Fit method, in a distributed system.

6.6.1 Centralized example

The method

Given:

fillfactor – the proportion of each page used in the initial allocation of records (heap is always 100%),

pagesize – the number of bytes on a page available for data,

pageid – the size of a page identifier or pointer.

For each table:

1. **Calculate the record size,** by adding up the sizes of all the fields in the record.

2. **Calculate the number of records per page** for a given fill factor,

   R_p = floor (pagesize × fillfactor / recordsize)

   (The *floor()* function returns the highest integer less than the value of its argument, equivalent to the *int()* function in many programming languages.)

3. **Calculate the number of data pages,**

   P_d = ceiling (cardinality / R_p)

   (The *ceiling()* function returns the lowest integer greater than the value of the argument.) For a hash organization this will give the number of pages required for the file.

4. **Calculate the height of the index,** for a B-tree or similar file organization. There are two ways of doing this:

   (a) The first is to perform calculations similar to that in Step 2, except that the record is the {Key, PageId} pair, where Key is the record identifier,

   R_i = floor (pagesize × fillfactor / indexrecordsize)

   This gives the number of index keys per page. The number of index pages at the lowest level of the index is calculated from the number of records per page and the number of data pages,

   P_i = ceiling (Pd / Ri)

   This calculation can be performed recursively to estimate the number of pages at each level of the index until the root is reached. The depth of the index is the number of times the calculation is performed; there are rarely more than three index levels. The index depth is required to calculate the I/O cost of accessing a record in a B-tree.

   (b) The second method is to estimate the approximate depth of the index directly,

   I_{depth} = ceiling (log $_{Ri}$ P$_d$)

which is equivalent to

$$= ceiling \ (log_{10} \ P_d \ / \ log_{10} \ R_i)$$

At the end of the first stage we have estimates of the file sizes and access cost (number of I/Os) for a single record. For a hash organization it is constant – a value of 1.2 I/Os per access is reasonable [Litwin 1980]. For a B-tree it is reasonable to assume that the root page will always be in memory and in many modern systems it is reasonable to expect most of the upper levels of the tree to be memory-resident. The access cost can easily be refined to take account of the probability of the required index pages being in memory.

The second stage is to estimate the access costs for range retrievals. This relies on some knowledge of the distribution of values of the fields used in the selection criterion, although it is conventional to assume a uniform distribution in the absence of specific knowledge.

5. **Calculate the number of records in a group.** For a uniform distribution this is simply the cardinality of the table divided by the number of distinct values of the selection criterion.

6. **Calculate the I/Os needed to retrieve a group.** There are three cases:

   (a) If the records in a group are stored contiguously (for example a B-tree is organized on the selection attribute) the cost will be that to retrieve a single record and any additional data pages containing members of the group.

   (b) If the records in the group are accessed through a secondary index the cost will be that of retrieving a single record multiplied by the number of records in the group.

   (c) For a hash organization the cost of retrieving a group of records involves retrieving each record singly, as in (b) above.

   For low-selectivity queries (that is, where the group is large) in cases (b) and (c) it will be cheaper to scan the entire table if the number of I/Os to retrieve single records is greater than the number of data pages in the table. A heap organization always requires a table scan.

At the end of this stage we have estimates for the I/O costs of each transaction for the types of file organization that are of interest.

The third stage is to:

7. **Calculate the total I/O load for each file organization.** To establish the total load for each file organization of interest we weight the costs by the frequency of each transaction type.

8. **Select the file organization with the lowest I/O total.** The total I/O load for a particular file organization can be determined by summing the loads for each transaction type. The most efficient organization can be determined by subtraction.

The method we have described above gives simple estimates for retrieval queries. For data modification queries (insert and delete) additional calculations may be required to allow for the extra overhead of partial index reorganizations. The relevant background for these is given in Chapter 8. This approach can be elaborated as more detailed estimates of the expected performance are required.

The schema

Given part of a database to record share trading, containing the following tables:

Share (CompanyId, CompanyName, CurrentPrice)

Shareholder (CustomerId, Name, Address, Phone)

Holding (CustomerId, CompanyId, Qty, PricePaid, DateBought, DateSold)

The Share table has 2000 shares listed.

The Account table has 5000 customer records.

The Holding table has approximately 600,000 records.

The transactions

The number of Buy and Sell transactions is approximately equal:

- on average a customer buys or sells 40 times per day, assuming a 10 hour day,
- approximately 20% of trades involve inserting or deleting a record.

The Status transaction is run once every hour during the day. It gives the current position of the firm's customers with a balance of less than 100,000; on average 10% of the firm's customers are included in this report. [Aside: this sort of query, if it is allowed on an operational database, can usually be run with a lower consistency level, typically allowing unrepeatable reads (*see* Chapter 10 for a description).]

The NewPrice transaction updates the current share price; on average it runs once per second during the day.

The important transactions, expressed in SQL (described in Chapter 14), are listed below:

Buy:

(Name, CompanyName and Qty are supplied as parameters)

```
/* abort the transaction if the customer is not found */
whenever not found rollback;

/* find the CustomerId given the customer Name*/
select CustomerId, Balance, CreditLimit
    into :CustomerId, :Balance, :CreditLimit
```

```
   from Account
   where Name = :Name;

/* find the CompanyId and CurrentPrice given the CompanyName */
select CompanyId, CurrentPrice
   into :CompanyId, :CurrentPrice
   from Share
   where CompanyName = :CompanyName;

/* check that customer's credit limit is not exceeded */
if (CreditLimit < Balance - Qty * CurrentPrice)
   rollback;

/* charge the customer's account */
update Account
   set Balance = Balance - :Qty * :CurrentPrice
   where CustomerId = :CustomerId;

/* if the customer does not hold this stock create a new
record, */
/* otherwise update the Holding record */
whenever not found goto newrec;

select Qty
   into :CurrentQty
   from Holding
   where CustomerId = :CustomerId
      and CompanyId = :CompanyId;

update holding
   set Qty = :CurrentQty + :Qty, DateBought = 'now'
   where CustomerId = :CustomerId
      and CompanyId = :CompanyId;

commit;

newrec:
insert into holding
   :CustomerId, :CompanyId, :Qty, :CurrentPrice, 'now';

commit;
```

Sell:

(Name, CompanyName and Qty are supplied as parameters)

```
/* abort the transaction if the customer is not found */

whenever not found rollback;

/* find the CustomerId given the customer Name*/
select CustomerId
   into :CustomerId
   from Account
   where Name = :Name;

/* find the CompanyId and CurrentPrice given the CompanyName */
select CompanyId, CurrentPrice
   into :CompanyId, :CurrentPrice
   from Share
   where CompanyName = :CompanyName;

select Qty
into :CurrentQty
   from Holding
   where CustomerId = :CustomerId
      and CompanyId = :CompanyId;

/* abort the transaction if the customer does not have the
stock to sell */
if (CurrentQty < Qty)
rollback;

/* charge the customer's account */
update Account
   set Balance = Balance + :Qty * :CurrentPrice
   where CustomerId = :CustomerId;
```

```
/* take the stock from the customer's Holding records */
update holding
   set Qty = :CurrentQty - :Qty, DateSold = 'now'
   where CustomerId = :CustomerId
      and CompanyId = :CompanyId;

commit;
```

NewPrice:
(CurrentPrice and CompanyId are given as parameters)

```
update Share
   set CurrentPrice = :CurrentPrice
   where CompanyId = :CompanyId;

commit;
```

Status:
```
select Account.CustomerName, Account.Balance,
Share.CompanyName, Holding.Qty,
      Value = Holding.Qty * Share.CurrentPrice
   from Share, Account, Holding
   where Account.CustomerId = Holding.CustomerId
      and Share.CompanyId = Holding.CompanyId
      and Account.Balance < 100000
   group by Balance
   order by Value;
```

Analysis

In addition to the assumptions listed in the previous section we assume that:

- There is enough memory that the root page and the next index level of a B-tree will not be flushed to disk.
- The system has a page size that allows 2000 bytes for data.
- Pages are initially filled 70% full.
- A page identifier is 32 bytes.

Constants	pagesize	2000					
	fillfactor	0.7					
	pageid	32					

Tables	**Share**		**Account**		**Holding**	
	CompanyId	16	CustomerId	16	CustomerId	16
	CompanyName	96	Balance	8	CompanyId	16
	CurrentPrice	16	CreditLimit	8	Qty	4
			Name	96	DateBought	32
			Address	116	DateSold	32
			Phone	12		

Records	Size	128	256	100
	Cardinality	2000	5000	60000
	records/page	10	5	14

Transaction	**frequency (per hour)**	
Buy	10000	(40/10*5000)
Sell	10000	(40/10*5000)
NewPrice	3600	(60*60)
Status	1	

B-tree size			
	Share	**Account**	**Holding**
Data pages	200	1000	4286
Btree level 1	7	35	147
Btree level 2	1	1	6
Btree level 3			1
Total pages	208	1036	4440
Hash I/O			
Buy	12000	12000	11400
Sell	12000	12000	12000
NewPrice	4320	0	0
Status	2400	6000	720
Total	**30720**	**30000**	**24120**
B-tree raw I/O			
Buy	1	1	2
Sell	1	1	2
NewPrice	1	0	0
Status	183	915	583.33
Total	**184**	**916**	**4287**

continues over...

...continued from previous page

B-tree weighted I/O			
Buy	10000	10000	20000
Sell	10000	10000	20000
NewPrice	3600	0	0
Status	201	1001	583.33
Total	**23801**	**21001**	**40583**
Difference			
(B-tree − hash)	−6919	−8999	

Therefore we should implement the Share and Account tables as B-trees and the Holding table using a hashed organization.

6.6.2   Distributed example

The calculations for a database modelled on a simplified version of the TPC-C benchmark relations and transactions (described in Chapter 7) are shown below. There are five transaction types and nine tables. For the distributed case we have assumed that there are three separate departments, the Distribution Depot, the Sales department and the Accounts department.

1. Workload characterization

The table in Figure 6.1 shows the names and relative frequencies of the different transaction types in the first two columns; the remaining columns show the originators of the transactions. This information enables us to determine the relative composition of the workload generated at each site (assuming each department represents a single site).

Workload	Frequency	Originating Site		
	(relative)	Depot	Sales	Accounts
T1 NewOrder	45	15%	85%	
T2 Payment	43	50%		95%
T3 OrderStatus	4		100%	
T4 Delivery	4	100%		
T5 StockLevel	4	95%		5%

Figure 6.1 Relative composition of the workload.

2. Access calculations

The next step is to calculate the number of accesses made by every transaction type to each table, shown in Figure 6.2. This simply counts the number of records referred to by each transaction (using an average where the number is not fixed). Read accesses should be distinguished from writes, as this information will usually be useful in a later refinement of the design. For this part of the process it is necessary to understand the behaviour of each transaction type. This can either be done by analysing the application semantics or obtained from information about the behaviour of the transactions (or their equivalents) in an existing operational or experimental system. Determining the access patterns by analysis is more common.

The second part of this step is to weight the raw access totals by the relative frequency of each transaction type (from the previous step). In the first instance we do not distinguish between read and write accesses. This gives an aggregated total of accesses for each table.

Reads	Warehouse	District	Customer	Stock	Item	Order	NewOrder	OrderLine	History
T1 NewOrder	1	1	1	10	10				
T2 Payment	1	1	1						
T3 OrderStatus			1			1		10	
T4 Delivery						10	10	100	
T5 StockLevel		1		200				200	
Writes									
T1 NewOrder				10		1	1	10	
T2 Payment	1	1							1
T3 OrderStatus									
T4 Delivery			10			10	10	100	
T5 StockLevel									
Raw Total									
T1 NewOrder	1	1	1	20	10	1	1	10	0
T2 Payment	2	2	1	0	0	0	0	0	1
T3 OrderStatus	0	0	1	0	0	1	0	10	0
T4 Delivery	0	0	10	0	0	20	20	200	0
T5 StockLevel	0	1	0	200	0	0	0	200	0
Weighted Accesses									
T1 NewOrder	45	43	43	860	430	43	43	430	0
T2 Payment	86	86	43	0	0	0	0	0	43
T3 OrderStatus	0	0	4	0	0	4	0	40	0
T4 Delivery	0	0	40	0	0	80	80	800	0
T5 StockLevel	0	4	0	800	0	0	0	800	0
Total	**131**	**133**	**130**	**1660**	**430**	**127**	**123**	**2070**	**43**

Figure 6.2 Access frequency calculations.

3. Distributed 'Best Fit' calculations

The third step in this method is to apportion the relative accesses to each site, using the information on the use of each transaction type at each site (columns 3–5 of Figure 6.1). From this information we can calculate the total number of accesses required by each site on every table (Figure 6.3). Each table is considered in turn and is allocated to the site having the most local accesses to it. This allocation is shown in the last two rows of the table in Figure 6.3.

L1 Depot	Warehouse	District	Customer	Stock	Item	Order	NewOrder	OrderLine	History
T1 NewOrder	6.75	6.45	6.45	129	64.5	6.45	6.45	64.5	0
T2 Payment	43	43	21.5	0	0	0	0	0	21.5
T3 OrderStatus	0	0	0	0	0	0	0	0	0
T4 Delivery	0	0	40	0	0	80	80	800	0
T5 StockLevel	0	3.8	0	760	0	0	0	760	0
Local Accesses	49.75	53.25	67.95	889	64.5	86.45	86.45	1624.5	21.5
L2 Sales									
T1 NewOrder	38.25	36.55	36.55	731	365.5	36.55	36.55	365.5	0
T2 Payment	0	0	0	0	0	0	0	0	0
T3 OrderStatus	0	0	4	0	0	4	0	40	0
T4 Delivery	0	0	0	0	0	0	0	0	0
T5 StockLevel	0	0	0	0	0	0	0	0	0
Local Accesses	38.25	36.55	40.55	731	365.5	40.55	36.55	405.5	0
L3 Accounts									
T1 NewOrder	0	0	0	0	0	0	0	0	0
T2 Payment	81.7	81.7	40.85	0	0	0	0	0	40.85
T3 OrderStatus	0	0	0	0	0	0	0	0	0
T4 Delivery	0	0	0	0	0	0	0	0	0
T5 StockLevel	0	0.2	0	40	0	0	0	40	0
Local Accesses	81.7	81.9	40.85	40	0	0	0	40	40.85

Allocation	Warehouse	District	Customer	Stock	Item	Order	NewOrder	OrderLine	History
Site	Accounts	Accounts	Depot	Depot	Sales	Depot	Depot	Depot	Accounts

Figure 6.3 Apportioning the accesses to sites.

In this example the simple Best Fit method gives a satisfactory result, although the placement of some relations is sensitive to the proportions of each transaction type originating at each of the three sites. It should be obvious that it is advantageous to maintain these calculations using a spreadsheet package.

6.7 Summary

We have described an approach to physical design that is based on estimating the number of I/Os, simple calculations of access times for deriving simple performance estimates and approaches to table fragmentation and allocation for distributed database design. We have included a relatively detailed discussion of disk access time calculations because of the importance of disk service to performance-critical database applications.

Exercises

1. A bank has a database system to record its banking transactions. The relational schema for this database is:
   Branch (Branch_id, Branch_name, Branch_balance)
   Teller (Teller_id, Branch_id, Teller_balance)
   Account (Account_id, Account_name, Branch_id, Account_balance)
   History (Account_id, Teller_id, Timestamp, Branch_id, Amount)
   The bank has 100 branches; each branch has (on average) 100,000 accounts and 10 tellers.
   The system has to handle two types of transaction:

   i) The banking transaction
       The logical sequence of events for this transaction is that:
       – money is debited or credited to an account and the balance updated;
       – the teller's balance is updated;
       – the branch balance is updated;
       – the details of the transaction are recorded in the history file;
       – the updated account details are returned to the application (so that they can be displayed on the teller's terminal).

   The application that runs this transaction can pass the amount, the Account_id and the Teller_id to the query(s) in this transaction. There are approximately 1,000,000 banking transactions a day.

   ii) The treasury transaction
       This transaction retrieves the identity and balance of every branch and the identity and balance of each teller in that branch. There are approximately 10,000 treasury transactions a day.

   The history file is emptied daily.
   The system should be designed to maximize throughput.
   Design the storage structures and indexes for this database, assuming that:

      – a page reference in an index is 20 bytes long;
      – each transaction has to fetch all the data it needs from disk;
      – the CPU is never a bottleneck;
      – each tuple is 100 bytes long;
      – Account_id, Teller_id and Branch_id are each 20 bytes long;
      – the page size is 4Kbytes, of which 4000 bytes are available for data or index keys;
      – the root page of any B-tree index is always in memory.

2. Using the information from the TPC-C design exercise in Section 6.6.2 derive an allocation using the All Beneficial Sites allocation method.

Chapter 7

PERFORMANCE ESTIMATION

7.1 Introduction

In this chapter we describe the principal approaches to performance measurement and estimation, and show how they can be incorporated into the wider design process.

Most software and systems development projects include a certain amount of performance evaluation work (modelling and experimental), but in many cases this is not sufficient to prevent major performance problems with newly developed systems. The approach of predicting performance almost entirely on the basis of expert judgement is becoming increasingly unreliable since the emerging generation of systems has many more significant interactions between software, hardware and communications systems. The applications' demands are much more stringent than those of the current generation of information systems in order to allow them to use audio, moving video and other complex data types.

Performance evaluation studies are used in many circumstances, in the design and procurement of new systems, and in the improvement and assessment of existing systems. Performance evaluation work is primarily oriented towards allowing users and developers to acquire or build systems that maximize performance and minimize cost [Jain 1991].

It is generally recognized that major design efforts can benefit considerably from suitable performance evaluation studies and experiments. However, it is frequently not easy to achieve this; typically, texts assume that performance evaluation work provides valuable input into the design process, without providing any discussion or guidance as to how this is achieved.

Despite the emphasis on mathematical technique, performance evaluation remains an art – the techniques may be rigorous, but their selection, combination and interpretation remain a matter for the skill of the analyst in the first instance.

The first two sections of this chapter describe the role of performance evaluation studies in database design. First, we describe the role of prototyping, the users of performance evaluation studies and outline some of the principal approaches. Second, we focus on their incorporation into the wider process of database application design. The second half of the chapter is concerned with database benchmarking, describing the history and process before outlining the main features of some of the more important database benchmarks. An appendix lists a sample implementation of the TPC-C benchmark.

7.2 Performance evaluation in database design

During the 1980s performance evaluation became a minor concern in the database design process as a result of three trends:

- The realization that the maintenance and enhancement of database systems was very significantly improved by having a good match between the logical design and the system implementation.
- Many commercial database applications, involving relatively simple data structures and query types, became sufficiently well understood to allow a few performance-enhancing heuristics to suffice for many designs.
- Most major hardware ranges were developed to be transparently upgradable over a large range of sizes. This meant that a large range of incremental performance improvements was possible by simple hardware upgrades, without having any effect on the applications.

A more sophisticated approach is needed to deliver the required performance from systems dealing in a wide variety of data types (video, audio and so on) with more demanding performance requirements in heterogeneous networked environments utilizing a variety of machine architectures (shared memory, pipelined and so on) and a greater range of storage devices (CD-ROM, PCMCIA and so on). In order to deal satisfactorily with these more complex environments a more structured integration of performance evaluation work into the systems development process is necessary. The incorporation of performance and modelling work into an explicit prototyping framework offers an effective solution to many of the frequently encountered integration problems.

The principal motivation for the development of prototyping techniques for software development came from difficulties in establishing user requirements. By the early 1980s it was apparent that many information systems development projects were delivering systems that failed to meet customer needs. In many cases a significant source of problems was inadequate communication and understanding of the requirements: the customer did not properly understand what was proposed and the developer did not understand what the customer really wanted. In addition the customer's requirements often change rapidly as the potential uses of a new system are appreciated.

One response to these problems has been the development of prototyping for systems development. A number of detailed approaches have been proposed and a useful classification of prototyping techniques is given by [Mayhew and Dearnley 1987]; this is summarized below.

7.2.1   Prototyping

The classification of information systems prototyping approaches can most readily be done on the basis of the participants involved in a particular prototype system (Prototyper, User, Software, Hardware) and the dominant interactions involved (Figure 7.1).

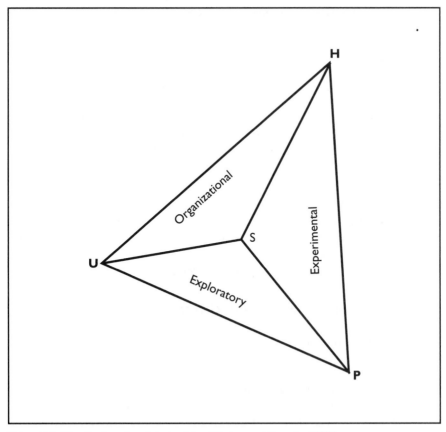

Figure 7.1 Classification of prototyping (after [Mayhew and Dearnley 1987]).

Exploratory

Exploratory prototyping is perhaps the most frequently used type of prototyping. It aims to enhance communication between prototyper and user in order to arrive at a better requirements specification.

Experimental

Experimental prototyping is directed towards testing the adequacy of solutions proposed for a particular problem; the principal interactions are between the prototyper, the hardware and software components of the system. Further subdivisions of this category are into experimental, hardware and performance prototyping.

Experimental and hardware prototyping are concerned with the validation of aspects of the software and hardware designs respectively.

Performance prototyping is the running of the application prototype in the operational situation with a synthetic workload, with the aim of detecting 'incompatible combinations of problem, hardware, software and workload' [Mayhew and Dearnley 1987].

Organizational

Organizational prototypes are used in the target environment and are designed to clarify aspects of the system requirements. They are subdivided into functional prototypes, which aim to reveal deficiencies in the proposed functionality of the system, and ergonomic prototypes, which are constructed to determine the adequacy of the proposed hardware in the operational environment.

Evolutionary

Evolutionary prototyping is defined as a prototype that is successfully refined until it becomes the final system. Mayhew and Dearnley see this as an extension of organizational prototyping. Some writers (for example, [Vonk 1990]) see this as one of the principal classes of prototype, contrasting it with rapid (experimental) prototypes which are thrown away before the final system is constructed.

7.2.2 Performance evaluation clients

Performance evaluation activity in a software development project has to satisfy a number of clients:

1. System Architects and Designers. These are the primary source of designs and the initial point for liaison and feedback. In the absence of performance evaluation results the system designers will rely on qualitative arguments, domain folklore and practice, and their own previous experience.

2. Project Managers. The prime focus of project management is in ensuring targets are met. One measure of project progress is the extent to which the current design meets defined performance targets. Another important activity for performance evaluation work is the definition of suitable performance targets.
3. Implementation team. The interaction with the implementors overlaps with the testing programme.

The performance of the finished system must ultimately satisfy the users.

7.2.3 Performance evaluation techniques

The classification of performance estimation approaches is well established and there is a wide consensus as to the strengths and value of many methods.

Analytic

Analytic models represent salient aspects of the target system in a series of linked equations. They vary in complexity from simple 'back of the envelope' calculations to sophisticated queuing models. The advantages of this class of model are that the models are usable in a very wide variety of situations, are relatively cheap, rapid to construct and do not demand expensive tools. Their disadvantages are that the results are rarely accurate and that it may be difficult to represent the desired features of the system in a mathematically tractable form.

Analytic models are most obviously used in the early stages of system design, where measurements are not possible. These models are also commonly used to supplement simulations and measurement experiments.

Simulation

Simulation models are timestep models, capturing critical aspects of the behaviour of the system being studied. Simulations have major strengths in situations where the problem to be studied is relatively stable and there is sufficient time to develop, run and analyse a simulation model. The model can be more complex, representing more of the target system's detail than analytic models, and the results are correspondingly more accurate.

The difficulties with this class of model are that, if the problem to be simulated is not sufficiently well defined, much effort can easily be wasted. The level of tool support for simulation modelling is considerable, with a number of well-established languages and packages.

Experimental

Measurements have the decisive presentational advantage of having been taken from something 'real'. However, there are usually considerable difficulties in deciding what to measure and then in obtaining the desired measurements without influence from extraneous factors.

Within the context of systems development, measurements of an existing system can be taken (in principle) at any time, but can only be taken for a new system after some sort of organizational prototype has been developed. If the target environment is not available then the measurements obtained must be extrapolated to that target. This can be a particular problem where the development environment and the target environment are significantly different (for example, the development is done on a uniprocessor workstation and the target is a massively parallel server).

It can be difficult to convince development managers of the time and resources needed to conduct measurement experiments, since they are usually conceptually simple (for example, 'Run the Wisconsin benchmark tests') and the pitfalls are not obvious. This is discussed further below.

7.3 A performance estimation strategy

In order to integrate performance evaluation and modelling activities into a wider systems development environment we suggest a broad strategy of:

1. constructing quick, simple models in the initial design phases of a project;
2. elaborating these where the results suggest particular problems and in critical regions of the overall design;
3. further elaborating key problem areas through the use of simulation models where the review of preceding activity suggests this is warranted (not forgetting that building a simulation model is a programming activity and must be treated as such);
4. running measurement experiments to verify key aspects of the design or to provide base figures for other performance evaluation tasks.

This strategy makes use of the ability to rapidly construct analytic models to feed timely results into the early phases of the design, when major changes will frequently be made. There is an explicit trade-off in favour of timeliness, at the cost of decreased accuracy of the performance estimates, although a well-constructed analytical model should give the correct rank order among design choices, even if the quantitative estimates are inaccurate.

The construction of simulation models must be treated as a programming task, with an appropriate infrastructure, goal definition, and so on. if it is to yield the desired results. Since successful programming projects are heavily dependent on a clearly defined set of objectives, we suggest that the construction of simulation models is best done when the main outlines, scope and goals of the project are stable.

Where there is an existing system there is scope for useful measurement experiments against which the projected performance of the new system can be compared and the improvements quantified. The problems to be solved are typically well-structured, with clearly defined goals, and hence will respond well to conventional linear development methods. The performance evaluation activity in these projects is easy to incorporate, since there is an obvious role in keeping the developers on track and auditing their progress in the attainment of performance objectives.

In many projects it is not possible to attempt meaningful measurement experiments until an advanced stage. In any case good measurement results are expensive to obtain and need a well-designed experimental framework, addressing specific issues, if they are to be useful.

In order to incorporate the more sophisticated performance evaluation needed by the emerging generation of systems some suggestions can be made:

1. Incorporate specific performance evaluation milestones into each iteration of the design process. Typically these will consist of short reports describing simple analytical models, with an emphasis on the assumptions and fundamental relationships modelled – the results cannot be expected to provide more than a rank order evaluation of options.
2. Do not embark on costly simulations without clear goals and a well-defined scope. Treat a simulation exercise like any other programming project of similar size.
3. Define an evaluation strategy for the developing system. Ensure that the results of specific experiments on aspects of the target environment are properly reported and visible at the appropriate reviews.

The designers and modellers must work closely together. The modellers must understand sufficient of the design issues to follow the designers' discussions and identify the critical points to be addressed by modelling. The results of modelling exercises must be fed back to the designers rapidly, before the issues have been decided. For their part the designers need to ensure that the modellers appreciate the critical design issues and have the necessary background material to do so (particularly where the design team have a shared history of past projects). The modellers must also be allowed time to develop their models if the results are to be of any use in the design process.

7.3.1 Integration into database development

We can identify a number of issues:

1. Project managers may not appreciate the nature of performance evaluation work and not allow sufficient time and resources.
2. Development staff may have unrealistic or conflicting expectations of modelling.
3. Performance evaluators may not have a sufficient appreciation of the technical issues being confronted in the system design.

4. Performance evaluation studies often have interesting aspects which are not critical to the project; these tangential aspects will take resources away from more productive work if evaluation teams feel detached from the main effort.
5. The problem to be modelled or the phenomena to be measured are not well defined – this will lead to wasted effort.
6. Evaluation results are not available in time or are presented in a form which the developers cannot assimilate.

The problems common to prototyping efforts are described in [Vonk 1990], and other texts; those of performance evaluation are discussed in detail in [Jain 1991].

As a general rule we can say that performance evaluation activity decreases in relevance to the implementation team as it becomes more detailed. This is because, with more detail, the implementors can detect differences between their model of the system and the performance evaluation model, making it easier to reject the conclusions of the evaluation if they are unwelcome.

7.3.2 Performance evaluation and modelling tools

The availability of suitable tools can be a major influence on the success of performance evaluation activities. The major distinctions are between:

- general-purpose, simple tools (for example, spreadsheet or simple queuing model package),
- more demanding general-purpose tools (for example, simulation language environment),
- specialist tools (for example, database cost evaluator [Andres et al. 1991], software testing package [Kersten and Kwakkel 1993]).

The last category of tools is, in general, in research or commercial prototype form. They differ from existing database administrator tools in providing a generality of function which is largely independent of a specific database management system or machine architecture.

7.4 Database benchmarking

A basic understanding of database benchmarking and of the principal characteristics of the most widely used database benchmarks is important for the database designer for three reasons:

- to better understand manufacturers' performance claims and evaluate their applicability to the target application;

- to assess the need to conduct benchmark tests or to specify appropriate benchmarks for competitive evaluations;
- to be able to use parts of existing benchmarks to conduct performance experiments for proposed system designs.

Here we present an overview of the benchmarking process, the development of database benchmarks and describe the main features of the principal database benchmarks.

7.4.1   History and rationale

Database benchmarks have been developed as a tool for comparing the performance of database management systems, attempting to summarize their relative performance in a single figure. We can distinguish two principal strands of development: the first arising from vendors' performance claims and the second from a desire to understand and compare the performance of the components of different database management systems. Other strands of database benchmark development include configurable test suites developed by consultancy groups and, of increasing importance, benchmarks targeted at specific application areas or types of database management system.

The origins of systematic database benchmarking can be traced to the development of the Wisconsin benchmark by DeWitt and his colleagues [Bitton *et al.* 1983] in response to their need for a scalable benchmark that could isolate the performance of various components of a database management system and allow comparisons between different systems (in their case the DIRECT database machine and the 'university' version of INGRES). Their results, which named the systems they tested, caused considerable controversy but ultimately led to a significant decrease in the performance differences between systems. The Wisconsin benchmark is still widely used for system testing and development work, although it has been superseded by other benchmarks for vendors' headline figures.

As a result of the commercial importance of performance to database vendors there were many disputes, sharp practices and misleading claims made for various systems in a series of 'benchmark wars' during the 1980s. In order to enable truly comparative figures to be produced, a consortium of manufacturers formed the Transaction Processing Performance Council (TPC) in 1988.

The TPC developed the specification of a simple transaction processing benchmark based on the DebitCredit or TP1 transaction [Anon *et al.* 1985]. This work resulted in the TPC-A and TPC-B benchmarks. These have been extremely influential, because they provide a strict definition of what is to be measured, consistent methods for presenting the results and calculating costs, and a requirement for independent audit of the benchmarking process. More recently there has been a general acceptance that these transactions are unrepresentative of many real workloads and that a wider series of measures is required. This has led to the development of TPC-C, based on an order entry system, and TPC-D, based on a decision support application.

The principal measure of commercial interest is the overall cost of ownership of a system that can deliver a certain level of performance. The performance of a database management system is most often expressed as transactions per second (tps) and the cost measure most widely used is the system cost over five years. The combination of these two gives cost per tps as the single measure.

7.4.2   Unwanted influences

Database benchmark tests involve many aspects of the system, and are therefore frequently confounded by extraneous variables; a partial list includes:

- data left in buffers from previous queries (for example, DBMS, operating system, disk controller);
- disk and network speed (that is, different from the expected speed);
- memory fragmentation;
- query parsing time (depends on the query processing strategy used by the database management system);
- limitations on the number of concurrent users (which may cause unexpected queuing or which may determine other system resources, such as memory, that are allocated to the database management system);
- number of attributes and number of sources of attributes in the result;
- formatting costs of result relations;
- allocation of resources to processes (in an environment with many processes it is easy for one to be starved of resources and become a bottleneck);
- size of buffer for large queries (for example loading 100,000 tuples using the SQL INSERT command generates either a very large log tail or incurs an extra overhead from frequent commits);
- variable disk fragmentation (in environments where the disk may be used for purposes other than database benchmarking).

7.4.3   Benchmarks for competitive evaluations

As part of a system procurement it is common to specify a series of tests or benchmarks. It is essential, in defining the tests to be carried out, that the manufacturers can implement them in a reasonable time and that the results will be pertinent to selecting the best system for the intended application. There are some dangers for the unwary:

- Vendors will try to persuade potential customers to use benchmarks that favour their products.

- Losing vendors will often cry 'foul', alleging that their competitors have used a three star wizard while they only used their local one star wizard. There is a danger that this can escalate until each party is using a full team of five star wizards.
- Any ambiguity in the specification will be exploited.
- If the purpose of the exercise is not clear at the start a great deal of time and effort will be wasted by all the parties involved.

7.5   Individual benchmarks

Database benchmarks are frequently referred to in academic, technical and commercial literature. Anybody concerned with database performance should have at least a nodding acquaintance with the characteristics of the most widely used benchmarks. In this section we provide brief descriptions of some of the more influential and interesting benchmarks. Full descriptions of these and other benchmarks can be found in [Gray 1993].

There are two principal uses for database benchmarks:

- providing comparative performance measures,
- as a source of data and queries that represent experimental approximations to other problems.

Benchmarks are all designed to fulfil the first point. In adopting a benchmark for an evaluation, or using reported results, it is important to understand the aspects of the database system being tested by each benchmark. There is no necessary correlation between a database management system's performance on different types of benchmark; for instance, a system that is good for on-line transaction processing is not necessarily good for complex decision-support queries.

In the second role the benchmark definition becomes a convenient approximation of an application that is being designed. The data is synthetic, with known properties and defined scaling characteristics, while the queries exhibit well-defined behaviour. In many cases it is possible to find a benchmark that captures the essence of a problem, thus providing the database designer with a convenient experimental framework to conduct performance experiments. The time and effort that can be saved by reusing part of a benchmark definition must always be balanced against the extent to which a meaningful representation of the target application is compromised.

There are two main approaches to data generation:

1. Artificial. Involves the generation of data with entirely artificial properties, designed to investigate particular aspects of a system. This approach is exemplified by the Wisconsin benchmark.
2. Synthetic workload. The aim in these benchmarks is to produce a simplified version of an application, using synthetically generated data with

approximately the same properties as the application data. The Transaction Processing Performance Council benchmarks are the best known examples of this type of benchmark.

The main features of selected benchmarks are described in the remainder of this section.

7.5.1 *Wisconsin*

The Wisconsin benchmark was the first systematic benchmark definition. It was designed to facilitate investigation and comparison of particular features of database management systems, rather than provide a simple overall performance metric. It is a single-user series of tests, comprising:

- selections and projections with varying selectivities on clustered, indexed non-indexed attributes;
- joins of varying selectivities;
- use of aggregate functions (min, max, sum);
- updates and deletions involving key and non-key attributes.

The original benchmark defined three relations: one with 1,000 records called Onektup and two others with 10,000 records called Tenktup1 and Tenktup2. Each relation has 13 integer attributes and three 52-byte strings. Some of the original methods for allocating values to records resulted in strong patterns, which influence the access patterns required for some queries and which a very sophisticated optimizer might be able to make use of. The current definition of the benchmark incorporates a number of modifications which eliminate this patterning and make the benchmark more readily scalable.

For a table with n records the attributes of each relation are:

unique1	0–(n − 1)	random
unique2	0–(n − 1)	sequential
two	0–1	(unique1 mod 2)
four	0–3	(unique1 mod 4)
ten	0–9	(unique1 mod 10)
twenty	0–19	(unique1 mod 20)
onePercent	0–99	(unique1 mod 100)
tenPercent	0–9	(unique1 mod 10)
twentyPercent	0–4	(unique1 mod 5)
fiftyPercent	0–1	(unique1 mod 2)
unique3	0–(n − 1)	unique1
evenOnePercent	0–198	(onePercent * 2)
OddOnePercent	1–199	(onePercent * 2) + 1
stringu1	unique string	random
stringu2	unique string	sequential
string4	4 values	cyclic

This structure is easy to build a generator for and can be readily scaled to very large sizes for testing large database systems (for example, massively parallel) which need many millions of records to stress them.

The Wisconsin benchmark has endured well because it is straightforward to implement, readily understandable and the results generally provide much useful information. The principal deficiencies of this benchmark for testing current relational systems are the lack of any highly skewed attribute distributions and the simplicity of the join queries.

7.5.2   TPC-A and TPC-B

The Transaction Processing Performance Council's first effort was directed towards producing a standard benchmark, applicable to a wide variety of systems. They developed the specification of the TPC-A benchmark from the earlier DebitCredit definition of a simplified bank teller system which was loosely based on the Bank of America's system in the 1970s.

The benchmark measures the performance of a simple banking transaction, from its initiation at a terminal (which may be a dumb terminal, workstation or any other machine on a user's desk) until the response arrives back from the server. This encompasses the time taken by the database server, network and any other components of the system, but excludes formatting and other user-directed work done by the terminal. The terminals are emulated, using a negative exponential transaction arrival distribution.

The tables and cardinalities used in the benchmark are:

branch	1
teller	10
account	100,000
history	2,592,000
terminals	10

This configuration is the minimum per tps (that is, the database is scaled in multiples of this configuration). Each record type is 100 bytes long.

The TPC-A transaction mimics the transfer of money to or from an account; the actions are:

update the account record
update the teller record
update the branch record
insert a history record
return the account balance.

The TPC-B benchmark is similar, except that it only measures the performance of the database server. The costs must include sufficient storage for 90 days' records, assuming an 8 hour day.

All these actions are performed on single records, so important aspects of database operation, such as query planning and join execution, are not measured.

7.5.3 TPC-C

The TPC-C benchmark is based around an order entry application. The range of queries and additional tables make it a significantly more complex benchmark than TPC-A. It is much closer to current typical database applications than previous TPC benchmarks and offers a much more comprehensive test of a database management system's abilities.

The scope of the system, its costing, and so on are similar to TPC-A and TPC-B.

The schema

There are nine tables in the benchmark, shown in Figure 7.2. The unit of scaling is the warehouse (W). The other tables (except Item) are expressed in terms of their size relative to the number of warehouses. The relationships are:

District	W * 10
Customer	W * 30,000
Order	W * 30,000
Order-Line	W * 300,000+
New-Order	W * 2,000+
History	W * 30,000+
Stock	W * 50,000
Item	50,000

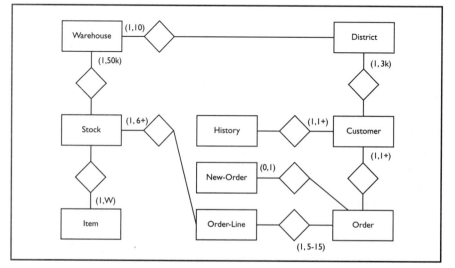

Figure 7.2 Logical schema for TPC-C.

Sample SQL definitions of the tables are listed in the appendix at the end of this chapter.

The transactions

There are five transaction types defined; four of them have minimum frequencies and the balance is made of New-Order transactions. The reported throughput measure is the number of completed New-Order transactions per minute (tpm). The transactions and their frequencies are:

> **New-Order** (n/a). Represents the entering of a complete order. It is a mid-weight read-write transaction with stringent performance constraints that forms the core of the benchmark workload.
> **Payment** (43%). Represents customers making payments into their accounts. It is a lightweight transaction, similar in style to the TPC-A transaction.
> **Order-Status** (4%). Represents an enquiry to determine the status of the customer's last order. This transaction is a mid-weight, read-only relatively infrequent on-line query.
> **Delivery** (4%). Represents the batch processing of a delivery consisting of 10 orders. It is low frequency, with relaxed performance constraints. It is executed off-line from the issuing terminal, to which a completion message is sent.
> **Stock-Level** (4%). Represents the enquiry to determine the numbers of recently sold items. It is a heavy read-only transaction with a low frequency, reduced consistency and relaxed performance requirements.

Sample implementations of these queries are listed in the appendix at the end of this chapter.

Evaluation

This benchmark is relatively new, but has been adopted by several manufacturers and is likely to supplant TPC-A and TPC-B as the most widely used performance metric. It is a good representation of a moderately complex application scenario and sample benchmark generation and execution programs are included in the definition. The range of queries is sufficient to allow portions of it to be used in a variety of performance estimation experiments.

7.5.4   AS3AP

The ANSI SQL Standard Scalable And Portable (AS3AP) benchmark tests [Turbyfill 1988; Turbyfill *et al.* 1993] are designed to provide an examination of the performance of different aspects of a database management system, following the philosophy underlying the Wisconsin benchmark [Bitton *et al.* 1983]. The benchmark is designed as two series of tests: single-user and multi-user. The single-user benchmark tests are designed to test the basic functions that a relational system should support:

1. Utilities for loading and structuring the database;
2. Queries designed to test access methods and basic query optimization.

The multi-user tests are designed to model significant characteristics of different types of database workload:

3. On-line transaction processing (OLTP);
4. Information retrieval (IR);
5. Mixed workloads which include short transactions, report queries, long transactions and relation scan.

Attention has been paid to the development of queries designed to test the performance of parallel and main memory database systems.

The metric

The measurement of performance is based on throughput and excludes think time, terminal emulation, and so on. The queries scale with the database size and there are rules specifying the number of concurrent users that are emulated for a given database size.

The actual measure proposed by Turbyfill is the equivalent database ratio, defined as the maximum database size that allows the queries to be completed in under 12 hours.

Database structure and characteristics

The AS3AP relations are:

tiny	A single value. Used to measure overhead.
uniques	All attributes have unique values.
hundred	Most attributes have 100 values and are correlated. The correlation permits the generation of projections containing 100 multi-attribute tuples.
tenpct	Most attributes have 10% selectivity.
updates	A relation customized for updates, using different distributions and three types of index.

The four principal relations each have 10 attributes, with the same names and data types. The tuple width is 100 bytes on average, comprising 9 fixed-length fields and a variable-length string with an average size of 20 bytes. The data types used comprise:

- 4-byte integers,
- 4-and 8-byte floating point,

- fixed-length string,
- variable length string,
- datetime (8 bytes),
- exact decimal (18 bytes).

Substitution rules allow for the replacement of unsupported types with a shorter type and a compensating field to maintain overall tuple size.

The SQL92 Level 1 standard does not define a DATE data type and the AS3AP designers assumed that date and time can be adequately represented in 8 bytes. DBMSs differ in the range of dates they will allow and this may be reflected in the length of the data type. Many application areas may need wide date ranges:

- Property, heritage and conservation databases frequently need date ranges of several hundred years.
- Scientific and sports databases often record sub-second times.

Several distributions are used for the attributes, including uniform, normal, Zipf and sparse values from a large range.

The required indexes are:

- clustered (primary) B-tree,
- non-clustered (secondary) B-tree,
- non-clustered hash.

Substitution is allowed, with the constraint that two different non-clustered and one clustered index type should be used if they are available in the system under test.

The queries

The single-user tests are divided into six logical parts:

- tests of output modes,
- selections,
- projections,
- joins,
- aggregate functions,
- updates.

These follow the Wisconsin approach of trying to isolate the effect of various components of the database management system on its overall performance.

Evaluation

The AS3AP benchmark represents an important attempt to incorporate a serious evaluation of database utilities into the benchmarking process, although these can have an unduly large influence on the overall measure. The equivalent database ratio is an innovative approach to incorporating database size and scaleup into the metric. However, it is not easily understood and does not seem to be very useful in practice. The queries cover a wide range but there are groups amongst them that do not contribute much to the understanding of a system (for example, the three-way joins do not add to the information from the two-and four-way joins). There is a good variety of data distributions in the benchmark, but the published definition does not give sufficient information to implement the specification accurately [Smith and Krabbe 1992]. The complexity of the data definition and the lack of widely available database generation programs has hindered the more widespread use of AS3AP[1].

Overall, the AS3AP benchmark provides a very useful set of queries and data for conducting performance evaluation experiments, although it suffers from a number of limitations as a complete relational benchmark.

7.5.5   OO7

The OO7 benchmark [Carey *et al.* 1993] has been designed to test various aspects of system performance for a generalized CAx application domain. It is influenced by the designers' previous experience of the Wisconsin benchmark and the lessons gained from the OO1 [Cattell and Skeen 1992] and HyperModel [Cattell 1991b] benchmarks.

The OO1 benchmark was designed to test the navigational and insert capabilities of object-oriented database systems (ODBS). The principal criticism of this benchmark is that the objects are linked in such a way as to prevent any semantic clustering – the transitive closure of any object is the whole database. This biases it heavily in favour of systems that have good pointer-chasing performance at the expense of any other operations.

The specification of HyperModel is more complex, including a wider range of operations and data types. These additions are not all very informative and the complexity of the benchmark makes implementation more difficult without delivering a corresponding benefit in information and understanding.

OO7 is designed to examine the performance characteristics of a number of different types of retrieval and traversal, object creation and deletion and the performance of the query processor. In order to facilitate its use the designers have provided a number of sample implementations[2]. Small, medium and large versions have been defined; the larger versions have more and more complex objects.

The schema

The OO7 schema represents a complex parts hierarchy. Each part has associated documentation and objects at the top level of the hierarchy, modules, each have an associated manual.

The schema and its refinements are shown in Figures 7.3 and 7.4.

---

1   A suite of generator programs for this benchmark was produced at UEA Norwich as part of the EDS project; they are available by anonymous ftp from ftp.sys.uea.ac.uk

2   Available by anonymous ftp from the OO7 directory at ftp.cs.wisc.edu

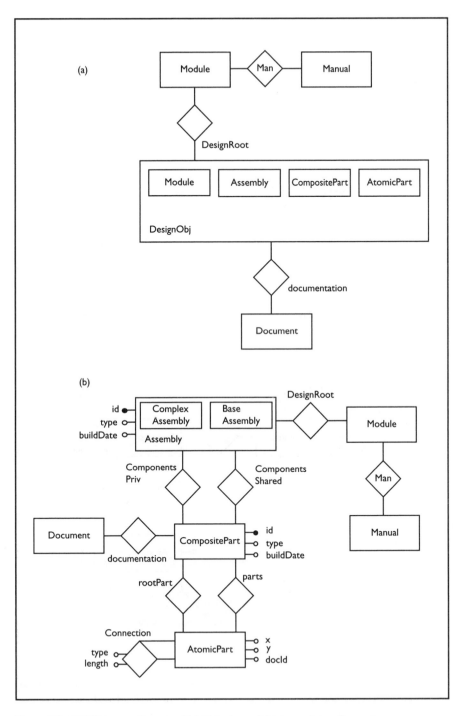

Figure 7.3 OO7 Schema refinement. (a) Initial schema, (b) Intermediate refinement.

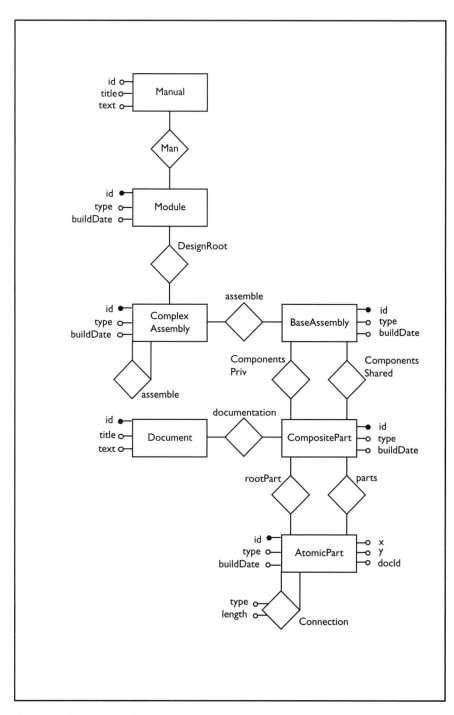

Figure 7.4 OO7 Refined schema.

The tests

The first group of tests is a series of traversals which have been designed to test:

1. Raw traversal speed. This is a simple test of navigational performance, similar to the measure emphasized by OO1.
2. Traversal with updates. Similar to 1, but performing a number of updates, using three patterns (every atomic part visited, a part in every composite part, every part in a composite part four times). A similar series of traversals is also done using an indexed field.
3. Operations on Manual. Two traversals, first to test whether the first and last characters of a 1Mb Manual are the same, second to count the number of 'I's in Manual.

By running combinations of these traversals with empty caches ('cold') and again after the caches are full from a previous execution ('hot') the effectiveness of caching strategies across transactions can be determined.

The second group of tests is a set of queries that are designed to be expressed declaratively:

1. Exact match. A straightforward indexed retrieval of a single atomic part.
2. Range searches with variable selectivity. These are designed to test the performance of range searches and examine query processing strategy for the search with 10% selectivity (when a scan should be quicker than using an index).
3. Path lookup. Find the assemblies that use a part corresponding to a document.
4. Scan. Accesses every atomic part.
5. Make. A query that simulates the behaviour of the make utility in determining which objects have changed since the last make operation.
6. Join. Examines the performance of a simple join query.

The third group of tests changes the database structure by inserting and deleting a group of composite parts.

Evaluation

The OO7 benchmark appears to have addressed the weaknesses of earlier ODBS benchmarks. The results described in [Carey *et al.* 1993] suggest that it provides a comprehensive examination of ODBS performance and can effectively isolate the contribution of various components to the overall system performance. We believe that this benchmark will fulfil a role for ODBS similar to that of the Wisconsin benchmark for relational systems.

7.6 Summary

In this chapter we first described an iterative approach to performance modelling activities, emphasizing the need for simple, rapid performance evaluation results which can be used as an integral part of the overall design process.

The second part of the chapter provided an overview of database benchmarking, outlining its history and the main features of the most widely used benchmarks. An important use of benchmarks for database designers, apart from comparing systems, is as a source of material for smaller-scale experiments to evaluate the performance of critical components of the system being designed.

Appendix

This appendix contains a template for a sample implementation of the TPC-C benchmark; it runs with INGRES 6.4. The sample implementation is included here to illustrate the nature and complexity of the benchmark. Any reader who is interested in implementing the benchmark should obtain a full copy of the standard specification, either from the TPC or from [Gray 1993].

```
create table warehouse (
        w_id                integer,
        w_name              varchar(10),
        w_street_1          varchar(20),
        w_street_2          varchar(20),
        w_city              varchar(20),
        w_state             char(2),
        w_zip               char(9),
        w_tax               float4 ,
        w_ytd               float4
);
create table item (
        i_id                integer,
        i_name              varchar(25),
        i_price             float4,
        i_data              varchar(50)
);
create table customer (
        c_id                integer,
        c_d_id              integer,
        c_w_id              integer,
        c_first             varchar(16),
        c_middle            char(2),
        c_last              varchar(16),
        c_street_1          varchar(20),
        c_street_2          varchar(20),
```

```
        c_city              varchar(20),
        c_state             char(2),
        c_zip               char(9),
        c_phone             char(16),
        c_since             date,
        c_credit            char(2),
        c_credit_lim        integer,
        c_discount          float4,
        c_balance           integer,
        c_ytd_payment       integer,
        c_payment_cnt       integer,
        c_delivery_cnt      integer,
        c_data              varchar(200)

);
create table history (
        h_c_id              integer,
        h_c_d_id            integer,
        h_c_w_id            integer,
        h_d_id              integer;
        h_w_id              integer,
        h_date              date,
        h_amount            float,
        h_data              varchar(24)
);
create table district (
        d_id                integer,
        d_w_id              integer,
        d_name              char(10),
        d_street_1          char(20),
        d_street_2          char(20),
        d_city              char(20),
        d_state             char(2),
        d_zip               char(9),
        d_tax               float4,
        d_ytd               float4,
        d_next_o_id         integer
);
create table stock (
        s_i_id              integer,
        s_w_id              integer,
        s_quantity          integer,
        s_dist_01           char(24),
        s_dist_02           char(24),
        s_dist_03           char(24),
```

```
            s_dist_04           char(24),
            s_dist_05           char(24),
            s_dist_06           char(24),
            s_dist_07           char(24),
            s_dist_08           char(24),
            s_dist_09           char(24),
            s_dist_10           char(24),
            s_ytd               integer,
            s_order_cnt         integer,
            s_remote_cnt        integer4,
            s_data              char(50)
    );
    create table order (
            o_id                integer,
            o_c_id              integer,
            o_d_id              integer,
            o_w_id              integer,
            o_entry_d           date,
            o_carrier_id        integer,
            o_ol_cnt            integer4,
            o_ol_local          integer4
    );
    create table order_line (
            ol_o_id             integer,
            ol_d_id             integer,
            ol_w_id             integer,
            ol_number           integer,
            ol_i_id             integer,
            ol_supply_w_id      integer,
            ol_quantity         integer,
            ol_amount           integer,
            ol_delivery_d       date,
            ol_dist_info        char(25)
    );
    create table new_order (
            no_o_id             integer,
            no_d_id             integer,
            no_w_id             integer
    );


    #include <stdio.h>
    #define FALSE -1
    #define DIST_PER_WARE    10

    EXEC SQL INCLUDE sqlca;
```

```
EXEC SQL BEGIN DECLARE SECTION;
        long    w_id;
        char    w_name[11];
        char    w_street_1[21];
        char    w_street_2[21];
        char    w_city[21];
        char    w_state[3];
        char    w_zip[10];
        double  w_tax;
        double  w_ytd;

        long    c_id;
        long    c_d_id;
        long    c_w_id;
        char    c_first[17];
        char    c_middle[3];
        char    c_last[17];
        char    c_street_1[21];
        char    c_street_2[21];
        char    c_city[21];
        char    c_state[3];
        char    c_zip[10];
        char    c_phone[17];
        char    c_since[26];
        char    c_credit[3];
        double  c_credit_lim;
        double  c_discount;
        double  c_balance;
        double  c_ytd_payment;
        double  c_payment_cnt;
        double  c_delivery_cnt;
        char    c_data[501];

        long    d_id;
        long    d_w_id;
        char    d_name[11];
        char    d_street_1[21];
        char    d_street_2[21];
        char    d_city[21];
        char    d_state[3];
        char    d_zip[10];
        double  d_tax;
        double  d_ytd;
        long    d_next_o_id;
```

```
long    o_id;
long    o_c_id;
long    o_d_id;
long    o_w_id;
char    o_entry_d[26];
long    o_carrier_id;
long    o_ol_cnt;
long    o_all_local;

long    no_o_id;
long    no_d_id;
long    no_w_id;

long    i_id;
char    i_name[26];
double  i_price;
char    i_data[51];

long    s_i_id;
long    s_w_id;
long    s_quantity;
char    s_dist_01[25];
char    s_dist_02[25];
char    s_dist_03[25];
char    s_dist_04[25];
char    s_dist_05[25];
char    s_dist_06[25];
char    s_dist_07[25];
char    s_dist_08[25];
char    s_dist_09[25];
char    s_dist_10[25];
double  s_ytd;
long    s_order_cnt;
long    s_remote_cnt;
char    s_data[51];

long    ol_o_id;
long    ol_d_id;
long    ol_w_id;
long    ol_number;
long    ol_i_id;
long    ol_supply_w_id;
double  ol_quantity;
long    ol_amount;
```

```
char    ol_delivery_d[26];
char    ol_dist_info[26];

char    datetime[32];
int     supware[100];
int     itemid[100];
int     qty[100];
int     price[100];
char*   iname[100];
char    bg[100];
int     amt[100];
int     total;
int     stock[100];
char    err_msg[255];
long    h_amount;
int     namecnt;
char    c_new_data[500];
char    h_data[500];
int     byname;
int     n;
char    h_date[32];
char    entdate[32];
int     i;
int     ol_total;
int     stock_count;
int     threshold;
int     ol_i_id_a[15];
int     ol_supply_w_id_a[15];
int     ol_quantity_a[15];
int     ol_amount_a[15];
int     ol_delivery_d_a[15];

EXEC SQL END DECLARE SECTION;
```

```
int main ()
{
  EXEC SQL CONNECT tpcc;

  EXEC SQL INSERT INTO benchmark ( queryname, date,
        time, elapsetime, cpums, dio, bio, faults )
        VALUES ( 'PRE_QUERIES',
                 _date( _bintim(0) ), _time( _bintim(0) ),
                 bintim(0), _cpu_ms(), _dio_cnt(), _bio_cnt(),
                 _pfault_cnt() );

  /*  Execute transactions here, according to TPCC transaction
      mix specifications */

  EXEC SQL INSERT INTO benchmark ( queryname, date,
        time, elapsetime, cpums, dio, bio, faults )
        VALUES ( 'POST_QUERIES',
                 _date( _bintim(0) ), _time( _bintim(0) ),
                 _bintim(0), _cpu_ms(), _dio_cnt(), _bio_cnt(),
                 _pfault_cnt() );
  EXEC SQL COMMIT;

  EXEC SQL DISCONNECT;

  return (1);

  sqlerr:
        exit(1);
}

void pick_dist_info(char* x, int y)
{
  strncpy(x, "abcdef");
}

int sql_notfound(int x)
{
  return (0);
}

/* The New-Order Transaction */

int neword()
```

```
{
   EXEC SQL WHENEVER NOT FOUND GOTO sqlerr;
   EXEC SQL WHENEVER SQLERROR GOTO sqlerr;


   EXEC SQL SELECT c_discount, c_last, c_credit, w_tax
         INTO :c_discount, :c_last, :c_credit, :w_tax
         FROM customer, warehouse
         WHERE w_id = :w_id AND c_w_id = :w_id
         AND c_d_id = :d_id AND c_id = :c_id;

   EXEC SQL SELECT d_next_o_id, d_tax
         INTO :d_next_o_id, :d_tax
         FROM district
         WHERE d_id = :d_id AND d_w_id = :w_id;

   EXEC SQL UPDATE district
         SET d_next_o_id =  d_next_o_id + 1
         WHERE d_id = :d_id AND d_w_id = :w_id;

   o_id = d_next_o_id;

   EXEC SQL INSERT INTO ORDERS
         (o_id, o_d_id, o_w_id, o_c_id, o_entry_d, o_ol_cnt,
          o_all_local)
         VALUES
         (:o_id, :d_id, :w_id, :c_id,
          :datetime, :o_ol_cnt, :o_all_local);

   EXEC SQL INSERT INTO NEW_ORDER (no_o_id, no_d_id, no_w_id)
         VALUES ( :o_id, :d_id, :w_id);

   for (ol_number = 1; ol_number <= o_ol_cnt; ol_number++)
   {
     ol_supply_w_id = atol(supware[ol_number - 1]);
     if (ol_supply_w_id != w_id) o_all_local = 0;
     ol_i_id = atol(itemid[ol_number-1]);
     ol_quantity = atol(qty[ol_number-1]);

     EXEC SQL WHENEVER NOT FOUND GOTO invaliditem;

     EXEC SQL SELECT i_price, i_name, i_data
         INTO :i_price, :i_name, :i_data
         FROM item
         WHERE i_id = :ol_i_id;
```

```
price[ol_number-1] = i_price;
strncpy(iname[ol_number-1], i_name, 24);

EXEC SQL WHENEVER NOT FOUND GOTO sqlerr;

/* The following query selects all s_dist .xx fields */
/* only the one which matches d_id is  required */

EXEC SQL SELECT s_quantity, s_data,
    s_dist_01, s_dist_02, s_dist_03, s_dist_04, s_dist_05,
    s_dist_06, s_dist_07, s_dist_08, s_dist_09, s_dist_10
    INTO :s_quantity, :s_data,
    :s_dist_01, :s_dist_02, :s_dist_03, :s_dist_04,
    :s_dist_05, :s_dist_06, :s_dist_07, :s_dist_08,
    :s_dist_09, :s_dist_10
    FROM stock
    WHERE s_i_id = :ol_i_id AND s_w_id = :ol_supply_w_id;

/* Copy proper s_dist_xx into ol_dist_info */
pick_dist_info(ol_dist_info, ol_w_id);
stock[ol_number-1] = s_quantity;

if ((strstr(i_data, "original") != NULL) &&
    (strstr(s_data, "original") != NULL) )
  bg[ol_number-1] = 'B';
else
  bg[ol_number-1] = 'G';

if (s_quantity > ol_quantity)
  s_quantity = s_quantity - ol_quantity;
else
  s_quantity = s_quantity - ol_quantity + 91;

EXEC SQL UPDATE stock SET s_quantity = :s_quantity
    WHERE s_i_id = :ol_i_id
    AND s_w_id = :ol_supply_w_id;

ol_amount = ol_quantity * i_price * (1+w_tax+d_tax) *
            (1-c_discount);
amt[ol_number-1]=ol_amount;
total += ol_amount;

EXEC SQL INSERT INTO order_line
    (ol_o_id, ol_d_id, ol_w_id, ol_number, ol_i_id,
    ol_supply_w_id, ol_quantity, ol_amount, ol_dist_info)
```

```
          VALUES
          (:o_id, :d_id, :w_id, :ol_number, :ol_i_id,
           :ol_supply_w_id, :ol_quantity, :ol_amount,
           :ol_dist_info);

    } /* End Order Lines */

EXEC SQL COMMIT WORK;
return(0);

invaliditem:
          EXEC SQL ROLLBACK WORK;
          printf("Item number is not valid");
          return(0);

sqlerr:
          exit(1);

} /* end neword */

/* Payment transaction */

int payment()
{
  EXEC SQL WHENEVER NOT FOUND GOTO sqlerr;
  EXEC SQL WHENEVER SQLERROR GOTO sqlerr;

  EXEC SQL UPDATE warehouse SET w_ytd = w_ytd + :h_amount
        WHERE w_id=:w_id;

  EXEC SQL SELECT w_street_1, w_street_2, w_city, w_state,
                  w_zip, w_name
        INTO :w_street_1, :w_street_2, :w_city, :w_state,
             :w_zip, :w_name
        FROM warehouse
        WHERE w_id=:w_id;

  EXEC SQL UPDATE district SET d_ytd = d_ytd + :h_amount
        WHERE d_w_id=:w_id AND d_id=:d_id;

  EXEC SQL SELECT d_street_1, d_street_2, d_city, d_state,
                  d_zip, d_name
        INTO :d_street_1, :d_street_2, :d_city, :d_state,
             :d_zip, :d_name
```

```
            FROM district
            WHERE d_w_id=:w_id AND d_id=:d_id;

    if (byname)
    {
      EXEC SQL SELECT count(c_id) INTO :namecnt
            FROM customer
            WHERE c_last=:c_last AND c_w_id = :c_w_id AND c_d_id =
                :c_d_id;

      EXEC SQL DECLARE c_byname CURSOR FOR
            SELECT c_first, c_middle, c_id,
            c_street_1, c_street_2, c_city, c_state, c_zip,
            c_phone, c_credit, c_credit_lim,
            c_discount, c_balance, c_since
            FROM customer
            WHERE c_w_id=:c_w_id AND c_d_id=:c_d_id AND
                c_last=:c_last
            ORDER BY c_first;

      EXEC SQL OPEN c_byname;

      if (namecnt%2) namecnt++;    /* Locate midpoint customer */;
      for (n=0; n<namecnt/2; n++)
      {
        EXEC SQL FETCH c_byname
          INTO :c_first, :c_middle, :c_id,
                :c_street_1, :c_street_2, :c_city, :c_state,
                :c_zip, :c_phone, :c_credit, :c_credit_lim,
                :c_discount, :c_balance, :c_since;
      }
        EXEC SQL CLOSE c_byname;
    }
    else
    {
      EXEC SQL SELECT c_first, c_middle, c_last,
          c_street_1, c_street_2, c_city, c_state, c_zip,
          c_phone, c_credit, c_credit_lim,
          c_discount, c_balance, c_since
          INTO :c_first, :c_middle, :c_last,
          :c_street_1, :c_street_2, :c_city, :c_state, :c_zip,
          :c_phone, :c_credit, :c_credit_lim,
          :c_discount, :c_balance, :c_since
          FROM customer
```

```
              WHERE c_w_id=:c_w_id AND c_d_id=:c_d_id AND c_id=:c_id;
}
c_balance += h_amount;
c_credit[2] = '\0';
if (strstr(c_credit, "BC"))
{
  EXEC SQL SELECT c_data INTO :c_data
          FROM customer
          WHERE c_w_id=:c_w_id AND c_d_id=:c_d_id AND
                c_id=:c_id;

  sprintf(c_new_data,"| %4d %2d %4d %2d %4d $%7.2f %12c %24c",
          c_id, c_d_id, c_w_id, d_id, w_id, h_amount, h_date,
          h_data);
  strncat(c_new_data, c_data, 500-strlen(c_new_data));

  EXEC SQL UPDATE customer
          SET c_balance = :c_balance, c_data = :c_new_data
          WHERE c_w_id = :c_w_id AND c_d_id = :c_d_id AND
                c_id = :c_id;
}
else
{
  EXEC SQL UPDATE customer SET c_balance = :c_balance
          WHERE c_w_id = :c_w_id AND c_d_id = :c_d_id AND
                c_id = :c_id;
}
strncpy(h_data, w_name, 10);
h_data[10] = '\0';
strncat(h_data, d_name, 10);
h_data[20] = ' ';
h_data[21] = ' ';
h_data[22] = ' ';
h_data[23] = ' ';

EXEC SQL INSERT INTO history (h_c_d_id, h_c_w_id, h_c_id,
                             h_d_id, h_w_id, h_date,
                             h_amount, h_data)
     VALUES (:c_d_id, :c_w_id, :c_id, :d_id,
             :w_id, :datetime, :h_amount, :h_data);

EXEC SQL COMMIT WORK;
return (0);
```

```
   sqlerr:
     printf("EXIT DUE TO sqlerr\n");
     exit(1);
} /* end payment transaction */

int ostat()
{
  EXEC SQL WHENEVER NOT FOUND GOTO sqlerr;
  EXEC SQL WHENEVER SQLERROR GOTO sqlerr;

  if (byname)
  {
    EXEC SQL SELECT count(c_id) INTO :namecnt
          FROM customer
          WHERE c_last=:c_last AND c_d_id=:d_id AND
                c_w_id =:w_id;

    EXEC SQL DECLARE c_name CURSOR FOR
          SELECT c_balance, c_first, c_middle, c_id
          FROM customer
          WHERE c_last=:c_last AND c_d_id = :d_id AND
                c_w_id = :w_id
          ORDER BY c_first;
    EXEC SQL OPEN c_name;

    if (namecnt%2) namecnt++;    /* Locate midpoint customer */;
    for (n=0; n<namecnt/2; n++)
    {
      EXEC SQL FETCH c_name
        INTO :c_balance, :c_first, :c_middle, :c_id;
    }

    EXEC SQL CLOSE c_name;
  }
  else {
    EXEC SQL SELECT c_balance, c_first, c_middle, c_last
        INTO :c_balance, :c_first, :c_middle, :c_last
        FROM customer
        WHERE c_id = :c_id AND c_d_id = :d_id AND
              c_w_id= :w_id;
  }
  EXEC SQL SELECT o_id, o_carrier_id, o_entry_d
        INTO :o_id, :o_carrier_id, :entdate
        FROM orders
        ORDER BY o_id DESC;
```

```
      EXEC SQL DECLARE c_line CURSOR FOR
          SELECT ol_i_id, ol_supply_w_id, ol_quantity,
          ol_amount, ol_delivery_d
          FROM order_line
          WHERE ol_o_id = :o_id AND ol_d_id = :d_id AND
                ol_w_id = :w_id;

   EXEC SQL OPEN c_line;
   EXEC SQL WHENEVER NOT FOUND CONTINUE;

   i=0;
   while (sql_notfound(FALSE))
   {
      i++;
      EXEC SQL FETCH c_line
          INTO :ol_i_id_a[i], :ol_supply_w_id_a[i],
               :ol_quantity_a[i], :ol_amount_a[i],
               :ol_delivery_d_a[i];
   }

   EXEC SQL CLOSE c_line;
   EXEC SQL COMMIT WORK;
   return (0);

   sqlerr:
     exit(1);

} /* end order status transaction */

int delivery()
{
   EXEC SQL WHENEVER SQLERROR GOTO sqlerr;

   /* For each district in warehouse */
   printf("W: %d\n", w_id);
   for (d_id=1; d_id<=DIST_PER_WARE; d_id++)
   {
      EXEC SQL WHENEVER NOT FOUND GOTO sqlerr;

      /* select entire key of new_order, not just no_o_id - see
next comment */

      EXEC SQL DECLARE c_no CURSOR FOR
          SELECT no_o_id, no_d_id, no_w_id
          FROM new_order
```

```
        WHERE no_d_id = :d_id AND no_w_id = :w_id AND
            no_o_id = :o_id
        ORDER BY no_o_id ASC;

EXEC SQL OPEN c_no;

EXEC SQL WHENEVER NOT FOUND continue;
EXEC SQL FETCH c_no INTO :no_o_id, :no_d_id, :no_w_id;

/* differs from published standard, uses key not cursor to
   delete row.
   INGRES does not allow an update cursor to contain an
   ORDER BY clause */

EXEC SQL DELETE FROM new_order WHERE no_o_id = :no_o_id AND
   no_d_id = :no_d_id AND no_w_id = :no_w_id;

EXEC SQL CLOSE c_no;

EXEC SQL SELECT o_c_id INTO :c_id FROM orders
        WHERE o_id = :no_o_id AND o_d_id = :d_id AND
        o_w_id = :w_id;

EXEC SQL UPDATE orders SET o_carrier_id = :o_carrier_id
        WHERE o_id = :no_o_id AND o_d_id = :d_id AND
        o_w_id = :w_id;

EXEC SQL UPDATE order_line SET ol_delivery_d = :datetime
        WHERE ol_o_id = :no_o_id AND ol_d_id = :d_id AND
        ol_w_id = :w_id;

EXEC SQL SELECT SUM(ol_amount) INTO :ol_total
        FROM order_line
        WHERE ol_o_id = :no_o_id AND ol_d_id = :d_id
        AND ol_w_id = :w_id;

EXEC SQL UPDATE customer SET c_balance = c_balance +
:ol_total
        WHERE c_id = : c_id AND c_d_id = :d_id AND
        c_w_id = :w_id;

EXEC SQL COMMIT WORK;
```

```
  EXEC SQL COMMIT WORK;
  return(0);

  sqlerr:
    exit(1);
} /* end delivery transaction */

int slev()
{
  EXEC SQL WHENEVER NOT FOUND GOTO sqlerr;
  EXEC SQL WHENEVER SQLERROR GOTO sqlerr;

  EXEC SQL SELECT d_next_o_id INTO :o_id
        FROM district
        WHERE d_w_id = :w_id AND d_id = :d_id;

  EXEC SQL SELECT COUNT(DISTINCT (s_i_id)) INTO :stock_count
        FROM order_line, stock
        WHERE ol_w_id = :w_id AND
        ol_d_id = : d_id AND ol_o_id < :o_id AND
        ol_o_id >= :o_id-21 AND s_w_id = : w_id AND
        s_i_id = ol_i_id AND s_quantity < :threshold;

  EXEC SQL COMMIT WORK;
  return(0);

  sqlerr:
    exit(1);
} /* end stock level transaction */
```

Part III

DATABASE SYSTEM ORGANIZATION

Chapter 8

FILE STRUCTURES AND ACCESS METHODS

The rate at which data can be transferred between secondary storage devices and main memory and the rapidity with which individual items can be located in a large body of stored data are major constraints on the performance of data-intensive applications. Hardware aspects of the major types of physical storage media ranging from the high-speed but volatile main memory to the slow but highly stable magnetic tape were described in Chapter 2. In this chapter we discuss file organizations and access methods. The coverage presented here illustrates the range of methods used in current database systems, not all of which will be found in any particular system.

The traditional requirements of database systems are essentially one-dimensional, providing access to stored data on the basis of a single key. The application of database technology to the management of spatial, scientific and CAD data introduces a requirement to manipulate complex data types and for efficient access using multi-dimensional search keys. Several suitable storage structures for multi-dimensional data are described.

We begin by discussing the various file performance characteristics and application access requirements, before moving on to consider several file organizations in greater detail. Our approach is informal and can only cover the main characteristics of each file type. Wiederhold [1987] provides a thorough quantitative approach to the analysis of performance characteristics, and Gray and Reuter [1993] cover algorithms and other implementation issues.

8.1 Introduction

Each of the file organizations described here can be directly compared with equivalent techniques for managing data held in main memory. The most significant difference in the case of disk files is the use of pages rather than direct addressing of single records by memory address. This distinction is imposed by the need to transfer data between disk and memory in fixed-size units, rather than as single stored records, so as to maximize the efficiency of disk access.

An alternative nomenclature will often be found in other literature. For consistency we will always use the term page here to refer to **logical** blocks containing one or more records. These logical blocks are equivalent to one or more **physical** disk blocks. However, the word bucket has long been used by others to describe these units. Usage of the terms block, page and bucket varies; some authors use the term bucket to denote logical blocks (I/O transfer units) and page to refer to physical disk blocks.

Files have a single storage structure, but may be used with several access methods. File structure refers to the physical organization of the file on the storage device. Access methods are the algorithms used to retrieve, update, insert and delete records. A file structure typically has one principal access method, but other methods may also be used to support other access patterns. In general, these other methods have lower performance than the main access method.

Selecting a suitable file structure for any application involves a compromise between conflicting file characteristics and conflicting access requirements. A major distinction is that of ordered versus random storage. Heap and hash files both provide random storage. The physical ordering of records is not related to any key value and, as a result, they cannot directly support ordered retrievals on the basis of some key field. In other structures, ordering is central to the organization of records. The ordered or sequential file and the various indexing methods all provide direct support for access in key value order. They are, therefore, also suited to applications that must retrieve a group of records matching a range of key values, or those requiring partial matches with the key.

Another important issue is uniformity of access. Access patterns may involve single records, groups of records, or the entire file, but the different file structures vary in their suitability for these tasks. We have already noted that ordering is a requirement for retrieving groups of records. The heap file is well suited to retrieval of the entire file, but is quite inappropriate for applications that need to access individual records. In contrast, the hash file is designed to support direct access to single records but is far less suited to a complete scan of all records. These file structures may be used where there is a single dominant access pattern, but in many cases a more general structure such as the B-tree is chosen because of its good all-round performance.

8.2 Performance characteristics

Wiederhold [Wiederhold 1987] lists seven principal quantitative measures for comparing the performance characteristics of files. These are:

1. The storage space needed for a record, and
2. The time taken to:

- fetch an arbitrary record,
- fetch the next record in a sequence,
- insert a new record,
- update an existing record,
- read all records,
- reorganize the file.

To these we can also add the time taken to delete a record which Wiederhold treats with insert and update operations.

Storage space requirements

An important characteristic of any page-oriented file structure is the fill factor. This is the proportion or percentage of the page that is currently occupied by records. Most file organizations use an initial fill factor of less than 100% when the file is first created to allow space for records to be inserted in their correct locations at a later date. Different strategies are used when pages fill up or are emptied. In some organizations a new page is allocated before a page is completely filled whenever the fill factor exceeds a predetermined level. Similarly, when the fill factor drops below a predetermined threshold, its contents may be redistributed amongst one or more other pages.

Besides the fill factor, the other main influence on space requirements is the presence of indexes to improve retrieval and update performance. An index structure may be part of the main data file, or it may be held in a separate file. In either case there is an overhead in the redundant storage of key and address information in the index.

Read one record

Read operations involve two stages; first the required record must be located, then it is read and copied to a main memory buffer. Once the record or page has been found, transfer to memory takes place in a more or less fixed time, independent of the file organization. The time taken to locate the required record varies greatly according to the file organization, whether the search term includes a primary key, secondary key or a non-key value, and whether the search involves partial or complete matching of values. In file organizations such as hashing, the storage address may be calculated directly from a primary key value. For ordered files it may be estimated and for indexed organizations it is obtained by lookup from a separate index file. Searches involving non-key values require a complete scan of the file, irrespective of its organization.

Fetch the next record

Records must often be read in some order, typically that of a primary or other key. The importance of ordering has already been discussed. Where records are physically ordered on the key the next record in the key sequence may be in the same, or immediately following, page. Such physical clustering is only possible on a single key and alternative orderings can only be supported with additional indexes. Fetching the next record using a secondary ordering will, almost always, require a page fetch.

Update a record

Fixed-length records are normally updated in place by first reading a page into main memory, modifying it, then writing it back to the storage device. Update performance is therefore usually dependent on the time taken to locate, read and write the required record. As with reading a single record, the read and write operations take a more or less constant time, but the time required to locate the record varies significantly between different file organizations.

Add a record

In the most straightforward case, new records may be added at the end of a file. This is equivalent to a simple update. The last page is fetched, updated and written back to the main storage. If the last page is full, a new page containing the new record is added at the end of the file. In other cases the record must be inserted at a specific location in the file. Again, if space is available this operation is similar to an update. However, an overhead is incurred if the location is already occupied by another record. Either the following records must be moved to make room, or the new record is placed in an overflow area.

Delete a record

Deletion is essentially the inverse of insertion of new records. However, in practice deleted records are rarely completely removed and are often simply marked by setting a flag to indicate that they are no longer current.

Read all records

Although many accesses involve single records or defined groups of records, some activities such as report generation may require access to every record in the file. Files that are optimized for individual record or group access may have relatively poor performance under these circumstances when compared with those using simpler organizations.

Reorganize the file

The need for reorganization arises from the progressive deterioration of performance as records are added or deleted. Insertions may lead to an increasing number of records being held in an overflow area. Records may have been marked as deleted, but not physically removed, and the unused space that they occupy must be reclaimed. File structures may be characterized as static or dynamic according to whether they need periodic intervention to maintain their structure, or are self-reorganizing. Most are static and, for those that are dynamic, performance considerations may dictate that they are not implemented in a way that performs a complete reorganization. The time needed to reorganize a file influences its availability.

8.3   File organizations

In the following sections we describe several widely used file organizations. For simplicity these are illustrated using fixed-length records each containing the same number of fields, but each can also be used with variable-length fields and records. We begin with the simple heap and sequential organizations. This is followed by a discussion of hashing techniques. We then discuss the use of primary and secondary indexes, and the indexed sequential and B-tree structures. Finally, we examine methods for multi-dimensional indexing.

8.3.1   *Heap*

The simplest form of file organization is the heap. Records are unordered and there is no means of ensuring that they are unique. New records are added at the end of the file. When the file is organized in pages, records are always added to the last page until there is insufficient room to hold a complete record. At this point a new page is allocated and the new record inserted (Figure 8.1).

	PatientId	Initials	LastName	DateOfBirth	Sex	...
(a) Page 1	93860211	AJ	Allan	23-Mar-1950	m	...
	28375134	ER	Barnes	18-Apr-1948	f	...
	49852044	DJ	Coles	29-Jan-1972	m	...
Page 2	81248650	ER	Jones	6-Aug-1960	f	...
	35083788	DW	Jones	29-Jan-1972	f	...

	PatientId	Initials	LastName	DateOfBirth	Sex	...
(b) Page 1	93860211	AJ	Allan	23-Mar-1950	m	...
	28375134	ER	Barnes	18-Apr-1948	f	...
	49852044	DJ	Coles	29-Jan-1972	m	...
Page 2	81248650	ER	Jones	6-Aug-1960	f	...
	35083788	DW	Jones	29-Jan-1972	f	...
	93484452	HJ	Williams	10-Jul-1952	f	...
Page 3	77759890	K	Bennett	16-Aug-1962	m	...

Figure 8.1   Adding records to a heap file of patient records. In (a) the next new record will be inserted at the end of the file using the available space in Page 2. In (b), Page 2 is already filled, so a new page must be allocated when inserting the next new record.

The heap has a fill factor of 100% because each page is filled to capacity as new records are added. Space utilization is high, making the heap suitable for conserving space in large files. As well as conserving space, the heap also benefits from simplicity. Other file organizations involve calculations of record location or manipulation of indexing structures, all of which add an overhead to record insertion. One result of this simplicity is that the heap is a very efficient structure for bulk-loading large volumes of data. It is also well suited to storing small files covering only a few pages. These can often be read directly into memory buffers and scanned for records matching a query condition using fewer disk accesses than might be needed for a more complex file organization.

The major disadvantage of the heap is that retrieval is slow for files covering more than few pages because the entire file must be searched for records matching a query. This would appear to limit its utility to applications that must search the entire file for each query. However, the heap is often used to conserve space in large files that are normally accessed by a secondary index (*see below*, Section 8.4).

With fixed-length records, updates can be performed by first locating the required record, modifying it in a memory buffer, then writing it back over the original. Variable-length records are more problematic. If the modification does not change, or reduces, the length of the record it can be treated in the same way as for fixed-length records. However, if the record length is increased, the new version must be inserted at the end of the file and the original deleted.

Record deletion involves marking a record as deleted by overwriting the record with null values or a special marker character. In a page-oriented file, deletion often involves no more than setting a flag in the page header. Because of the requirement to add new records at the end of the file, the space occupied by a deleted record is not normally reused. The only common exception is where the deleted record is located in the final page of the file. Heap files that are subject to frequent deletions must be reorganized periodically to reclaim lost space.

8.3.2   Ordered or sequential files

Sequential file organization provides some improved retrieval qualities by storing records ordered on a particular key field or combination of fields. A sequential file can be created by sorting the records in a heap file. The ordering is often based on the primary key of the file and can also be used as a mechanism to ensure that each record is unique.

Unlike the heap, where all records must be scanned to locate those matching a search key, the sequential scan can stop as soon as a greater value is found. If the ordering is based on a unique key, the scan stops when one matching record has been found. On average, queries can be performed in half the time taken for a similar query on a heap file with a similar fill factor.

The sequential file can also be used for range queries and some partial match queries without the need for a complete scan of the file. Range queries must locate the first matching record by a sequential scan, then read all subsequent records while the key remains in the search range. Partial matches on the leftmost part of a character field are performed in a similar way, locating the first match and then continuing to read until a non-matching record is found. In both cases the query is terminated as soon as the first non-matching record is found, and the remaining records can be ignored.

Ordering may also be beneficial for displaying information. It is often important to be able to present information in a sorted form so that an additional sorting phase which would be needed for the heap organization can be avoided when the records are retrieved in this order. Similarly, performance of operations such as the relational join can be improved if the need to sort at least one file can be avoided.

The improved retrieval characteristics of the sequential file only apply to queries involving the key. From the viewpoint of a non-key field the file is simply a heap and any attempt to retrieve records based on the value of such a field requires a full scan of the table. As with the heap, retrieval performance can be improved by providing secondary indexes on frequently used non-key fields.

Although more commonly used for in-memory searching, the binary search method can also be applied to sequential files. This works by progressively halving the section of the file to be searched. Given a file of N records, the $N/2$th record is fetched and its key compared with the search key. The result of this comparison determines whether the required record should be located in the first or second half of the file. The appropriate section is chosen and the record at the mid-point of this section is fetched and the keys are compared. This comparison then determines which quarter of the file should be searched next. The progressive halving continues until the required record is located in a single block or page.

	PatientId	Initials	LastName	DateOfBirth	Sex	...		
Page 1	28375134	ER	Barnes	18-Apr-1948	f	...		
	35083788	DW	Jones	29-Jan-1972	f	...		
							null	overflow pointer
Page 2	49852044	DJ	Coles	29-Jan-1972	m	...		
	77759890	K	Bennett	16-Aug-1962	m	...		
	79811211	R	Shah	19-Dec-1982	m	...		
	79967341	JK	Evans	22-Feb-1977	f	...		
							50	overflow pointer
Page 3	81248650	ER	Jones	6-Aug-1960	f	...		
	93484452	HJ	Williams	10-Jly-1952	f	...		
	93860211	AJ	Allan	23-Mar-1950	m	...		
							null	overflow pointer
Page 50 (overflow page)	80044110	AH	Fisher	3-Aug-1968	f	...		
							null	overflow pointer

Figure 8.2 The use of overflow pages in a sequential page structured file. The file is ordered on PatientId. The record for A.H. Fisher cannot be inserted in its correct place on Page 2, so an overflow page (Page 50) is used. The overflow pointer on Page 2 is set to indicate the next page in the overflow chain.

Inserting a new record in its correct position would incur a large overhead if all subsequent records had to be moved to make space. In a page-based organization the onset of this problem can be delayed by creating the file with a low initial fill factor, typically 50–80%, to allow space for future insertions. When pages are eventually filled, new records are inserted into a part of the file reserved for use as an **overflow area** (Figure 8.2). Periodically the file is reorganized by merging the overflow records into the main sorted sequence. If the overflow area is small its contents can be kept in sorted order. When an overflow area is used, retrieval is complicated by the need to scan the overflow records if a search of the main sequence fails to locate the required data.

If the value of the sort key is modified the record must be moved to a new position in the file. This is achieved by copying the old record to a buffer where the changes are made, then deleting the old record and inserting the changed record into its new position. Updates that do not involve the sort key value can be handled by overwriting the old record. With variable-length records updates that increase the length of a record are handled by deleting the old and inserting the modified records. Deletion can be achieved by marking a record as deleted, overwriting it with null characters or adjusting the page header entries. The space occupied by the record then becomes available for reuse. Reorganization to reclaim space is only worthwhile if the number of deletes heavily outweighs the number of inserts.

8.3.3   Hashing

Hashing determines the location of a record by an algorithmic transformation from the key value to a storage address. The address may be a physical location in terms of track, cylinder and block, or, more simply, a page number within a file. When a new record is inserted, the **hashing algorithm**, or **key-to-address transform**, is applied to the key to derive a **hash value** representing the storage address at which the record will be written. The same algorithm is used when searching for a record containing a particular key value.

There are many possible hashing algorithms, each of which involves applying various arithmetic or logical operations to the key value to derive an integer. The normal approach is to use a randomizing function that does not preserve key order, but instead attempts to distribute records throughout the file.[1] Character values can be used by first summing the ASCII codes representing each individual character. The derived integer value I can then be mapped onto the available file addresses. If there are N distinct addresses ranging from 0 to $N - 1$ then the hash address can be given by the remainder of the integer division of I by N, or $I \bmod N$. In Figure 8.3 we assume that the file has 1000 possible address slots. The *Patient_id* field is used to derive an address in the range 0 to 999 by taking the remainder of a division by 1000.

---

1   The approach to hashing in page-oriented files is similar to that used for simple in-memory hash tables, except that the hash value is always used to locate a bucket or page, usually containing several records, rather than pointing to a single record or table entry.

Hash value	PatientId	Initials	LastName	DateOfBirth	Sex	...
134	28375134	ER	Barnes	18-Apr-1948	f	...
788	35083788	DW	Jones	29-Jan-1972	f	...
44	49852044	DJ	Coles	29-Jan-1972	m	...
890	77759890	K	Bennett	16-Aug-1962	m	...
*211	79811211	R	Shah	19-Dec-1982	m	...
341	79967341	JK	Evans	22-Feb-1977	f	...
110	80044110	AH	Fisher	3-Aug-1968	f	...
650	81248650	ER	Jones	6-Aug-1960	f	...
452	93484452	HJ	Williams	10-Jly-1952	f	...
*211	93860211	AJ	Allan	23-Mar-1950	m	...

Figure 8.3   Storage addresses in the range 0 to 999 derived from PatientId by taking the remainder of a division by 1000. Note that two keys (marked *) transform to the same address value. If space permits, they will be placed on the same page.

A record in a hash file can ideally be read or written using only single disk accesses, although in practice this is not always possible. Typically, there will be many more possible values of a hash key than need to be recorded in the file. For example, a medical practice may use a nationally issued number as the key to its patient records. Every person in the country may have a unique number, but the practice may only ever have a few hundred registered patients. It would only be possible to ensure that the hashing algorithm produces a unique address for each patient number if either the file contained sufficient distinct addresses to store records for the entire national population, or all of the patient numbers for the practice were known in advance. Neither assumption is realistic.

In practice, sufficient space is allocated in a hash file for the maximum expected number of records, and it is accepted that the hashing algorithm will map several key values onto the same address value, as in Figure 8.3. When a new record is inserted, the location indicated by the hashing algorithm may already be occupied. Such **collisions** are a normal feature of hashing and there are several approaches to their resolution, including **open addressing**, **multiple hashing** and **chaining**.

The open addressing method places the new record in the next available free location. If, when searching, the key value is not found in the location given by the hashing algorithm, the following records are read sequentially until the required record is found. Multiple hashing makes use of two or more hashing algorithms. If the first fails to provide a free location, the second is used, and so on. If each fails to find a free location then open addressing can be used.

The chaining method allocates additional blocks in the file as an overflow area to store records that cannot be inserted at their computed hash address (Figure 8.4). Each record also contains a pointer to the next record with the same hash value. The first inserted record with a particular hash address is placed at the correct address and its pointer set to null. The next record with the same address is placed in the overflow area and the pointer in the first record is updated to indicate this new

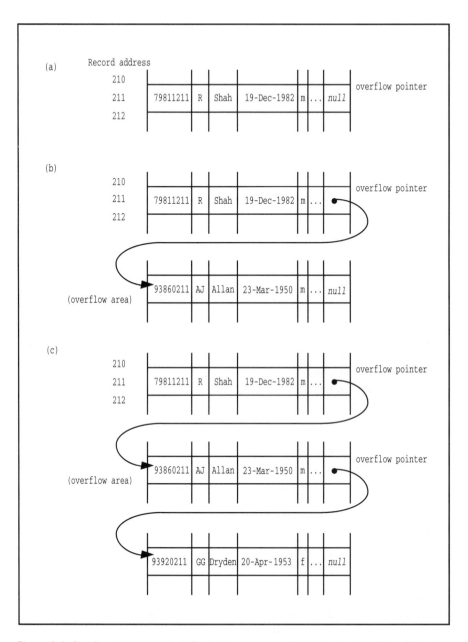

Figure 8.4 Overflow chaining in a hash file. In (a) a new record key hashes to the address 211 and the record is inserted at this location. In (b) a second record 'collides' with the first. It is placed in an available slot in the overflow area, and the original record's overflow pointer is set to indicate this address. In (c) a further collision results in another overflow record. The pointer in the first overflow record is set to point to the new record. For simplicity, this example assumes one record per page.

location. The pointer in the new record is set to null. In this way a chain of records is established and searching proceeds by following the pointers chain until the required record is located.

Chaining is easily extended to files where records are stored within pages. Indeed, the ability to store several records with the same hash value on a single page is itself a way of reducing collisions comparable with the open addressing method. In this case a chain of pages is formed using a pointer stored in each page rather than in each record. The pointer indicates the location of the next overflow page. Record deletion is simplified because in most cases a slot within a page can be marked and reused. Empty pages can be reclaimed by pointer adjustment as in the single record form.

Hashed files are usually created with a fixed number of primary data pages and an initial page fill factor of 50–80%. This allows space for further records to be inserted with a minimum of overflow pages. The fill factor can be adjusted to suit the characteristics of the key and the hashing algorithm. Fixing the number of primary data pages when the file is created ensures that overflow pages will be used increasingly if the file grows. As the number of overflow pages increases, the performance of the file will decrease because of the extra disk accesses needed to read the overflow pages. If the decrease in performance becomes too great the file must be reorganized. Similarly, a large number of deletions may leave many overflow pages sparsely populated, with similar effects on performance. A new hashed file can be created with a larger number of primary data pages and a suitable initial fill factor. The data is then copied from the old to the new file.

Rehashing the keys using the same file size and the same hashing algorithm would result in the same distribution of records as before. Reorganization of a hashed file therefore involves adjusting the file size to maintain the optimum density or fill factor and, possibly, changing the hashing algorithm to one that behaves more randomly with the given key value distribution. It is a time-consuming operation during which the file is not available for normal processing.

The major benefit of hashing is that it is particularly efficient for retrieval queries based on known key values, where the storage address can be calculated from the key. Hashing algorithms typically do not preserve the relative ordering of key values so it is impossible to use hashing for queries involving ranges of key values.[2] Similarly, queries involving partial matching of keys are not supported because hashing requires the complete key value. Queries involving non-key fields do not, of course, benefit from hashing. In each of these cases the file must be treated as a heap and scanned from start to finish until all matching records are found.

Because hashing randomizes the location of records, retrieval in key order requires an additional sorting phase so performance is inferior to that of a sequential file. The lower fill factor means that a hash file may be up to twice the size of a heap with the same number of records. Consequently, when searching for a non-key value, the performance can be significantly worse than that of the heap, unless secondary indexes are employed.

---

2   In special cases where the distribution of keys is known in advance, 'order-preserving' hash functions may be used, but such static conditions do not normally apply to databases.

8.3.4   Other hashing methods

In addition to the simple hashing method described here there are also a number of techniques intended to overcome the problem of declining performance as new records are inserted. Both **dynamic hashing** and **extendible hashing** make use of indexing structures instead of pointer chains to find the required overflow pages. These methods require some additional disk accesses to read the index, but avoid long overflow chains by allowing data pages to split whenever they are filled. Some implementations attempt to keep the index pages in main memory so as to reduce the overhead in accessing them.

A third and more popular method, known as **linear hashing**, avoids the overhead of an index by splitting primary data pages and redistributing records from overflow pages to new primary pages. It is a dynamic method that avoids the need for reorganization by adjusting both the size of the file and the hashing algorithm. A split is made whenever a data page fills up. Instead of dividing the filled page, the first split is performed on the first page in the file, the next on the second page, and so on through the file. When the last page has been split the process starts again with the first page. This linear progression of splitting gives the method its name. The number of primary data pages doubles during each splitting cycle. Overflow pages are used when needed, and their contents are redistributed as the splitting progresses through the file.

As pages are split the hashing algorithm is adjusted to suit the increased number of pages. Suppose the file starts with N pages and addresses are given by $I \bmod N - 1$. A counter n is used to indicate the highest split page. During the first splitting cycle page addresses are found using $I \bmod N - 1$. For pages greater than n this address is used directly; for those less than n the two split pages are distinguished by computing a second hash value using $I \bmod 2(N - 1)$. At the end of the first splitting cycle this becomes the primary hashing function, and split pages are distinguished using $I \bmod 4(N - 1)$, and so on.

8.4   Indexed methods

The file structures discussed so far each have particular benefits. The heap has good storage utilization, the sequential file is well suited to ordered retrieval and hashing provides direct access to single records using exact values of a key. None, however, shows more than one of these benefits and all exhibit poor performance under other conditions. Index-based approaches typically provide more general solutions that can give satisfactory, though not necessarily optimal, performance over a wider range of query types.

Indexing techniques are based on key-to-address lookup. The index consists of records holding key value and address pairs. In a simple index each record contains a search key value and a data record or page address (Figure 8.5). More complex multi-level or tree-structured indexes contain tree nodes where the address points to another tree node, or to a leaf node. Typically, data addresses are only held at the leaf nodes. The index may be stored as a separate file, distinct from the main data file, or it may form part of the structure of the data file itself.

Key	Address			PatientId	Initials	LastName	...	Record address
Allan	10			28375134	ER	Barnes	...	1
Barnes	1			35083788	DW	Jones	...	2
Bennett	4			49852044	DJ	Coles	...	3
Coles	3			77759890	K	Bennett	...	4
Evans	6			79811211	R	Shah	...	5
Fisher	7			79967341	JK	Evans	...	6
Jones	2			80044110	AH	Fisher	...	7
Jones	8			81248650	ER	Jones	...	8
Shah	5			93484452	HJ	Williams	...	9
Williams	9			93860211	AJ	Allan	...	10

Figure 8.5 A simple dense index (left) providing an access path to the data file (right) on values of **LastName**.

With the exception of the heap, each of the file organizations described so far provides a means of improving retrieval performance for queries involving a single, possibly compound, key. In each case, searches based on non-key values must treat the file as a heap and scan from start to finish until all matching records are found. The same is true of the indexed file organizations described in the following section. Because each organization typically employs a fill factor of less than 100%, performance under these conditions is invariably inferior to that of a simple heap file.

In applications where such non-key searches are used and the response time for a full scan is unacceptable, **secondary indexes** may be used. These are called **dense indexes** because they contain an entry for each record in the main data file. In the simplest cases they are organized as separate sequential files ordered on the key value. It is also possible to create indexes using other file structures such as hash or B-tree. In the hash index, the hashing algorithm is used to locate a small record containing a page number or key/page pair that gives the record location in the associated data file. B-tree indexes are discussed below in Section 8.4.2. The associated data file can have any suitable file organization.

8.4.1   Indexed sequential

The indexed sequential file organization retains the ability of the sequential file to retrieve records in key order, but adds an index to improve access to single records. Instead of scanning from the start of the file a search is first made in the index to locate the record or page containing the required key value. Once a single record is located, range queries can proceed by sequential scanning.

In its simplest form the index is implemented as a separate file. In other implementations the index may be stored as part of the main file using a group of reserved pages. It is a **primary index**. In other words, it contains values of the primary key or ordering key of the data file. There is no need to include an index entry for every record in the data file because the data records are already sorted on the key. Instead the index holds key and page number pairs where the highest key value in each data page is recorded (Figure 8.6). It is therefore said to be a **sparse index**, in contrast to a dense secondary indexes discussed above in which there is an entry for every data record.

Key	Address
49852044	1
80044110	2
93860211	3

PatientId	Initials	LastName		Page address
28375134	ER	Barnes	...	1
35083788	DW	Jones	...	
49852044	DJ	Coles	...	
77759890	K	Bennett	...	2
79811211	R	Shah	...	
79967341	JK	Evans	...	
80044110	AH	Fisher	...	
81248650	ER	Jones	...	3
93484452	HJ	Williams	...	
93860211	AJ	Allan	...	

Figure 8.6   An indexed sequential file ordered on the PatientId field.

To locate a record, the index is scanned until a value greater than the search key is found. The required record, if it exists, will then be found in the associated data page. The index is typically much smaller than the main data file. When implemented as a separate file it can be regarded as a sequential file in which the records contain only the key field(s) and the page number. It also contains fewer records than the data file.

These factors make it possible to scan the index more rapidly using fewer disk accesses than would be needed for an equivalent scan of the main file. However, whereas the absence of a matching record can be determined directly from a dense index, in most cases the data page must be fetched to discover whether or not a matching record exists because only one key value per page is held in the sparse index.

Another form uses a multi-level or tree-structured index (Figure 8.7). The first-level index is a single page containing key/pointer pairs that reference individual index pages at the second level. As with the simple form, the key value represents the highest value found on the associated page. Subsequent levels are similar, except that the lowest level of index points directly to a data page. The number of levels used is dependent on the number of pages in the data file and the number of index entries that can be accommodated per page.

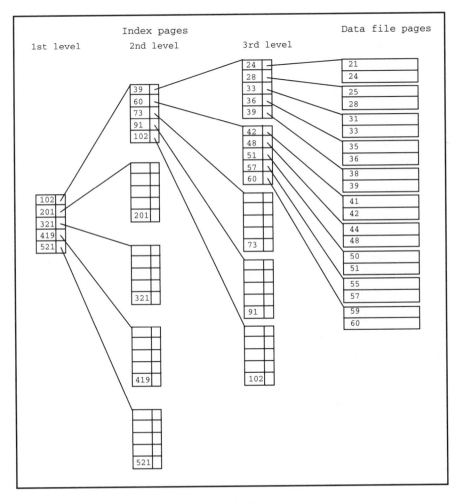

Figure 8.7   A multi-level index in an indexed sequential structure.

The example shown in Figure 8.7 has five index records per index page and two data records per data page. At the second level there is a maximum of five index pages, one for each first-level index entry, each of which points to a further five at the third level. There are, then, 25 index pages at the third level, each referencing five data pages of two records each. This permits a maximum of 125 data pages (250 records) before the index needs to expand to accommodate an additional level.

Insertion, deletion and updating of records proceed as for the sequential file, with records that cannot be inserted in their correct location being placed in an overflow area. The overflow area must also be scanned when searching. Reorganization of the index can represent a significant overhead and is rarely performed as the file changes. The indexes are static because they are only rebuilt when reorganizing the file. As reorganization is also necessary to merge overflow records into the correct sequence, the two tasks can be accomplished at the same time.

Indexed sequential organization is suitable for files that will be accessed by queries involving single values, ranges of key values, or the leftmost part of partial or multi-column keys, provided that the table is relatively static. It is less suitable for rapidly growing tables because of the need for frequent reorganization.

The term **indexed sequential access method (ISAM)** is often used to refer to variations of this file organization. The name was first used by IBM to describe a structure that was closely linked to the physical arrangement of the file on disk. The index was organized in two levels referencing the cylinders and tracks, with the track index pointing to sequentially ordered data records within the blocks of each track.

8.4.2   B-Tree

The B-tree organization, and its derivatives the **B$^+$-tree** and **B*-tree**, use a dynamic multi-level index in the form of a balanced tree. A balanced tree is one in which all leaf nodes are at the same depth. The index is dynamic because it is automatically reorganized as records are inserted and deleted. The overhead for these operations is typically much less than would be required for the dynamic reorganization of other file structures. The overhead remains low as the file grows and may often be less than that caused by the need to deal with overflow records, making B-tree particularly suitable for rapidly growing files and high-availability applications.

The B+-tree form is perhaps the most widely used and will be described here. The structure is composed of two types of page, known as **internal** (or index) and **leaf** pages (Figure 8.8). The internal pages contain keys and pointers. The maximum number of pointers in each node is known as the **order** of the tree, and there is always one less key value than the number of pointers. Implementation is, however, simplified by using a set of key/pointer pairs in which the first key is unused. Each pointer references a sub-tree and points directly to either a further index page at a lower level of the tree, or to a leaf page at the lowest level of the tree. The internal pages thus provide a sparse index to the leaf pages.

The keys within each node are ordered, thus each pointer provides a route to nodes containing key values less than or equal to the key to its immediate right, and greater than the key to its immediate left.

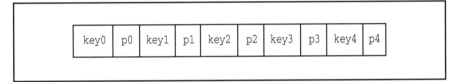

Figure 8.8   A B-Tree node of order 5. Note that `key0` is unused in index nodes.

The contents of the leaf pages may be either key and pointer pairs, or data tuples. In the former case the pointers reference the pages of the main data file. In this form, the B-tree is used solely as an index and may be stored separately from the data file. B-tree secondary indexes are frequently used to provide access to files of any other structure.

Where the B-tree is used as the main organizing structure of a file, the leaf pages either contain the data tuples, or act as an index into a separate area of data pages. A leaf page index may be either a sparse index to data pages, or a dense index indicating both page number and location within the page for each record. The latter provides greater flexibility when inserting and deleting records. Additionally, the leaf nodes are normally connected together in a chain to provide a sequential access path once a single record has been located.

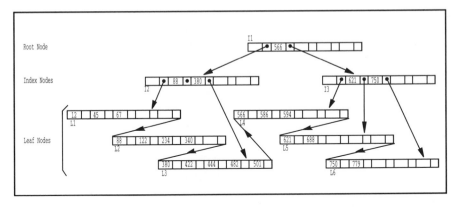

Figure 8.9   A small B-tree. The leaf nodes may contain data tuples or key/pointer pairs that reference data pages stored elsewhere.

When new records are inserted into a B⁺-tree the location is determined by traversing the tree until the appropriate leaf node is found. If there is room in the leaf node the new data is inserted, otherwise the node must be split into two and its contents divided between the old and new leaf pages.

A reference to the new leaf page must now be added to its parent index node, together with a key value that distinguishes the old and new leaf nodes. If there is no space in the parent node for a new key and pointer, then it too must be split. The keys and pointers of the original node are then divided between the old and new nodes.

This, in turn, means that a new key/pointer pair must be added to the parent of the original internal node. If necessary, this splitting process passes on up the tree until a node with sufficient space to accommodate the new key/pointer pair is found, or until the root itself is reached.

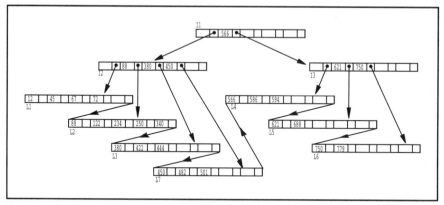

Figure 8.10   The B-tree of Figure 8.9 after insertion of the key values 72, 250 and 450. The first two values are added to existing leaf nodes L2 and L3, but the third results in a split. The new node L7 is allocated and a reference to it is added to index node I2.

Where the leaf node entries contain pointers into associated data pages, records are inserted into the data page until it is full. The key/pointer pair is added to the leaf node as described above. If the data page is full, a new page must be allocated.

As an example, consider the insertion of key values 72, 250, 450, 52, 77 and 160 into the B-tree index shown in Figure 8.9. The first value, 72, is inserted into the next available slot in the leaf page L1. Similarly, 260 is added to page L2. Here, greater values must be moved to the right to make room for the new value and so maintain the ordering of keys within the node.

The third value, 450, lies in the range covered by page L3 but, because there are no free slots on this page, the node must be divided. The new value and the contents of L3 are divided between L3 and the new node L7. A new key/pointer pair is added to the parent index node I2 to provide the correct access paths to L3 and L7. The sequence pointers joining the leaf nodes L3 and L4 are also adjusted to include the new node. The resulting B-tree at this stage is shown in Figure 8.10.

The next value, 52, is added to L1, moving greater values to the right. At this point, both L1 and L2 are full and inserting the final two values in our list causes both of them to split. Their contents are divided using the new nodes L8 and L9. The first of these splits can be accommodated by the parent index node I2, but the second causes the parent to overflow, hence it too must be split. This, in turn, requires an additional key/pointer pair in the root node I1, so that the paths to its three descendants can be distinguished. The result is shown in Figure 8.11.

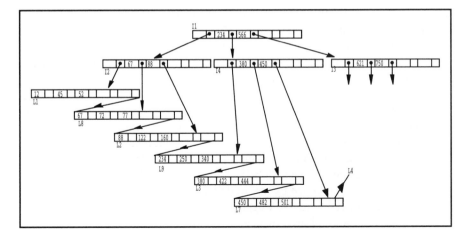

Figure 8.11   The B-tree of Figure 8.10 after insertion of the key values 52, 77 and 160. The leaf
pages L1 and L2 and the index page I2 have been split. Descendants of I3 have been
omitted for clarity.

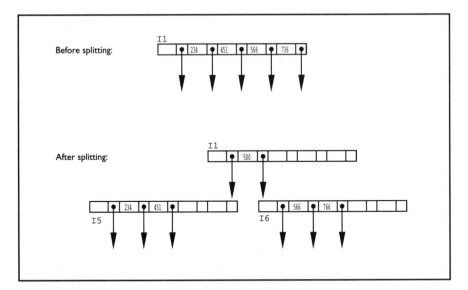

Figure 8.12   Splitting the root node involves creating two new nodes I5 and I6 between which all the
original root's key/pointer pairs are divided. The single dividing key with pointers to I5
and I6 is then placed in the original root node.

So far, the depth of the tree has remained constant. Eventually, however, further
insertions may cause the root node to fill and then to split. Splitting the root node is
different to splitting other index nodes because there is no parent node to contain the
new key/pointer pair. Also, because pointers to the root node may be cached by the

system, we must ensure that the same node acts as the root after redistributing the keys. Two new nodes are created (Figure 8.12) and the entire contents of the root are divided between them. The dividing key causing the split is then inserted into the original root node. Notice that the tree retains its balance because increases in depth can only occur as the result of a root split.

Deletion of records follows a reverse process. If the number of entries in the leaf node falls below the predetermined minimum fill factor, an attempt is made to redistribute its entries between one or other of its adjacent leaf nodes. If this is not possible, the leaf node may be merged with both adjacent nodes to form two leaves. This change must then be propagated up through the tree. This may in turn lead to merging of internal nodes if they fall below their required fill factor.

Data pages that are emptied by record deletion usually remain associated with a leaf page so that they can be reused whenever the leaf requires a new data page. When a leaf or internal page is released by merging, it and any associated data pages may be added to a list of free pages from which demands for new pages can be satisfied. This is typically less expensive than extending the size of the file. If necessary the file can be reorganized to reclaim disk space allocated to unused pages. This strategy is effective provided that deletions do not significantly outweigh insertions.

As with splitting, the upward propagation of page merges ensures that the tree remains balanced as the file grows and contracts. In other words, the depth remains constant for all leaf nodes, thus ensuring that all searches will need the same, minimal, number of disk or page accesses to reach their required data records. In this way the index not only adjusts to suit the changing file contents, but it also maintains its most efficient form so that performance degradation is minimized.

As with an indexed sequential file, a B-tree index contains explicit key values, making it suitable for queries involving some forms of pattern matching, ranges of key values or the leftmost part of multi-column keys. It outperforms indexed sequential when the table is growing rapidly, but is generally slightly inferior for relatively static tables.

8.5   Multi-dimensional file organizations

Geographical Information Systems (GIS) and Computer Aided Design (CAD) are based on multi-dimensional data such as points and regions in two dimensions, and points and volumes in three dimensions. The extension of GIS to include information that changes through time adds a further dimension. Statistical and scientific applications may need to manipulate data that is organized in yet higher-dimensional space. Other than the unordered heap, each of the file structures and indexing methods described so far provides a one-dimensional ordering of records. This is adequate for simple data types that have a single key value, but is less suitable for ordering multi-dimensional objects.

To understand the limitations of one-dimensional organizations, consider the following example. Figure 8.13a shows a number of points distributed in two-dimensional space. The points might represent the location of towns, villages or other objects on a map. Each point has a pair of coordinates x, y. Simple range queries applied to this data would attempt to locate all points within a rectangle with its lower left corner at *x0, y0* and its upper right corner at *x1, y1*.

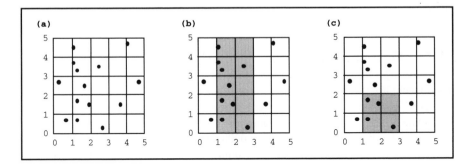

Figure 8.13   (a) Points on a map. (b) Selectivity of a one-dimensional index on *x* or *x,y* values. (c) Desired selectivity for two-dimensional range queries.

A simple index on, say, the *x* coordinate would only serve to isolate the points in a vertical strip of the map. A search for *x* values between 1 and 3 would locate all points in the shaded area of Figure 8.13b. Each of these would then need to be retrieved from the data file to check whether their y coordinate was in the target range *y0–y1*. If the required *y* range was between 0 and 2, an ideal indexing method would locate only those points shown in Figure 8.13c. This cannot be achieved by simple one-dimensional indexing methods.

Even if both of the *x* and *y* coordinates appear in the index, many entries that satisfy the condition on *x*, but not that on *y*, would have to be checked and rejected. An index on the compound key (*x, y*) orders the full range of possible *y* values within each distinct *x* value and so must be scanned for points within the required *x* range, rejecting those that are not in the required *y* range. Although better than scanning the entire data file to select or reject points, there may still be a significant overhead when attempting to isolate a small number of points in a large dense index.

A pair of separate indexes on *x* and *y* would be no better as each must be searched for points within the range of one coordinate. Each search would produce many more points than are required, and the two result lists must be compared to find those points that occur in both lists. The scale of the problem increases with the number of dimensions.

For applications with small volumes of point data these might not be significant problems, but even a relatively simple mapping system may contain hundreds of thousands of points. The poor selectivity of one-dimensional indexing strategies imposes severe limitations on performance, so an alternative approach must be sought.

In the following sections we describe some of the better known multi-dimensional file organizations; for an extensive survey of these techniques, *see* [Samet 1989a, 1989b]. We concentrate on point-and region-based methods, most of which are based on extended forms of the tree and hash structures discussed above. Although presented here in a two-dimensional form, most of these methods may be extended to higher-dimensional search spaces. As with the one-dimensional methods each technique is directly comparable with equivalent main memory techniques where records are addressed directly, rather than by page or bucket.

8.5.1   Grid-based methods

Several techniques retain a one-dimensional index based on bit interleaving. The key is formed by taking each bit in turn from the binary representation of each coordinate to form a code. As a simple example, the x, y pair 0, 15 might be represented by the 4-bit binary numbers 0000 and 1111. Alternately interleaving bits from the x and y values yields the 8-bit number 01010101. This 8-bit number can then be used as a pointer to one of 256 pages, each of which contains records for all points within a small square region or cell in a two-dimensional grid.

This approach works well for point-based retrievals and for some types of areal query. The biggest advantage is that it can be readily implemented over an existing B-tree implementation. A one-dimensional representation of this structure gives an ordering in which most points which are close together in the map are close in the index. It is commonly referred to as a z-order [Orenstein 1986], shown in Figure 8.14. Algorithms for z-order-based indexes are fully described in [Orenstein and Manola 1988].

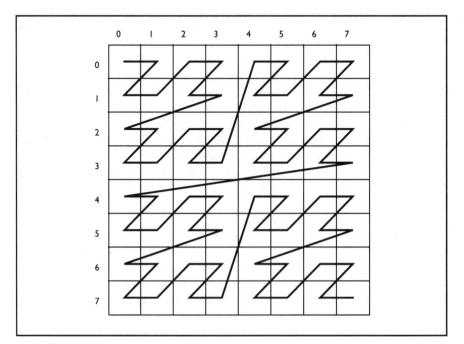

Figure 8.14   The spatial representation of z-order.

Figure 8.15 shows this method applied to the search space of Figure 8.13. Although an improvement on a simple or compound one-dimensional index, this approach does suffer from variable selectivity. In some cases the multi-dimensional search range may map directly to a contiguous range of cells in the key space (Figure 8.15a), while others may result in key ranges with many cells outside the query rectangle (Figure 8.15b and c).

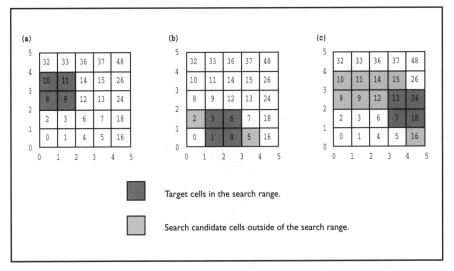

Figure 8.15   Bit-interleaving, a 2-dimensional example showing the variable selectivity of range queries. Cells contain values obtained by interleaving *x* and *y* coordinate values.

(a) The search range *0 < x < 2, 2 < y < 4* maps to the key value range 8–11.

(b) The range *1 < x < 3, 0 < y < 2* maps to the key range 1–6 leading to a 50% overhead in candidate cells that must be searched for matching values.

(c) The range *3 < x < 5, 1 < y < 3* maps to the key range 7–24 with a 200% overhead.

The simplest explicitly multi-dimensional file structures suited to point data are also based on a division of the search space into a regular grid. Points located within a single grid cell are assigned to the same data page (Figure 8.16). If this primary page overflows when new points are added an overflow chain is created. The size of the grid is chosen to suit the expected distribution of data points and to minimize the number of overflow pages attached to each primary cell page.

Access to data records is by a directory in the form of a *k*-dimensional array, where *k* is the number of dimensions. The grid size is fixed so there is no need to store cell coordinates or size information with the page pointer in the directory. A query of the form 'Find the object at x, y' can be performed by calculating which directory cell to examine from the input coordinates and the cell size. To locate all points within an arbitrarily sized rectangle with sides parallel to the grid, it is necessary to calculate which cells are overlapped by the search rectangle, then each corresponding directory entry is examined. If it contains a valid pointer the associated data page and any overflow pages are retrieved. If the sides of the rectangle do not lie on grid lines, there may be some loss of selectivity in the query because points outside the search rectangle, but inside the affected cells, must be excluded from the returned data pages. Nevertheless, the number of unwanted records is typically very much less than for a one-dimensional index.

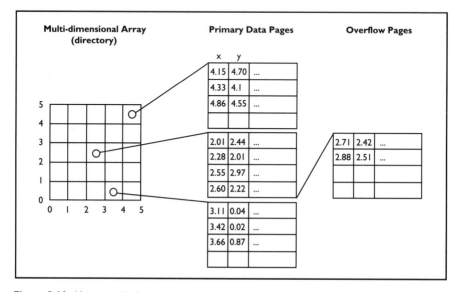

Figure 8.16   Using a multi-dimensional array as an index to data pages. Each array cell corresponds to a single page, with additional records handled by overflow pages.

Finding objects within a given search radius, an irregularly shaped region, or a rectangle at an angle to the grid can be achieved by first calculating the bounding rectangle of the required region, then proceeding as for the rectangle query.

The major limitation of the fixed grid approach comes from the division of the search space into equal-sized cells irrespective of the distribution of points. It is best suited to uniformly distributed point data because this allows a suitable choice of cell size. For other distributions, especially when points show a tendency to cluster, the regular cell size may result in large numbers of empty cells in areas of low point density. Equally, long overflow chains of data pages may be formed for areas of high point density. Clearly, the grid size needs to be carefully chosen to balance these problems.

8.5.2   The grid file

The **grid file** [Nievergeldt *et al.* 1984] improves on the fixed grid approach by using a dynamic directory in which the number of cells may increase or decrease as data points are inserted or deleted. It avoids the problems of empty data pages caused by clustering of points by only allocating pages as needed to hold data points. There is no longer a direct one-to-one relationship between a directory cell and a corresponding data page. All records for points within a single directory grid cell are located on the same data page, but a data page may contain points corresponding to more than one grid cell, provided that the cells can be grouped to form a rectangle.

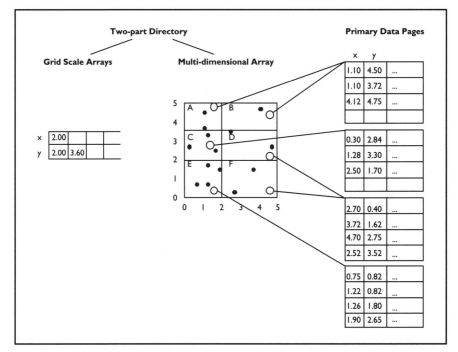

Figure 8.17 A two-dimensional grid file. Each data page holds four records. The directory cells C and E each have their own data pages; A and B share one page, D and F share another. The grid scale arrays locate the current grid splits at x=2.00, y=2.00 and y=3.60.

The directory is in two parts, the first consisting of a k-dimensional array corresponding to the grid cells. As before, each array element contains a single pointer to a data page. The second part, the grid scale arrays, contains k one-dimensional arrays containing the current coordinates of the divisions between cells (Figure 8.17). If these one-dimensional arrays are held in memory, the data record for any single point in a grid file can be found with exactly two disk accesses, one to read the directory array, the second to read the required data page. It thus offers higher performance than a simple regular grid method where many disk accesses may be needed to follow long overflow chains.

Insertion proceeds by adding records to the appropriate page until it is full. At this point a split is made along one or other axis. Typically the division alternates between the x and y axes, and the split is located at the mid-point of the divided cell. Adaptive methods may also be used to relate splitting to the data point distribution.

When deletion leads to underflow (typically <70% full), data pages can be merged with their neighbours.

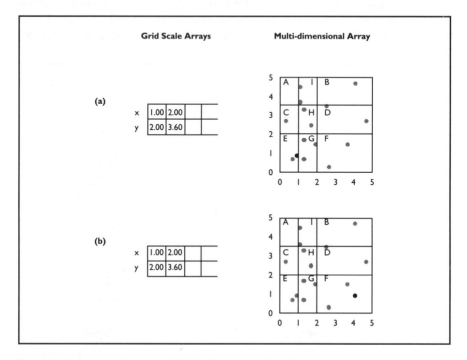

Figure 8.18 Inserting the points (a) *0.90, 1.00* and (b) *4.00, 1.00* into the grid file of Figure 8.17.

Adding the point 'x=0.90, y=1.00' to the example in Figure 8.16 would fill the page associated with grid cell E. The x axis is the next candidate to be divided and a split is made at the mid-point of the affected cell (x=1). The x scale array is updated to reflect the new division point (Figure 8.18a). Three points previously in the data page associated with cell E are moved to a new page pointed to by the new cell G. Two other new cells are created by the grid split (H and I), but as these contain fewer than four points they share their data pages with A and C respectively.

When a page that is shared by two or more grid cells fills up, a new page is allocated and the records are redistributed to maintain the association between each cell and a single data page. For example, adding the point 'x=4.00, y=1.00' to the data in Figure 8.17 would fill the data page used by grid cells D and F. The data page would be split and the records redistributed so that the cells each have their own data page (Figure 8.18b).

8.5.3 Hierarchical or tree-based methods

The grid-based methods for structuring multi-dimensional data make use of directories that parallel simple indexes in the one-dimensional case. A second class of multi-dimensional structures use directories in the form of a tree and can be compared with the multi-level indexing and B-tree techniques of their one-dimensional counterparts. Several methods for dealing with multi-dimensional points are based on the **k-d-tree**. This is a form of binary search tree in which branching represents a splitting of the data space on a different dimension at each successive level of the tree (Figure 8.19). Other, specifically two-dimensional, structures are derived from the **quadtree** and have corresponding **octree** forms for three-dimensional points.

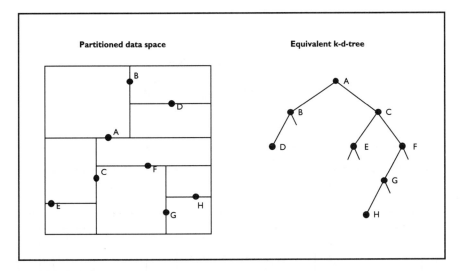

Figure 8.19 The k-d-tree is built by partitioning the data space along different dimensions at each level of the tree. Here, the first tree level (node A) has its children divided in the y direction, the second level (nodes B and C) has children divided in the x direction, the third level divides again in the x direction, and so on.

The nodes of a quadtree contain four pointers to child nodes. Like the k-d-tree, the **point quadtree** contains nodes representing data points. However, instead of dividing the data space on a single dimension at each node, the quadtree divides on two dimensions. Thus each child is located within a quadrant of the space 'below' its parent (Figure 8.20).

In the region quadtree, each node represents a square area of the data space, and each child represents one quadrant of the area covered by the parent. The successive subdivision of the data space into quadrants permits variable-sized squares at the leaf nodes. Large areas can be located more rapidly than small ones because their leaf nodes are placed at a shallower depth in the tree. Region quadtrees are widely used to store raster graphics data such as areas of specific land use in a geographical information system. Figure 8.21 shows how the successive division of quadrants is used to represent the extent of a geographical feature such as a river.

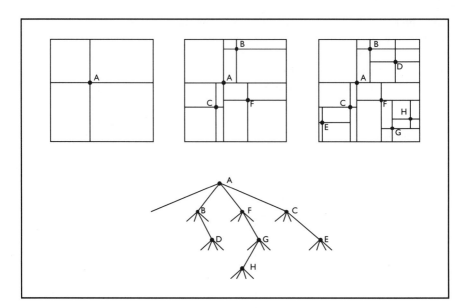

Figure 8.20 A point quadtree. Diagram showing the successive division of space by data points and the corresponding quadtree.

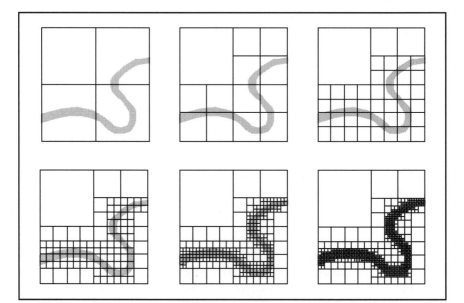

Figure 8.21 Successive subdivision of quadrants in a region quadtree representing part of a raster image.

There are several ways in which the region quadtree can be adapted to store point data. The PR quadtree subdivides its data space until the areas covered by each leaf node contain a single point object (Figure 8.22). When adapted to disk storage, the PR **quadtree** provides an index to data pages used for point storage. Here, each leaf node contains a pointer to a data page holding records for a number of points.

The example in Figure 8.22 can be viewed as such an index in which the data pages hold only one point record but, typically, there will be many more records per data page. When one of these pages fills up it is split and its contents divided between up to four pages. At the same time the leaf node in the quadtree index is replaced by a new internal node and the data page pointers are distributed between the attached leaf nodes.

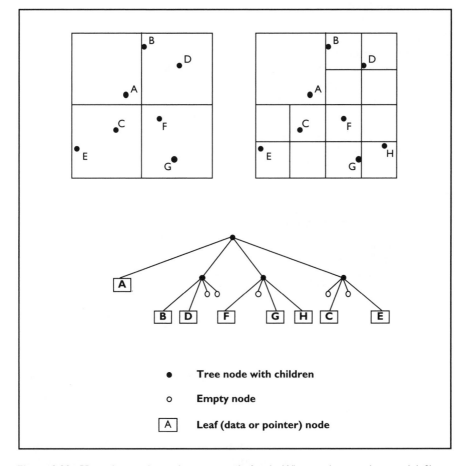

Figure 8.22 PR quadtree with one data point per leaf node. When used as an index to a disk file, the leaf nodes each contain a pointer to a data page containing records of objects located within the quadrant.

As with some grid-based methods there are disadvantages in a regular division of the data space. Several other methods employ adaptive splitting techniques in which the partitioning is located to optimize the distribution of points between data pages. For a detailed discussion of a wide range of methods based on both quadtrees and k-d-trees, *see* [Samet 1989a].

8.5.4   R-tree

Each of the multi-dimensional techniques described so far is primarily intended for managing point data. They are less suited to queries involving other spatial data types such as regions. Although point-based methods could be used to access a region characterized by its centre point, this is of little help in determining whether an arbitrary point is contained within a region, or whether two regions overlap. Many region-based methods store the bounding rectangles of objects in their indexes so that tests for overlap can be used in searches.

One of the most widely used region methods is the **R-tree** [Guttman 1984]. It is a multi-dimensional extension of the B-tree in which each tree node represents the bounding rectangle of all its children (Figure 8.23). Each node contains a rectangle and pointer pair for each of its children. The rectangle indicates the maximum extent of all children in the associated branch, and the pointer references a further tree node or leaf node. The leaf nodes contain the bounding rectangles of stored spatial objects, each with a corresponding data page pointer.

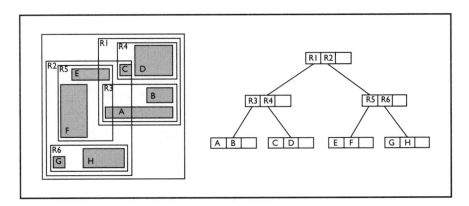

Figure 8.23   A simple R-tree showing data objects A–H and the spatial extents of the bounding rectangles R1–R6.

A significant difference from the quadtree-based methods is that, in an R-tree, spatial objects and their bounding rectangles may overlap, so each object might be reached by more than one route through the tree. In practice, only one of these routes is used and each data page, and hence each record, is associated with only one leaf node. For example, the rectangle labelled 'C' in Figure 8.23 could have been placed in either the 'R1' or 'R2' branches of the tree. The overlapping of tree nodes can have an adverse effect on search times because it may be necessary to traverse many branches of the tree before finding the required object.

When a record is inserted, the location is chosen by finding the rectangle that would be least extended by the addition of the new object. As with the B-tree, overflow of data and leaf pages is handled by splitting and propagation of the split upwards through the tree. Because there is no linear order an alternative method is needed to determine which entries should be moved to the new page. Two approaches are possible: the first is to minimize the spatial overlap of the bounding rectangles, the second to minimize the area covered by each of the new rectangles.

Deletion proceeds by removing the data record and associated leaf node entry as for the B-tree with the addition that the bounding rectangles of parent nodes are adjusted to reflect the changes in their children. Underflow is handled differently. The lack of a linear ordering means that there are no adjacent nodes that can be used for merging. All entries from underflowing nodes are therefore removed and held in a temporary list. Once all rectangle adjustments are completed, these removed nodes are reinserted as if they were new records.

As with the B-tree, both **R⁺-tree** [Sellis *et al.* 1987] and **R*-tree** [Beckmann *et al.* 1990] forms have been described. The R⁺-tree allows bounding rectangles to be split between their parents, thus allowing multiple paths to the same data record at the expense of increasing tree depth.

The R*-tree method concentrates on improving performance by careful optimizations of the choice of insertion paths and node splitting based on empirical observations of the effects of area, margin (total side length) and overlap of rectangles. It also uses removal and reinsertion instead of simpler partitioning whenever overflow occurs in an insert operation.

8.6   Summary

In this chapter we have described the principal factors that determine the performance of files and the characteristics of the most widely used database file storage structures. An understanding of these issues is an essential complement to the techniques of physical database design discussed in Chapter 6.

Many DBMSs provide only limited choice over storage structures; rarely do they provide more than heap, hash and B-tree methods, and in some cases only B-tree may be used. However, the increasing range of applications of database systems, particularly in areas such as Computer Aided Design and Geographical Information Systems, requires a broadening of the range of file structures to cope with the special characteristics of multi-dimensional data. Some specialized systems now provide suitable methods while others, at present largely experimental, have introduced the possibility of adding 'user-defined' access methods. We return to this topic in the description of extended relational and object-oriented systems in Chapters 15 and 16.

Exercises

1. What factors influence the choice of fill factor in sequential, hash and B-tree files? If you have access to a DBMS that supports user-specified fill factors, what are the default values for the available file types, and why have these values been chosen as defaults?

2. The following diagram represents a B-tree index of order 3.
   Describe the effects of the following sequence of operations:
   • Insert key values 790, 75, 572, 200
   • Delete key values 67, 88, 122, 340

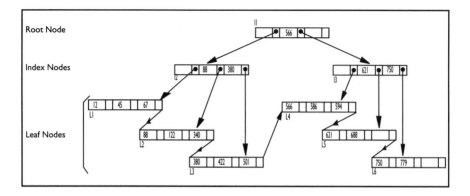

Chapter 9

RULES, TRIGGERS AND STORED PROCEDURES

9.1 Introduction

Traditional database systems provide passive repositories for secure persistent data. All operations on the stored data and metadata take place as a result of externally initiated actions, usually the execution of a query language statement submitted by an interactive user or an application. Most, if not all, behavioural aspects of the system are handled outside the database by application programs.

In Chapters 3, 4 and 5 we described methods for developing data, functional and behavioural schemas. Although these are treated separately we emphasize the need for an integrated approach in order to develop a satisfactory model of the static and dynamic aspects of a system. In this chapter we describe several ways in which in modern database systems support the implementation of integrated data and behavioural schemas.

A clear separation of data and process at the implementation level might appear attractive, but this earlier approach suffers from several major disadvantages. Not the least of these is the need for applications to support all the operational behaviour and semantic constraint rules governing the data objects on which they operate. In a large system this may lead to many applications containing a large proportion of duplicated code with consequent effects on the complexity of the software maintenance task.

Another major limitation is that any operational rules enforced only by applications can be bypassed by interactive queries or other applications that do not embody the same rules. Until recently, few commercial systems have provided more than minimal support for the automatic enforcement of even the most basic integrity constraints. Consequently, it has been easy for an interactive user or an inadequately specified application to violate the integrity of the database.

These problems explain why a large part of recent database research and of the developments by commercial systems vendors have been directed towards methods of supporting integrity constraints and behavioural semantics as part of the stored database. The trend is to increase the capability of the database to support the functional and behavioural schemas in addition to the normal data schema.

In effect, this means that an increasing proportion of the work previously done by applications can now be encapsulated within the stored database. Not only does this prevent interactive users and rogue applications from violating integrity, it also reduces the potential problems of application maintenance. Applications can be simplified because they no longer have to perform many routine operations, and code redundancy is reduced with analogous benefits to the reduction in data redundancy. With client–server systems there are also potential performance gains from a significant reduction in the volume of commands and data passing between the application and database engine.

It is no coincidence that the development of object-oriented programming techniques has also been driven by the aims of combining representations of state and behaviour, while hiding details of the implementation of behaviour from the users of the data objects. The object-oriented approach takes these ideas further than anything discussed in this chapter by encapsulating behaviour in each distinct class of object, rather than simply within the database. However, it has come to be a major influence on the development of database systems, particularly those intended to support a wider range of data types than traditional systems. We return to these issues in Chapters 15 and 16.

The two main areas of interest here are **active databases** and **deductive databases** (Figure 9.1). The term 'reactive' might better describe the former, but 'active' has gained a wide currency. It covers the ability of the system to respond to events by performing specified actions. Events may include conventional database operations or external stimuli such as clock events, and actions are typically further database operations, execution of procedures or functions, or passing messages to external processes. Production rules, defined as part of the database schema, may be used to specify the conditions under which a particular action is performed. Thus a conventional operation such as updating a record may result in a chain of further actions, often not visible to the user or application that initiates the sequence.

Deductive database systems provide the ability to derive further information from existing stored data. The approach is closely associated with that of logic programming and languages such as PROLOG [Clocksin and Mellish 1981]. Indeed, much of the experimental work in this area employs a subset of PROLOG known as **Datalog** which is specialized for database use (*see, for example,* [Ullman 1988]). As with a PROLOG program, a typical deductive database contains a collection of facts specifying the associations between attribute values and a collection of logic rules. Facts provide an extensional database equivalent to the stored data of a conventional database. An inference mechanism is used to derive new facts by applying the rules to the data. Whereas conventional systems support only limited mechanisms for defining intensional (derived) data, the rulebase of a deductive system is intended to be a major component of the database.

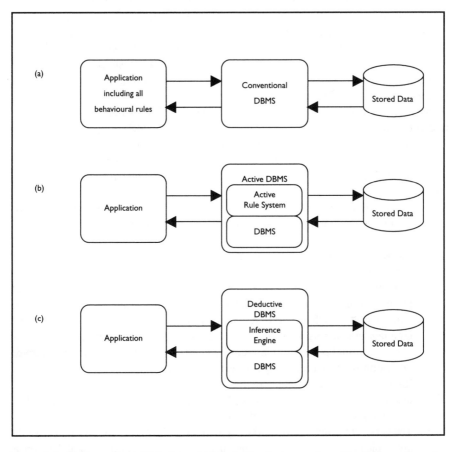

Figure 9.1   (a) Conventional, (b) Active and (c) Deductive database systems. The tightness of coupling between the active rule system or inference engine and the DBMS varies between implementations.

Although both involve the storage and management of rule systems, they approach the problem from quite different directions. The active approach can be seen as part of the continuing evolution of conventional database systems. Deductive databases are a development of knowledge-based systems that address the problems of managing much larger collections of facts and rules than are possible with conventional logic programming methods. Both are significant research areas, but whereas many current commercial systems provide some active capabilities, work on deductive systems has been largely confined to the research community with, so far, only limited effects on commercial systems.

9.2 Active database systems

The initial impetus behind active database development came from the need to support integrity constraints in conventional relational systems, and has since been broadened to cover more generalized constraints and behaviour.

Although entity integrity has long been supported in relational DBMSs by indirect methods such as the creation of unique indexes on keys, enforcing referential integrity has been more problematic. Indeed, this lack of support led to early implementations of active database mechanisms being promoted primarily as a means of enforcing referential integrity.

With the increasing adoption of the SQL 2 standard (*see* Chapter 14), entity and referential integrity constraints are now becoming more widely supported as part of the data schema. More general constraints can be handled by the assertion mechanism but, as with SQL entity and referential constraints, the resulting action is limited to raising an exception whenever the condition specified in a search condition fails.

The basic components of an active system are now provided in some form by an increasing number of commercial system vendors. They include:

- **Stored procedures**: programs or procedures stored in the database and executed either in response to a trigger, or from an application in a manner analogous with a conventional remote procedure call. Typically they allow parameter passing and return of result values to the calling program and are written in a fourth generation language that combines conventional query language statements with the looping, conditional and assignment constructs of conventional procedural languages. They may be used to perform database operations or to pass messages to external processes.
- **Rules**: stored rules usually in the form *if <condition> then do <action>*, usually fired by triggers. The condition is typically a predicate logic expression or a valid database search condition, as in an SQL 'where' clause.
- **Triggers**: a mechanism for initiating an action in response to an event. Events are typically database operations such as an insert, update or delete on a stored record. Actions can include executing one or more query language statements, executing a stored procedure, or firing a rule which, if its condition is true, may in turn initiate further actions.
- **Alerters**: a mechanism that may be used to pass a message to a listening application via the medium of the DBMS. Typically, applications register an interest in one or more alerters, rather than being notified of all such events. Notification may be received either by polling or by callback.

The terms rule and trigger are often used interchangeably to describe simple forms of **Event–Condition–Action (ECA)** rules [McCarthy and Dayal 1989]. These subsume rules within triggers as described above by adding conditional execution of the action. The basic format of such rules is:

ON <event>
IF <condition>
DO <action>

Many implementations add the ability to specify whether rule firing takes place before or after execution of the triggering event. When the event is one that changes the database state, commands executed in the action part may also be allowed to access 'before' and 'after' values. For example, the action part of a rule fired on an insert might need to access the new values even if it is performed before the insert takes place. Similarly the old values may need to be accessible after a delete operation, and both old and new values may need to be visible to an action resulting from an update.

There are clear benefits to be gained from incorporating rule systems into a DBMS. We have already mentioned the potential to simplify applications and to improve performance by minimizing client–server messaging. A well-integrated rule system will handle rules as first-class database objects and make full use of optimization, concurrency control and recovery mechanisms in their execution.

Rules, however, should not be seen simply as an 'add-on' feature, rather as an opportunity to provide a single mechanism capable of supporting a wide range of both existing and new database functions. An effective production rules system can be used as an underlying mechanism for implementing views, versions, and other forms of virtual or derived data such as function valued attributes. It has been argued that there are significant benefits to be gained by concentrating efforts on the development of a single, powerful, rules system rather than implementing separate support for each of these facilities [Stonebraker *et al.* 1990b].

9.2.1   *Event–Condition–Action (ECA) rules*

The ECA model is more general than that supported by most current commercial systems. For example, it allows for a wide variety of primitive event types and complex events representing various combinations of primitive events.

Primitive event types include the following:

- Start or end of basic data manipulation or definition operations.
- Start or end of specific transactions.
- Abstract events such as messages from external processes and firing of alerters.
- Temporal events, including those specified to take place at absolute and relative times, and repetition at defined intervals.

Complex events may be formed by combinations of primitive events using the Boolean operators AND, OR and NOT. By introducing a temporal element to the event model, other combinations of events such as sequences (*event1* followed by *event2*) or events occurring within an interval can be specified.

Few systems have so far supported temporal events. Schwiderski and Saake [1994] propose a method for extending the ECA model to include initialized temporal logic expressions. The initialization is an additional event that defines the start of the period of interest to the rule. The end of the period is then signalled as the event, at which time the action is performed if the condition has been satisfied during the period of interest. The condition part of the rule is a temporal logic formula.

9.2.2 Rule execution

Consideration of the relationship between the triggering event and rule execution leads to several possible approaches to processing ECA rules (Figure 9.2):

- **Immediate**: the rule is fired immediately on detection of the event in the main transaction. The execution sequence of the main transaction is then suspended until after any actions performed by the rule (Figure 9.2a). If nesting of rules is allowed and the action part of a rule triggers the firing of a further rule, the first rule is suspended until the second completes, and so on. All rules are executed as part of the main transaction, and any error aborts the entire transaction.
- **Deferred**: triggering events in the main transaction are recorded until it is ready to commit. All rules are then executed as the final part of the transaction before it commits (Figure 9.2b). As with the immediate approach, rules are executed as part of the main transaction. If rule nesting is permitted, further rules may be executed immediately or deferred until completion of the triggering rule.
- **Decoupled**: the rule is executed in a separate transaction initiated by the triggering event (Figure 9.2c). The rule transaction executes concurrently with the main (parent) transaction. Serializability of nested rules can be dealt with by the conventional concurrency control system.
- **Hybrid** execution modes are also possible by dividing the rule into condition and action phases. A mixed immediate and deferred strategy arises from performing the condition test on detection of the event, but deferring the action until the main transaction is ready to commit (Figure 9.2d). Decoupling may also be employed within the rule itself by executing the condition and action parts in separate transactions (Figure 9.2e).

A limitation of immediate execution is that all rules are executed in turn, even if subsequent operations in the parent transaction nullify the effect of their triggering event. For example, inserting a tuple and later updating it within the same transaction is logically equivalent to a single insertion using the final updated values. Similarly, any number of updates to a tuple followed by its deletion have the net effect of a single delete operation. If each of these operations result in rule firing, some of the ensuing actions will be redundant.

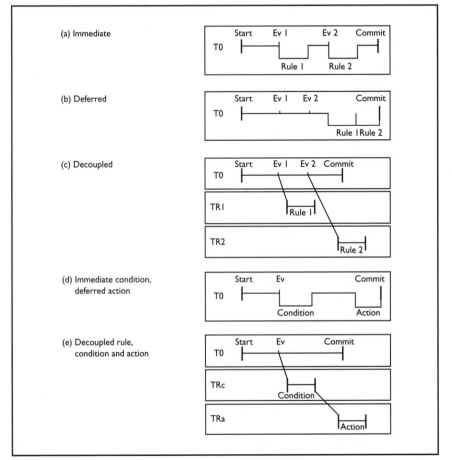

Figure 9.2 ECA Rule execution methods. T0 is the main transaction in which the event leading to rule firing occurs. Transactions labelled TRx are subtransactions in which some or all of the rule processing takes place.

Deferred execution allows the possibility of firing rules as a result of logical events that is, as a result of the net effect of a sequence of operations within a transaction. Firing rules on logical rather than physical events simplifies rule programming because it allows the programmer to concentrate on the effects, not the expression of database operations. This approach is taken by several experimental active database systems including Ariel [Hanson 1992] and Starburst [Widom and Finkelstein 1990; Widom *et al.* 1991].

9.2.3 Views and other virtual data

Unlike the approach taken in a deductive database, most of the data in a conventional database is present in an extensional form. The intensional database is normally limited to view definitions, but can be extended to cover many types of virtual data by supporting rules of the form:

```
INSTEAD OF <event>
IF <condition>
DO <action>
```

Conventional view definitions are equivalent to rules in which the underlying query is executed instead of one on the virtual table. For example:

```
INSTEAD OF select from viewname
DO view definition query
```

Similar rules can also be defined to cover insert, update and delete operations. Rules can be generated automatically when executing conventional view and table definition statements rather than being written by the user but, by allowing this form of rule, a single mechanism can support these and user-defined 'instead' rules.

Other forms of virtual data may be supported by a rule mechanism. For example, function-valued attributes can be provided using rules of the form:

```
INSTEAD OF select table.column
DO execute function to calculate and return value
```

The experimental POSTGRES system employs a single rules system designed to support logical, partial and materialized views, versions, and procedure- or function-valued attributes [Stonebraker *et al.* 1990b]. This allows many of the problems of view update semantics to be overcome by generating additional rules to handle insert, update and delete operations on the view. These additional rules may be generated automatically for simple single relation views, or the user may specify a group of rules to realize the required update semantics for views covering more than one base relation.

In addition to the conventional approach of activating rules at the tuple level during query execution, POSTGRES also provides a 'query rewrite' mechanism. This mechanism inspects the commands output from the parser and, if they fire a query rewrite rule, modifies them before passing them on to the optimizer. Rules in which the event part has no 'where' clause, and those that can be expected to access a large proportion of tuples in the affected relations, may be handled by this mechanism, thus avoiding large numbers of rule activations during execution.

Separating this form of rule activation from the query execution allows the action part of a rule to be cached as a separate stored object, effectively a materialized view.

A separate caching demon is used to ensure that these materializations are periodically updated to reflect changes in base tables. The action query only needs to be executed when the rule is activated if the cached data has been invalidated.

9.2.4   Rule management

Although techniques for managing large collections of interdependencies are well established elsewhere, for example in the compilation of programs from many source code units, there has been relatively little attention paid to the problems of interdependencies in complex collections of rules. Most current implementations allow new rules to be added to a database without any check on their possible interactions with existing rules.

There are several possible sources of interaction and non-determinism problems in rule systems. To avoid such problems, any collection of rules should exhibit the following characteristics:

- **Lack of conflicts**. If more than one rule is allowed for a particular event there is a possibility that their firing or actions may conflict. Multiple rules may be fired before or after an event without necessarily conflicting, but if any of the rules specifies 'instead of' there will always be a conflict.
- **Guaranteed termination**. If the action part of a rule is allowed to trigger further rules, there must be a suitable mechanism for ensuring that cycles in a chain of rules either are avoided or can be guaranteed to terminate. Several strategies are possible, ranging from terminating as soon as the first cycle is detected, to applying an arbitrary limit to the depth of nesting and recursion.
- **Confluence**. When there are several rules that may fire at one time, the order of firing may affect the final database state. Clearly this is undesirable and a rule system should behave in a deterministic manner. If the outcome is independent of firing order, the rules are said to be confluent.
- **Observable determinism**. Determinism is also desirable in any observable effects of rule execution. For example, consider two rules fired by the same event, one performing an update and the other retrieving data. If both act on the same data items and the effect of the update is visible to subsequent rules, the result of the retrieval will depend on the order in which the rules are executed. Rules that are free of such interactions are said to be observably deterministic.

An increasing number of systems permit rules to be prioritized, often by giving each a numeric priority. An interesting alternative method employed in Starburst supports specific ordering by specifying that a given rule precedes or follows other named rules.

[Aiken *et al.* 1992] comment that 'The unstructured, unpredictable, and often non-deterministic behaviour of rule processing can be a nightmare for the database programmer.' They describe techniques for determining whether a collection of rules will terminate, produce a unique final database state and produce a unique sequence of observable actions. There is, however, an urgent need to develop CASE tools that implement such techniques and aid the database designer and programmer in both developing and maintaining complex rule systems.

9.2.5   Current commercial implementations

Although many commercial systems now provide rule mechanisms in some form, they are as yet not standardized and most are limited to simple database events. The current draft of the SQL 3 standard contains a detailed specification for stored procedures and triggers that combines features of several current implementations, including ORACLE, INGRES and SYBASE. This standard is, however, unlikely to be adopted before 1996. A simplified outline of the proposed syntax is shown below:

```
1  CREATE TRIGGER <trigger_name>
2  [BEFORE | AFTER | INSTEAD OF]
3  [INSERT | UPDATE [ OF <column_list>] | DELETE] ON <table_name>
4  [REFERENCING [OLD AS <correlation_name1>]
                [NEW AS <correlation_name2>]]
5  WHEN <search_condition>
6  <SQL statement list> ;
```

In this form, the event part of the rule (line 3) is limited to insert, update and delete operations on a named table. The rule firing time, and hence the action time, may be specified as before or after the database operation, or the action may be performed instead of the operation that caused the event (line 2).The update event may be limited to named columns within the table and the old and new versions of affected tuples may be given different correlation names for use in the action statements (line 4).

The condition (line 5) is a simple predicate logic expression equivalent to a conventional SQL WHERE clause. If the condition evaluates to 'True', the action part (line 6) is executed. The SQL 3 proposal allows the action to be a single SQL statement or a block of statements. The statements may include calls to execute stored procedures, either synchronously or asynchronously.

Several current implementations provide a subset of this specification, in some cases replacing the term 'trigger' by 'rule'. The rule mechanism provided in the 'Knowledge Management Extension' of INGRES version 6 restricts rule firing to after the event, and the action is limited to executing stored procedures [INGRES 1991b]. For example, the following rule might be used in maintaining a hospital's stock of drugs. It executes the reorder_drug_proc procedure whenever an update to the drugs table results in a stock quantity (qty) of less than 20. The name of the drug and the new stock quantity are passed as parameters to the procedure:

```
CREATE RULE reorder_drug_rule
AFTER UPDATE (qty) OF drugs
WHERE new.qty < 20
EXECUTE PROCEDURE reorder_drug_proc (name = old.name, qty =
new.qty);
```

Other systems provide more extensive facilities. Illustra, an SQL-based commercial DBMS with origins in the POSTGRES project [Stonebraker *et al.* 1987; 1990a], can perform actions within the same transaction as well as before, after or instead of the triggering event. It also adds the ability to fire a rule in response to a 'select' query in addition to inserts, updates and deletes [Illustra 1994]. It is perhaps surprising that many other implementations have not recognized the obvious potential of this extension for monitoring applications. For example, the following would log the user name and current time in the drug_log table whenever anyone retrieved information about restricted drugs from the drug table:

```
CREATE RULE monitor_drug_select AS
ON SELECT TO drugs
WHERE category = 'restricted'
DO BEFORE insert into drug_log
             values (user, 'select', current_timestamp);
```

A second example shows how the ability to respond to select events can be used for access control. Here, if the user is not listed in the drug_staff table a tuple containing null values is returned instead of the name and quantity expected as the normal query result.

```
CREATE RULE restrict_drug_select AS
ON SELECT TO drugs
WHERE category = 'restricted'
  AND user not in (select uid from drug_staff)
DO INSTEAD return NULL::CHAR(40), NULL::INTEGER;
```

Different approaches to conflict and cycle avoidance or resolution are found in current implementations. Invariably, stored procedures can only perform data manipulation functions or raise alerters. Data definition operations are not allowed, so avoiding one source of potential conflict. To date, few systems implement rule firing 'instead of' the triggering event. Those that do may detect conflicts between two or more such rules at run time, whereas it would be preferable to do so when the rules are defined.

Most systems appear to allow multiple rules to be triggered by a single event. Typically, they lack any means of prioritizing rules and fire all candidates in an arbitrary order. Methods of dealing with cyclical rules include flattening the cycle and aborting if a preset maximum depth of recursion is reached.

Some systems provide an alerter mechanism that may be used to pass arbitrary messages to applications. Typically, an alerter (for example, a 'dbevent' in INGRES) is created as a named object within a database schema. Any application or stored procedure running with the appropriate permissions may then raise the alerter. In some cases the alerter may also be raised directly in the action part of a rule or trigger. Applications that need to respond to alerters typically register their interest in one or more named alerters and use either a polling or callback method to receive notification.

The draft SQL 3 standard specification for triggers provides an indication of current trends, but may be modified further before the standard is finalized. Both rules and alerters are active development areas for many commercial systems and standards tend to reflect current commercial practice. The importance of these mechanisms and the continued striving for competitive advantage can be expected to result in many vendors implementing extensions beyond the proposed standard, even before it is adopted.

At present, however, one of the most pressing needs is for tools to support the implementation and management of complex rule systems. The absence of mechanisms for checking rule interactions puts a considerable responsibility on the database designer and programmer to ensure that as new rules are added they do not compromise the stability of the database. As is often the case, the development of support tools lags well behind the introduction of new features. In the meantime, tasks such as dependency checking and conflict resolution are typically performed by hand or by locally built applications that query the system catalogues. As with other CASE tools, this need may be increasingly satisfied by third-party vendors.

9.3 Deductive database systems

Deductive systems represent a bringing together of two different technologies, those of databases and expert systems. They are intended to combine large- scale data storage and manipulation facilities with domain knowledge in the form of a collection of rules. As with logic-based languages, an inferencing mechanism is used to derive further information by applying the intensional rules to the extensional stored data.

There are two basic approaches to building deductive database systems:

- extending logic languages to provide database facilities such as access control, transaction control and recovery mechanisms, thus making them adequately robust for use in multi-user environments and with large volumes of data and rules;
- adding logic language constructs to conventional database systems, either by adding a separate high-level rule specification language, or by extending a logic language to provide the full range of data definition and manipulation functions.

These approaches have led to a variety of experimental systems ranging from a loose coupling of expert system and conventional database, to integrated or 'tightly coupled' systems in which the rule-handling mechanisms form an integral part of the DBMS.

9.3.1   *Logic languages*

In this section, we first outline the way in which both extensional and intensional data are expressed in the logic languages PROLOG and Datalog. Datalog is a subset of PROLOG intended for use in deductive database systems. It uses a different inference mechanism from that of PROLOG systems, but the examples presented below are applicable to both languages. Our purpose here is not to describe these languages in detail, but simply to illustrate their use as rule specification languages. For detailed descriptions of PROLOG, *see* [Clocksin and Mellish 1981] and for Datalog, *see* [Ullman 1988; 1989].

A PROLOG or Datalog 'program' is a form of database. It contains collections of clauses representing both facts and rules. Facts are expressed as predicates, or relationships, indicating a named association of one or more values. In this respect they resemble the tuples of a relation in a relational DBMS. However, a PROLOG predicate is a pure tuple in which values are identified by position rather than by name.

For example, the following facts might represent part of a health centre database:

```
doctor('Cameron', 1).
doctor('Finlay', 2).
patient('Williams', 'Cameron').
patient('Garcia', 'Cameron').
patient('Fisher', 'Finlay').
patient('Waldon', 'Finlay').
appointment('Cameron', 'Williams', '1994-08-10 10:00').
appointment('Finlay', 'Garcia', '1994-08-10 10:00').
appointment('Cameron', 'Fisher', '1994-08-10 10:20').
appointment('Finlay', 'Waldon', '1994-08-10 10:20').
```

For the purposes of this discussion we can regard these facts as an extension of the following relational schema:

```
DOCTOR ( Name, Room_no )
PATIENT ( Name, Registered_with_doctor )
APPOINTMENT ( Doctor_name, Patient_name, Appt_date )
```

Queries against this database can be expressed as simple clauses. The interpreter then treats the clause as a goal to be solved by finding matching predicates in the database. For example, to find the name of the doctor with whom the patient 'Williams' is registered:

```
?- patient('Williams',D).
```

Here, the '?-' is the PROLOG interpreter prompt and the required value is expressed as an arbitrary variable name starting with an upper-case letter. Assuming the above facts, this query would return:

```
D = 'Cameron'
```

A conventional PROLOG interpreter would then allow the user to step through all possible matching values, although in this case there is only one. A Datalog system would typically return all results as a multi-set of tuples, as with a more conventional query language.

The deductive capabilities of these languages come from their ability to express intensions as rules. These are clauses in the form:

```
Head :- body.
```

The head is a single predicate expressing an intensional goal. The body contains one or more predicates that must be solved for the rule to succeed. For example

```
isapatient(X)  :- patient(X, Y).
```

is a rule that says that X is a patient if there exists a patient fact with X as its first argument. With this rule the query:

```
?- isapatient(P).
```

would produce in turn each of the patient names, whereas

```
?- isapatient('Williams').
```

would succeed and produce the answer 'yes'. The following would produce the answer 'no' because the rule fails to find a patient named 'Bloggs':

```
?- isapatient('Bloggs').
```

To determine whether a patient is registered with a doctor, a rule needs to succeed for a valid patient, to match the second argument of the patient fact against the first argument of a doctor fact, and perhaps also to check that the doctor's name is not blank. This conjunction of multiple predicates is achieved by placing them all in the body of the rule, separated by commas or '&':

```
isregistered(X)  :- patient(X, Y), doctor(Y, Z), Y != ''.
```

Multiple rules with the same name allow disjunctions by providing alternative ways of solving a single goal. This pair of rules defines both doctors and patients as persons:

```
person(X)  :- doctor(X, Y).
person(X)  :- patient(X, Y).
```

One or other of these rules will succeed when a doctor or patient name is used as the argument, and the query:

```
?- person(P).
```

will retrieve in turn every match found by each rule.

Logic rules can be used as equivalents of relational views expressed in SQL. The view:

```
CREATE VIEW diary AS
SELECT p.name AS patient, d.name AS doctor,
       a.appt_date, d.room, p.registered_with
FROM patient p, appointment a, doctor d
WHERE a.doctor = d.name
  AND a.patient = p.name;
```

can be expressed in rule form as:

```
diary(Patient, Doctor, Date, Room, Registeredwith)  :-
   patient(Patient, Registeredwith),
   appointment(Doctor, Patient, Date),
   doctor(Doctor, Room).
```

The rule head predicate can be used to formulate queries such as:

```
?- diary(P, Doc, Date, Rm, Reg).
```

This would return a tuple for each appointment in the database, together with the doctor's name and the name of the doctor with whom the patient is registered. Substituting a constant value for any of the query arguments instructs the interpreter to evaluate the sub-goals using that value instead of testing all possible values. For example:

```
?- diary('Fisher', Doc, Date, Rm, Reg).
```

would find any appointments for the patient name 'Fisher' and list the values of the remaining arguments. The result would then be:

```
Doc = 'Cameron'
Date = '1994-08-10 10:20'
Rm = 1
Reg = 'Finlay'
```

As with active database rules, logic-based deductive rules are considerably more powerful than a conventional view mechanism. Consider the following rules:

```
ancestor(X, Y)  :- parent(X, Y).
ancestor(X, Z)  :- parent(Y, Z), ancestor(X, Y).
```

Together, these form a recursive definition of 'ancestor'. Note also that, because of the equivalence between facts and rules, a rule predicate may appear in the body of another rule, or even within its own body. The first leads to the evaluation of a chain of rules, the second to recursion.

9.3.2   Rule evaluation

PROLOG interpreters evaluate rules by a method known as **backward chaining**. This is a top-down approach that works back from the rule to the stored facts. Each predicate in the rule body is checked in turn for matches between query variables and database facts or other rules. This approach is not well suited to handling large databases. However, its main limitation is that it is dependent on the ordering both of facts and rules in the database, and of predicates in the body of the rule. For example, if the second rule of the above ancestor definition were written in the logically equivalent form:

```
ancestor(X, Z)  :- ancestor(X, Y), parent(Y, Z).
```

the first clause in the body would be evaluated first, thus leading to infinite recursion.

The alternative **forward chaining** approach works in a bottom-up manner from the stored facts towards the goal. It generates new facts by applying rules to existing facts. Each new fact is then checked against the goal. The major drawback of this approach is the potential to generate an enormous number of irrelevant facts unless some way of constraining fact generation to those relevant to the query, or to subsequent rules, is used. This is the main reason why it is not used in PROLOG interpreters.

Logic rules can be used to express any relational algebra operation (*see* Chapter 13), and so can be used to perform any retrieval query that is possible using a conventional relational query language such as SQL. Other than the recursive example, each of the rules discussed in the previous section can also be expressed as a combination of the basic relational operators select, project, join and union.

The ease of mapping between logic rules and relational operators has made it possible to implement Datalog on top of conventional relational DBMS. In this way the limitations of both forward chaining and backward chaining are avoided. The evaluation of rules proceeds in a conventional bottom-up manner just as with conventional relational queries. This leads to a set-oriented behaviour in which, unlike PROLOG, query results are independent of rule and fact ordering. Unlike most relational languages, however, Datalog and other logic languages support recursive queries.

In its simplest form Datalog lacks several features of both PROLOG and conventional database languages. Various extensions have been proposed to overcome these limitations. They include support for functions as predicate arguments, negation, set arguments and database updates. We are not concerned here with the details of these extensions, other than to note that these extensions are required to provide an integrated rule language for database systems. The interested reader can find accessible descriptions in [Gardarin and Valduriez 1989].

9.3.3   *Adding deductive capabilities to a conventional DBMS*

Logic languages also have the potential to support extended features as well as the conventional features of relational database systems. We have seen that the specification of ECA rules requires a very low-level approach. Even simple constraints may require separate rules to cover insert, update and delete operations. Where there is a high-level language for defining views or referential integrity constraints, these additional rules may be generated automatically but, for most other application-specific constraints, the programmer must specify each individual rule.

Houtsma and Apers [1990] propose a data model that combines conventional ER modelling with rule specification. Whereas the current SQL standard only allows constraints to be included in a table definition or as assertions, their language includes specification of constraints and virtual attributes as Datalog-like clauses. They also include separate relationship definitions that may themselves contain constraint clauses.

Simon *et al.* [1992] argue that, in contrast to current active database rule systems, deductive database languages have a well-understood syntax and can provide a superior basis for defining an active database rule language. They observe that because logic rules may be translated into triggers it is possible to specify rules using a high-level logic language without needing to decompose the rule into many separate triggers. Decomposition of any rules may be handled by the system in much the same way as Ariel and POSTGRES generate the necessary set of rules to match the definition of a simple view or referential integrity constraint.

By extending the deductive language RDL1 [Kiernan *et al.* 1990] to overcome its inherent inability to manage events, Simon *et al.* [1992] propose a rule language that combines both active and deductive database rules. Their approach employs a 'trigger monitor' to detect trigger events by parsing submitted queries before passing them to the database server. Rules are linked with the monitor by incremental compilation and executed whenever a trigger event is detected. They include the ability to handle both immediate and deferred rules. This system benefits from flexibility and portability because it could be implemented alongside any conventional DBMS. However, a major shortcoming is that rule activation is separated from query execution and cannot therefore benefit from the optimization facilities of the DBMS.

9.4   Summary

In this chapter we have described the production rule systems that are at the heart of current active database developments, and the deductive database approach to building 'knowledge-base' systems. Most work on the latter remains largely within the research community. Apart, perhaps, from specialized application areas where the need for a logic programming language is dominant, it seems most likely that the major commercial developments in the foreseeable future will focus on extending conventional database systems with production rule systems.

Together with other enhancements, such as user-defined data types and function-valued attributes (*see* Chapter 15), active database systems based on current relational practice can provide much of the functionality of their deductive counterparts. The benefits of a familiar environment seem likely to be perceived by most database designers and programmers as outweighing those of deductive systems using a logic-based approach.

The development of rule systems is playing a significant part in the commercial vendors' pursuit of competitive advantage. Despite moves towards standardization of rule specification and semantics, there is likely to be a wide variation in capabilities between different systems for some time to come.

Exercise

If you have access to a DBMS that supports rules or triggers, design and test a set of simple rules to examine its behaviour under the following conditions:

- Multiple rules triggered by a single event.
- Conflicting 'instead of' rules (if supported).
- Rules with actions that trigger other rules.
- Cycles of rules.

Examine how information about triggers, stored procedures and alerters is stored in the system catalogues. Write a simple application to generate a report listing these objects and any dependencies between them.

Chapter 10

TRANSACTIONS AND CONCURRENCY CONTROL

10.1 Introduction

A transaction is a sequence of read and write actions that are grouped together to form a database access. In order to preserve the integrity of the database a database transaction is **atomic**, that is, either all the actions happen or none of them are reflected in the database. This basic abstraction frees the database application programmer from concerns about:

- inconsistencies caused by conflicting updates from concurrent users,
- partially completed transactions in the event of systems failures,
- user-directed undoing of transactions.

Much of the complexity of database management systems can be hidden behind the transaction interface. The notion of a transaction interface is currently finding favour with many designers of distributed and multimedia systems as a means of making the system complexity transparent to the user and insulating applications from implementation details.

We will start by giving a description of simple transactions and the problems that a practical concurrency control scheme must deal with.

We discuss the concept of atomic transactions which, in conventional database applications, are typically of very short duration. This is followed by a discussion of the particular problems encountered with applications such as CAD where individual transactions may last for several hours or more.

The second half of the chapter describes mechanisms for maintaining consistency and we conclude with a discussion of methods for dealing with the special problems of distributed transactions. We concentrate on locking, as it is used by all major systems and outperforms other methods in most realistic situations [Agrawal and DeWitt 1985]. We restrict our coverage to a basic overview of the principal variants of other methods of concurrency control, based on timestamps and certification (optimistic concurrency control); a comprehensive exposition of these methods is given in [Bernstein *et al.* 1987]. Readers requiring a thorough formal treatment of the material covered in this chapter are referred to [Lynch *et al.* 1994].

The properties of the database system that we are concerned with here are commonly referred to as the ACID properties; these are:

Atomic – completes or fails as one unit,
Consistent – all resources must always be in a consistent state,
Isolated – transactions do not interfere with each other,
Durable – the result of transactions is not lost even in the presence of failure.

10.2 Motivation and definitions

10.2.1 Problem

The simplest case of a transaction processing system forces all transactions into a single stream and executes them serially, allowing no concurrent execution at all. This is not a practical strategy for large multi-user databases, so mechanisms to enable multiple transactions to execute without causing conflicts or inconsistencies are necessary.

In a multi-user environment there are three problems of conflicting transactions:

- **Lost Update**. If T1 and T2 both read a record and then update it, the effects of the first update will be overwritten by the second (Figure 10.1).

  For example, suppose two clerks in the Finance Department of Dunwich General Hospital are updating Edgar's salary record, the first to give an annual salary adjustment and the second to reimburse his travel expenses for attending the annual Nordic Colloquium on Emergency Medicine. Without a suitable concurrency control mechanism the effect of the first update will be overwritten by the second.

- **Dirty Read**. In this case T1 updates a record, which is read by T2; T1 aborts and T2 has values which have never formed part of the stable database (Figure 10.2).

  For instance, a nurse records a dose of 2500 mg of Paracetamol to be given every four hours. This value is read by a report-generating transaction which includes it in the report before the nurse realizes the error and changes the dose to 250 mg. The problem arises because the second transaction sees the first's updates before it commits.

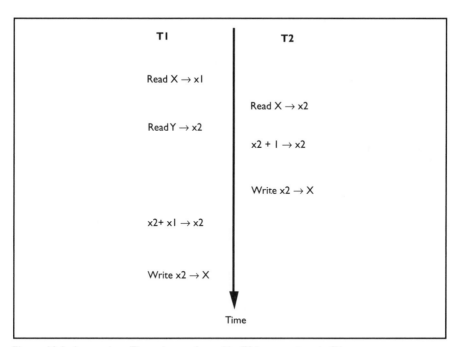

Figure 10.1   Lost update. The update performed by T2 is overwritten by T1.

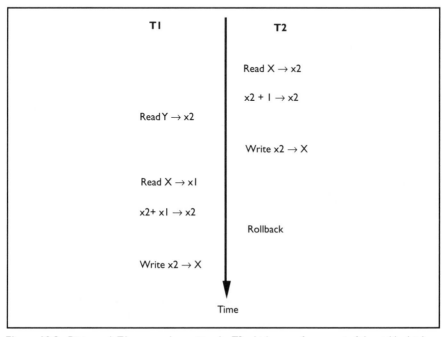

Figure 10.2   Dirty read. T1 uses a value written by T2 which never forms part of the stable database.

- **Unrepeatable Read.** This problem arises when T1 reads a record and then does some other processing during which T2 updates the record. If T1 rereads the record the new value will be inconsistent with the previous value (Figure 10.3).

  A report transaction produces a profile of drug usage for every clinic whose prescriptions are more than 5% different from the previous month's. If the prescription records are updated after this transaction has started it is likely to show details and totals which do not meet the criterion for generating the report.

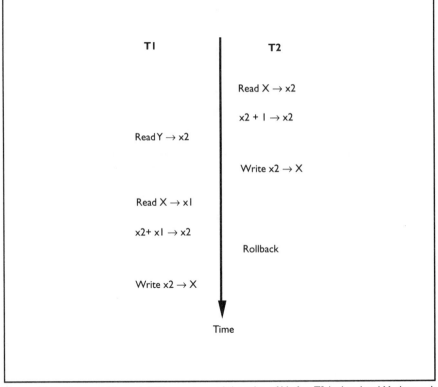

Figure 10.3   Unrepeatable read. If T1 were to read the value of X after T2 had updated X, the result of T1 would be different.

None of these problems arise if there is a single stream of transactions executed in serial order.

A common problem for all methods of concurrency control is that of **phantoms.** A phantom may arise when what is logically a single transaction is implemented as two separate transactions, between which another transaction can perform its updates.

Consider a bed-booking system with the following operations:

T1(i)	List patients' names and hospital numbers for each ward,
T1(ii)	Total the number of free beds in each ward,
T2	Book a patient in to a free bed.

If the execution order is T1(i) $\Rightarrow$ T2 $\Rightarrow$ T1(ii) the free bed totals will be incorrect and the patient added by T2 will be a phantom with respect to T1.

A number of approaches are possible to deal with the problems of maintaining database consistency in the presence of concurrent updating transactions. (Concurrent read-only transactions do not pose a problem, as they do not change the database state.)

10.2.2   Definitions

In order to define the characteristics of concurrency control schemes we need a number of (informal) definitions:

Granule
A unit of data individually controlled by the concurrency control subsystem (in a lock-based concurrency control scheme this is a lockable unit). Most often the granule is a page, although smaller or larger units (for example, tuple, relation) can be used and most commercial systems provide a variety of locking granularities.

Action
A unit of processing that is indivisible from the DBMS's perspective. In systems where the granule is a page the actions are typically read-page and write-page. The actions provided are determined by the system designers, but in all cases they are independent of side-effects and do not produce side-effects.

Permutable actions
A pair of actions is permutable if every execution of Ai followed by Aj has the same result as the execution of Aj followed by Ai on the same granule. Actions on different granules are always permutable. For the actions read and write we have:

> *Read-Read.* Permutable.

> *Read-Write.* Not permutable, since the result is different depending on whether read is first or second.

> *Write-Write.* Not permutable, as the second write always nullifies the effects of the first.

Transaction
A sequence of actions for a given user that respects database consistency. The database is consistent before and after a transaction, but may be inconsistent during it.

Schedule
A sequence of actions that is constructed by merging the actions of a set of transactions, respecting the sequence of actions within each transaction.

Serializable schedule
A schedule that allows a set of transactions to execute in some order such that the effects are equivalent to executing them in some serial order.

10.2.3 Degrees of consistency

Four levels of transaction consistency have been defined [Gray *et al.* 1976]:

Level 0 consistency:
T does not overwrite other transactions' dirty data.

Level 1 consistency:
T does not overwrite other transactions' dirty data,
T does not make any of its updates visible before it commits.

Level 2 consistency:
T does not overwrite other transactions' dirty data,
T does not make any of its updates visible before it commits,
T does not read other transactions' dirty data.

Level 3 consistency:
T does not overwrite other transactions' dirty data,
T does not make any of its updates visible before it commits,
T does not read other transactions' dirty data,
T can perform consistent reads (that is, no other transaction can update data read by T before T has committed).

Level 0 transactions are not, in general, recoverable since they may have interactions with the external world which cannot be undone. Level 1 is the minimum consistency requirement that allows a transaction to be recovered in the event of system failure. Level 2 consistency isolates the transaction from the updates of other transactions. Finally, Level 3 adds consistent reads, so that successive reads of a record will always give the same values.

Most conventional database applications require Level 3 consistency and this is provided by all major commercial DBMSs; mechanisms for providing this consistency are described below. However, there a number of circumstances where this level of consistency (and the attendant isolation) can either be dispensed with, usually for performance reasons, or where it is a hindrance, for example in many design applications where a related group of transactions need to see each others' partial results. The issues involved in complex transaction management are discussed in Section 10.5.

10.2.4 Serializable schedules

The execution of transactions in a serializable schedule is a sufficient condition for preventing conflicts. Given the existence of non-permutable actions and the sequence of actions in a transaction it is possible to define a partial order of transactions by constructing a **precedence graph**.

We can define a precedence relationship, T1 precedes T2, between T1 and T2 if there are two non-permutable actions a1 and a2 and a1 is executed by T1 before a2 is executed by T2.

A precedence graph is a directed graph in which:

- the set of vertices is the set of transactions,
- an arc exists between T1 and T2 if T1 precedes T2.

A schedule is serializable if the precedence graph is acyclic. (This condition is sufficient but not necessary.)

10.3 Locking

Locking is the most widely used form of concurrency control and is the method of choice for most applications. Locking schemes aim to allow the concurrent execution of compatible operations; permutable actions are compatible. The simplest type of locking scheme has two types of lock:

> S – shared (read) lock,
> X – exclusive (write) lock.

Locks are granted and released by a lock manager. The principal data structure of a lock manager is the **lock table**, in which an entry consists of a transaction identifier, a granule identifier and the lock type. The lock manager refuses incompatible requests, so if:

1. T1 holds an S lock on granule g1. A request by T2 for an S lock will be granted. (Read-Read are permutable.)
2. T1 holds an S lock on granule g1. A request by T2 for an X lock will be refused. (Read-Write are not permutable.)
3. T1 holds an X lock on granule g1. No request by T2 for a lock on g1 will be granted. (Write is not permutable.)

Transactions refused lock requests are queued until the lock can be granted. It is possible for two (or more) transactions to be waiting for locks held by the other; this is a **deadlock**. Deadlock detection and resolution are discussed below.

Two-phase locking (2PL) [Eswaran *et al.* 1976] is the standard scheme used to maintain Level 3 consistency. The essential discipline is that after a transaction has released a lock it may not obtain any further locks. In practice this means that transactions hold all their locks until they are ready to commit (Figure 10.4).

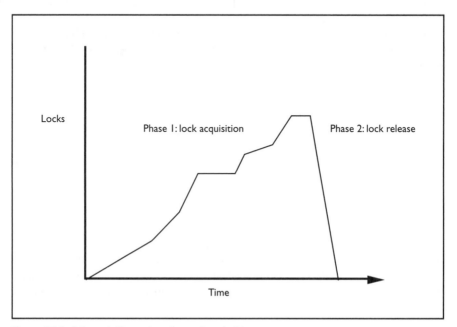

Figure 10.4 Schematic illustration of two-phase locking.

Deadlock

Deadlock is a circular waiting condition where two transactions are waiting (directly or indirectly) for each other. Many proposals have been made for detecting and resolving deadlocks, all of which rely on detecting cycles in a waits-for graph.

A waits-for graph is a directed graph in which the nodes represent transactions and a directed arc links a node waiting for a lock[1] with the node that has the lock.

The frequency of deadlocks is primarily dependent on the query load and the physical organization of the database. The only general estimate of deadlock frequency has been proposed by Gray: '...it appears that deadlocks per second rise as the square of the degree of multiprogramming and as the fourth power of transaction size...' [Gray 1981].

There are three basic schemes for when to do deadlock detection:

- Never. In this case a timeout is used to abort transactions that have been idle for too long. A simple but indiscriminate approach.

---

1   A waits-for graph can be used to represent conflict for any resource, although we restrict the discussion to lock conflicts.

- Every time a transaction is blocked. This is expensive, since most blocked transactions are not involved in deadlocks.
- Periodically. Generally the optimal scheme if the detection period is suitable. The ideal period is that which, on average, detects one deadlock cycle. A shorter period than this means that deadlock detection is done unnecessarily and a longer period involves transactions in unnecessarily long waits until the deadlock is broken.

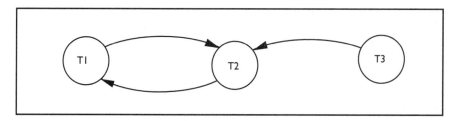

Figure 10.5   Fragment of simple waits-for graph. The cycle T1–T2 represents a deadlock and T3 is waiting for T2.

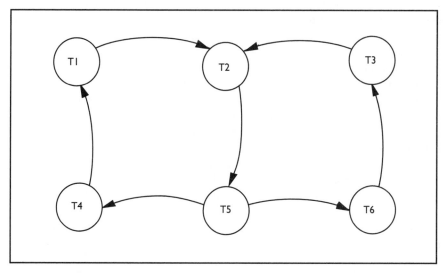

Figure 10.6   Fragment of more complex waits-for graph.

In the simple case a deadlock only involves two transactions; more complex deadlock situations may occur, involving several transactions (as shown in Figures 10.5 and 10.6 respectively).

In the simple case the deadlock may be broken by aborting one of the transactions involved and restarting it. Since it is expensive to abort and restart a transaction it is desirable to abort the one that has done least work. However, if the victim is always the transaction that has done least it is possible that a transaction may be repeatedly aborted and thus prevented from completing. In practice it is generally better to abort the most recent transaction, which is likely to have done least work, and restart it with its original identifier. This scheme ensures that a transaction that is repeatedly aborted will eventually become the oldest active transaction in the system and will eventually complete. We assume that transaction identifiers are a monotonically increasing sequence, for example, based on the system clock value.

In the second case there are two alternatives: to minimize the amount of work done by the transactions to be aborted, or to find the minimal cut-set of the graph and abort the corresponding transactions. The second approach has a number of attractions, but suffers from the problem that finding the minimal cut-set is NP-complete if the waits-for graph is non-planar. This consideration means that repeatedly selecting the youngest transaction involved in a deadlock until there are no deadlocks left provides a practical solution to the resolution of complex deadlock situations.

For example, in Figure 10.6 the minimal solution is to abort T2 or T5, but a simple policy of aborting the youngest victim involved in a deadlock would first abort T6 and then abort T5 to break the remaining deadlock cycle.

The most difficult deadlock detection problem is to detect **global** (or distributed) **deadlock** detection which can occur in distributed systems, where there is a cycle involving several nodes. Many algorithms have been proposed for distributed deadlock detection; we describe a simple version, based on [Gray 1978] and [Obermarck 1982].

A distributed transaction has a number of cohorts, each operating on a separate node of the system. A cohort is a process and so may be in one of a number of states (executing, processor wait, I/O wait, and so on); the states of interest for deadlock detection are session wait (where a cohort is waiting for data from one or more other cohorts) and lock wait.

A deadlock in a distributed system may be either local or global; local deadlocks are handled in the same way as deadlocks in centralized systems. Global deadlock occurs when there is a cycle in the global waits-for graph involving cohorts in session wait and lock wait (Figure 10.7).

Cycles in a distributed waits-for graph are detected through the actions of a designated process at one node which:

1. Periodically requests fragments of local waits-for graph from all other sites;
2. Receives from each site its local graph containing cohorts in session wait;
3. Constructs the global waits-for graph by matching up the local fragments;
4. Selects victims until there are no remaining cycles in the global graph;
5. Broadcasts the result, so that the session managers at the sites coordinating the victims can abort them.

The deadlock detection processes do not have to be synchronized if the list of victims from the previous round of deadlock detection is remembered, since this allows the global deadlock detector to eliminate from the graph any transactions that have previously been aborted.

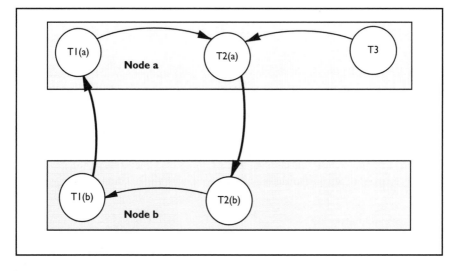

Figure 10.7   Distributed deadlock.

10.4 Other methods of concurrency control

Locking is the most widely used form of concurrency control scheme and is the method of choice for most applications; here we describe the less widely used timestamping and optimistic approaches. Although of limited use for conventional database applications we anticipate that they may be of interest in some highly distributed multimedia and similar areas where locking is difficult to implement efficiently.

10.4.1   Timestamping

A number of methods of concurrency control based on timestamps, first proposed in [Bernstein and Goodman 1980], have been proposed and have been implemented in prototype systems. In timestamp-based concurrency control methods each transaction is assigned a **transaction timestamp**: a monotonically increasing number (often based on the system clock). The transactions are managed so that they appear to run in timestamp order.

Granule timestamps

Each granule accessed by an active transaction must have a **granule timestamp**: a record of the timestamp of the last transaction to access it. A separate record of the last read and write accesses may be kept.

Granule timestamps may cause additional write operations for read accesses if they are stored with the granules. The problem can be avoided by maintaining granule timestamps as an in-memory table; the table may be of limited size, since conflicts may only occur between current transactions. An entry in a granule timestamp table consists of the granule identifier and the transaction timestamp. A record containing the largest (latest) granule timestamp removed from the table is also maintained. A search for a granule timestamp, using the granule identifier, will either be successful or will use the largest removed timestamp.

There are three basic variants of timestamp-based methods: total timestamp ordering, partial timestamp ordering and multiversion timestamp ordering.

Total timestamp ordering

The total timestamp ordering algorithm relies on maintaining access to granules in timestamp order by aborting one of the transactions involved in any conflicting access. No distinction is made between read and write access, so only a single value is required for each granule timestamp.

Partial timestamp ordering

An obvious improvement on the total timestamp ordering algorithm is to only order non-permutable actions. This requires storing both read and write granule timestamps. The algorithm allows the granule to be read by any transaction younger than the last transaction that updated the granule. A transaction is aborted if it tries to update a granule that has previously been accessed by a younger transaction.

This algorithm aborts fewer transactions than the total timestamp ordering algorithm, at the cost of extra storage for granule timestamps.

Conflict resolution

The approach to dealing with conflicts in timestamp algorithms is to make some transactions involved in conflicts wait and to abort others; the main strategies are:

> **Wait-Die**: The older transaction waits for the younger if the younger has accessed the granule first. The younger transaction is aborted (dies) and restarted if it tries to access a granule after an older concurrent transaction.
>
> **Wound-Wait**: The older transaction preempts the younger by suspending (wounding) it if the younger transaction tries to access a granule after an older concurrent transaction. An older transaction will wait for a younger one to commit if the younger has accessed a granule that both want.

The handling of aborted transactions is a significant aspect of this algorithm. In the case that the aborted transaction is the one requesting access it must be restarted with a new (younger) timestamp. It is possible that the transaction can be repeatedly aborted if there are conflicts with other transactions. An aborted transaction that had prior access to a granule where conflict occurred can be restarted with the same timestamp; this will take priority, eliminating the possibility of the transaction being continuously locked out.

Multiversion timestamp ordering

This variant of the scheme stores several versions of an updated granule, allowing transactions to see a consistent set of versions for all granules it accesses and so reduces the conflicts that result in transaction restarts to those where there is a Write-Write conflict.

Each update of a granule creates a new version, with an associated granule timestamp. A transaction that requires read access to the granule sees the youngest version that is older than the transaction (that is, the version with a timestamp equal to or immediately below the transaction's timestamp).

10.4.2 Optimistic concurrency control

Optimistic concurrency control algorithms are based on the notion that conflicts are rare and that it is better to let transactions run to completion and only check for conflicts before they commit. In an optimistic scheme a transaction has three phases:

1. a **Read** phase, where updates are prepared using a private copy of the granule;
2. a **Certification** phase, where the list of granules is checked for conflicts;
3. a **Write** phase, where the updated granules are made public.

If conflicts are detected in the certification phase the transaction is aborted and restarted.

The certification algorithm must check that the transaction has:

1. seen all modifications of transactions committed after its start;
2. not read granules updated by a transaction committed after its start.

It is convenient to allocate a timestamp to each transaction at the end of its Read phase to determine the set of transactions that must be examined by the certification procedure (those transactions that have finished their Read phases since the start of the transaction being verified).

Optimistic concurrency control methods suffer from the problems that:

- conflicts are expensive to deal with, since the conflicting transaction must be rolled back;

- longer transactions are more likely to have conflicts and may be repeatedly rolled back because of conflicts with short transactions.

These considerations suggest that optimistic methods are only suitable for environments where there are few conflicts and no long transactions.

10.5 Long transactions

So far we have assumed that a transaction is a simple linear sequence of actions. This model is inadequate for many applications, particularly in CAx domains. Here we discuss more complex transaction structures. Typically these types of transaction may be large (involving many database objects), computationally intensive, wait for significant user action and can last for hours or days. Transactions with some combination of these characteristics are generically termed **long-lived transactions** (LLTs) [Garcia-Molina and Salem 1987].

In a conventional locking scheme LLTs cause performance problems by locking resources for long periods; they are also more likely to be involved in deadlocks and consequent restarts. Timestamp and optimistic concurrency control schemes have analogous problems.

Many concurrency control schemes have been proposed to address these problems. Solutions are generally sought by a combination of:

- relaxing consistency requirements;
- allowing some other transactions to see uncommitted updates;
- providing more sophisticated transaction control mechanisms (for example, conditional execution);
- utilizing knowledge of the semantics of the transaction to allow more flexible concurrency control.

These are described below.

10.5.1 Reduced consistency requirements

Some types of transaction can execute without the requirement of strict consistency. For example, the result of a transaction counting the number of outpatients for every clinic is not significantly affected by the activity of a concurrent referral transaction. The acceptability of inconsistent reads for many large reporting transactions allows them (in principle) to be run concurrently with conventional transactions.

Current commercial systems generally allow certain transactions to be run with reduced consistency for performance reasons, most often to allow unrepeatable reads, thereby saving the overhead of setting and maintaining read locks.

10.5.2   Using semantic knowledge

The simplest case of increasing concurrency by utilizing semantic knowledge of the database is the case of a source of identifiers or similar sequential values ('id server', 'number fountain', and so on). Here the operation is always to read the current value and then increment the server value; the server never needs to be decremented. A simple latch, to prevent concurrent access to the server, released immediately the server is incremented, is all that is required. Maintaining a lock until end of transaction on resources of this type causes large bottlenecks under any but the lightest transaction loads.

The second straightforward case is that of a high-contention item (typically numeric) whose consistency can be maintained by running a compensating transaction if an earlier updating transaction aborts. Other transactions that update the item between the initial (aborted) transaction and the compensating transaction are not affected by the compensating actions. The action of the compensating transaction must be commutative with the original action, so this type of scheme is generally applicable to quantities that are simply incremented and decremented. These schemes have been developed into an escrow model [O'Neil 1986].

Other schemes utilize:

- Constraints defined on the database to allow controlled relaxation of access restrictions.
- Annotations provided by the programmer to make explicit relaxations of concurrency rules for particular transactions [Salem *et al.* 1994]. The information provided may be of several types:

    1. **complete access** information that describes the complete set of database entities the transaction will access;
    2. **negative access** information that describes database entities that the transaction will not access;
    3. **positive access** information that describes entities that the transaction will access;
    4. **access pattern** information that states rules such as 'T1 will access G1 no more than once per execution'.

    The language used to describe this information must be either one in which the programmer and the concurrency system refer to the same entities (for example, SQL level entities) or one where there is a clear mapping between the entities seen by the programmer and those seen by the concurrency control system. There is an obvious mismatch where the programmer sees the database through SQL entities and the concurrency control system views the database in terms of disk pages.
- Query languages that are semantically richer than current SQL dialects and permit the concurrency controller to reason about the behaviour of a transaction.

There are a number of important open issues and difficult problems with this work.

10.5.3   Access to uncommitted updates

The motivation behind allowing controlled access to uncommitted updates is to maintain throughput in the presence of **long-lived transactions (LLTs)** in environments where there are few LLTs and many short transactions.

The essential feature of uncommitted update schemes is that a large transaction (the **flagship**) proceeds and other transactions follow in its wake (the **flotilla**), utilizing the large transaction's uncommitted updates.[2] The flagship makes its (uncommitted) updated granules available to transactions in the flotilla after it has finished with them.

If a flotilla transaction accesses a granule which is subsequently modified by the flagship it will have seen an inconsistent database (that is, a partial state before the flagship and a partial state after it). To overcome this problem we introduce a rule that flotilla transactions may only reference granules accessed by the flagship. Additional flexibility may be gained by allowing a flotilla transaction to ask the flagship to access granules on its behalf and thereby allow it to proceed without having to wait for the flagship to commit.

If multiple flagships are allowed, the database must contain structures to record the identities of flagships and their flotilla transactions. The flotilla transactions also need the ability to query the flagship's access set and to make access requests through the flagship. The special case where only a single flagship is allowed is described by the black-and-white algorithm (*see* Chapter 11).

Flagship transactions behave like simple transactions towards any transaction outside their wake; the updates of flotilla transactions are invisible to transactions outside that flotilla. Obviously, flagship transactions should not abort if at all possible, since the abort cost includes the cost of aborting every transaction in the flotilla.

Unlike nested transaction schemes, flotilla transactions need have no semantic link with each other or with the flagship.

An accessible example of such a scheme is the altruistic locking proposal described in [Salem *et al.* 1989; Salem *et al.* 1994], which has many of the same underlying concepts as the black-and-white scheme for reading complete (or large parts of) databases proposed in [Pu 1986] and developed to checkpoint memory-resident databases [Salem and Garcia-Molina 1990].

Sagas

Sagas are a simple scheme for LLTs developed by Garcia-Molina [Garcia-Molina and Salem 1987]. Sagas rely on the observation that many LLTs can be broken into

---

2   In this framework a checkpoint can be regarded as a large, system-generated, transaction with smaller, user-generated, transactions following in its wake.

a sequence of relatively independent subtransactions need to see a consistent database, but do not have to see identical versions of the database.

The LLT is broken into a series of subtransactions which each commit atomically and so a saga can be viewed as a nested transaction with exactly two levels of control. The subtransactions can be interleaved with other transactions provided that appropriate compensating transactions are defined, so that if a subtransaction aborts it can be compensated for without having to roll back any other (sub)transactions that have used its results. Ultimately the whole saga is either successfully completed or it is aborted.

The most difficult problem with sagas is to capture the application code needed for redoing transactions in the event of failure. In principle the problem can be overcome by capturing the application code as a BLOB, although there may be a significant performance penalty. Developments of the saga scheme, using database procedures (*see* Chapter 9) and methods (in object-oriented contexts, *see* Chapter 16), are likely.

10.5.4   Nested transactions

Nested transactions are transactions that are composed of series of smaller atomic units of execution: subtransactions. In general, a subtransaction may itself be nested. A number of schemes have been proposed based around such improved control structures.

The general model is that a transaction controls the execution of its subtransactions. A subtransaction either commits or aborts, returning its execution status and results (if any) to the controlling transaction. The controlling transaction may vary its execution, depending on the results of subtransactions. The execution of a group subtransactions may be

- in parallel, that is, there are no dependencies between them, so the order of execution is immaterial;
- in sequence (that is, the execution of a subtransaction is dependent on the results of one or more others).

A number of specific instances of limited nested transaction implementations exist in current commercial systems, although more general facilities are confined to research prototypes.

10.6 Summary

In this chapter we have described many of the core ideas that motivate database consistency. We have described the ACID properties that database systems should meet and how they are commonly implemented using concurrency control schemes based on locking. The latter part of the chapter contains descriptions of alternative implementations of concurrency mechanisms and the issues involved in implementing long transactions.

Exercise

Given a hospital blood bank transaction system which records:

- deliveries of different blood products, in standard units;
- issues of blood products to hospital wards, clinics and operating theatres – assume that each issue is for an identified patient and each unit is uniquely identified;
- returns of unused blood products from hospital wards, and so on.

Describe a concurrency control scheme for this system which allows maximum concurrency, always allows read access to the stock and accurately records the blood products used by each patient.

Chapter 11

RELIABILITY

11.1 Introduction

In this chapter we describe the principal techniques used to maintain the physical consistency of a database, so that transactions can be reliably executed. These techniques are important elements in the construction of high-availability and fault-tolerant systems.

In most database systems the component responsible for these functions is the **recovery manager**. The recovery code is complex to write and difficult to debug and, since it will only be exercised in failure situations, it is essential that it performs correctly.

The aim of the recovery manager is to guarantee the consistency of the physical storage structures and their resilience in the presence of various types of failure, noting that it is impossible to guard against all eventualities. These tasks must have a minimal impact on normal processing.

The chapter is organized as follows. In Section 11.2 we describe the concepts involved in reliability mechanisms. Section 11.3 contains a description of the principal choices involved in log-based recovery schemes, concentrating on recovery mechanisms for centralized systems. Checkpointing methods are described in Section 11.4. In the next section, 11.5, we describe commit protocols for centralized and distributed systems. Disk shadowing, replication and the use of RAID are presented in Section 11.6.

Although we have divided the material into distinct sections for ease of exposition, the reader should bear in mind that the design of a recovery system must simultaneously consider all aspects of the problem, as the elements are all closely interrelated. The performance criteria for a (log-based) recovery system [Reuter 1984] are:

- overhead in normal processing,
- speed of recovery after failure,
- degree of reliability,
- space requirements of log files,
- software complexity of logging and recovery components.

11.2 Basic concepts

11.2.1 Transactions

The essential unit of processing that must be considered for recovery operations is the **atomic transaction**. The actions performed by a transaction are either entirely done or not done. Thus, if a database is in a consistent state before the transaction starts it should be in a consistent state when it finishes. For simplicity, here we view a transaction as a sequence of read and write actions.

This definition implies two outcomes for a transaction:

- *commit*, where the newly written or modified values (*updates*) written by the transaction are incorporated into the database;
- *abort*, where a transaction fails and none of its updates is incorporated into the database. This may be either as a result of a user action or through the operation of a recovery procedure.

For a transaction's updates to be permanent they must be recorded onto *stable storage*, that is, storage where a write is either completely executed or not executed at all. Here we will consider secondary memory (usually disk) to be stable storage.

11.2.2 The storage hierarchy

The essential characteristics of the storage hierarchy were introduced in Chapter 2. For many years the combination of relatively small amounts of main memory, disks (either fixed or removable) and tape as an archiving medium has been almost universal, but the combination of hardware developments and increased demands from a wider range of applications is resulting in a greater variety of configurations. In many cases these developments have no impact on the choices of recovery strategy, but the use of large main memory is likely to have a wider impact.

There have been a number of proposals for recovery systems that involve the use of stable RAM to enhance performance [Copeland *et al.* 1989]; some research prototypes have put these ideas into practice (for example, EDS [Haworth *et al.* 1990]). The increasing availability of large main memory for data storage (hundreds of megabytes are not uncommon in current servers and workstations) brings the possibility that some novel reliability mechanisms may have a distinct performance advantage over conventional techniques. These mechanisms are outlined in Section 11.4.2.

Disk striping, shadowing and parallel disk arrays can make some improvements in the speed of disk accesses and may also improve system reliability; these topics are discussed in Section 11.6 below.

11.2.3 Types of failure

Failures may be classified:

Transaction failure. Occurs when a transaction cannot continue for some reason such as a deadlock situation, an action failure or a concurrency violation. Transaction failures may occur several times a minute and are generally dealt with by aborting and then requeuing the transaction. This type of failure is the easiest to detect and rectify (*see* Chapter 10).

System failure. The contents of main memory are lost as a result of system tables being corrupted, a power failure or other problem that necessitates a system restart.

Media failure. A failure, such as a disk head crash, that results in the complete or partial loss of stable storage. This type of failure is the most serious.

Communications failure. A communications failure may occur when a message is either not delivered or incorrectly delivered. In any distributed system the possibility of messages failing to reach their destination must be allowed for. The problems of ensuring correct delivery of messages are outside the scope of this chapter.

11.2.4 Frequency of failure

The expected frequency of failures, the severity of their consequences and the applications' requirements together determine the acceptable costs that should be incurred in avoiding or reducing any particular type of failure.

The figures in Table 11.1 give an approximate idea of the failure rates that may be expected from contemporary hardware.

Component	Failures / 10^6 hours
Memory	1.2
Processor	2.0
Cabinet	5.0
Network	10.3
Power Supply	24.9
Disk	25.0[1]

Table 11.1 Hardware component failure rates.

1 Based on manufacturer's data for an Imprimis Wren VIII 1.2Gb SCSI disk. There are several methods used by manufacturers to calculate or estimate these figures; for example, Digital quote an MTBF of 500,000 hours for their DSP3100 series disks.

We will assume (for simplicity) that failure rates are independent and that each node in a system contains a processor, memory, a disk, cabinet and power supply. In this case the expected failure rates for systems of varying sizes are shown in Table 11.2. These figures illustrate the importance of designing complex systems so that they are minimally impacted by failures.

No. nodes	Failures / 10^6 hours	MTBF (days)
1	68	610
4	153	272
16	491	85
64	1812	23
256	6944	6

Table 11.2   System failure rates.

The assumptions used for these illustrations are very simple; in practice, failures are rarely independent and recovery mechanisms must allow for multiple failures and for failures during the recovery process.

11.3 Log-based recovery

Any recovery mechanism must record all updates in stable storage before the transaction commits, but must also retain all the previous values in case the transaction aborts. All commercial systems achieve this through the use of a log, in which before-images and after-images are recorded, providing the data duplication needed for recovery.

A log may record transactions (operations), objects (logical structures) or pages (physical state). We assume that pages are the unit of logging, in line with common practice.

Logging is generally coupled to an **update in place** discipline, where the system contains a single permanent copy of each item in stable storage. This minimizes the storage space needed for the database, in contrast to shadowing schemes which maintain a duplicate copy of the database.

The basic processing model is that a transaction reads pages from stable storage into buffers (slots) in memory where they are updated. A record of the updates is written to the log file. When the transaction commits, its log records are forced to stable storage and its locks are released, making its updates visible to other transactions.

The buffer pool is an area of memory controlled by the buffer manager, which handles all requests for pages. The buffer manager fetches pages from disk as required, typically using a least recently used (LRU) discipline to free buffers. Dirty (modified) pages are flushed to disk.

Within this basic framework a number of trade-offs are possible to improve various aspects of the basic scheme.

In the remainder of this section we describe the principal elements and operations of logging schemes in more detail.

11.3.1   Data structures

A log file is used to record the progress of transactions. The data structures it may contain are:

> **Before-image**. The page value before update, tagged with the transaction identifier.
>
> **After-image**. The page value after update, tagged with the transaction identifier. This is often stored as a differential image (that is, only the differences with the previous value are stored) to minimize the storage overhead of the log file. A single page may become several pages after update. For simplicity, we assume that it is a single page, as the extensions for multiple pages are conceptually straightforward.
>
> **Begin-transaction record**. An entry that records the start of a transaction, containing the transaction's identifier and timestamp.
>
> **Commit record**. An entry showing that a transaction has committed and all its updates have been copied to stable storage.
>
> **Abort record**. An entry showing that a transaction was aborted.
>
> **System checkpoint**. Consistent state of the database (including execution state information such as the contents of memory, file pointers and program states) stored on secondary storage which can be used to restore database consistency.
>
> **Backup copy**. Complete consistent copy of a database, usually stored on an archival medium. Used in the recovery from media failures.

11.3.2   Recovery procedures

There are three sets of recovery operations that a recovery manager must implement:

Normal recovery. A restart after normal system termination. In this case the last record on the log is a checkpoint and the job of the recovery algorithm is simply to restore the execution state of the system.

Warm recovery. A restart after a system failure (that is, memory contents have been lost). All committed updates are preserved on stable storage. The job of the recovery algorithm in this case is to restore the system to its state at the last checkpoint and then to process the log, incorporating the effects of all committed transactions and eliminating any updates of uncommitted transactions.

Cold recovery. Recovery after a media failure which involves starting from a backup copy of the database and applying the log to it to reach the last consistent database state.

In the case of disasters, automatic methods of recovery are not feasible and the database administrator must reconstruct the database from a backup copy, the application of whatever portion of the log is available and suitable manual transactions to test and restore the database's consistency and integrity.

11.3.3 Recovery manager operations

The recovery manager must implement five basic operations:

Begin (T)	Records the start of transaction T
Read (T, P, B)	Reads page P into buffer B for T
Write (T, P, B)	Writes buffer B into page P for T
Commit (T)	Commits T
Abort (T)	Aborts T
Restart	Invokes the recovery mechanisms to restore the database after a system failure.

These operations must be atomic with respect to each other. Additionally restart operations must be idempotent, so that the partial execution of one or more restart operations followed by a complete execution of a restart operation is equivalent to a single complete execution of the restart operation on that database.

11.3.4 Recovery algorithms

From the perspective of a recovery procedure transactions fall into five types (shown in Figure 11.1):

1. Transactions committed before the last checkpoint;
2. Transactions that started before the last checkpoint, but committed before the system failure;
3. Transactions started before the last checkpoint and still in progress when the system failed;
4. Transactions started after last the checkpoint and committed before the system failure;
5. Transactions started after last the checkpoint and in progress when the system failed.

At each checkpoint the records of committed transactions (T1) can be removed from the 'active' part of the log, since they do not participate in recovery from system failures. They are kept in the archive log, where they are still needed for cold recovery.

There are several algorithms for recovery, which may be characterized by whether or not they require undo and redo transactions to recover from system failures. This results in four categories: Undo/Redo, Undo/No-redo, No-undo/Redo, No-undo/No-redo. All four types are feasible and are considered in more detail below.

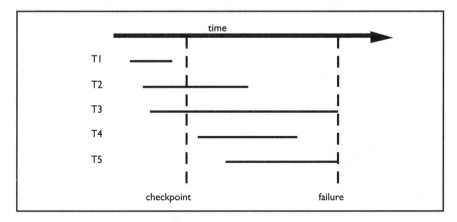

Figure 11.1   Transaction types for recovery processing.

UNDO/REDO

The strength of this algorithm, which is used by most systems, is that it allows dirty pages to be flushed to disk before, during or after commit. The scheduling of disk writes is left to the buffer manager.

This algorithm optimizes the normal case at the expense of abort and recovery processing.

Recovery using this algorithm proceeds as follows:

Create two empty lists: UNDO and REDO

1. Read the log file backwards to the last checkpoint.
2. Put all transactions that were active then on the UNDO list (T2, T3).
3. Read the log forwards:

   • Remove transaction T from the UNDO list and put it on the REDO list if a commit record is found for it.
   • Add transaction T to the UNDO list if a begin-transaction record is found.

   At the end of this, the UNDO list contains T3, T5 and the REDO list contains T2, T4.
4. Use the before-images to undo the updates of all transactions on the UNDO list.
5. Use the after-images to redo the updates of all transactions on the REDO list.

UNDO/No-REDO

This strategy flushes all dirty pages to stable storage before commit, thereby avoiding the need to redo a transaction during recovery processing as no updated pages can be lost.

The principal features of the algorithm are:

- After-images are not needed in the log.
- Restart is cheap, as updates of committed transactions cannot be lost as a result of system failure.
- Since all updates must be flushed before commit, writes cannot be buffered, so normal processing is more costly.
- Aborting a transaction is expensive, as it means undoing updates that have been flushed to disk.

The principal steps in recovery processing are:

Create an empty list: UNDO
1. Read the log file backwards to the last checkpoint.
2. Put all transactions that were active then on the UNDO list (T2, T3).
3. Read the log forwards:

- Remove transaction T from the UNDO list if a commit record is found for it.
- Add transaction T to the UNDO list if a begin-transaction record is found.

At the end of this, the UNDO list contains T3, T5.
4. Use the before-images to undo the updates of all transactions on the UNDO list.

No-UNDO/REDO

If dirty pages are never flushed to disk before a transaction commits, it is never necessary to UNDO a transaction. This strategy makes transaction aborts cheap, as the after-images are simply discarded; for this reason it is the normal choice for optimistic concurrency control algorithms, which tend to abort transactions frequently.

The principal features of the algorithm are:

- Before-images are not needed in the log.
- Aborts are cheap, as after-images are all in memory and are simply discarded.
- Recovery procedure may have to REDO transactions as dirty pages may not have been written to disk before failure.

Recovery using this algorithm proceeds as follows:

Create an empty list: REDO
1. Read the log file backwards to the last checkpoint:

- Put transaction T on the REDO list if a commit record is found for it.

At the end of this the REDO list contains T2, T4.
2. Use the after-images to redo the updates of all transactions on the REDO list.

No-UNDO/No-REDO

This algorithm relies on maintaining shadow copies of all uncommitted updates in stable storage, using two lists (directories) pointing to the current and shadow copies. A transaction is committed by changing the pointer from the current directory (before-images) to the shadow directory (after-images). Shadowing techniques are described further in Section 11.6.

This strategy results in inexpensive recovery processing and transaction aborts, but at the cost of more expensive normal processing. For this reason it is rarely considered.

11.4 Checkpointing

The purpose of checkpointing operations is to provide a snapshot of the database state from which the recovery manager can operate. Since the checkpoints provide the starting point for the recovery operations the frequency with which they are taken is an important cost consideration.

11.4.1 Checkpointing for disk-based systems

The classification of checkpointing strategies is fully described in [Haerder and Reuter 1983]. The type of checkpoint taken is linked to other aspects of the recovery architecture (analysed by [Reuter 1984] and [Agrawal and DeWitt 1985]). All checkpointing strategies start by writing a BEGIN-CHECKPOINT record to the log, followed by the checkpoint information; the checkpoint is finished by writing an END-CHECKPOINT record.

Transaction-consistent checkpoints (TCC)

This checkpointing strategy requires that the database is quiesced – executing update transactions are allowed to finish and new ones are not allowed to start. All modified pages in the buffer pool are written to the database and the checkpoint is then complete. Recovery operations never have to go back further than the latest end-checkpoint record.

Although this strategy is attractive its costs rule it out for most applications. In a large system the time to quiesce the system and then write the dirty pages to disk will be excessive. For instance, in a system performing 100 tps with two dirty pages per transaction a checkpoint every 30 seconds will need to write up to 6,000 pages to the database, to which must be added the time for all existing transactions to complete; these actions may easily result in a delay of several seconds. However, the simplicity of the scheme makes it attractive for small, low-volume systems.

Action-consistent checkpoints (ACC)

A transaction can be viewed as a series of actions operating on records. In this strategy the database is quiesced with relation to update actions at the start of the checkpoint. The strategy is similar to TCC, except that the system only waits for existing actions to complete before starting to write the dirty pages to the database.

The strategy limits the amount of REDO processing required, but UNDO information must be retained for all transactions in progress when the checkpoint is taken. The costs of this strategy can still be unacceptable if there are large numbers of dirty pages.

Fuzzy checkpoints

The most widely used variant of this strategy entails writing the identifiers and status (modified or not) of every page in the buffer pool to the log file. Only if a modified page is found in the buffer on two successive checkpoints is it written to the database. This technique limits the REDO information to two checkpoint intervals.

Since recovery is a relatively rare event and this technique imposes a minimal overhead on normal processing it has been widely adopted.

11.4.2   Checkpointing for memory-resident systems

The use of large memory for database systems increases the importance of I/O operations for logging and recovery operations, since they form a larger proportion of the total I/O performed. Although any recovery strategy that works for a disk-based system will also work for a memory-based system it is unlikely to be optimal. The System M prototype was built to explore a number of these issues [Salem and Garcia-Molina 1990]. We briefly describe two approaches designed to reduce the overhead of logging activities.

Stable memory

The first approach is to include a portion of stable memory in the system (typically implemented as battery-backed RAM) which is both fast and stable. The stable memory is then used as a write cache from which pages can be written to disk. The idea is generally accepted and is being implemented in some systems, although there is little experience reported in the literature.

The important implementation issues for stable memory are: ensuring that the backup power supply is sufficiently independent of other components to function properly, and ensuring that the contents of stable memory cannot easily be overwritten by rogue software.

Black-white checkpointing

This group of checkpointing algorithms constitute the most promising approach to the problem of efficient checkpointing for memory-based systems. The approach involves attaching to each page[2] in memory:

- a paint bit,
- one or two dirty bits.

The number of dirty bits depends on whether one or two copies of the database are maintained on disk. Maintaining a single copy implies fuzzy checkpointing, since a failure during checkpointing may leave the database in an inconsistent state; action or transaction consistent checkpoints are possible if two disk copies are maintained [Salem and Garcia-Molina 1990]. A transaction sets the dirty bit(s) when it modifies a page.

Assuming that the paint bit is 'white' to start with, the checkpointing algorithm proceeds as follows:

Write a BEGIN-CHECKPOINT record to the log.

For every segment:

1. Lock a segment
2. If the dirty bit is set, flush the segment to disk.
3. Clear the dirty bit (if it is set).
4. Make the paint bit 'black'.
5. Unlock the segment.

Write an END-CHECKPOINT record to the log.

If two disk copies of the database are maintained an update sets both and each checkpoint clears one bit. The two copies of the disk database are updated with successive checkpoints, thus ensuring that any update is propagated to both disk copies. The identity of the most recently updated disk copy must be kept in a safe place.

In order to avoid blocking, transactions (or actions) may be active, accessing only 'black' or only 'white' segments. Transactions preceding the checkpoint that try to access 'black' segments are aborted; those in the wake of the checkpoint wanting to access 'white' segments are blocked.

---

2   We retain the term for consistency – segment is more generally used.

11.5 Commit protocols

11.5.1 Distributed transactions

So far we have implicitly assumed a single centralized process, where the commit action involves a single write to stable storage. In order to deal with transaction commit for a distributed system additional mechanisms are needed.

If a transaction performs updates at several sites mechanisms are needed to ensure that:

- the transaction fragment executing at each site is atomic (this is the same requirement as for a single site transaction);
- all transaction fragments of a single transaction are either committed or aborted.

The essence of the problem is that reliable communication cannot be guaranteed between sites, so there is no certainty that any message will be received. (We assume that the communications protocol ensures the correctness of a delivered message.)

The generally accepted solution to the problem is a protocol called **Two-Phase Commit** (2PC).

In order to synchronize the commit operations at each site we designate one site as the coordinator.

The coordinator distributes the query fragments, which are executed at each site participating in the transaction. When the coordinator is ready it sends a PREPARE-TO-COMMIT message to all participants (which may be piggybacked onto the transaction fragment). This is the **precommit** stage of the protocol.

As each participant finishes its processing it replies with either a READY-TO-COMMIT or a NOT-READY message. A participant must be able to recover from any failure before it can issue its READY message, by ensuring that concurrency requirements are satisfied and writing all necessary log records, ending with a READY record.

If every participant replies READY-TO-COMMIT the coordinator records the decision in its log and broadcasts a COMMIT message.

In the event that any participant replies not-ready or fails to reply within a specified time the coordinator records the decision in its log and broadcasts an ABORT message.

After broadcasting the decision the coordinator records END-COMMIT in its log.

The failures that may occur are:

1. A participant fails before receiving the PREPARE-TO-COMMIT message. The coordinator will abort the transaction as it will receive no message before the timeout.
2. A participant fails after sending a READY-TO-COMMIT message. When it recovers it must resend the READY-TO-COMMIT and the coordinator will inform it of the decision.

3. The coordinator fails after sending PREPARE-TO-COMMIT but before receiving READY-TO-COMMIT. When the coordinator recovers it sends the PREPARE-TO-COMMIT message again and the participants reply appropriately.
4. The coordinator fails after recording the decision in its log but before END-COMMIT. Not all participants may have received the decision, so it is broadcast again to allow the participants to terminate.

11.5.2   Commit for large transactions

Large transactions, locking many pages (possibly for a long time), are likely to cause significant resource contention, leading to a large number of deadlocks and blocked transactions. This results in a significant deterioration in system throughput.

From the perspective of the recovery manager large transactions may be generated by a user or by the system. A number of types of event, which we term **flagship** events, fall into this classification:

- system checkpoints,
- group commit,
- long transactions,
- nested transactions.

We can take a common view of them since they all share the characteristic of having a **flotilla** of dependants which can see uncommitted updates (or updates which have not been written to stable storage) in the wake of the flagship. If the flagship aborts or fails because of a system failure all the transactions in the flotilla must also be aborted.

The generalized log entries for a flotilla are:

begin-flagship (F)   Begin record for a flagship transaction

The flagship's own reads and writes may be treated in the same way as those of ordinary transactions.

begin (T)	Transaction begin (non-flagship)
in-flotilla (T, F)	Log record locating a transaction in a flotilla.
commit-flagship (F)	or abort-flagship(F)

The recovery processing depends on the other aspects of the recovery architecture, but consistency can be maintained by UNDOing the effects of a flagship and its dependants, although this is obviously wasteful, making a REDO discipline more attractive.

Nested transactions

A nested transaction consists of a high-level transaction which initiates sub-transactions, each of which commits or aborts atomically, making its updates visible to the rest of the nested transaction. A transaction may dynamically initiate a series of subtransactions. The sequence may depend on the results of other subtransactions.

In the event of the main transaction aborting, the effects of other subtransactions must be undone by a series of compensating transactions. These transactions can be prepared by the system, using before-images and record-level update statements.

An obvious example for this type of processing is a travel-agency booking which involves several airlines and hotel reservations. The precise itinerary will depend on the availability of airline and hotel places, so the sequence of subtransactions cannot be determined until run time. The nested transaction model is also a useful approach for implementing triggers and rule systems.

This outline shows how a nested transaction forms a large transaction with the subtransactions in its wake.

Group commit

The basic model described in Section 11.2 was developed for systems running small transactions, using a simple write-ahead logging rule. A small transaction of this type (such as those of the TPC-A and TPC-B benchmark transactions [Serlin 1991]) typically does 3–4 page reads or writes which generate 400 bytes of log data. Assuming that writing this log data takes 10 ms (the time to write a 4Kb page without a disk seek), using a single log device, the transaction throughput is restricted to 100 tps[3] [DeWitt *et al.* 1984].

The observation behind group commit is that it is possible to buffer log records until they fill a page; the cost of writing that page is then shared by several transactions. Database consistency is maintained if the log records are written in strict commit order and, in the example above, theoretical throughput could rise to 1000 tps.

In this case the log buffering effectively forms a large system transaction which contains the group of user transactions in its wake.

11.6 Shadowing and replication

In a conventional computer system each functional unit – power supply, processor, disk controller, disks, communications links, and so on – represents a potential single point of failure (Figure 11.2). If any one unit fails the entire system may be unusable until it is replaced. The backup and recovery mechanisms discussed so far in this chapter enable a stable state to be restored once a failed unit has been replaced, but the delays incurred in replacing hardware and restoring software or data may be unacceptably long.

---

3   Transactions per second.

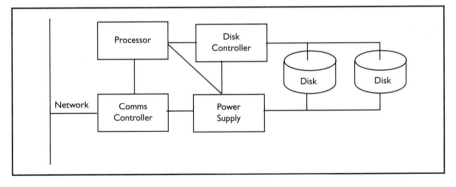

Figure 11.2 Conventional computer system. (Every component represents a point of failure.)

Backup and recovery mechanisms are a secondary component of reliable systems. Secure air-conditioned machine rooms, backup power generators and carefully designed operational procedures have long been employed as a first line of defence for mainframe and minicomputer installations. In this section we focus on primary reliability, methods of minimizing the risk of time-consuming failures. This is an extensive topic, much of which is beyond the scope of this book (for a detailed discussion of the problems and one manufacturer's solutions, *see* [DEC 1991]). Here we concentrate on the reliability of secondary storage devices.

In Section 11.2 we noted that disk drives are one of the least reliable components of a system. Database files and log system files are typically stored on separate devices so that, in the event of failure of either disk, disruptions can be minimized. Indeed the files used by the logging and recovery systems may be split over two or more disks, and may include on-line backups of the database.

Primary reliability can be improved by providing duplicate disks for each function. All disk write operations must then update both disks before signalling their completion. In some cases increased read performance can be achieved because read requests need only be serviced once and can be divided between the identical devices.

This technique is known variously as replication, mirroring or shadowing. Although it could be performed by a DBMS, the replication of storage is best handled at the operating system or device driver level. After all, replication of the database disks may reduce recovery time but is of little help if any of the disks serving the operating system or important system utilities fails.

If spare disks are kept on site failed units can be swapped with minimal disruption of service. It may be necessary to close the machine while the disks are changed, although 'hot swapping' may be possible. Rebuilding the file store on the replacement unit may also be automated.

The reliability of disk systems can be further enhanced by providing separate controllers for each set of disks (Figure 11.3). This configuration is capable of surviving the failure of a single disk or controller. Some systems employ 'dual-ported' disks that can be connected to two controllers. If a pair of controllers is used to service each set of disks (Figure 11.4), simultaneous failures of disk and controller become survivable.

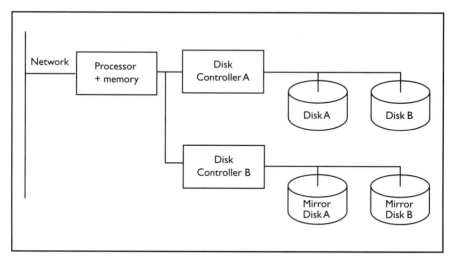

Figure 11.3 Multiple controllers and disk mirroring reduce the likelihood of total disk system failure. (In this case the system can survive the failure of any single disk or of either disk controller.)

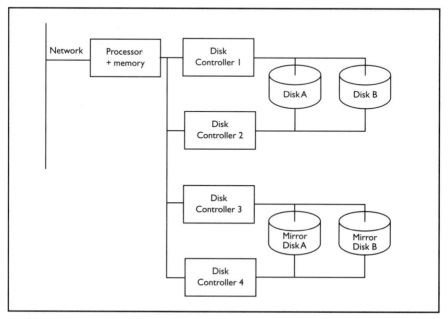

Figure 11.4 Dual-ported disks with multiple controllers further enhance fault tolerance. (In this configuration the failure of a disk and controller can be tolerated.)

The only way to eliminate single points of failure is to use redundant units throughout the system; in other words, to eliminate all single points. Each functional unit is duplicated, and each is capable of remaining fully operational should its duplicate unit fail (Figure 11.5). Provided that a failed unit can be replaced before its partner fails, the system remains operational. This approach leads to a fault-tolerant system capable of continuous operation in the event of single, and some multiple, failures.

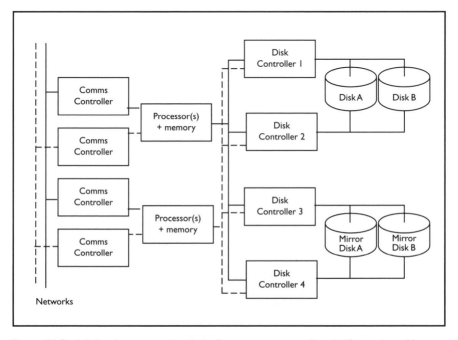

Figure 11.5   A fault-tolerant system in which all components are replicated. (Connection cables between processors and disk controllers may also be replicated.)

The approach can be extended to distributed systems. Redundant nodes can be added to a network with the express purpose of shadowing other nodes, or existing nodes can shadow each other as part of their normal function. Of course, the network itself must include multiple physical circuits and each node should be equipped with additional network adapters.

Shadowing with large disk units is expensive. Although their performance in terms of speed, capacity and price continues to improve, it does so at a much slower rate than the performance of processor and memory subsystems. With the ever increasing demands on storage performance of modern database applications, disk units frequently impose a limit to overall system throughput.

The problem of differential rates of improvement in subsystem performance has long been recognized [Amdahl 1967], and much effort has been devoted to techniques for alleviating the disk I/O bottleneck. Main memory buffering of I/O is often employed by the operating system, but this is of little benefit to database systems with high volumes of small transactions, or indeed, those with low volumes of very large transactions.

Small transactions lead to a quite random pattern of reading with a consequent low hit rate on cached data. Very large transactions may require data volumes that are too big to fit in a cache and so each must be fetched directly from disk. Similarly with output, each transaction must be physically flushed to stable storage. It is not acceptable for a logging system to mark a transaction as committed if its updates are waiting in a buffer.

Another approach to improving disk performance is 'striping', in which single read and write operations are distributed over several devices. For example, a single 2Kb data page might be split into four 512-byte units, each of which is written to a different disk. The limitation on throughput is now that of the disk controller and disk subsystem as a whole, rather than that of any individual disk drive. Striping can achieve significant performance improvements, but in a fault-tolerant system the costs of the increased numbers of disks and controllers can be high.

11.6.1 Redundant Arrays of Inexpensive Disks (RAID)

The performance of disks intended for small computers is in some respects comparable to, or even better than, disks used on larger systems [Patterson *et al.* 1988]. They compared the 3.5 inch diameter Conner CP3100 100Mb SCSI disk with the 7.5Gb IBM 3380 mainframe disk and the 600Mb Fujitsu 'Super Eagle' minicomputer disk. On measures such as power consumption and price per megabyte, the SCSI disk was better than the larger units. Claimed failure rates were comparable, and the data transfer rate of the small disk was about one third of that of the larger disks.

Based on these figures, they noted that an array of 75 100Mb disks would provide equivalent capacity to the large IBM unit, but with twelve times the I/O bandwidth as well as lower cost and power consumption. However, the anticipated failure rate of a subsystem containing large numbers of disks would be unacceptably high.

These factors led Patterson and his colleagues to propose five 'levels' of Redundant Arrays of Inexpensive Disks (RAID). The levels are distinguished by the method of distribution of data across a group of disks and the way in which error correcting information is stored (Table 11.3). The use of redundant disks at each level improves the expected failure time for the subsystem to figures well beyond its useful life.

RAID techniques are not limited to mainframe and minicomputer installations. In the past few years microcomputer networks have become increasingly powerful and widespread; these trends are surveyed in [Chen *et al.* 1994]. Recent releases of network operating systems from both Novell and Microsoft include support for RAID systems on servers. The capacity and performance of small SCSI disks continues to improve, and a number of specialist hardware suppliers now offer arrays employing 3.5 inch disks with individual capacities of 1Gb or more.

The RAID Levels

Level 1 uses simple disk mirroring or shadowing as described earlier in this section. This approach is equally suited to large reads and small transactions, but carries a high overhead in additional storage capacity.

Level 2 systems use bit interleaving of data across all data disks, thus a single read or write operation involves a read or write to all data disks. In addition, a Hamming code is used for error correction. To be able to locate and correct single errors a group of ten data disks requires an additional four disks to hold the ECC. Much of the error-correcting information stored by a Level 2 system is used to locate which disk has failed. The disk controller is usually quite capable of detecting a failure by comparing data with error-correcting information stored with each data sector.

Level 3 uses a single parity disk to correct a failure. The missing data can be recovered by a bitwise comparison between the original parity sum and one calculated from the surviving disks.

Level 4 again uses a single parity disk but unlike Levels 2 and 3 does not employ bit interleaving. Instead it allows independent read and write operations on each data disk. Read performance is improved because small reads involve only a single disk, and large reads can take place in parallel across the group. Each write operation now involves only one data disk and the parity disk as the new parity value can be calculated from the previous value and the new data. Write operations on a Level 4 array must be performed sequentially because each must update the single parity disk.

Level 5 lifts this restriction by spreading parity information evenly across all data disks. There is no longer a separate disk for error checking as all disks are now both data and check disks. With this arrangement writes still involve two disks, but several writes can take place in parallel if they use different disks for data and parity.

The performance of Level 5 approaches that of Level 1 for small transaction-based applications. Levels 3 and 4 are not suited to this type of application because of their limited write performance. Levels 3, 4 and 5 provide somewhat better performance for large reads than Level 1. Level 2 has little to recommend it and is usually only included in discussions for completeness.

RAID level	Method	Usable capacity as %age of total	Cost overhead of extra disks (group size =10)
1	Simple mirroring	50%	100%
2	Bit interleaving plus check disks	40%	71%
3	Bit interleaving with single parity disk	91%	10%
4	Independent read/write to each data disk	91%	10%
5	Check data spread over all disks	91%	10%

Table 11.3   RAID levels 1–5 showing the usable capacity as a percentage of total capacity for small disks in groups of 10.

11.7 Summary

In this chapter we described software techniques used to ensure the physical consistency of a database by enabling recovery from failures, as well as hardware configurations that can help to minimize the risk of serious failures. We began by introducing the central concept of a transaction and its two possible outcomes, **commit** or **abort**. A successful transaction is committed by permanently recording all of its updates on stable storage. When a failed transaction is aborted none of its updates are stored.

We then described the types and frequencies of failure and emphasized the inevitability of failure in any complex system.

Section 11.3 introduced the techniques of **log-based recovery** in which a **log file** is used to record transaction progress. Next we described four categories of recovery algorithms characterized by whether or not they UNDO and REDO transactions. The **checkpoint**, a static snapshot of the state of the database, provides a starting point for recovery operations. Checkpointing strategies for both disk-based and memory-resident systems were described in Section 11.4.

Next we returned to the transaction concept to consider the special problems of commit operations for distributed systems. Here we introduced the widely used **Two-Phase Commit** protocol used to synchronize commit and abort when a transaction is distributed over two or more sites. Section 11.5 also included discussion of several categories of large transactions and presented a general model for a suitable commit strategy.

The ability to recover from failure is fundamental to a reliable system. Many applications, however, also require high availability and need to minimize interruptions due to hardware failures. In Section 11.6 we described the use of redundant hardware components in a **fault-tolerant** system. This discussion concentrated on disk storage systems and led to a description of **RAID** both as a low-cost form of reliable storage and as a means of improving disk I/O performance.

Chapter 12

QUERY PROCESSING

12.1 Introduction

This chapter first describes techniques used to split complex queries into multiple simple operations. Next we describe methods of implementing these low-level operations. The efficiency of query processing algorithms is crucial to the performance of a DBMS. There are many different ways in which a complex query can be performed and in the second half of the chapter we concentrate on optimization techniques used to choose an efficient execution plan. The discussion is couched in relational terms (since this is where most of the development of query processing techniques has been done), although it is generally applicable to other types of system that have a high-level language interface.

In order to deal satisfactorily with the more complex and demanding queries of many emerging database applications the techniques used for the current generation of relational systems will have to be extended and enhanced: '... query processing algorithms and software will become more complex and a solid understanding of algorithm and architectural issues is essential...' [Graefe 1993].

Non-procedural languages such as SQL specify the result, not how to obtain that result. In the DBMS the high-level statement is transformed into an **execution plan** that contains the detailed sequence of actions to obtain the result. The problem of deciding the optimal query plan is NP-complete in the number of relations, with the additional complication that for some operations (notably join) there is usually a choice of several algorithms, each of which is efficient for certain types of problem.

The function of a query processor is to transform a high-level query into an execution plan that performs the required retrievals and manipulations. These activities can be divided into three main phases: decomposition, optimization and execution.

12.2 Query decomposition

The query decomposition phase of query processing starts with a high-level query and transforms it into a graph of low-level operations which will satisfy the query.
  The stages of query decomposition are most conveniently enumerated as:

1. **Analysis**. The query is lexically and syntactically analysed in the same way as a conventional programming language. These processes are described fully in texts on compiler design (for example, [Aho and Ullman 1977]; [Levine *et al.* 1992]). A syntactically legal query is then validated, using the system catalogues, to ensure that all the database objects referred to by the query are in the database; the type specification of the query qualifiers and result is also checked at this stage.
2. **Normalization**. The normalization phase rewrites the query into a normal form which can be readily manipulated in later steps. Disjunctive normal form is most often used, as it allows the query to be broken into a series of independent subqueries linked by unions. In practice the query is usually held as a graph structure by the query processor.
3. **Semantic analysis**. It is relatively easy to analyse a normalized query to detect any contradictory clauses. The purpose of this phase of query processing is to reduce the number of predicates that must be evaluated by refuting incorrect or contradictory queries or qualifications.
4. **Simplification**. Further analysis of the query graph can detect redundant qualifications, eliminate common sub-expressions and transform sub-graphs to semantically equivalent but more easily computed forms. Commonly integrity constraints, view definitions and access restrictions are introduced into the graph at this stage of the analysis, so that the query can be simplified as much as possible. Integrity constraints define constants which must hold for all states of the database, so any query that contradicts an integrity constraint must be void and can be rejected without accessing the database. Queries expressed in terms of views can be simplified by substituting the view definition, since this will avoid having to materialize the view before evaluating the query predicate on it. A query that violates an access restriction cannot have an answer returned to the user, so can be answered without accessing the database. The final form of simplification is obtained by applying the idempotence rules of Boolean algebra:

   $$A \wedge \neg A \equiv \bot$$
   $$\neg (A \vee B) \equiv \neg A \wedge \neg B$$
   $$A \vee \bot \equiv A$$

   where the symbol $\bot$ is the value false and $\equiv$ denotes logical equivalence.
5. **Query restructuring**. In the final phase of query decomposition the query can be restructured to give a more efficient implementation. The query can now

be regarded as a relational algebra program, consisting of a series of operations on relations. This program can be transformed into a tree where:

- a leaf represents a base relation;
- an internal node represents an intermediate relation which is the result of applying an operation in the algebra;
- the root represents the result;
- data flows from the leaves to the root.

12.2.1   Query restructuring

Query restructuring rules

Restructuring rules can then be applied to this tree. Proofs and further discussion of restructuring rules are given in [Ullman 1988]. Here we will restrict ourselves to the principal restructuring rules concerned with restriction, projection and join operations.

1. Commutativity of joins

$R \bowtie S \equiv S \bowtie R$
that is, the order in which relations are specified in joins does not affect the result.

2. Associativity of joins

$(R \bowtie S) \bowtie T \equiv (S \bowtie T) \bowtie R$
that is, the order of evaluation of a series of joins does not affect the result.

3. Grouping of restrictions

$\sigma_{R(a)-x}$ *and* $\sigma_{R(b)-y} \equiv \sigma_{R(a)-x \wedge R(b)-y}$

that is, the result of a series of separate restrictions is the same as that obtained by grouping all the restrictions together.

4. Commuting restriction with projection

$\sigma_{R(a)=x}$ *and* $\pi_{R(a,b,c)} \equiv \pi_{R(a,b,c)}$ *and* $\sigma_{R(a)=x}$

that is, the result of a restriction followed by a projection is equivalent to a projection followed by a restriction, assuming that the attribute(s) defining the restriction are also in the projection.

5. Commuting restriction and joi

$R \bowtie S$ *and* $\sigma_{R(a)=x} \equiv \sigma_{R(a)=x}$ *and* $R \bowtie S$

that is, a join followed by a restriction is equivalent to a restriction followed by a join.

6. Commuting projection and join

$R \bowtie S$ *and* $\pi_{R(a,b,c)} \equiv \pi_{R(a,b,c)}$ *and* $R \bowtie S$

that is, a join followed by a projection is equivalent to a projection followed by a join, assuming that the join attributes are included in the projection.

7. Grouping of projections

$\pi_{R(a,b,c,d)}$ *and* $\pi_{R(a,b,c)} \equiv \pi_{R(a,b,c)}$

that is, the result of a series of separate projections is the same as that obtained by grouping all the projections together.

Query restructuring algorithms

Query restructuring algorithms rely on heuristics to produce a relational algebra tree that is likely to minimize the work done by the database. In this phase of query processing no reference is made to any physical characteristics of the database (query selectivity, attribute distributions, physical organization, and so on).

The most common heuristic is to push restriction and projection before join wherever possible. The justification for this is that projection and restriction reduce the size of the intermediate results and so reduce the cost of subsequent operations. Using this heuristic the steps in the query restructuring process are:

1. Apply Rule 3 to separate restrictions involving several predicates into series of restrictions each using a single predicate.
2. Apply Rules 4 and 5 to push restrictions as far down the query tree as possible.
3. Apply Rule 3 again to group sequences of restrictions.
4. Push projections down the query tree using Rule 6.
5. Group sequences of projections using Rule 7.

Other rules, covering union, difference, semijoin, and so on, can also be applied in a similar way. Rules 1 and 2 are not used at this stage, since the most efficient ordering of joins requires information about the relative sizes of the input relations.

Most query processors can recognize a common sub-expression, since the query execution plan is not a tree, but a directed acyclic graph. The usual approach is to execute the common sub-expression separately and save the results in a temporary file. This temporary file is deleted after the last query fragment has used it. This approach avoids multiple evaluations of the same expression.

12.3 Cost evaluation

The cost of an operation is heavily dependent on its selectivity, that is, the proportion of the input relation(s) that forms the output. In general, different algorithms are suitable for low-and high-selectivity queries. In order for the query optimizer to choose a suitable algorithm for an operation an estimate of the cost of executing that algorithm must be provided. The cost of an algorithm is dependent on the cardinality of its inputs.

To estimate the costs of different query execution strategies we view the query tree as containing a series of basic operations which are linked in order to perform the query. Each basic operation has an associated cost function whose argument(s) are the cardinality of its input(s). It is also important to know the expected cardinality of an operation's output, since this forms the input to the next operation in the tree. The expected cardinalities are derived from statistical estimates of a query's selectivity, that is, the proportion of tuples satisfying the query. These statistics are usually referred to as **optimization statistics**.

Optimization statistics

The number of tuples satisfying a condition is determined by:

- the number of distinct values of the attribute(s) concerned,
- the distribution of those values,
- correlations between attributes.

For instance, in a Patient table there are many more values of PatientId than DoctorId; the job title Nurse is much more common than Medical Director; there is a strong correlation between grade and salary.

The simplest and least expensive assumptions to make are that values are uniformly distributed, the number of values is a simple function of the cardinality of the table and attributes are independent. A DBMS usually has a set of defaults which it can use if no more detailed statistics are available (for example INGRES assumes that any selection predicate has a selectivity of 10% if there is no other information).

The most commonly used optimization statistics are histograms which typically partition the range of an attribute into a number of segments and record the numbers of values in each segment. Since this process is expensive, involving a scan, it is usually done periodically by the database administrator. The statistics are not maintained dynamically, since this would add to the cost of normal processing and query planning is insensitive to modest variations in the statistical estimates [Kumar and Stonebraker 1987]. This is an important result, since it indicates that crude selectivity estimates are generally adequate, at least for current relational systems. However, recent developments which provide increased functionality through a wider range of basic operations and increased performance through the use of parallelism suggest that more sophisticated statistics may be required.

12.4 Buffer management

The purpose of any buffer management policy is to maximize the number of page requests that can be satisfied from the buffer pool, rather than requiring a disk access.

The standard buffer replacement policy, Least Recently Used (LRU), is not appropriate for all situations [Stonebraker 1981]. For instance, pages from a serial scan are only used once, but will force out other pages, such as index pages, that are much more likely to be used again.

Work on improving buffer pool management policies has focused on two main tactics:

- Subdividing the pool to prevent an operation filling the whole pool with pages of no use in the future. The aim is to give scans (and other operations that pull in many infrequently referenced pages) a small buffer pool, just adequate for their needs, and so prevent them from sweeping out other useful pages. The replacement policy for each of the small pools can be determined by the reference pattern of the particular operation. Buffer size has a non-linear effect on the performance of many relational algorithms, so if an operation does not have a suitable minimum number of pages its performance will be adversely affected. A hot-set model for database buffer sizing is presented in [Sacco and Schkolnick 1986].

- Pinning pages in the buffer pool. Pages that are frequently needed (for example, internal pages of B-tree indexes) are pinned in the buffer pool and so not swept out by the LRU process. This reduces the size of pool available to active operations and, in the extreme case, if too many pages are pinned the buffer manager may have to suspend some operations until some pages are unpinned. A variant of this approach is to employ 'hints', which can be used to recommend that a page is retained, although the buffer manager can flush it if the space is needed for another operation.

12.5 Implementation of operations

12.5.1 Join algorithms

The join operation is the characteristic relational operation. It is essential for relational systems, since at a logical level it is the usual way of combining data from two relations. In practice, many queries require information from several tables, retrieved as a multi-way join, but this is implemented as a series of two-way joins. The join operation is the usual method of choice for any associative or value-based merging of information. Algorithms for the join operation have been extensively studied; a recent survey is provided by [Mishra and Eich 1992].

A naïve implementation of join has a complexity of $O(n^2)$, so there is considerable scope for efficient algorithms. Here we describe the main features of the three principal algorithms: nested loops, sort-merge and hash join. Given the importance of join processing for overall performance, efficient implementations contain many enhancements to maximize performance by taking advantage of the detailed structures of the target DBS. Since these complicate the explanation of the basic algorithm they are omitted here.

In the discussion of the algorithms we refer to the inner (R) and the outer (S) relations, with the assumption that the inner relation is the smaller of the two. The numbers of tuples are m and n respectively (that is, $m < n$). Since the cost of preparing the result relation is the same in all cases we ignore it here.

Nested loops

The nested loops algorithm works by taking each tuple in the outer relation and comparing it with every tuple in the inner relation. It is implemented in all systems because it is the only algorithm that can cope with all cases. It can cope with any condition and does not require any indexing or ordering of the inputs. The performance of the nested loops algorithm has a performance of $O(n \times m)$. The basic algorithm is:

> for each tuple in S
> test it against each tuple in R
> if the condition is satisfied concatenate the tuples
> put the concatenated tuple on the result

In the worst case the whole of the inner relation must be paged in for each tuple in the outer relation; here the I/O cost will be that of paging once through the outer relation and n times through the inner, that is, $n + (n \times m)$,

In the more realistic case where a substantial part of the inner relation can be buffered in memory the performance of the algorithm can be improved by starting the comparisons of alternate tuples from the end of the inner relation. This strategy makes use of the portion of the inner relation that is already in memory.

If the whole of the inner relation (R) can be accommodated in memory its performance is significantly improved, since the I/O cost is just that of paging through both relations, that is, $m + n$.

The relative performance of nested loops is better for joins with a high selectivity (that is, a high proportion of comparisons result in a match). The algorithm is readily parallelized and good parallel performance is not difficult to obtain.

Sort-merge

The sort-merge algorithm has two phases:

1. The input relations are sorted on the join attribute.
2. The relations are scanned, and matching tuples are concatenated and put on the result.

The basic steps of the algorithm are:
Sort R on R(a)
Sort S on S(b)

read first tuple from R
read first tuple from S

```
while (R(a) > S(b))
    read next tuple of S
    if R(a) = S(b)
        concatenate the tuples
        put the concatenated tuple on the result
read next tuple of R
```

The algorithm is complicated by the presence of duplicate values. The result of joining two sets of tuples with the same value of the join attribute is equivalent to the Cartesian product of those two sets. For instance, given a set of three tuples of R with the same value of R(a) which join with two tuples of S with identical values of S(b), there should be six tuples put on the result. The implementation of this requires two loops and flags to keep track of which combinations have been used. The cost of dealing with duplicates becomes substantial if one of the duplicate sets is too large to fit in memory.

The algorithm extends readily to deal with outer joins. Its parallel performance depends largely on how the input relations are partitioned. The ideal case is that they are both partitioned on the same divisions of the join attribute, since this eliminates any data transfers between nodes, and the linear speedup should be obtainable. In the case where one or both of the input relations must be sorted and the sorted tuples redistributed, the performance will be dominated by the amounts of data to be transferred between nodes.

Sort-merge is efficient on large relations, especially where one or both have indexes on the join attribute. The algorithm is most efficient when both relations are clustered on the join attribute. The efficiency of the algorithm when one of the relations has a secondary index on the join attribute depends on the selectivity of the query. A semijoin on a relation with a secondary index on the join attribute is very efficient, since no access is required to the base relation, only to the secondary index (which is in sorted order).

The performance of the sort-merge algorithm is, in general, dominated by the sort phase, which is $O(n \log n)$for each relation. The performance of the merge phase depends on the selectivity of the join and the number of duplicate values of the join attribute. Overall, sort-merge offers good performance because it reduces the number of comparisons that have to be made. It has the added advantage of being able to use existing sort mechanisms (which are usually heavily optimized).

Hash join

Hash joins attempt to reduce the number of comparisons by hashing tuples from the first relation into buckets and then, using the same hash function, probing the second relation for matching tuples. A great many variants of hash joins have been proposed and a large number implemented. Many hash join algorithms are well suited to large memory and to parallel implementation; for these reasons they have been the focus of considerable attention over the past few years and are now the algorithm of choice in many situations. Here we describe two variants of the technique; techniques for hash joins are described in [DeWitt *et al.* 1984; Valduriez and Gardarin 1984; DeWitt and Gerber 1985].

The **simple hash join** strategy is:

for each tuple in R
    hash on join attribute
    place the tuple in a bucket of the hash table
for each tuple in S
    hash it on the join attribute
    if it hashes to a non-empty bucket
        compare it with the tuples in that bucket
        if the join attributes match
            concatenate the tuples
            put the concatenated tuple on the result

Joins on any condition other than equality must use an order-preserving hash function, but these often do not lead to an even distribution of hashed values. Since joins on other conditions are uncommon they can usually be handled satisfactorily by a nested loops algorithm, avoiding the additional complexities of order-preserving hashing.

The simple hash join algorithm is substantially improved if the whole of the hash table fits into memory, since this reduces the I/O complexity to $O(m + n)$. A uniform distribution improves the performance of the algorithm because it eliminates the unnecessary comparisons that result from many values of the join attribute hashing to the same bucket.

The principal improvement to be made to the simple hash join algorithm is to partition the problem into parts so that each part can be processed in memory or on a separate node of a parallel machine. The approach is to partition both input relations so that the tuples in each partition have only to be compared with those in the corresponding partition of the other relation.

The **hybrid hash join** algorithm consists of two largely disjoint phases: partitioning and joining. The aim of the partitioning phase is to produce the smallest number of partitions of R such that each will fit into memory. The algorithm for the partitioning phase is:

Create a large number of buckets for R, allocating one page of memory per
    bucket
Hash the tuples of R into the buckets
For all but the first bucket, if a page becomes full, flush it to disk
For the first bucket, if the page becomes full, allocate another page
Merge any small buckets into larger partitions

This algorithm uses some of the available memory to retain the contents of the first partition, so that at the end of the partitioning phase the first bucket is already in memory. Small buckets are merged so that they come as close as possible to filling the available memory. This is called bucket tuning and is useful because it reduces the likelihood of a bucket overflowing and becoming larger than the available memory.

In the case of a bucket overflow the bucket is recursively partitioned so that it does fit into memory.

After the first relation, R, has been partitioned the same algorithm is applied to the second, S. The partitioning proceeds in the same way as for the first relation, except that tuples hashing to the first bucket of S are immediately used to probe the part of R which is still in memory and any matches are put on the output.

The probing phase of the algorithm is similar to the simple hash join algorithm. After S has been partitioned the next partition of R is brought into memory and the tuples of the corresponding partition of S are retrieved, hashed and any matches with the tuples of R are concatenated and placed on the output.

The hybrid hash join algorithm offers good performance provided that there is sufficient memory for the partitions of R and is readily adapted to parallel execution. The use of bucket tuning minimizes the chance of overflow (which is costly to deal with) and maximizes the use of large memory.

12.5.2   Recursive retrievals

In many types of advanced database application, particularly those discussed in Chapter 1, and in knowledge-based systems (discussed in Chapter 9) it is necessary to support recursive queries. The archetypal example of the recursive query is the ancestor relation.

Parent

Parent	Child
Charles	Thomas
Thomas	John
Thomas	Luke
John	William
William	James

Figure 12.1   The Parent relation.

The query we are interested in answering is 'Who are the ancestors of William?' In this section we outline some of the principal approaches to executing queries of this type. Recursive query processing has been the subject of considerable research over the past decade; the classic starting point for the reader interested in further detail is [Bancilhon and Ramakrishnan 1986].

A **recursive query** can be defined as a query on a **recursive relation**. A recursive relation is a derived relation that includes the recursive relation on the right-hand side of the rules that define it. For example, the recursive relation Ancestor can be derived from Parent in our example using the following rules:

$ancestor(x,y) \leftarrow parent(x,y)$ (1)

$ancestor(x,z) \leftarrow parent(x,z), ancestor(z,y)$ (2)

The second of these rules is recursive.

A number of methods for optimizing and executing recursive queries are restricted to **linear recursive relations**. A relation is linearly recursive if the recursive predicate only appears once on the right-hand side of the definition, as in the example above.

We can take a simple view of the database consisting of a set of facts (tuples) and a set of rules. A query may be evaluated using one of two approaches:

- **Top-down.** These methods start from the query, applying the rules, using backward chaining, until the query is answered. They are often efficient but complex to evaluate, since they only generate tuples that form part of the answer.
- **Bottom-up.** This strategy starts from the database extension and applies rules until the query is answered. The principal disadvantage of this approach is that large numbers of intermediate relations, containing many unwanted tuples, may be generated.

A strategy may be either **interpreted** or **compiled**. Here we describe only compiled strategies, since they are generally easier to integrate with conventional database technology.

We first describe two basic approaches to recursive query processing, which Bancilhon and Ramakrishnan term **naïve evaluation** and **semi-naïve evaluation**. Then we briefly describe some ways in which the execution of these strategies may be improved.

Naïve evaluation

The naïve evaluation strategy computes a derived relation by applying all the rules at each step in the inference. It is a bottom-up, compiled approach. The computation proceeds as follows:

1. Initialize the relation, using tuples from the base relation(s). In our example this is achieved by the application of Rule 1.
2. Expand the initial relation using all the rules in the definition by repeatedly applying them until no new derived tuples are produced. At each iteration the rules are applied to the cumulative result of the previous iterations. The process can alternatively be represented:

$R = R0;$
while (R changes)
$R = R \cup E(R);$

where R is the relation and $E(R)$ is the evaluation of the rules defining R. The conditional parts of the rules defining R can be represented as a relational algebra expression, which turns $E(R)$ into the execution of a relational algebra program.

This is shown for our example in Figure 12.2, answering the query 'Who are William's ancestors?', that is, instantiating Rule 2,

$$ancestor(William,z) \leftarrow parent(x,z), ancestor(z,y).$$

The derived tuples computed at each iteration are shaded.

(a) The initial Forbear relation (after applying rule 1).

Forbear(0)

Ancestor	Descendent
Charles	Thomas
Thomas	John
Thomas	Luke
John	William
Luke	Henry

(b) The Forbear relation after the first iteration.

Forbear(1)

Ancestor	Descendent
Charles	Thomas
Thomas	John
Thomas	Luke
John	William
Luke	Henry
Charles	John
Charles	Luke
Thomas	William
Thomas	Henry

(c) The Forbear relation after the second iteration.

Forbear(2)

Ancestor	Descendent
Charles	Thomas
Thomas	John
Thomas	Luke
John	William
Luke	Henry
Charles	John
Charles	Luke
Thomas	William
Thomas	Henry
Charles	William
Charles	Henry

(d) The Forbear result relation.

Forbear

Ancestor	Descendent
John	William
Thomas	William
Charles	William

Figure 12.2 Naïve evaluation of *ancestor(William, z)*.

The method has two significant disadvantages:

- No account is taken of constants in the query until after the evaluation of the recursive relation. This leads to the evaluation of many unnecessary tuples.
- At each iteration the whole relation is evaluated, leading to the repeated evaluation of many tuples.

Semi-naïve evaluation

Semi-naïve evaluation is a bottom-up, compiled approach which is an extension of naïve evaluation. The major advance in this approach is that it reduces the reevaluation of tuples produced in previous iterations.

Using the notation from the previous section, the process can be represented:

Rd = R0;
R = Rd
while (Rd ≠ 0)
    Rd = df(R, Rd);
    Rd = Rd – R;
    R = R ∪ Rd;

It is difficult to find a good expression for df() in the general case. If the system is restricted to linear rules the inference at each iteration only requires the tuples from the previous iteration. The method can be implemented to produce relational algebra programs. An unthinking execution strategy of these programs will be very inefficient if there is inadequate memory, because they contain repeated sequences of joins, unions and differences.

The successive iterations are shown for our example in Figure 12.3. Note the smaller number of tuples computed in the second iteration. This effect would be greater for queries with a greater depth of recursion.

(a) The initial Forbear relation (after applying rule 1).

Forbear(0)

Ancestor	Descendent
Charles	Thomas
Thomas	John
Thomas	Luke
John	William
Luke	Henry

(b) The Forbear relation after the first iteration.

Forbear(1)

Ancestor	Descendent
Charles	Thomas
Thomas	John
Thomas	Luke
John	William
Luke	Henry
Charles	John
Charles	Luke
Thomas	William
Thomas	Henry

(c) The Forbear relation after the second iteration.

Forbear(2)

Ancestor	Descendent
Charles	Thomas
Thomas	John
Thomas	Luke
John	William
Luke	Henry
Charles	John
Charles	Luke
Thomas	William
Thomas	Henry
Charles	William
Charles	Henry

(d) The Forbear result relation.

Forbear

Ancestor	Descendent
John	William
Thomas	William
Charles	William

Figure 12.3 Semi-naïve evaluation of *ancestor(William, z)*.

12.5.3   Recursive query optimization

The naïve and semi-naïve execution strategies described above are both compiled approaches which answer a query by executing a relational algebra program. It is not easy to derive efficient relational algebra programs and there have been many proposals for improving their efficiency, mostly by pushing selection before recursion. Optimizing a relational algebra program is difficult, so the more promising approaches use rewriting rules to achieve this.

The Alexander method is a widely used recursive query optimization method. The basis of the method is to split each recursive rule containing a constant into two parts: the problem (PB) and the solution (SOL). For example, to find William's ancestors we rewrite Rule 2:

$PB \_ ancestor(William)$
$SOL \_ ancestor(x, y) \leftarrow PB \_ ancestor(y) \wedge parent(x, y)$
$PB \_ ancestor(x) \leftarrow PB \_ ancestor(y) \wedge parent(x, y)$

Many other methods have been developed; several are described in [Bancilhon and Ramakrishnan 1986; Gardarin and Valduriez 1989].

12.5.4   Aggregates and duplicate removal

Aggregates are useful for summarizing data in a database. Most systems support maximum, minimum, sum, average, and count. These can be divided into scalar aggregates and aggregate functions.

Scalar aggregates are typically evaluated by performing a single pass over the data and returning a single value (for example, the average length of stay in hospital). Many systems will exploit an index for maximum, minimum and count, if a suitable one exists, since this avoids having to scan the base data.

Aggregate functions return a set of values (for example, the average length of stay in each ward of a hospital). Since the calculation of aggregate functions requires grouping, they are usually implemented in the same module as duplicate removal. In the calculation of an aggregate function a record is compared on its grouping attribute and some computation is performed before it is dropped by the function. Currently the direct specification of complex aggregate functions, involving several levels of nesting and a richer set of functions, is not generally possible. Consequently the logic for these aggregates is usually specified in application programs and is not optimized – an optimizer cannot tell that three nested cursors are really implementing a complex grouping condition and generate an appropriate plan. Direct support of more complex aggregates could improve their performance considerably, by allowing the optimizer to generate efficient query plans for them.

Duplicate removal also involves grouping records. There are two differences from the treatment of records in aggregate functions:

- records are compared on all their attributes,
- a record that matches one that was examined previously is immediately dropped.

These functions are implemented using algorithms based on sorting and in many DBMSs they use the same code as the sorting routines. From this it follows that the complexity of aggregate functions and duplicate removal is roughly $O(n \log n)$. Other approaches, based on hashing or on nested loops, are feasible, given large main memories [Graefe 1993].

12.6 Optimization strategies and techniques

12.6.1 Problem statement

Finding the optimal query plan is a hard problem, for which a number of basic approaches have been investigated. The most important underlying considerations are:

- **Balancing the query requirements of *ad hoc* against compiled queries.** At one end of this spectrum is the view that all access is by way of compiled queries which will be executed many times, so it is worth trying to find the truly optimum plan. At the other extreme is the view that the queries are dynamic and should be optimized at run time. In this case the queries are usually executed using a dynamic query planning strategy. The intermediate position compiles query plans for the first invocation of the query and then caches them for the remainder of the session, so the cost of optimization is spread over the whole session. The optimization process is run until a 'good' solution is found and then the query is run.
- **Responding to changes in the database schema**. If the database schema (either logical or physical) changes this may invalidate the plan of any precompiled query. This is of no concern if queries are planned dynamically, but if they are precompiled and stored a mechanism for invalidating and recompiling the plans is needed (generally at the next execution), unless changes to the database schema are seen as sufficiently infrequent to make it a manual task to be performed by the database administrator.

The DBMS designers' views of the intended pattern of use of the system determine the approaches to query planning. Experience has led to the predominance of static query planning methods, as they avoid extra run-time overhead for frequently executed queries. The remainder of this section reflects the practical importance of static approaches.

Query execution plans

Query execution plans may be classified as **left-deep**, **bushy** or **right-deep** [Graefe and DeWitt 1987]. These terms refer to how operations are combined to execute the query. The naming convention relates to the way the inputs of binary operations, particularly join, are treated. Most operations treat their inputs in different ways, so the performance characteristics differ according to the ordering of the inputs. For example, in the conventional representation of the nested loops algorithm the outer loop iterates over the left input and the inner loop iterates over the right input.

Left-deep query execution plans (Figure 12.4a) start from a table and construct the result by successively adding operations involving a single table until the query is completed; that is, only one input into a binary operation is an intermediate result. This strategy has the advantages of reducing the search space and allowing the query optimizer to be based on dynamic programming techniques. The price of this simplification of the optimizer is that it misses some optimal plans. The System R optimizer [Selinger *et al*. 1979] used this approach.

Bushy execution plans (Figure 12.4b) allow both inputs into a binary operation to be intermediate results and are therefore the most general type of plan; left-deep and right-deep plans are special cases of bushy plans. The added flexibility allows a wide variety of plans to be considered, which yields better plans for some queries. However, this flexibility can considerably increase the search space.

Right-deep execution plans (Figure 12.4c) have only recently been studied and appear to have considerable promise for systems where there is large main memory [Schneider and DeWitt 1990].

12.6.2   Exhaustive search

Exhaustive search is the method of choice if a query is to be precompiled and then executed many times, since the high initial cost of constructing the query execution plan is amortized over many executions of the query. The query plan is determined statically, using statistics (or default assumptions if no suitable statistics are available). All possible plans that the optimizer can generate are examined and the cheapest is retained.

A variant of this approach keeps track of the time taken to produce the query plan and stops searching if the time taken equals the current best estimate for executing the query. This allows for good dynamic query performance without burdening frequently executed queries, within the scope of a database session.

12.6.3   Reduction approach

The reduction approach is conceptually attractive, since it is dynamic and does not require any statistics. The algorithm uses simple heuristics, typically always to perform selections before joins, to select an initial operation and dynamically evaluates each subsequent operation using the actual result of the previous operation. The use of actual results rather than estimates reduces the likelihood of picking a poor execution plan. This approach was used in the first INGRES optimizer [Stonebraker *et al*. 1976]. Despite its simplicity the method has some serious disadvantages:

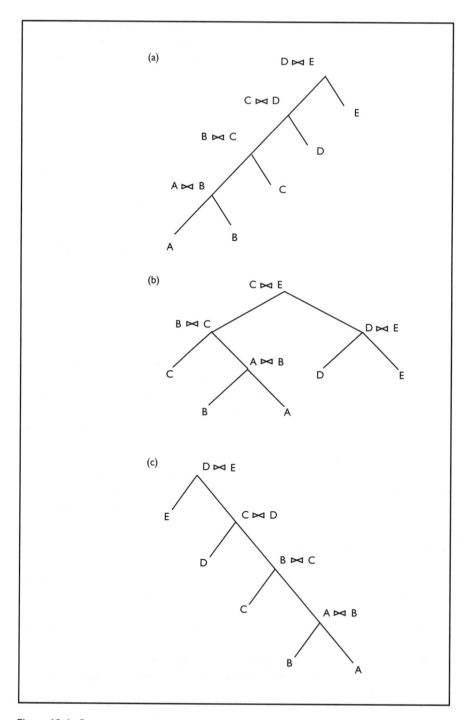

Figure 12.4 Query execution plans: (a) Left-deep, (b) Bushy, (c) Right-deep.

- Choosing which implementation of any basic operation to use dynamically imposes an extra overhead at run time.
- Queries cannot be precompiled.
- Operations cannot be pipelined if the plan is built dynamically.

12.6.4   Optimization challenges

The queries needed to support many modern applications are substantially more complex than those needed for conventional applications, often involving multiple joins or complex retrievals. Since exhaustive optimization strategies are NP-complete in the number of relations, the expansion of the search space makes a simple exhaustive strategy infeasible.

There is therefore considerable interest in techniques for improving query optimization and the execution of complex queries.

Improvements to query optimizers

Significant work has been done in recent years to make query optimizers more tailored to types of query typical of specific domains, pioneered by the EXODUS optimizer generator [Graefe and DeWitt 1987].

Join indexes and other ancillary data structures

A join index is an ancillary data structure, proposed by Valduriez [Valduriez 1987], which maintains a list (index) of the identifiers of matching tuples for frequently executed joins. This replaces the execution of a join algorithm with a scan of a small table followed by retrieval of the records, using their identifiers. These identifiers are typically a tuple identifier, surrogate or other form of logical pointer which can be hashed to a physical location.

Recently there has been renewed interest in ancillary data structures for reassembling composite objects (for example, [Kemper and Moerkotte 1990]) and for improving the performance of complex queries. These approaches are characterized by the use of several small data structures, represented as internal data structures or as an additional layer on top of a relational system. The memory available to a typical modern system is sufficient to allow these structures to be memory-resident, when they can provide the effect of navigational retrieval within a declarative framework. Research tends to suggest that unless the schema is extremely dynamic (entailing extensive maintenance of any access structures), there are substantial overall performance benefits.

We believe that future database systems will increasingly make use of a variety of ancillary data structures to improve the performance of complex queries. These are significant challenges in integrating these into existing query planning and execution strategies and not burdening the programmer with managing their use and maintenance.

12.7 Summary

The decomposition, planning and optimization of queries were described here. We gave a broad overview of the approaches involved at each stage of the mapping of a query from a high-level declarative specification (typically SQL) through to execution. The field of query optimization contains many difficult problems and open issues which must be addressed in order to provide efficient execution of the complex queries of modern applications.

Part IV

DATABASE MODELS AND ARCHITECTURES

Chapter 13

THE RELATIONAL MODEL

13.1 Introduction

The relational model owes its origins to the mathematical concept of a relation and to set theory. It was first proposed as an approach to data modelling by E. F. Codd in 1970, but development of a DBMS based on it had to wait until the later years of the decade [Codd 1970]. Although of similar antiquity to the CODASYL (network) model [Tschritzis and Klug 1978] which dominated commercial database systems until the mid-1980s, it can be regarded as a more recent form of database model.

Apart from the widespread success of the hierarchical and network approaches in commercial data processing, the main reasons for this delay in implementation lay with the capabilities of the contemporary hardware, and the need to develop efficient implementations for the simple relational operations and for automatic query optimization.

As well as efficient software techniques, the relational model required a significant increase in processing power and disk I/O speeds to achieve comparable performance on non-trivial applications. It was only during the 1980s that suitable hardware became generally available. From then until quite recently, much of the development of commercial DBMSs has concentrated on relational systems.

In this chapter we first describe the structure of the relational model and then the operators of the relational algebra. Although providing a simple language to describe low-level data manipulation, the algebra is rarely used as the basis for relational query languages. Instead, declarative languages such as SQL are based on the relational calculus and permit users to specify queries in terms of what is required, rather than how it should be performed. Consequently there is considerable scope for optimizing queries when they are translated into algebra-like operations prior to execution (*see* Chapter 12).

Since the mid-1980s much research has been directed towards extending the relational model to deal with the requirements of a wider range of applications. This period has also seen the emergence of the object-oriented approach to data management. These approaches are discussed in Chapter 16.

13.1.1   Objectives

The relational model was intended to overcome several shortcomings of the earlier generations of hierarchical and network database systems. These suffered from limited independence of application programs from the physical methods used to store data. Although physical design remains an important issue with relational systems, the use of declarative query languages and a uniform logical data model insulates the programmer from concerns with physical storage.

Earlier systems required a 'navigational' approach to locating and accessing data. Both earlier models rely on nested structures encapsulating one-to-many (1:N) relationships. To retrieve instances of related entity types, a program must start from a predefined access point and locate a record of one type. It then iterates over the related records of the next type, and so on until all required data has been found. For example, given a 1:N relationship between the two record types *doctor* and *patient*, the task of finding patients registered with a particular doctor might proceed by first locating the required doctor's record, then retrieving all related patient records. These separate actions must be explicitly coded in an application program.

Access paths are defined as part of the data definition process and the selection of suitable paths during the implementation phase is critical to the efficiency of the system. If a direct path does not exist, the required information can only be found by traversing other record types that may be irrelevant to the query. In the above example, the doctor records might be nested within those of medical practices or health centres. If the doctor record could not be accessed directly, but only via those of the practice, an extra loop would be added to the program to iterate over the practice records to locate the particular doctor.

Where multiple access routes are available, efficiency may depend on the programmer's ability to select the one that is most appropriate to the query. This may require a detailed knowledge of not just the structure but also the contents of the database.

The navigational approach is well suited to certain classes of problems, particularly those involving complex nested objects, recursive relationships and graph traversal. We return to this topic in the context of object-oriented and extended relational systems in Chapters 15 and 16. However, in earlier generations of database systems, a reliance on navigation and defined access paths meant that access was only possible through application programs and so there was no mechanism for performing *ad hoc* queries. The set-oriented approach of the relational model opened the way to declarative query languages which, together with automatic query optimization, provide an effective basis for interactive query systems.

Codd's main objective in developing the relational model was to provide a sound theoretical basis for a simple means of manipulating stored data. The model was intended to maximize data independence and minimize redundancy. Wherever possible, application programs should be shielded from changes in the structure and organization of stored data. If possible, all data values should be stored once only. This not only minimizes storage requirements, but avoids the possibility of update anomalies when more than one copy of a value needs to be changed. The relational model does not completely abolish redundancy. Indeed a form of redundancy is used to represent relationships between stored entities. However, the application of normalization theory ensures that this necessary redundancy is controlled.

13.1.2   Structure

The relational model is based on the core concept of a **relation**. Informally a relation may be viewed as a named two-dimensional table representing an entity set. A relation has a fixed number of named columns, or **attributes**, and a variable number of rows, or **tuples**. A relational schema contains a collection of relation definitions.

Each tuple represents an instance of the entity set and each attribute contains a single value of some recorded property for the particular instance. All members of the entity set have the same attributes. Thus Figure 13.1 shows an instance, or extension, of a relation called PERSON. This has four attributes, *Initials*, *LastName*, *DateOfBirth* and *Sex*. The extension has eleven tuples, each of which describes a single person.

PERSON	Initials	LastName	DateOfBirth	Sex
	T	Williams	1972-01-12	m
	J	Garcia	1981-03-18	f
	W	Fisher	1950-10-22	m
	K	Waldon	1942-06-01	m
	P	Timms	1928-06-03	m
	A	Dryden	1944-06-23	m
	F	Fogg	1955-10-16	f
	A	Cameron	1937-04-04	m
	B	Finlay	1948-12-01	m
	C	King	1965-06-06	f
	D	Waldon	1938-07-08	f

Figure 13.1   Example PERSON relation.

Each attribute contains values drawn from a particular **domain**. This is a named set of atomic (indivisible) data values, and is usually specified by name, data type and, possibly, a constrained range of values. For example, the person information in Figure 13.1 would be drawn from four different domains:

Attribute	Domain	Description
Initials	PersonInitials	The set of all possible initials
LastName	PersonLastNames	The set of all possible last names
DateOfBirth	Dates	The set of all possible past dates
Sex	Sex	The set {m, f}

Within each tuple, the value of each attribute is **atomic**. In other words, it is a single value drawn from the domain of the attribute. Multiple or repeating values are not permitted.

More formally a relation may be defined as follows. Given n domains $D_1, D_2, ...,$ D_n, a relation on these domains consists of an unordered set of n-tuples $(a_1, a_2, ..., a_n)$ where each value a_1 is drawn from the corresponding domain D_1. Thus $a_1 \in D_1, a_2 \in D_2, ..., a_n \in D_n$.

Each tuple is a member of the set formed by the Cartesian product (all possible distinct combinations) of the domains $D_1 \times D_2, ... \times D_n$. Thus each tuple is distinct from all others and any instance of the relation is a subset of the Cartesian product of its domains.

Because each tuple is distinct, it follows that it may be identified by the values of one or more of its attributes. This unique identifier is known as a **key**. Keys are always minimal sequences of attributes. Where more than one attribute, or group of attributes, could serve as a unique identifier they are known as **candidate keys**. Only one of these candidates, called the **primary key**, is selected for the purpose of identifying tuples.

We have already discussed the limitations of value-based identifiers in Chapter 3. The PERSON relation of Figure 13.1 illustrates why care must be taken to select a suitable identifier for a relation. Here, no one attribute is sufficient to identify an individual person. On the basis of the values shown several pairs of attributes could serve as a key, but none of these would be a wise choice. If further tuples are added to the relation there is a high probability that another person might have the same values for one or more of the attributes as one already recorded. In terms of these attributes the two individuals would be indistinguishable, and only one tuple with these values can exist in the relation.

Another reason for not choosing an attribute such as *LastName* as part of the key is that a person might change his or her name during the lifetime of the data. Because of the dependence on key values to represent relationships, the attributes chosen to form the identifier should be ones whose values can be expected to remain constant so as to avoid key maintenance problems.

Many entities will have suitable identifiers amongst their attributes. For example, electronic equipment such as a computer or television set will usually have a manufacturer's serial number, and a vehicle will have a chassis or body number. These values clearly identify individual instances of the class and can usually be expected to remain constant throughout its lifetime.

Where no such identifying attribute exists it is necessary to add an attribute specifically for this purpose. Figure 13.2 shows the PERSON relation with a PersonId attribute added to serve as the primary key. It is conventional to underline the primary key, thus the relation may be specified in intensional form as PERSON (PersonId, Initials, LastName, DateOfBirth, Sex).

PERSON	PersonId	Initials	LastName	DateOfBirth	Sex
	100	T	Williams	1972-01-12	m
	101	J	Garcia	1981-03-18	f
	102	W	Fisher	1950-10-22	m
	103	K	Waldon	1942-06-01	m
	104	P	Timms	1928-06-03	m
	105	A	Dryden	1944-06-23	m
	106	F	Fogg	1955-10-16	f
	50	A	Cameron	1937-04-04	m
	51	B	Finlay	1948-12-01	m
	52	C	King	1965-06-06	f
	53	D	Waldon	1938-07-08	f

Figure 13.2   Example PERSON relation with an artificial key.

Null values

In any particular tuple, some values may be missing because they are either unknown or inappropriate. In the relational model, these are represented by **null** values. Nulls should not be thought of as values in a conventional sense. They are not the same as empty character strings or numeric zeros. Indeed, a null is not equal to any other value, and two nulls are never equal to each other. However, in general, null values are application or query dependent and an adequate implementation should allow user-defined nulls.

Relationships

Relationships between relations are expressed through foreign keys. A foreign key is an attribute in one relation that is drawn from the same domain as the primary key of the related relation. Figure 13.3 shows a relationship formed between two relations PATIENT and DOCTOR. The relationship, which here indicates registration of the patient with a particular doctor, is represented by including the RegisteredWith attribute in the PATIENT relation. This attribute contains the value of DoctorId from the tuple in the DOCTOR relation representing the doctor with whom the patient is registered.

The foreign key method supports representation of 1:N relationships. The value placed in the foreign key attribute can refer to no more than one tuple in the other relation, but the primary key value may be referenced by the foreign key in many tuples. In this case, each patient tuple may contain at most one reference to a doctor, so the cardinality of PATIENT in this relationship is (0, 1). Any tuple in the DOCTOR relation may be referenced by many foreign key values, so its cardinality is (0, n).

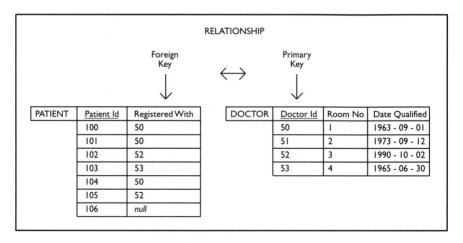

Figure 13.3 The use of a foreign key attribute to represent a relationship between two relations.

The method may also be used to represent a 1:1 relationship (cardinality (0, 1) or (1, 1) in both directions). Typically in these cases the corresponding tuples have the same primary key value, and the primary key attribute also serves as the foreign key.

An M:N relationship may be represented using a relationship relation. This is a simple relation that exists solely to represent the relationship and contains two attributes, both of which are foreign keys. For example, two relations

```
PROBLEM ( ProblemId, ... )
TREATMENT ( TreatmentId, ... )
```

might contain details of problems and treatments. As an ailment might be treated in several different ways and a treatment might be used for several ailments, the relationship is M:N (cardinality (0, n) or (1, n) in both directions). The relationship may be represented using a relationship relation containing only the primary key values of both related tuples as foreign keys:

```
PROBLEM-TREATMENT ( ProblemId, TreatmentId )
```

Note that the primary key of this relation is the concatenation of the foreign key attributes. This approach can be extended to cover ternary and higher-order relationships by adding additional foreign key columns.

Entity and referential integrity

Two simple rules govern the integrity of a relation. The first, known as the **entity integrity** rule or the **entity constraint**, states that no part of the primary key may have a null value. This ensures that every tuple has a complete identifier.

The **referential integrity** rule states that the value of a foreign key must either be wholly null, or equate to an existing value of the primary key in the related relation. The inclusion of null values permits the expression of optional relationships.

The relational model provides no means of representing other semantic integrity constraints.

13.2 Mapping a logical model to a relational schema

Figure 13.4 shows a simple logical data model for part of a health centre database. The model is deliberately simplistic and contains no more than is needed for immediate illustrative purposes. In particular, no attempt has been made to include any group of health care workers other than doctors. Consequently there is no distinction between appointments with, or treatments given by, doctors, nurses or other specialists. Also omitted are prescriptions, laboratory samples and other important entity classes that might appear in a real health centre database.

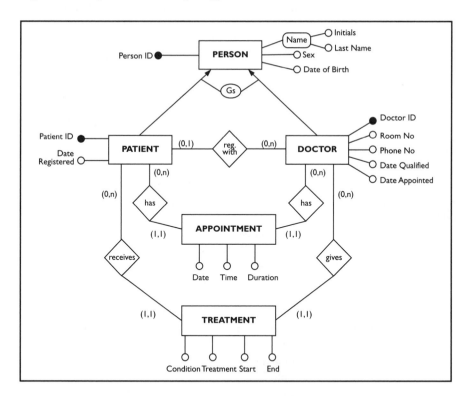

Figure 13.4 Logical data model for part of a health centre database.

There are two parts of the model that cannot be represented directly in a relational schema. Firstly, the compound attribute Name in the Person entity class must be decomposed into its component single-valued attributes Initials and LastName. Secondly, the overlapping generalization hierarchy involving Person, Patient and Doctor can be implemented in one of three ways:

- As one Person relation containing all attributes of the component classes, with null values in the unused attributes:
  PERSON (PersonId, Initials, LastName, DateOfBirth, Sex,
              RoomNo, PhoneNo, DateQualified, DateAppointed,
              DateRegistered)

- As two separate Patient and Doctor relations, each containing the generalized attributes from Person in addition to their own specialized attributes:
  DOCTOR (DoctorId, RoomNo, PhoneNo, DateQualified,
              DateAppointed, Initials, LastName, DateOfBirth, Sex)
  PATIENT (PatientId, DateRegistered, Initials, LastName,
              DateOfBirth, Sex)
- As three separate relations with IS-A relationships between the subclasses and the superclass:
  PERSON (PersonId, Initials, LastName, DateOfBirth, Sex)
  DOCTOR (DoctorId, RoomNo, PhoneNo, DateQualified,
              DateAppointed)
  PATIENT (PatientId, DateRegistered)

The first approach has the benefit of simplicity. Each person is represented by a single tuple in a single relation. Because any doctor may also be a patient, their tuples will contain values for each, if not all, of the attributes. However, most patients are not doctors and their tuples will contain null values in all of the doctor subtype attributes. Despite this limitation, the approach may offer performance benefits where the dominant query load relates to the supertype or simultaneously to both subtypes.

The distinction between doctor and patient is entirely dependent on the presence or absence of valid values in certain attributes. A preferable alternative is to add an additional 'flag' column for each of the subtypes to indicate subtype membership. Here we would use a separate flag attribute for each of doctor and patient. In the case of an exclusive generalization, a single 'type' column containing the name of the subtype may be used. For each of these variations the method relies heavily on the application programmer and query language user performing valid updates and adding necessary restrictions to their queries. The relational model provides no way of ensuring that a tuple representing a patient who is not a doctor will always contain null values in the doctor specific attributes.

The second approach is more suited to generalizations with exclusive membership. There is an optional 1:1 relationship between the two relations. The PatientId and DoctorId attributes act both as primary keys within their own relation, and as foreign keys to the matching tuple in the other relation. Typically this method may be employed when the majority of queries refer to one subtype or other, rather than both together. It may also be used where the complexity of the third approach imposes unacceptably high performance costs.

A significant limitation of this method when used for overlapping generalizations is that where a person has both roles, the supertype attributes Initials, LastName, *DateOfBirth*, and *Sex* will be stored redundantly in one tuple of each relation, with the attendant danger of update anomalies. Again this places a greater responsibility on the application programmer and query language user to maintain semantic integrity by ensuring that only valid updates are performed.

The third method minimizes redundancy and null-valued attributes at the cost of query complexity and hence performance. This arises from the need to join at least two relations whenever both supertype and subtype information is required. Where a person is both a doctor and a patient, his or her details will be spread over three relations. The PersonId, PatientId and DoctorId attributes act both as primary keys within their own relation, and as foreign keys to the matching tuples in the other two relations.

Clearly, physical design considerations would influence the final decision on which of these approaches is most appropriate for a particular application. In a practical system, any of the three approaches could be used. However, in the present case, the need to support overlapping membership, the freedom from potential update anomalies and faithfulness to the original logical model make the third option an acceptable choice.

We now turn to the more 'conventional' relationships in the logical model. That between doctor and patient is optional because the MIN–CARD is zero at both ends. The MAX–CARD values indicate that it is 1:N from doctor to patient. In other words, a patient may be registered with zero or one doctor, whereas a doctor may have zero or more registered patients. This relationship may be implemented by using the primary key of the 'one' end as a foreign key at the 'many' end. In other words, a new column called RegisteredWith is added to the Patient relation to act as a foreign key to Doctor. The Patient relation becomes:

PATIENT (PatientId, DateRegistered, RegisteredWith)

The relationships between Appointment and both Patient and Doctor are also implemented using foreign keys in the relation at the 'many' end. Again, the cardinality values indicate that the relationships are 1:N. A patient or doctor may be involved in zero or many appointments, but a single appointment must involve one patient and one doctor. The Appointment relation becomes:

APPOINTMENT (DoctorId, PatientId, Date, Time, Duration)

So far, this relation has no primary key. There are several possible candidates:

DoctorId, PatientId, Date, Time
DoctorId, Date, Time
PatientId, Date, Time

The first of these allows for the possibility that a patient and doctor might meet more than once on the same day. If this was not required the Time column could be removed from the key. The others are based on the fact that neither doctors or patients can attend simultaneous appointments. In its longer form, the first is the least attractive because of its greater length and complexity than the others. Between the others the choice is more arbitrary. Here, physical design considerations may affect the final decision, influencing both the choice of key and the ordering of elements within the key. However, for present purposes, we might decide that the correspondence of the sequence DoctorId, Date, Time to the concept of a doctor's schedule makes it the preferred choice.

The Treatment entity class has similar relationships with both *Doctor* and *Patient* to those of Appointment, and these can be represented in the same way by adding foreign key columns to Treatment.

TREATMENT (DoctorId, PatientId, Condition, Treatment, Start, End)

The selection of a primary key is again problematic. In this case both doctor and patient could be involved in more than one treatment at any time, and these treatments may start and end on the same date. The combination of DoctorId, PatientId, Condition, Treatment is unlikely to be unique because treatments could be repeated at different times. Only by adding one or other of the Start and End dates can a unique key be found. Again physical design considerations may influence decisions about the ordering of elements within the key.

After mapping from the logical model to a relational schema we have the following relations. These will be used in subsequent sections of this chapter to illustrate the operations of the relational algebra and the SQL language.

PERSON (<u>PersonId</u>, Initials, LastName, DateOfBirth, Sex)
DOCTOR (<u>DoctorId</u>, RoomNo, PhoneNo, DateQualified, DateAppointed)
PATIENT (<u>PatientId</u>, DateRegistered, RegisteredWith)
APPOINTMENT (<u>DoctorId</u>, PatientId, <u>Date</u>, <u>Time</u>, Duration)
TREATMENT (<u>DoctorId</u>, <u>PatientId</u>, <u>Condition</u>, <u>Treatment</u>, <u>Start</u>, End)

13.3 Relational algebra

Relations provides a simple, but static, structure that can be used to represent both entities and relationships. The relational algebra provides the operations needed to manipulate information stored logically in this form. The operators may be classified as unary or binary, depending on the number of their operands. Unary operators act on a single relation, binary operators act on two relations, and both produce a single relation as their result.

Because relations are sets of tuples, four binary operators, **Cartesian product**, **union**, **difference** and **intersection**, are borrowed directly from mathematical set theory. These are all binary operators that treat the tuples of their operands as atomic objects. In addition, several specifically relational operators are required for operations that must take account of the attributes and attribute values within the tuples of their operands. These are the unary operators **select** and **project**, and the binary operators **join** and **divide**. With the exception of the relatively unimportant division, each of these operators is described in the following sections.

13.3.1   Select

The select (also sometimes called restrict) operator creates a new relation by extracting specific tuples from an input relation. The result contains the subset of tuples from the input relation that match a Boolean **selection** or **restriction condition**, expressed as

> *<attribute name> <operator> <value expression | attribute name>*

The comparison operators is typically one of $\{<\leq, =\geq>, \neq\}$ when dealing with ordered domains, or $\{=, \neq\}$ for unordered domains. More complex conditions may be constructed using the Boolean operators AND, OR and NOT.

For example, given the PERSON relation in Figure 13.2, tuples referring to people born before 1 January 1961 could be retrieved using a selection condition on the DateOfBirth attribute. This can be expressed as:

σPERSON (DateOfBirth)<1961-01-01

The result is shown in Figure 13.5.

R	PersonId	Initials	LastName	DateOfBirth	Sex
	102	W	Fisher	1950-10-22	m
	103	K	Waldon	1942-06-01	m
	104	P	Timms	1928-06-03	m
	105	A	Dryden	1944-06-23	m
	106	F	Fogg	1955-10-16	f
	50	A	Cameron	1937-04-04	m
	51	B	Finlay	1948-12-01	m
	53	D	Waldon	1938-07-08	f

Figure 13.5   Result of the select operation σPERSON (DateOfBirth)<1961-01-01.

13.3.2   Project

The project operator creates a new relation by extracting named attributes from an input relation. The result contains only the attributes specified in a **target list**. It is therefore a subset of the attributes of the input relation. For example, the operation to extract the LastName and DateOfBirth attributes from the PERSON relation can be expressed as:

πPERSON (LastName, DateOfBirth)

The result is shown in Figure 13.6.

RI	LastName	DateOfBirth
	Williams	1972-01-12
	Garcia	1981-03-18
	Fisher	1950-10-22
	Waldon	1942-06-01
	Timms	1928-06-03
	Dryden	1944-06-23
	Fogg	1955-10-16
	Cameron	1937-04-04
	Finlay	1948-12-01
	King	1965-06-06
	Waldon	1938-07-08

Figure 13.6   Result of the project operation πPERSON (LastName, DateOfBirth).

Note that, if we project just the *LastName* attribute from PERSON, the result has only ten tuples (Figure 13.7). The name 'Waldon' occurs twice in the input, but only once in the output. Remember that each tuple in a relation must be distinct from all others. Projection extracts the required columns and also removes any duplicate rows from the result.

RI	LastName
	Williams
	Garcia
	Fisher
	Waldon
	Timms
	Dryden
	Fogg
	Cameron
	Finlay
	King

Figure 13.7   Result of the project operation πPERSON (LastName).

13.3.3   Cartesian product

The Cartesian product is often also referred to as cross-product or just product. It is a binary operation combining (concatenating) each tuple from the first operand with each tuple in the second operand. If the first operand contains n tuples and the second m, the resulting relation contains $m \times n$ tuples, one for every possible combination of tuples in the input relations.

In Figure 13.8 the two relations PATIENT and DOCTOR are combined by the Cartesian product operation PATIENT × DOCTOR.

PATIENT	LastName	DateOfBirth	×	DOCTOR	DoctorName	RoomNo	DateQualified
	Williams	1972-01-12			Cameron	1	1963 - 09 - 01
	Garcia	1981-03-18			Finlay	2	1973 - 09 - 12

R	LastName	DateOfBirth	DoctorName	RoomNo	DateQualified
	Williams	1972-01-12	Cameron	1	1963 - 09 - 01
	Williams	1972-01-12	Finlay	2	1963 - 09 - 01
	Garcia	1981-03-18	Cameron	1	1973 - 09 - 12
	Garcia	1981-03-18	Finlay	2	1973 - 09 - 12

Figure 13.8   The Cartesian product operation PATIENT × DOCTOR.

13.3.4   Join

The relational model divides all objects, no matter how complex, into simple normalized relations and represents relationships between them by common values in shared attributes. Information retrieval thus depends on the ability to realize relationships by combining relations according to these shared attributes. This is achieved using the join operator. For this reason, join is the characteristic relational operation.

Joins are made according to a join or linkage condition over a pair of (possibly compound) attributes, one in each relation, which are drawn from the same domain. A number of terms are used to describe different types of join. The notation for a join of R and S is $R \bowtie S$. Elaborating this to give the join attributes and a join condition gives $R \bowtie R_{(a) = S(b)}$. This is the theta join, where $R(a)$ is an attribute of R, $S(b)$ is an attribute of S and θ is a condition that must be met in order for the tuples to which $R(a)$ and $S(b)$ belong to participate in the result of the join. The condition may be any of the normal comparison operators.

The most frequent condition for a join is equality between the join attributes; this type of join is called an **equijoin**, $R \bowtie R_{(a) = S(b)}$. The result contains both the join attributes, which frequently results in a relation with two differently named attributes with identical values. For example, the equijoin of the relations PATIENT and DOCTOR over RegisteredWith = DoctorId is shown in Figure 13.9.

PATIENT	Patient Id	Registered With
	100	50
	101	50
	102	52
	103	53
	104	50
	105	52
	106	null

DOCTOR	Doctor Id	Room No	Date Qualified
	50	1	1963 - 09 - 01
	51	2	1973 - 09 - 12
	52	3	1990 - 10 - 02
	53	4	1965 - 06 - 30

R	Patient Id	Registered With	Doctor Id	Room No	Date Qualified
	100	50	50	1	1903 - 09 - 01
	101	50	50	1	1963 - 09 - 01
	102	52	52	3	1990 - 10 - 02
	103	53	53	4	1965 - 09 - 01
	104	50	50	1	1963 - 09 - 01
	105	52	52	3	1990 -10 - 02

Figure 13.9 The equijoin of PATIENT and DOCTOR over *RegisteredWith* = *DoctorId*. Note the repetition of values in the *RegisteredWith* and *DoctorId* columns.

The case where the joining attribute is a primary key (or candidate key) in one relation and an identically named foreign key in the other is so frequent that this type of join is known as the **natural join**, represented by the notation $R*S$. This is identical to an equijoin of R and S over the primary key of R (present in S as a foreign key), followed by a projection to eliminate the duplicate attribute. Figure 13.10 shows the natural join of DOCTOR and APPOINTMENT over the common attribute *DoctorId*.

DOCTOR	Doctor Id	Room No
	50	1
	51	2
	52	3
	53	4

APPOINTMENT	Doctor Id	Patient Id	Appt Date	Appt Time
	50	100	1994-08-10	10:00:00
	50	100	1994-08-16	10:50:00
	50	101	1994-08-21	11:20:00
	50	102	1994-08-10	10:10:00
	50	103	1994-08-10	10:20:00
	50	104	1994-08-10	10:00:00
	52	105	1994-08-10	10:10:00
	53	106	1994-08-10	11:30:00

R	Doctor Id	Room No	Patient Id	Appt Date	Appt Time
	50	1	100	1994-08-10	10:00:00
	50	1	100	1994-08-16	10:50:00
	50	1	101	1994-08-21	11:20:00
	50	1	102	1994-08-10	10:10:00
	50	1	103	1994-08-10	10:20:00
	50	3	104	1994-08-10	10:00:00
	52	3	105	1994-08-10	10:10:00
	53	4	106	1994-08-10	11:30:00

Figure 13.10 The natural join R ←DOCTOR * APPOINTMENT. Note the single occurrence of the join attribute *DoctorId* in the result.

Semijoin

A semijoin is a join where the result is composed entirely of tuples from one of the relations; $R \bowtie R(a) = S(b)$ is the semijoin of R and S over $R(a)$ and $S(b)$ with only the attributes of R forming the result. Semijoin operations are very frequently used in the internal processing trees of relational systems, where they are used to select tuples that match in a secondary index and a base relation. In terms of the previous example a request for the DOCTOR tuples of all doctors who have an appointment scheduled for 21/08/1994 gives

DOCTOR	DoctorId	RoomNo
	50	I

Outer join

The join operation only includes tuples from a relation if there is a match with the other relation. In some cases it is desirable to include tuples from one or both the relations even if they do not match; this is an outer join. Depending on which relations supply non-matching tuples we can distinguish **left outer join**, $R = \bowtie S$, (where non-matching tuples are supplied from the first-named relation), **right outer join**, $R \bowtie = S$, (where non-matching tuples are supplied from the second-named relation) and **full outer join**, $R = \bowtie = S$, (where non-matching tuples are supplied from both relations). The non-matching tuples are padded with null values for the missing attributes.

The natural join of DOCTOR and APPOINTMENT in Figure 13.10 omitted doctors without appointments from the result. The request for a list of *all* doctors and their appointments is an outer join. If we specify the DOCTOR relation first it is a left outer join, $DOCTOR = \bowtie APPOINTMENT$, with the result shown in Figure 13.11.

R	DoctorId	RoomNo	PatientId	ApptDate	ApptTime
	50	I	100	1994-08-10	10:00:00
	50	I	100	1994-08-16	10:50:00
	50	I	102	1994-08-21	11:20:00
	50	I	103	1994-08-10	10:10:00
	50	I	104	1994-08-10	10:20:00
	51	2	null	null	null
	52	3	102	1994-08-10	10:00:00
	52	3	105	1994-08-10	10:10:00
	53	4	106	1994-08-10	11:30:00

Figure 13.11 The left outer join of DOCTOR and APPOINTMENT over *DoctorId*.

13.3.5 Union

The result of the union operation contains all tuples from one operand together with all non-duplicate tuples from the other. Both operands must be *union compatible*; they must contain the same number of attributes which must correspond pairwise in their domains. Attribute names need not be the same. Union may be used to add new rows to relations, and to combine the results of two different, but union compatible, queries.

PATIENT 1 ∪ PATIENT 2

PATIENT 1	Patient Id	Registered With
	100	50
	101	50
	102	52
	103	53

∪

PATIENT 2	Patient Id	Registered With
	103	53
	104	50
	105	52

→

R	Patient Id	Registered With
	100	50
	101	50
	102	52
	103	53
	104	50
	105	52

Figure 13.12   The UNION operator applied to a pair of union compatible relations. Note the removal of duplicate tuples from the result.

13.3.6 Intersection

Intersection is also a binary operation on union compatible relations. The result contains one copy of each tuple found in both of the operand relations. Using the same operands as the previous union example, only one tuple (103, 53) appears in both operands, and this is copied to the result.

Figure 13.13 shows the result of applying the intersection operator to the PATIENT_1 and PATIENT_2 relations of Figure 13.12.

PATIENT1 ∩ PATIENT2

→

R	PatientId	RegisteredWith
	103	53

Figure 13.13   The INTERSECTION operator, ∩, applied to the PATIENT1 and PATIENT2 relations of Figure 13.12.

13.3.7   Difference

The difference operator also requires union compatible relations. The result contains all tuples in the first operand that are not found in the second. Unlike the union and difference operators, the order in which the operands are specified is significant because difference is not commutative.

Figure 13.14 shows the two possible results of applying the difference operator to the PATIENT1 and PATIENT2 relations of Figure 13.12.

PATIENT1 – PATIENT2

→	R	PatientId	RegisteredWith
		100	50
		101	50
		102	52

PATIENT2 – PATIENT1

→	R	PatientId	RegisteredWith
		104	50
		105	52

Figure 13.14   The DIFFERENCE operator applied to the PATIENT1 and PATIENT2 relations of Figure 13.12. Note that the order of the operands is significant.

13.4 Codd's twelve rules

In the early years of relational database systems many products were advertised as relational despite limited, or even questionable, adherence to the relational model. As a response to this wide variation in claims, Codd proposed a set of rules that were intended to define the important characteristics and capabilities of any relational system [Codd 1986]. Today, relational purity is less of an issue but Codd's rules remain a useful yardstick for what can be expected from a conventional relational DBMS.

Despite being invariably referred to as 'Codd's twelve rules', there are in fact thirteen rules. The first, Rule Zero or the Foundation Rule, requires that a relational database management system must manage the database entirely through its relational capabilities.

The remaining twelve rules may be summarized as follows:

1. **Information Rule**: All information is represented logically by values in tables.
2. **Guaranteed Access Rule**: Every data value is logically accessible by a combination of table name, column name, and primary key value.

3. **Missing Information Rule**: Null values are systematically supported independent of data type.
4. **System Catalogue Rule**: The logical description of the database is represented, and may be interrogated by authorized users, in the same way as for normal data.
5. **Comprehensive Language Rule**: A high-level relational language with a well-defined syntax expressible as character strings must be provided to support all of the following: data and view definition, integrity constraints, interactive and programmable data manipulation, and transaction start, commit and rollback.
6. **View Update Rule**: The system should be able to perform all theoretically possible updates on views.
7. **Set Level Updates Rule**: The ability to treat whole tables as single objects applies to insertion, modification and deletion, as well as retrieval of data.
8. **Physical Data Independence Rule**: User operations and application programs should be independent of any changes in physical storage or access methods.
9. **Logical Data Independence Rule**: User operations and application programs should be independent of changes in the logical structure of base tables provided they involve no loss of information.
10. **Integrity Independence Rule**: Entity and referential integrity constraints should be defined in the high-level relational language referred to in Rule 5, stored in the system catalogues and enforced by the system, not by application programs.
11. **Distribution Independence Rule**: User operations and application programs should be independent of the location of data when it is distributed over multiple computers.
12. **Non-subversion Rule**: If a low-level procedural language is supported, it must not be able to subvert integrity or security constraints expressed in the high-level relational language.

Of these, Rules 1 to 5, 7 and 8 are reasonably well supported by the majority of current commercial relational DBMSs. The increasing number that conform to the SQL2 standard (discussed below) also provide a limited degree of support for Rules 6, 9 and 10. Rule 11 applies only to distributed systems, and the difficulties of Rule 12 are largely avoided by the simple expedient of not providing a low-level procedural language.

13.5 Summary

We have described the relational model and relational algebra, concentrating on descriptions of the operations of the algebra. Although relational query languages do not generally use relational algebra it is important as an intermediate language which can be manipulated by query processors, described in Chapter 12.

Chapter 14

SQL

14.1 Introduction

SQL (Structured Query Language) is an ISO standard database language designed for relational database systems. It has been developed from a language originally called SEQUEL (Structured English QUEry Language) designed by an IBM research team as part of the experimental relational database project System R [Chamberlin *et al.* 1976]. It was subsequently adopted as the query language for IBM's commercial systems SQL/DS and DB2. The first ANSI standard for the language was published in 1986 and adopted the following year.

The language is not without critics, for example [Date 1984], and system vendors have introduced many extensions to address some of the limitations. The second edition of the standard, widely known as SQL2, has regularized some of this independent development. At present, most vendors have issued new releases that comply with this standard. In the meantime, a third edition of the standard is under discussion. This will in due course provide a common basis for many of the vendor-specific extensions that were not addressed in, or have been introduced since, the second edition.

All commercial relational database vendors now support some variant of the SQL standard. It is also the basis of most database interoperability products and proposals (for example, ODBC). The use of SQL has become so widespread that: 'For better or worse, SQL is intergalactic dataspeak.' [Manifesto 1990]. Consequently, a grasp of the language is essential for anybody involved with the design, construction and maintenance of data-intensive applications.

In the following sections we describe the main data definition and manipulation statements of SQL2. This is not intended as a complete description of the standard (*see* [Date and Darwen 1993] and the standards documents [ISO 1992]). The standard defines three levels of compliance: full, intermediate and entry level. Few implementations reach the full compliance level, so not all of the language features discussed here will be supported by any particular implementation.

14.2 Data definition

SQL2 introduces a number of new features not found in earlier editions of the standard. At the highest level these include the **catalog**, which provides a standardized system catalog interface, and the schema. The catalog contains the Information Schema (named INFORMATION_SCHEMA) which is publicly accessible and contains details of all database elements in each of one or more schemas. The Information Schema is a collection of views on an underlying Definition Schema. This provides a mapping from the implementation-specific catalogs to the standard form and is not accessible in SQL statements.

14.2.1 The schema

A schema is created using the CREATE SCHEMA statement in one of the following forms:

- Create a schema called healthcentre using the authorization (that is, user id) of the current session:

  ```
  CREATE SCHEMA healthcentre;
  ```

- Create a schema using the authorization abc. The schema will be named abc:

  ```
  CREATE SCHEMA AUTHORIZATION abc;
  ```

- Create a schema called healthcentre using the authorization abc

  ```
  CREATE SCHEMA healthcentre AUTHORIZATION abc:
  ```

Each of these forms may be followed by any number of schema element definitions, including domains, tables, views (virtual tables), and so on. Other schema elements such as character sets, collation sequences and translations are not discussed here.

14.2.2 SQL2 data types

Table 14.1 lists the SQL2 data types. The maximum precision of numeric types and maximum lengths of bit and character types is implementation defined. For example, the INTEGER type is typically implemented as a 32-bit integer number, giving a range of –2,147,483,648 to +2,147,483,648, and SMALLINT as a 16-bit integer ranging from –32768 to +32767.

Some implementations permit alternative display and entry formats for dates such as DD/MM/YYYY, MM-DD-YYYY or DD-MMM-YYYY to cover international variation in conventions.

Type name with alternatives	Description
FLOAT(p)	Floating point number with precision equal to or greater than p.
REAL	Single precision floating point number.
DOUBLE PRECISION	Double precision floating point number.
INTEGER	
INT	Integer number.
SMALLINT	Integer number of lower precision than INTEGER.
DECIMAL(p,s)	
DEC(p,s)	
NUMERIC(p,s)	Exact decimal numeric value. The number of decimal digits or precision is given by p, and the number of digits after the decimal point (the scale) by s.
BIT(n)	Fixed-length bit string of n bits, numbered 1–n.
BIT VARYING(n)	Variable-length bit string, maximum length n
CHAR(n)	
CHARACTER(n)	Fixed-length character string of length n.
VARCHAR(n)	
CHARACTER VARYING(n)	Variable-length character string of maximum length n.
DATE	Date expressed as YYYY-MM-DD
TIME	Time expressed in HH:MM:SS
TIME(p)	The optional fractional seconds precision (p) extends the format to include fractions of seconds. for example TIME(2) HH:MM:SS.SS WITH TIMEZONE adds six positions for a relative displacement from 12:59 to +13:00 in
TIME WITH TIMEZONE	hours:minutes.
TIME(p) WITH TIMEZONE	
INTERVAL	Relative time interval (positive or negative). Intervals are either year/month expressed as 'YYYY-MM' YEAR TO MONTH, or day/time, for example, 'DD HH:MM:SS' DAY TO SECOND(p).
	Intervals may be expressed as any sub-range within these two types, but may not cross the month/day boundary. Used in date arithmetic to increment or decrement DATE or TIME
TIMESTAMP	Absolute time expressed as YYYY-MM-DD HH:MM:SS
TIMESTAMP(p)	The optional fractional seconds precision (p) extends the format as for TIME.
	Timestamps are guaranteed to be unique and to increase monotonically.
TIMESTAMP WITH TIMEZONE	
TIMESTAMP(p) WITH TIMEZONE	See TIME WITH TIMEZONE.

Table 14.1   SQL2 data types.

Limited support for domains is provided by the CREATE DOMAIN statement which associates a domain name with a data type and, optionally, a default value. For example, in a schema where several tables include a person identifier column, each which should be of the same type:

```
CREATE DOMAIN personid AS CHAR(10);
```

or

```
CREATE DOMAIN healthcentre.personid AS CHAR(10);
```

The second form includes the schema name. This qualified form may be used when creating all types of schema element, but it is rarely needed because a normal SQL session connects with a single schema. Domain definitions may also be followed by a constraint definition that limits the range of possible values. This employs a CHECK clause of the same type as described later under assertions (Section 14.3.11).

14.2.3 Tables

The CREATE TABLE statement specifies a logical definition of a stored table, or **base table**. Physical storage structures are not defined by the standard. Constraints (*see below*) defined as part of the CREATE TABLE statement may influence the choice of physical structure, but this and any mechanisms for modifying the physical structure are implementation dependent. Figure 14.1 shows the CREATE TABLE statements in a possible schema for a local health centre database.

In its minimal form the CREATE TABLE statement specifies the table name and lists the name and type of each column. The type may be either a standard data type or a domain name. As with domain names, the table name may be qualified by a schema name. Null values will be permitted unless the NOT NULL constraint is specified. This should be used for primary keys, foreign keys in mandatory relationships and any other column that must contain a valid non-null value.

A DEFAULT clause may be used to set column values automatically whenever a new row is inserted. In the absence of a specified default value, nullable columns will contain nulls and a type-dependent value, such as zero or an empty string, will be used for non-nullable columns.

Optional table constraints may be included in the CREATE TABLE statement after the column definitions:

- The PRIMARY KEY clause lists one or more columns that form the primary key.
- If the table contains other unique keys these columns can be specified in a UNIQUE clause.

- The FOREIGN KEY clause is used to specify referential integrity constraints and, optionally, the actions to be taken if the related tuple is deleted or the value of its primary key is updated.

Optionally, a constraint may be named by preceding it with CONSTRAINT <constraint_name>. A named constraint may be changed or removed using the ALTER TABLE statement (see below).

The events used to trigger referential integrity checks and their corresponding actions are specified in ON UPDATE and ON DELETE clauses. The possible actions are SET NULL, SET DEFAULT and CASCADE. Both SET NULL and SET DEFAULT remove the relationship by resetting the foreign key value to null or, if it has one, to its default. These are typically used for optional relationships. The action is the same for both updates and deletes.

The effect of CASCADE depends on the event. With ON UPDATE, a change to the primary key value in the related tuple is reflected in the foreign key. Changing a primary key should normally be avoided but it may be necessary when a value has been entered incorrectly. Cascaded updates ensure that referential integrity is maintained. With ON DELETE, if the related tuple is deleted then the tuple containing the foreign key is also deleted. Cascaded deletes are therefore appropriate for mandatory relationships such as those involving weak entity classes.

```
CREATE TABLE person (
      person_id          personid        NOT NULL,
      initials           CHAR(4)         NOT NULL,
      last_name          CHAR(24)        NOT NULL,
      date_of_birth      DATE,
      sex                CHAR(1),
   PRIMARY KEY (person_id)
);
CREATE TABLE doctor (
      doctor_id          personid        NOT NULL,
      phone_no           CHAR(10)        NOT NULL,
      room_no            CHAR(4)         NOT NULL,
      date_qualified     DATE,
      date_appointed     DATE,
   PRIMARY KEY (doctor_id),
   UNIQUE (room_no),
   FOREIGN KEY (doctor_id) REFERENCES person (person_id)
      ON DELETE CASCADE
      ON UPDATE CASCADE
);
CREATE TABLE patient (
      patient_id         personid        NOT NULL,
      date_registered    DATE            NOT NULL,
```

```
        registered_with      personid,
     PRIMARY KEY (patient_id),
     FOREIGN KEY (patient_id) REFERENCES person (person_id)
          ON DELETE CASCADE
          ON UPDATE CASCADE,
     CONSTRAINT patientreg
        FOREIGN KEY (registered_with) REFERENCES doctor (doctor_id)
          ON DELETE SET NULL
          ON UPDATE CASCADE
  );
  CREATE TABLE appointment (
        doctor_id            personid       NOT NULL,
        patient_id           personid       NOT NULL,
        appt_date            DATE           NOT NULL,
        appt_time            TIME           NOT NULL,
        appt_duration        INTEGER        DEFAULT 10,
     PRIMARY KEY (doctor_id, appt_date, appt_time),
     FOREIGN KEY (doctor_id) REFERENCES doctor (doctor_id)
          ON DELETE CASCADE
          ON UPDATE CASCADE,
     FOREIGN KEY (patient_id) REFERENCES patient (patient_id)
          ON DELETE CASCADE
          ON UPDATE CASCADE
  );
  CREATE TABLE treatment (
        doctor_id            personid       NOT NULL,
        patient_id           personid       NOT NULL,
        condition            CHAR(20)       NOT NULL,
        treatment            CHAR(20)       NOT NULL,
        start_date           DATE           NOT NULL,
        end_date             DATE,
     PRIMARY KEY (doctor_id, patient_id, condition, treatment,
                  start_date),
     FOREIGN KEY (doctor_id) REFERENCES doctor (doctor_id)
          ON DELETE CASCADE
          ON UPDATE CASCADE,
     FOREIGN KEY (patient_id) REFERENCES patient (patient_id)
          ON DELETE CASCADE
          ON UPDATE CASCADE
  );
```

Figure 14.1 SQL table definitions for part of an imaginary health centre schema.

In the example schema, the patient table includes the named referential integrity constraint

```
CONSTRAINT patientreg
   FOREIGN KEY (registered_with) REFERENCES DOCTOR (doctor_id)
      ON DELETE SET NULL
      ON UPDATE CASCADE
```

The registration of a patient with a doctor is optional to enable patient details to be entered before the patient is assigned to a doctor, and to simplify the task of transferring a patient from one doctor to another. The foreign key registered_with will be updated to reflect any change in the primary key of the doctor table but, if the related doctor tuple is deleted, it will be set to null.

Both doctor and patient are subclasses of person and have a mandatory relationship with this superclass. In the patient table, the constraint

```
FOREIGN KEY (patient_id) REFERENCES PERSON (person_id)
      ON DELETE CASCADE
      ON UPDATE CASCADE,
```

ensures that changes to the primary key of the person table are reflected in the associated member of the patient subclass, and that the patient tuple is removed when the person tuple is deleted.

By default, all constraints are immediate and not deferrable. This means that they are checked immediately after any change is made, and that this behaviour cannot be changed. The initial behaviour may be changed by adding 'INITIALLY DEFERRED' at the end of the definition. This delays constraint checking until the end of the current transaction.

Both 'INITIALLY DEFERRED' and the alternative 'INITIALLY IMMEDIATE' may be followed by 'DEFERRABLE' or 'NOT DEFERRABLE' to indicate whether or not the behaviour can be later changed by a SET CONSTRAINTS command (*see below*).

In addition to persistent base tables it is also possible to create local or global temporary tables within a transaction. These may be preserved or deleted when the transaction is committed. For example:

```
CREATE LOCAL TEMPORARY TABLE tmptable1 (
    col1  INTEGER,
    col2  CHAR(10)
)ON COMMIT DELETE ROWS ;
```

or

```
CREATE GLOBAL TEMPORARY TABLE tmptable2 (
    col1  INTEGER,
    col2  CHAR(10)
)ON COMMIT PRESERVE ROWS ;
```

Derived, or **virtual**, tables are known in SQL as **views**. They are defined as stored queries on base tables and so are introduced after we have discussed SQL queries. Similarly we delay discussion of **assertions**. These provide an additional mechanism for specifying semantic integrity constraints and are defined in terms of search conditions identical to those used in queries.

14.2.4 Schema evolution

SQL2 provides several methods for altering an existing schema. In general, a named schema element may be removed by a DROP statement and, in several cases, its definition may be changed by an ALTER statement.

The schema itself may be dropped using:

```
DROP SCHEMA health centre RESTRICT
```

The keyword RESTRICT describes the behaviour of the command. In this case the command will succeed only if the schema is empty, otherwise an exception will be raised. The alternative:

```
DROP SCHEMA health centre CASCADE
```

effectively applies the appropriate drop command to all schema elements, thus removing the entire schema irrespective of its content.

Domains may be removed using either of the following statements:

```
DROP DOMAIN personid RESTRICT
DROP DOMAIN personid CASCADE
```

The first of these will fail if the domain is in use in any existing column definition, whereas the effect of CASCADE is to replace all uses of the domain by its corresponding data type. In our example schema, the first of these statements would raise an exception, but the second would set the data type of the person_id, patient_id, doctor_id and registered_with columns to CHAR(10).

If the domain has any associated constraints, the keyword CASCADE may be followed by either of:

```
DROP COLUMN CONSTRAINT <constraint name list>
KEEP COLUMN CONSTRAINT <constraint name list>
```

to specify whether the applicability of the constraint to columns of this domain type should be removed or retained.

Tables may be removed using the DROP TABLE statement:

```
DROP TABLE appointment RESTRICT
DROP TABLE appointment CASCADE
```

Here, CASCADE drops all associated referential integrity constraints and views that depend on this base table, whereas RESTRICT raises an exception if any of these exist.

Several changes are possible within a table. New columns may be added or existing ones dropped. For example, to add or remove a column to indicate the patient's response to a course of treatment:

```
ALTER TABLE treatment ADD COLUMN columnname
ALTER TABLE treatment DROP COLUMN columnname RESTRICT
ALTER TABLE treatment DROP COLUMN columnname CASCADE
```

Again, CASCADE and RESTRICT determine the drop behaviour when constraints or views depend on the affected column.

Column default values may be altered or dropped. For example, the default value of 10 for the duration of an appointment may be changed to 15, or the default may be removed:

```
ALTER TABLE appointment ALTER COLUMN appt_duration SET DEFAULT 15
ALTER TABLE appointment ALTER COLUMN appt_duration DROP DEFAULT
```

The association of a column with a domain may be removed, resetting the column to the underlying data type of the domain. The next command changes the person_id column in the Person table to CHAR(10). Other columns using the personid domain are unchanged.

```
ALTER TABLE person ALTER COLUMN person_id DROP DOMAIN
```

This statement may optionally be followed by one of

```
DROP COLUMN CONSTRAINT <constraint name list>
KEEP COLUMN CONSTRAINT <constraint name list>
```

which determine whether domain constraints should also be removed or should continue to apply to the column.

Finally, table constraints may be added:

```
ALTER TABLE tablename ADD <table constraint>
```

Here, the table constraint is specified in the same way as in a CREATE TABLE statement. Named table constraints may be removed:

```
ALTER TABLE tablename DROP CONSTRAINT <constraint name list>
```

followed by CASCADE or RESTRICT to specify the behaviour when there are further dependencies.

14.3 Data manipulation

The four main SQL data manipulation statements are:

SELECT – retrieve information
INSERT – add new rows to a table
DELETE – delete existing rows from a table
UPDATE – modify data in existing rows

The examples in the following sections assume that the tables in the health centre schema are populated with data as shown in Figure 14.2.

PERSON	person_id	initials	last_name	date_of_birth	sex
	100	T	Williams	1972-01-12	m
	101	J	Garcia	1981-03-18	f
	102	W	Fisher	1950-10-22	m
	103	K	Waldon	1942-06-01	m
	104	P	Timms	1928-06-03	m
	105	A	Dryden	1944-06-23	m
	106	F	Fogg	1955-10-16	f
	50	A	Cameron	1937-04-04	m
	51	B	Finlay	1948-12-01	m
	52	C	King	1965-06-06	f
	53	D	Waldon	1938-07-08	f

DOCTOR	doctor_id	phone_no	room_no	date_qualified	date_appointed
	50	1234	1	1963-09-01	1991-05-10
	51	1235	2	1973-09-12	1991-05-10
	52	1236	3	1990-10-02	1993-04-01
	53	1237	4	1965-06-30	1994-03-01

PATIENT	patient_id	date_registered	registered_with
	100	1992-01-01	50
	101	1992-10-12	50
	102	1993-09-03	52
	103	1994-10-01	53
	104	1994-05-01	50
	105	1994-06-15	52
	106	1994-06-24	null

APPOINTMENT	doctor_id	patient_id	appt_date	appt_time	appt_duration
	50	100	1994-08-10	10:00:00	10
	50	100	1994-08-16	10:50:00	10
	50	102	1994-08-21	11:20:00	20
	50	103	1994-08-10	10:10:00	10
	50	104	1994-08-10	10:20:00	20
	52	102	1994-08-10	10:00:00	10
	52	105	1994-08-10	10:10:00	10
	53	106	1994-08-10	11:30:00	10

TREATMENT	doctor_id	patient_id	condition	treatment	start_date	end_date
	50	100	c1	t1	1992-07-02	1992-08-15
	50	100	c2	t2	1992-07-02	1992-08-15
	50	102	c3	t3	1993-09-03	1993-09-10
	50	100	c4	t4	1993-02-05	1992-02-19
	50	104	c5	t5	1994-07-12	1994-08-10
	50	104	c6	t6	1994-08-02	1994-08-14

Figure 14.2 Sample data for the health centre schema.

14.3.1   The SELECT statement

The SELECT statement is a declarative specification for a query that retrieves information from tables. In doing so it produces a result which is itself a table, albeit normally a temporary table that ceases to exist when the transaction is committed. An SQL table departs from the strict definition of a relation in that unique rows are not enforced. Thus a query result may contain duplicate rows. In other words, whereas a relation is a set of tuples, a table is a bag or multiset of rows.

In its most basic form the SELECT statement consists of three clauses, SELECT, FROM and WHERE, of which only the WHERE clause is optional. The SELECT clause contains a list of columns that are to appear in the result. The FROM clause specifies the tables to be used, and the WHERE clause specifies conditions that determine which rows appear in the result.

The SELECT clause should not be confused with the relational algebra select or restrict operator. Somewhat misleadingly, the SQL SELECT clause approximates to the relational project, and the relational selection or restriction operation is supported by the WHERE clause.

The simplest retrieval statement must contain both a SELECT and a FROM clause. For example, to find the `initials` and `last_name` of all persons in the person table:

```
SELECT initials, last_name
FROM person;
```

initials	last_name
T	Williams
J	Garcia
W	Fisher
K	Waldon
P	Timms
A	Dryden
F	Fogg
A	Cameron
B	Finlay
C	King
D	Waldon

The symbol * may be used to stand for all columns in the table. The entire person table shown in Figure 14.2 may be retrieved using the statement

```
SELECT *
FROM person;
```

which is equivalent to:

```
SELECT person_id, initials, last_name, date_of_birth, sex
FROM person;
```

A WHERE clause may be added to restrict the rows displayed to those which match a particular condition. To find the initials and last name of the person whose id is 104:

```
SELECT initials, last_name
FROM person
WHERE person_id = '104';
```

initials	last_name
P	Timms

Simple Boolean selection conditions, or predicates, use any of the operators {=, <>, <, <=, >, >=}, and multiple conditions may be linked using the logical operators AND, OR, NOT.

As mentioned earlier, SQL tables are bags or multisets of rows, possibly containing duplicate values. To retrieve only unique values, that is, to apply the proper semantics of the relational algebra project operator, the list of columns in the SELECT clause is qualified by DISTINCT. This query returns the list of unique values of last_name in the person table. Notice that the duplicate name 'Waldon' appears only once in the result.

```
SELECT DISTINCT last_name
FROM person;
```

last_name
Cameron
Dryden
Finlay
Fisher
Fogg
Garcia
King
Timms
Waldon
Williams

The order in which rows are returned by a SELECT statement is implementation dependent. The apparent ordering of the above example is typical of many systems but this behaviour cannot be guaranteed. To sort the result, use the ORDER BY clause:

```
SELECT DISTINCT initials, last_name
FROM person
ORDER BY last_name, initials;
```

initials	last_name
A	Cameron
A	Dryden
B	Finlay
W	Fisher
F	Fogg
J	Garcia
C	King
P	Timms
D	Waldon
K	Waldon
T	Williams

This query sorts the result in ascending order of last name then initials. The keywords ASC and DESC may be used to select ascending or descending order on each sort key. For example,

```
ORDER BY last_name ASC, initials DESC;
```

would produce a result sorted in ascending order of last name and, within each last name, on descending order of initials. Using this ordering the two 'Waldon' entries in the previous example would be reversed.

14.3.2   Aliases, derived tables and derived columns

Column names may be qualified by the name of the table in which they are found. Strictly, this is only necessary where queries involve more than one table containing columns with the same name. Where the column name is unique the table qualification may be omitted. Queries can also be shortened by using a correlation name or alias for a table name. The alias is specified in the FROM clause:

```
SELECT p.initials, p.last_name
FROM person p
WHERE p.last_name = 'Cameron';
```

is equivalent to:

```
SELECT person.initials, person.last_name
FROM person
WHERE person.last_name = 'Cameron';
```

Both return the same result:

initials	last_name
A	Cameron

SQL2 extends aliasing to include column names. For example a derived table may be expressed in a FROM clause using the keyword AS:

```
SELECT p.init, p.name
FROM person AS p(id, init, name);
```

Here, p is an alias for the person table and id, init, and name are aliases for the person_id, initials and last_name columns. Both table and column aliases are used here in the SELECT clause. Derived columns may also be specified in the SELECT clause as constant values:

```
SELECT 'Dr' AS title, initials, last_name
FROM person
WHERE last_name = 'Cameron';
```

title	initials	last_name
Dr	A	Cameron

or as the result of operations on base table columns. For example, using the concatenation operator ||:

```
SELECT 'Dr ' || initials || last_name AS name
FROM person
WHERE last_name = 'Cameron';
```

name
Dr A Cameron

14.3.3 Joining multiple tables

Earlier forms of SQL and systems conforming to Entry Level SQL2 only allow joins to be expressed as join or linkage conditions in the WHERE clause. For example, to find the id numbers and dates of registration for each registered patient, together with the id number and appointment date of the doctor with whom each is registered:

```
SELECT p.patient_id, p.date_registered,
    d.doctor_id, d.date_appointed AS doctor_appointed
FROM patient p, doctor d
WHERE p.registered_with = d.doctor_id;
```

The method of expressing the join condition in the WHERE clause allows conventional theta, or inner, join operations and, by omitting the condition, the Cartesian product. However, there is no direct provision in this method for supporting left, right or full outer joins. SQL2 provides specific support for these and other types of join through the use of a JOIN expression in the FROM clause. For example, the previous query specified an inner join in the WHERE clause. In SQL2, this can also be expressed as:

```
SELECT p.patient_id, p.date_registered,
    d.doctor_id, d.date_appointed AS doctor_appointed
FROM patient p INNER JOIN doctor d ON p.registered_with =
d.doctor_id;
```

The result of the inner join query only includes rows representing those patients who are registered with a doctor. If the registered_with column contains a null, the patient is not included in the result.

patient_id	date_registered	doctor_id	doctor_appointed
100	1992-01-01	50	1991-05-10
101	1992-10-12	50	1991-05-10
102	1993-09-03	52	1993-04-01
103	1994-10-01	53	1994-03-01
104	1994-05-01	50	1991-05-10
105	1994-06-15	52	1993-04-01

To include any unregistered patients, an outer join is used. In this case it is a left outer join because the patient table is specified as the left-hand side of the join expression:

```
SELECT p.patient_id, p.date_registered,
    d.doctor_id, d.date_appointed AS doctor_appointed
FROM patient p LEFT OUTER JOIN doctor d
        ON p.registered_with = d.doctor_id;
```

The result contains all of the rows that would be produced by an inner join, together with those rows from the left-hand table that are not matched by rows in the right-hand table.

patient_id	date_registered	doctor_id	doctor_appointed
100	1992-01-01	50	1991-05-10
101	1992-10-12	50	1991-05-10
102	1993-09-03	52	1993-04-01
103	1994-10-01	53	1994-03-01
104	1994-05-01	50	1991-05-10
105	1994-06-15	52	1993-04-01
106	1994-06-24	null	null

Alternatively, to include details of doctors whether or not they have registered patients, a right outer join is used:

```
SELECT p.patient_id, p.date_registered,
       d.doctor_id, d.date_appointed AS doctor_appointed
FROM patient p RIGHT OUTER JOIN doctor d
       ON p.registered_with = d.doctor_id;
```

The result contains the rows produced by an inner join, together with those rows from the right-hand table that are not matched by rows in the left hand table.

patient_id	date_registered	doctor_id	doctor_appointed
100	1992-01-01	50	1991-05-10
101	1992-10-12	50	1991-05-10
104	1994-05-01	50	1991-05-10
null	null	51	1991-05-10
102	1993-09-03	52	1993-04-01
105	1994-06-15	52	1993-04-01
103	1994-10-01	53	1994-03-01

The full outer join combines the effect of both left and right outer joins. In the next query the result contains the rows produced by an inner join, plus rows representing each patient with a null value in the registered_with column, and rows representing each doctor whose id number does not appear in any patient's registered_with column.

```
SELECT p.patient_id, p.date_registered,
       d.doctor_id, d.date_appointed AS doctor_appointed
FROM patient p FULL OUTER JOIN doctor d
       ON p.registered_with = d.doctor_id;
```

patient_id	date_registered	doctor_id	doctor_appointed
100	1992-01-01	50	1991-05-10
101	1992-10-12	50	1991-05-10
null	null	51	1991-05-10
102	1993-09-03	52	1994-03-01
103	1994-10-01	53	1994-03-01
104	1994-05-01	50	1991-05-10
105	1994-06-15	52	1993-04-01
106	1994-06-24	null	null

SQL2 also allows natural joins to be specified in a JOIN expression. This query joins the patient and appointment tables using a condition specified in the WHERE clause:

```
SELECT p.patient_id, p.registered_with,
    a.doctor_id, a.appt_date, a.appt_time
FROM patient p, appointment a
WHERE p.patient_id = a.patient_id;
```

The join condition involves two columns with identical names, so the query may be simplified to:

```
SELECT p.patient_id, p.registered_with,
    a.doctor_id, a.appt_date, a.appt_time
FROM patient p NATURAL JOIN appointment a;
```

patient_id	registered_with	doctor_id	appt_date	appt_time
100	50	50	1994-08-10	10:00:00
100	50	50	1994-08-16	10:50:00
102	52	50	1994-08-21	11:20:00
103	53	50	1994-08-10	10:10:00
104	50	50	1994-08-10	10:20:00
102	52	52	1994-08-10	10:00:00
105	52	52	1994-08-10	10:10:00
106	null	53	1994-08-10	11:30:00

14.3.4 Aggregate functions and the GROUP BY clause

SQL provides several set, or aggregate, functions for summarizing the content of columns. These act upon a set, or multiset, of values indicated by the function argument.

- COUNT (expr).   The number of rows or values matching the query.
- MIN (expr).   The minimum value of expr.
- MAX (expr).   The maximum value of expr.
- SUM (expr).   The sum of values of expr.
- AVG (expr).   The average or mean of values of expr.

In each case *expr* is a value expression, optionally preceded by ALL or DISTINCT. The value expression is typically a column name, the most frequent exception being the use of COUNT(*) to determine the number of rows matching a query. For example, the total number of appointments (rows) in the appointments table can be found using:

```
SELECT num_appt = COUNT(*)
FROM appointment;
```

num_appt
8

The number of appointments for a particular doctor could be found by:

```
SELECT num_appt = COUNT(*)
FROM appointment
WHERE doctor_id = '50';
```

num_appt
5

Any column name could be used instead of *, but if the column is nullable the query will return the number of non-null values, rather than the total number of rows.

```
SELECT COUNT (appt_duration) AS num_appt,
    MIN (appt_duration) AS min_appt,
    MAX (appt_duration) AS max_appt,
    AVG (appt_duration) AS avg_appt,
    SUM (appt_duration) AS total_appt
FROM appointment
WHERE doctor_id = '50';
```

returns the count, minimum, maximum, average and sum of all non-null values of appt_duration for the specified doctor.

num_appt	min_appt	max_appt	avg_appt	total_appt
5	10	20	14	70

In this case the value returned by COUNT(appt_duration) is the same as that returned by COUNT(*) in the previous query. However, because appt_duration is a nullable column it could return a lesser value if any row contained a null. In the Patient table there is a null value in the registered_with column, so the query

```
SELECT COUNT(*) as n, COUNT(patient_id) AS n_id,
    COUNT(registered_with) as n_reg
FROM patient;
```

returns the following result:

n	n_id	n_reg
7	7	6

The value expression may be qualified by DISTINCT, in which case the function operates only on the unique non-null values. For example, to determine how many different patients have appointments with a particular doctor:

```
SELECT COUNT ndp = (DISTINCT patient_id)
FROM appointment
WHERE doctor_id = '50';
```

ndp
4

The ALL qualifier may also be used, but is redundant because it is implied when neither qualifier is used. ALL and DISTINCT have no meaning with MIN and MAX.

So far we have applied the aggregate functions to an entire table or to a subset of the rows. In each case the result has been a single row containing the aggregated values. It is also possible to group rows on the value in a particular column and apply the aggregate functions within each group. For example, to produce summary statistics on each doctor's appointments, a GROUP BY clause is added to indicate that the grouping should be within values of doctor_id:

```
SELECT doctor_id, COUNT (appt_duration) AS num_appt,
    MIN (appt_duration) AS min_appt,
    MAX (appt_duration) AS max_appt,
    AVG (appt_duration) AS avg_appt,
    SUM (appt_duration) AS total_appt
FROM appointment
GROUP BY doctor_id;
```

doctor_id	num_appt	min_appt	max_appt	avg_appt	total_appt
50	5	10	20	14	70
52	2	10	10	10	20
53	1	10	10	10	10

The result contains one row for each distinct value of the columns specified in the GROUP BY clause. Note that the grouping columns must correspond to the non-aggregate columns specified in the SELECT clause.

In a grouped query, the WHERE clause determines which rows participate in the groups. In other words, the grouping is applied after selection of the required rows. The HAVING clause may be used to apply a restriction to the groups, that is, one that determines which groups will appear in the result. For example, to limit the previous query to those groups containing two or more appointments:

```
SELECT doctor_id, COUNT (appt_duration) AS num_appt,
    MIN (appt_duration) AS min_appt,
    MAX (appt_duration) AS max_appt,
    AVG (appt_duration) AS avg_appt,
    SUM (appt_duration) AS total_appt
FROM appointment
GROUP BY doctor_id
HAVING COUNT (appt_duration) > 1;
```

doctor_id	num_appt	min_appt	max_appt	avg_appt	total_appt
50	5	10	20	14	70
52	2	10	10	10	20

14.3.5 Set operators: UNION, EXCEPT and INTERSECT

SQL includes explicit support for the relational algebra set operators UNION, difference (EXCEPT) and INTERSECT. These act on the results of a pair of subqueries, both of which must have compatible SELECT clauses to ensure union compatibility. The basic form of a statement using any of these operators is

```
<SELECT statement> <set operator> <SELECT statement>
```

The following examples each use an additional table PERSON2(initials, last_name) which is union compatible with the projection of Initials and Last_name from the main Person table:

PERSON2	initials	last_name
	P	Timms
	A	Dryden
	F	Fogg
	B	Timms
	R	Timms

The UNION operator combines rows from two separate SELECT queries. By default it maintains the normal semantics of sets and relations by removing duplicate rows. For example, this query finds the names of people born before 1950 in the Person table and combines them with the names in the `Person2` table:

```
SELECT initials, last_name
FROM person
WHERE date_of_birth < '1950-01-01'
UNION
SELECT initials, last_name
FROM person2;
```

initials	last_name
A	Cameron
A	Dryden
B	Finlay
B	Timms
D	Waldon
F	Fogg
K	Waldon
P	Timms
R	Timms

If necessary, the more normal SQL multiset semantics may be enforced by using UNION ALL. In this example, duplicate rows appear for 'P. Timms and A. Dryden':

```
SELECT initials, last_name
FROM person
WHERE date_of_birth < '1950-01-01'
UNION ALL
SELECT initials, last_name
FROM person2;
```

initials	last_name	
A	Cameron	
B	Finlay	
K	Waldon	
D	Waldon	
P	Timms	
A	Dryden	
P	Timms	duplicate row
A	Dryden	duplicate row
F	Fogg	
B	Timms	
R	Timms	

The EXCEPT operator implements set difference. The result contains all those returned by the first subquery that are not in the set of rows returned by the second. Again, the ALL keyword may be added to allow duplicate rows to appear in the result.

Here, both 'P. Timms' and 'A. Dryden' occur in the result of both subqueries, so they are removed from the result:

```
SELECT initials, last_name
FROM person
WHERE date_of_birth < '1950-01-01'
EXCEPT
SELECT initials, last_name
FROM person2;
```

initials	last_name
A	Cameron
B	Finlay
K	Waldon
D	Waldon

The result of the INTERSECT operator contains only those rows that are returned by both subqueries:

```
SELECT initials, last_name
FROM person
WHERE date_of_birth < '1950-01-01'
INTERSECT
SELECT initials, last_name
FROM person2;
```

initials	last_name
A	Dryden
P	Timms

14.3.6 Other predicates used in search conditions

We have already seen the use of simple Boolean predicates for comparing values in a search condition. Here we discuss several other SQL predicates that may be used in the WHERE clause:

- Character string comparison: the LIKE predicate.
- Range comparison: the BETWEEN predicate.
- Testing for Null values: the IS NULL predicate.
- Set comparisons: the IN, EXISTS, ANY, SOME, and ALL predicates.
- Date and time range comparison: the OVERLAPS predicate.

The LIKE predicate

The LIKE predicate is used for partial matching of character strings. The following meta-characters may be used:

% matches zero or more characters
_ matches any single character

For example, to find details of all persons whose last name begins with F:

```
SELECT * FROM person
WHERE last_name LIKE 'F%';
```

person_id	initials	last_name	date_of_birth	sex
102	W	Fisher	1950-10-22	m
106	F	Fogg	1955-10-16	f
51	B	Finlay	1948-12-01	m

or, to find the details of all persons whose last name has six characters beginning with F:

```
SELECT * FROM person
WHERE last_name LIKE 'F_____';
```

person_id	initials	last_name	date_of_birth	sex
102	W	Fisher	1950-10-22	m
51	B	Finlay	1948-12-01	m

Where the meta-characters must be interpreted literally an optional ESCAPE clause is used:

```
WHERE name LIKE '!%%' ESCAPE '!';
```

indicates that any character following '!' should be interpreted literally, so the predicate matches all values of name beginning with %. Note that the second % in the predicate is the normal wildcard meta-character.

The BETWEEN predicate

The BETWEEN predicate tests whether a value lies in a specified range. It may be used with any data type.

```
SELECT * FROM person
WHERE last_name BETWEEN 'Dryden' AND 'King';
```

is equivalent to

```
SELECT * FROM person
WHERE last_name >= 'Dryden' AND last_name <= 'King';
```

person_id	initials	last_name	date_of_birth	sex
101	J	Garcia	1981-03-18	f
102	W	Fisher	1950-10-22	m
105	A	Dryden	1944-06-23	m
106	F	Fogg	1955-10-16	f
51	B	Finlay	1948-12-01	m
52	C	King	1965-06-06	f

The IS NULL predicate

The IS NULL predicate is used to test for NULL values. Because a NULL is not a value in the conventional sense and two NULLs are never equal to each other, search conditions of the form

```
expression1 <operator> expression2
```

are always FALSE if either expression1 or expression2 evaluates to NULL. Similarly, the expression

```
column = NULL
```

cannot be used to test whether the value of column is NULL. Instead, an explicit test using the IS NULL predicate is required. For example, to find the id numbers of any patients who are not registered with a doctor:

```
SELECT patient_id FROM patient
WHERE registered_with IS NULL;
```

patient_id
106

Unlike the other predicates described here, the inverse form may be expressed as IS NOT NULL:

```
SELECT patient_id FROM patient
WHERE registered_with IS NOT NULL;
```

patient_id
100
101
102
103
104
105

Set comparison predicates: IN

The multiset membership operator IN may be used with an explicit set of values as an alternative to multiple Boolean conditions joined by OR. The statement

```
SELECT * FROM person
WHERE last_name IN ('Williams', 'Waldon', 'Cameron');
```

returns all rows in which the last_name column contains one of the listed values. It is directly equivalent to

```
SELECT * FROM person
WHERE last_name = 'Williams'
    OR last_name = 'Waldon'
    OR last_name = 'Cameron';
```

person_id	initials	last_name	date_of_birth	sex
50	A	Cameron	1937-04-04	m
100	T	Williams	1972-01-12	m
103	K	Waldon	1942-06-01	m
53	D	Waldon	1938-07-08	f

The (multi)set of values may also be provided by a query statement. For example, the following query finds the details of all persons who are also patients and are registered with doctor whose id is 50. For each row in the `Person` table the IN predicate evaluates to TRUE if the `person_id` is a member of the (multi)set of `Patient_id` values retrieved by the nested SELECT statement from the `Patient` table.

```
SELECT * FROM person
WHERE person_id IN ( SELECT patient_id FROM patient
            WHERE registered_with = '50' );
```

person_id	initials	last_name	date_of_birth	sex
100	T	Williams	1972-01-12	m
101	J	Garcia	1981-03-18	f
104	P	Timms	1928-06-03	m

The EXISTS predicate

The EXISTS predicate provides a means of testing for the existence of one or more rows in a multiset. The previous query using an IN predicate can also be expressed as:

```
SELECT * FROM person p
WHERE EXISTS ( SELECT * FROM patient
        WHERE patient_id = p.person_id
        AND registered_with = '50' );
```

For each row in `Person`, the EXISTS predicate evaluates to TRUE if the nested SELECT statement returns one or more rows.

The EXISTS predicate is often used in negated form to test for the non-existence of matching rows. This query finds all doctors who do not appear in the `Appointment` table:

```
SELECT * FROM doctor d
WHERE NOT EXISTS ( SELECT * FROM appointment
        WHERE doctor_id = d.doctor_id );
```

doctor_id	phone_no	room_no	date_qualified	date_appointed
51	1235	2	1973-09-12	1991-05-10

The quantified comparison predicates ANY, SOME and ALL

The quantified comparison predicates are used to quantify normal comparison operators {=, <>, <, <=, >, >=} when they are used in set comparisons. The SOME keyword is interchangeable with ANY. They are used to test whether any of the values in the expression match the specified condition. When used as '= ANY' it is equivalent to IN, so the query to find persons who are also patients and are registered with the doctor whose id is '50' can also be expressed as:

```
SELECT * FROM person
WHERE person_id = ANY ( SELECT patient_id FROM patient
            WHERE registered_with = '50' );
```

ANY is perhaps more useful when used in inequality tests. For example, the following query finds persons whose date of birth is less than that of any male in the Person table. In other words, it returns the Person records of anyone who is older than the youngest male in the table (100, T, Williams, m, 1981-01-12). The only row not matching this condition is (101, J, Garcia, 1981-03-18, f).

```
SELECT * FROM person
WHERE date_of_birth < ANY ( SELECT date_of_birth FROM person
            WHERE sex = 'm' );
```

person_id	initials	last_name	date_of_birth	sex
50	A	Cameron	1937-04-04	m
51	B	Finlay	1948-12-01	m
52	C	King	1965-06-06	f
102	W	Fisher	1950-10-22	m
103	K	Waldon	1942-06-01	m
53	D	Waldon	1938-07-08	f
104	P	Timms	1928-06-03	m
105	A	Dryden	1944-06-23	m
106	F	Fogg	1955-10-16	f

The ALL predicate is used to test whether all of the values in the expression match the specified condition. This example finds persons who are older than all of the females in the table:

```
SELECT * FROM person
WHERE date_of_birth < ALL ( SELECT date_of_birth FROM person
             WHERE sex = 'f' );
```

person_id	initials	last_name	date_of_birth	sex
50	A	Cameron	1937-04-04	m
104	P	Timms	1928-06-03	m

The OVERLAPS predicate

The OVERLAPS predicate is provided to support temporal queries involving the overlap of two time periods. Each operand has two components, a start point specified as a DATE, TIME or TIMESTAMP type, and an end point or duration. If the second component is a duration then it is of type INTERVAL. For example, the expressions

```
(TIME '11:30:00', TIME '12:30:00')
OVERLAPS
(TIME '12:00:00', TIME '14:00:00')
```

and

```
(TIME '11:30:00', TIME '12:30:00')
OVERLAPS
(TIME '12:00:00', INTERVAL '2' HOUR)
```

both return TRUE. Thus, given a table containing treatment histories:

TREATMENT (patient_id, doctor_id, ailment, treatment, date_started, date_ended)

This query would list treatment and condition details for patients with overlapping treatments:

```
SELECT t1.patient_id,
     t1.condition, t1.treatment,
     t2.condition, t2.treatment
FROM treatment t1, treatment t2
WHERE t1.patient_id = t2.patient_id
  AND (t1.start_date, t1.end_date)
    OVERLAPS
    (t2.start_date, t2.end_date);
```

14.3.7 Adding new rows: the INSERT statement

New rows are added to a table using the INSERT statement. The inserted values may be specified either as a list of values in a VALUES clause, or as the result of a SELECT statement. For example, adding a new row to the person table:

```
INSERT INTO person
VALUES ('107', 'B', 'Timms', '1955-02-21', 'm');
```

and the patient table:

```
INSERT INTO patient
VALUES ('107', '1994-08-11', '53');
```

Here, the table name is indicated in the INSERT clause and the VALUES list contains one value for each column in the table. The list of values must correspond to, and be in the same order as, that specified in the CREATE TABLE statement used when the table was created.

When the values are listed in a different order or only a subset of column values are specified, the columns must be listed in the INSERT clause. In these cases the VALUE list must correspond in order and type to the columns in the INSERT list. The order need not match that used when the table was created. For example, omitting the date_of_birth from Person:

```
INSERT INTO person (person_id, initials, last_name, sex)
VALUES ('108', 'R', 'Timms', 'f');
```

or the registered_with column from Patient:

```
INSERT INTO patient (patient_id, date_registered)
VALUES ('108', '1994-08-11');
```

or specifying columns in an arbitrary order:

```
INSERT INTO appointment (appt_date, appt_time, patient_id,
doctor_id)
VALUES ('1994-08-11', '10:30:00', '107', '53');
```

Columns omitted from the insert list take their default value if one has been specified, otherwise they are set to NULL. However, if a column that was specified as NOT NULL is omitted the insert is rejected.

INSERT statements using the VALUES clause can add only one row at a time to the table. Using a SELECT statement enables a set (or multiset) of rows to be added by a single command. For example, given a table

NEW_PATIENT (patient_id)

containing a list of id numbers of new patients, the new patients could be inserted in the `Patient` table with `date_registered` set to the current date and `registered_with` set to NULL:

```
INSERT INTO patient (patient_id, date_registered)
SELECT patient_id, current_date
FROM new_patient;
```

The 'current_date' value in the SELECT clause is a datetime function that returns the current date. Also available are 'current_time' and 'current_timestamp'.

14.3.8   Removing rows: the DELETE statement

In its simplest form, the DELETE statement removes every row from the specified table. For example

```
DELETE FROM person;
```

leaves the `Person` table empty. The range of affected rows is restricted by a WHERE clause. Thus to remove a specific record from the Person table:

```
DELETE FROM person
WHERE person_id = '100';
```

Note that in our example schema, FOREIGN KEY constraints (ON DELETE CASCADE) were specified in both the `Patient` and `Doctor` tables for their relationships with `Person`, so the above deletions would have side-effects that maintain referential integrity. In both cases the delete operation is cascaded and removes the corresponding rows from the Patient and Doctor tables.

The WHERE clause of a DELETE statement may contain a subquery. In this statement rows are deleted from the Patient table if the patient does not have an entry in the Appointment table:

```
DELETE FROM patient
WHERE patient_id NOT IN ( SELECT patient_id
                          FROM appointment );
```

Here, the `patient_id` column of each row in the `Patient` table is tested for membership of the multiset returned by the subquery. Any row that fails this test is deleted.

14.3.9 Modifying existing rows: the UPDATE statement

As with the INSERT statement, UPDATE may be used with values specified explicitly in the statement or derived from another table. The columns to be updated and their new values are indicated by a SET clause. For example, the statement

```
UPDATE appointment
SET doctor_id = '53';
```

changes the doctor_id of every row in the appointment table to '53'. The range of affected rows may be restricted by a WHERE clause. To give all of one doctor's appointments to another:

```
UPDATE appointment
SET doctor_id = '53'
WHERE doctor_id = '52';
```

As with other statements an update may be performed according to the result of a search condition involving other tables. This query changes the registered_with column of any patient born on or after 1 January 1980 so that they are registered with the doctor whose id is 51:

```
UPDATE patient
SET registered_with = '51'
WHERE patient_id IN ( SELECT person_id FROM person
                      WHERE date_of_birth >= '1980-01-01');
```

14.3.10 Views

SQL views act as virtual tables and are derived from existing base tables or other views. They are used where data is often retrieved from one or more existing tables. Views are defined in terms of the results of SELECT statements. They may be used to simplify queries by combining the results of one or more joins into a single virtual table, or to restrict access to the base table columns included in the view. The data in the underlying tables is not physically replicated; instead the view is usually stored as a query definition.

This view definition combines all matching details from both Person and Patient records into a single virtual table:

```
CREATE VIEW named_patient AS
SELECT pt.patient_id,
    ps.initials, ps.last_name, ps.date_of_birth, ps.sex,
    pt.date_registered, pt.registered_with
FROM person ps, patient pt
WHERE ps.person_id = pt.patient_id;
```

The next view also joins the Person and Patient tables, but here the name information from `Person` is omitted so that the virtual patient records remain anonymous. Where necessary, access to the base tables can be restricted using the GRANT statement to ensure that such information is only available to privileged users.

```
CREATE VIEW unnamed_patient AS
SELECT pt.patient_id,
       ps.date_of_birth, ps.sex,
       pt.date_registered, pt.registered_with
FROM person ps, patient pt
WHERE ps.person_id = pt.patient_id;
```

Views may be particularly useful where the underlying query is complex. This view joins `Person` (twice), `Patient`, `Doctor` and `Appointment` to form a single `Diary` table containing appointment details together with the names of doctors and patients:

```
CREATE VIEW diary AS
SELECT pp.initials || pp.last_name AS patient,
       pd.last_name AS doctor, a.appt_date, a.appt_time
FROM person pp, patient p, appointment a, doctor d, person pd
WHERE pp.person_id = p.patient_id
  AND p.patient_id = a.patient_id
  AND a.doctor_id = d.doctor_id
  AND d.doctor_id = pd.person_id;
```

The names of columns in the view may be derived, as in the above examples, from the underlying query, or may be specified in a list of column names following the view name. A column list is only required if two columns in the SELECT clause have the same name. The previous view definition could also be expressed as:

```
CREATE VIEW diary (patient, doctor, appt_date, appt_time) AS
SELECT pp.initials || pp.last_name,
       pd.last_name, a.appt_date, a.appt_time
...
```

Once created, views may be queried in the same way as normal base tables:

```
SELECT initials, last_name
FROM named_patient
WHERE registered_with IS NULL;
```

initials	last_name
F	Fogg

```
SELECT patient, doctor, appt_time
FROM diary
WHERE appt_date = '1994-08-10'
ORDER BY doctor, appt_time;
```

patient	doctor	appt_time
T Williams	Cameron	10:00:00
K Waldon	Cameron	10:10:00
P Timms	Cameron	10:20:00
W Fisher	King	10:00:00
A Dryden	King	10:10:00
F Fogg	Waldon	11:30:00

So far we have only considered retrieving information from views. Updates on views are more problematic. In general, views on multiple joined tables are not updatable because they may map to several possible updates on base tables with no way for the system to choose between them. Views containing aggregates or other derived columns, such as the Patient column in Diary, are also not updatable because there can be no reverse mapping from the derived columns to their source.

SQL2 views may only be updated if they fulfil all of the following conditions:

- The FROM clause contains only a single table, or single updatable view.
- The SELECT clause only contains column names, and any column occurs once only.
- The query does not use SELECT DISTINCT, GROUP BY, HAVING, UNION, INTERSECT or EXCEPT.

For any view that is intended to be updated, a WITH CHECK OPTION clause may be added to the view definition so that the system may check the validity of updates and generate suitable execution plans. For example:

```
CREATE VIEW anon_person AS
SELECT person_id, date_of_birth, sex
FROM person
WITH CHECK OPTION;
```

As with base tables, views may be removed using the DROP command, for example:

```
DROP VIEW diary;
```

14.3.11 Assertions

Table constraints support the basic requirements of entity and referential integrity. Other semantic constraints may be added using the CREATE ASSERTION statement. Assertions are defined in terms of a search condition which is tested whenever an update affects any tuple referenced in the search condition. If the search condition returns true, the constraint is satisfied but, if it returns false, the constraint is violated and an exception is raised.

Any search condition that can appear in a WHERE clause may be used in an assertion. For example, the doctor whose id is '51' may not be available during the afternoon. This assertion will be violated by any attempt to update or insert an appointment for a time after 13:00 which involves this doctor:

```
CREATE ASSERTION pm_appointment
CHECK ( NOT EXISTS ( SELECT * FROM appointment
                     WHERE doctor_id = '52'
                     AND appt_time > '13:00' ));
```

14.4 Transactions

SQL supports the transaction model discussed in Chapter 10 through the use of four transaction statements. There is no 'begin transaction' statement. A transaction is started by the first schema or data manipulation statement of a session, or the first following a COMMIT WORK or ROLLBACK WORK command.

All of the changes made within a transaction are made permanent and visible to other transactions by the COMMIT WORK command. The ROLLBACK WORK command aborts the current transaction and cancels any changes made during the transaction and makes affected database objects visible to other transactions.

These two commands suffice for most purposes. However, SQL2 also defines a constraint mode, an access mode and an isolation level that may be set individually for each transaction. The constraint mode is set using the SET CONSTRAINTS statement, and all of the others by the SET TRANSACTION statement.

The SET CONSTRAINTS statement allows the mode of any named constraint to be set to IMMEDIATE or DEFERRED, provided that the original constraint definition specified that it was DEFERRABLE. The command may be issued at any time during a transaction, and the changed mode remains in force for the rest of the transaction, or until changed by another SET CONSTRAINTS statement. For example:

```
SET CONSTRAINTS ALL DEFERRED;
SET CONSTRAINTS constraint1, constraint2 IMMEDIATE;
```

The first example sets all deferrable constraints to deferred, and the second sets the constraints named constraint1 and constraint2 to immediate. The second case assumes that the named constraints were defined as deferrable and were either initially, or have subsequently been, set to deferred.

The SET TRANSACTION command must be issued before the first command of a transaction, and is valid only for that transaction. The access mode is either 'read-only' or 'read-write', the latter being the default. The read-only mode prevents modification of base tables and views during a transaction. The isolation level decreases from the default 3 down to 0 as follows:

3 The default level. Provides the full isolation of serializable transactions.
2 'Phantoms' are permitted. If T1 retrieves a set of rows matching a search condition, and T2 then inserts rows that would match that condition, a subsequent read by T1 using the same search condition retrieves a different set of rows.
1 Unrepeatable reads are also permitted. If T1 reads a row and T2 later modifies that row and commits, a subsequent read by T1 will retrieve the modified row. If T2 deletes the row and commits, the row will no longer be found by T1.
0 Dirty reads are also permitted. If T1 modifies a row which is then read by T2, a subsequent rollback by T1 will leave T2 with a row that should not have existed. At this level, all changes made within a transaction are visible to other transactions, thus transactions may read changes that are subsequently rolled back.

Examples:

```
SET TRANSACTION READ ONLY;
SET TRANSACTION ISOLATION LEVEL 2;
```

14.5 Access control

The owner of a database may control access to tables and views by other users through the grant command.[1] The privileges that may be granted are SELECT, INSERT, UPDATE, DELETE or REFERENCES. INSERT, UPDATE and REFERENCES may optionally be followed by a list of columns to restrict the privilege to only part of the table. The REFERENCES privilege enables a user to create a table that references a named column or a column in the named table, whether or not they have other permissions on the table or column.

The GRANT statement may include a single privilege or a list of privileges. Where all privileges are to be granted the keywords ALL PRIVILEGES may be used instead of the explicit list. The grantee (the recipient of the privileges) may be a single user identifier, a list of users or the keyword PUBLIC standing for all users.

---

1 The USAGE privileges may also be granted on domains, character sets, collation sequences and translations. Other than domains, these objects are not discussed here. For details, *see* [ISO 1992].

The optional clause WITH GRANT OPTION may be added to the end of the statement to enable the grantee in turn to grant the privilege to others.

For example, to enable all users to perform retrieval operations on the Patient, Doctor and Appointment tables:

```
GRANT SELECT ON patient, doctor, appointment TO PUBLIC;
```

To enable users abc and def to execute select, insert and update operations on the Appointment table:

```
GRANT SELECT, INSERT, UPDATE ON appointment TO abc, def;
```

To enable user ghi to perform any operation on the Person table:

```
GRANT ALL PRIVILEGES ON person TO ghi;
```

To enable user abc to update only the appt_date, appt_time and appt_duration columns of the Appointment table:

```
GRANT UPDATE ( appt_date, appt_time, appt_duration )
ON appointment TO abc;
```

14.6 Embedded SQL

So far in this chapter we have assumed implicitly that SQL statements will be executed by an interactive or, possibly, batch interpreter. Such an interpreter is one form of **SQL Agent,** a program that manages a connection with the database system, allows text commands to be composed and passed to it, and receives and formats any returned results.

When SQL statements are embedded in a host programming language the program produced is also an agent and must be able to perform these tasks. The SQL standard defines additional statements for these purposes, and specifies a binding with the standard languages Ada, C, COBOL, FORTRAN, MUMPS, Pascal, and PL/1.

The format of Embedded SQL commands is similar in most of the specified host languages. In all host languages except MUMPS every statement begins with 'EXEC SQL'. In COBOL, each statement must also be terminated with 'END-EXEC'. A semicolon is used to terminate statements in Ada, C, Pascal and PL/1, but no terminator is required in FORTRAN. In MUMPS, statements begin with '@SQL(' and end with ')'.

The following sections provide an outline of the main features of Embedded SQL. We cannot hope to provide a complete description here as much depends on the particular host language used and, as with the interactive language, there is considerable variation between implementations. The examples used here show standard Embedded SQL statements in C language host programs.

14.6.1 Handling exceptions

The WHENEVER statement provides a simple error directive. Two error conditions are recognized, the general-purpose SQLERROR and the more specific NOT FOUND, used when a search condition fails. The possible actions that may be associated with these are GOTO <label>, where <label> is the identifier of a label in the host language program, and CONTINUE.

For example, the command

```
WHENEVER SQLERROR GOTO <label>;
```

transfers control to the labelled statement in the host program whenever any error condition occurs. The second example ignores any search condition failure by forcing execution to continue with the next statement following the one that caused the exception:

```
WHENEVER NOT FOUND CONTINUE;
```

Multiple WHENEVER statements may be used throughout an Embedded SQL program. Each applies to all following SQL statements until another WHENEVER statement is encountered for the same error condition. Note that the word 'following' here refers to the simple text sequence of the program, not to its flow of control or execution sequence. When more information about an exception or statement completion is required, the GET DIAGNOSTICS command may be used.

14.6.2 Managing connections and sessions

An SQL agent may manage one or more sessions at a time. A session is initiated using the CONNECT TO statement. For example:

```
EXEC SQL CONNECT TO 'healthcentre' AS 'conn1' USER 'abc';
```

Here, user abc establishes a connection to an SQL environment called healthcentre. The mapping between an environment name and a database object is implementation defined; in this case we may assume that it corresponds to the healthcentre schema in our example database. The connection name conn1 allows a particular session to be identified when multiple connections are used. For single session connections the name may be replaced by the keyword DEFAULT.

Several CONNECT TO statements may be issued to start different sessions, but there is only one active session at a time. All other sessions are said to be dormant.

Each CONNECT TO statement makes its own session active and any current session dormant. The SET CONNECTION statement is used to make a dormant session active.

Any or all sessions may be terminated by the DISCONNECT command. This is followed by the name of the session to be disconnected, the keyword CURRENT to indicate the current active session, or ALL to terminate all sessions. Any open transactions are rolled back when a session is terminated.

The following example illustrates a sequence of connection management commands for two sessions:

```
EXEC SQL CONNECT TO 'healthcentre' AS 'conn1' USER 'abc';
// conn1 is active
EXEC SQL CONNECT TO 'other' AS 'conn2' USER 'abc';
// conn2 is active
EXEC SQL SET CONNECTION 'conn1';
// conn1 is active
EXEC SQL SET CONNECTION 'conn2';
// conn2 is active
EXEC SQL DISCONNECT 'conn1';
// conn1 is closed, conn2 still active
EXEC SQL DISCONNECT CURRENT;
// conn2 is closed
```

For systems that support the full level of SQL2 compliance, it is possible to select a catalog or schema within a session using the SET CATALOG and SET SCHEMA commands. Both are followed by the name of the required object.

14.6.3 Declarations

Any host language variable that must also be visible within SQL statements must be declared in an SQL declaration section. For example, the following declares C language variables matching columns in the Appointment table:

```
EXEC SQL BEGIN DECLARE SECTION;
    char    doctor[11];
    char    patient[11];
    char    date[11];
    char    time[9];
    long    duration;
EXEC SQL END DECLARE SECTION;
```

The correspondence between SQL and host language data types differs between languages. Here, the C character arrays have one more byte than the SQL types to accommodate the conventional null-terminated strings used in this language. The

SQL date and time types are converted to their external character representation, and again one extra byte is allowed. The SQL integer type is assumed here to correspond to a C 'long integer'.

Given the above declaration, the C language variables can be used in SQL statements that transfer data between host language and database, and vice versa. For example, the following INSERT statement uses host language variables in the VALUES clause. Host variables are indicated here by an initial colon when they are used in an SQL statement.

```
EXEC SQL INSERT INTO appointment (doctor_id, patient_id,
                    appt_date, appt_time)
        VALUES (:doctor, :patient, :date, :time);
```

14.6.4 Indicator variables

The following query will set the values of the host variables init, lname and dob to those of the person whose id is 101. The host variables used to receive values from the database are placed in the additional INTO clause.

```
EXEC SQL BEGIN DECLARE SECTION;
    char        init[5];
    char        lname[20];
    char        dob[11];
EXEC SQL END DECLARE SECTION;
EXEC SQL SELECT initials, last_name, date_of_birth
        INTO :init, :lname, :dob
        FROM person
        WHERE person_id = '101';
```

In this case the query is guaranteed to return only a single row, so there is no problem caused by the mismatch between the single record view of the host language and the set of rows returned by most SQL queries. However, there are two potential problems. Firstly, date_of_birth is a nullable column and there is no equivalent of a null value in the host languages. This is one aspect of the impedance mismatch between database and host language type systems. Secondly, if the size of the host variable was declared incorrectly, or that of the database column was increased, the transferred value could be truncated. In this case, lname has been declared with a length of 20 bytes, whereas the corresponding column requires 24. Both of these problems may be addressed by the use of **indicator variables**.

An indicator variable is a host language integer variable that can be used to communicate a null value in both retrieval and update statements. In the case of character columns it also serves as a truncation indicator in retrieval queries. The previous query may be changed to use this method by declaring three suitable integer variables and changing the INTO clause as follows:

```
EXEC SQL BEGIN DECLARE SECTION;
    char        init[5];
    char        lname[25];
    char        dob[11];
    int         ind1, ind2, ind3;
EXEC SQL END DECLARE SECTION;
EXEC SQL SELECT initials, last_name, date_of_birth
        INTO :init:ind1, :lname:ind2, :dob:ind3
        FROM person
        WHERE person_id = '101'
```

Now, if the query executes successfully, each of the indicator variables will be set to zero. If, however, any of the variables overflows the corresponding indicator will be set to the true length of the returned string. If the `date_of_birth` value is null the `ind3` variable will be set to a negative value. Similarly, when used in an insert statement the indicator may be set to a negative value (typically 1) to pass a null value to the database.

14.6.5 Cursors

The previous example showed an Embedded SQL SELECT statement retrieving data directly into host variables. This is only possible when the query is guaranteed to return only a single row. In this case the WHERE clause specified a single value of the primary key, so only one row will be returned.

In the more general case, the number of rows returned is not known in advance and may exceed one. This is another aspect of the impedance mismatch problem. The standard host languages have no direct support for sets of compound types. To overcome this problem a **cursor** is used to enable the program to loop over the multiset of rows and process them one at a time.

The cursor is declared together with the query it serves, and acts as a reference to the current row in the result table. For example, the following command associates the cursor name csr1 with a SELECT statement that will return the initials and names of persons born on or after 1 January 1980:

```
EXEC SQL DECLARE csr1 CURSOR FOR
        SELECT initials, last_name
        FROM person WHERE date_of_birth >= '1980-01-01';
```

The declaration has no immediate effect on the database. The query is only executed when the cursor is opened, after which the cursor refers to the first record in the result set. Data values are then copied from the table structure into program variables using the FETCH statement. When no more records are available, the cursor is closed. The next example shows a fragment of an Embedded SQL C program that uses a cursor to retrieve one row at a time and print the row number, initials and name:

```
            /* host variables visible to SQL commands */
            EXEC SQL BEGIN DECLARE SECTION;
                char      init[5];
                char      lname[25];
            EXEC SQL END DECLARE SECTION;

            /* local variable, not used in SQL commands */
            int     rowcount = 0;

            /* error directives transfer control to label */
            EXEC SQL WHENEVER NOT FOUND GOTO lab1;
            /* declare the cursor and the query */
            EXEC SQL DECLARE csr1 CURSOR FOR
                  SELECT initials, last_name
                  FROM person WHERE date_of_birth >= '1980-01-01';

            /* open the cursor (execute the statement) */
            EXEC SQL OPEN csr1;

            /* loop forever fetching rows - i.e. until NOT FOUND */
            for ( ; ; ) {
               EXEC SQL FETCH csr1 INTO :init, :lname;
               /* process a row: e.g. increment rowcount
                * then print rowcount, initials and last_name
                */
               ++rowcount;
               printf ("%d %s %s\n", rowcount, init, lname );
            }
    lab1:
        EXEC SQL CLOSE csr1;

        if ( rowcount > 0 )   /* one or more rows retrieved */
            ...
```

The variable declarations distinguish those that need to be visible in SQL statements from those that are only used in host language statements. Next, the error directive ensures that control passes to the label lab1 when no data is found. The cursor is declared and opened, then the program enters a loop which fetches each row in turn from the result. Of itself, the loop has no end. It relies on the NOT FOUND error directive to provide the terminating condition when the FETCH statement fails to return a new row.

Update and delete operations on the current row may also be included in a cursor loop. For updates, the cursor declaration includes a FOR UPDATE OF clause to indicate which columns are expected to be updated. Within the loop, the current row may then be changed by an UPDATE statement that specifies WHERE CURRENT OF <cursor_name> in place of a conventional WHERE clause.

In the next example, rows are fetched from the Person table with the intention to update the registered_with column. Values of this column that match the string held in the old_doc host variable are updated to the value held in new_doc:

```
/* host variables visible to SQL commands */
EXEC SQL BEGIN DECLARE SECTION;
   char    patient[11];
   char    doctor[11];
   char    new_doc[11];
EXEC SQL END DECLARE SECTION;

/* local variable, not used in SQL commands */
char    old_doc[11];

/* error directives transfer control to label */
EXEC SQL WHENEVER NOT FOUND GOTO lab2;
/* declare the cursor and the query */
EXEC SQL DECLARE csr2 CURSOR FOR
     SELECT patient_id, registered_with
     FROM patient
     FOR UPDATE OF registered_with;

strcpy ( old_doc, "52" );
strcpy ( new_doc, "53" );

/* open the cursor (execute the statement) */
EXEC SQL OPEN csr2;

/* loop forever fetching rows - i.e. until NOT FOUND */
for ( ; ; ) {
  EXEC SQL FETCH csr2 INTO :patient, :doctor;
  /* if the doctor is old_doc then update to new_doc */
  if ( strcmp ( doctor, old_doc ) == 0 ) {
    EXEC SQL UPDATE person SET registered_with = :new_doc
       WHERE CURRENT OF csr2;
  }
}
```

```
lab2:
      EXEC SQL CLOSE csr2;
```

Delete operations within the cursor loop may be performed using:

```
EXEC SQL DELETE FROM <table_name> WHERE CURRENT OF
                                   <cursor_name>;
```

The cursors described so far iterate over the result set in one direction only; starting with the first row each fetch returns the next until there are no more rows. If a scrolling cursor is declared the direction of each fetch may also be specified. A scrolling cursor is declared using

```
EXEC SQL DECLARE csr SCROLL CURSOR FOR ...;
```

The fetch orientation can then be specified as NEXT, PRIOR, FIRST, LAST, ABSOLUTE n or RELATIVE n, where n is a positive integer indicating the absolute row number or a signed integer for the relative offset from the current row. For example:

```
FETCH PRIOR csr INTO ...;
```

Cursor names must be unique within a session, and cursor operations cannot span a transaction. If a transaction with an open cursor performs a commit or rollback the cursor is automatically closed.

14.6.6 Preparing and executing dynamic statements

In the form discussed so far, the Embedded SQL statements are fixed at compile time. For many applications it is preferable to compose statements at run time. This is the purpose of 'Dynamic SQL' programming. Dynamic SQL includes provision for preparing, executing and describing the results of SQL statements generated at run time and held in host language character string variables.

The EXECUTE IMMEDIATE command is used to prepare and execute non-SELECT commands intended for once-only use. The statement may be specified in a host variable or a literal string. For example:

```
EXEC SQL BEGIN DECLARE SECTION;
    char  *stmt = "INSERT INTO appointment \
           ( doctor_id, patient_id, appt_date, appt_time) \
           VALUES ('102', '52', '1994-10-19', '11:30:00')";
EXEC SQL END DECLARE SECTION;

EXEC SQL EXECUTE IMMEDIATE :stmt;
```

The statement string might also be read from an external file or constructed using host language statements.

SELECT statements, and others, requiring parameter substitution when executed must first be prepared. A prepared statement is encoded in a form ready for execution, and may be executed repeatedly. For example, the statements

```
EXEC SQL PREPARE s1 FROM :stmt;
EXEC SQL EXECUTE s1;
```

encode the statement in the string variable stmt, naming it s1. Subsequently, s1 is executed. These two commands have the same effect as the EXECUTE IMMEDIATE in the previous example but, because the statement is only encoded once in the PREPARE statement, repeated executions can be more efficient.

The EXECUTE statement may be used to associate parameter values with a prepared statement and then execute it. The following fragment declares two character variables, one to hold a skeleton statement, the other for values to be used when the statement is executed. The skeleton statement, including a '?' parameter indicator, is then copied to the stmt variable and the statement is prepared. Before each execution a value is copied into the doctor variable which is then specified in the USING clause of the following EXECUTE statement. The variables listed in the USING clause are substituted for the parameter indicators in the prepared statement. Parameter substitution may be used for any constant expression in WHERE clauses, the VALUES clause of INSERT statements and the SET clause of UPDATE statements.

```
EXEC SQL BEGIN DECLARE SECTION;
    char    stmt[100];
    char    doctor[11];
EXEC SQL END DECLARE SECTION;

strcpy ( stmt, "DELETE FROM appointment WHERE doctor_id = ?" );
EXEC SQL PREPARE s2 FROM :stmt;
...
strcpy ( doctor, "52" );
EXEC SQL EXECUTE s2 USING :doctor;
```

The complexity of a dynamic SELECT depends on whether the types of the retrieved columns are known. The next example demonstrates the simpler case where the types are known at compile time. The statement is prepared as before and a cursor declared for the prepared statement. Before execution, the parameter variable dob is set. Parameter substitution again takes place at execution time, but here the query is executed by opening the cursor rather than by an EXECUTE statement. The OPEN CURSOR statement includes a USING clause, identical to that of the EXECUTE command in the previous example.

The cursor loop is identical to that used with a non-dynamic cursor. The FETCH statement transfers each row of data into the named host variables until the NOT FOUND condition is true, when control passes to the label following the cursor loop.

```
          /* host variables visible to SQL commands */
          EXEC SQL BEGIN DECLARE SECTION;
            char    stmt[100];
            char    dob[11];
            char    init[5];
            char    lname[25];
          EXEC SQL END DECLARE SECTION;

          /* local variable, not used in SQL commands */
          int    rowcount = 0;

          /* error directives transfer control to label */
          EXEC SQL WHENEVER NOT FOUND GOTO lab3;
          /* set up statement string, prepare statement
           * and declare cursor
           */
          strcpy ( stmt, "SELECT initials, last_name \
                  FROM person WHERE date_of_birth > ? ");
          EXEC SQL PREPARE s2 FROM :stmt;
          EXEC SQL DECLARE csr3 CURSOR FOR s2;

          /* set the parameter and open the cursor */
          strcpy ( dob, "1979-12-31" );
          EXEC SQL OPEN csr3 USING :dob;

          /* loop forever fetching rows - i.e. until NOT FOUND */
          for ( ; ; ) {
            EXEC SQL FETCH csr3 INTO :init, :lname;
            /* process a row: e.g. increment rowcount
             * then print rowcount, initials and last_name
             */
            ++rowcount;
            printf ("%d %s %s\n", rowcount, init, lname );
          }
      lab3:
          EXEC SQL CLOSE csr3;
          if ( rowcount > 0 )   /* one or more rows retrieved */
          ...
```

Where the types of the retrieved columns are not known at compile time an SQL **descriptor area** must be used to obtain type, size and other information. The descriptor area contains **item descriptors** for each column returned by the statement. Each item descriptor holds the name, type, length, scale, precision, and current value of a column, together with a flag indicating whether it is nullable and a null indicator. Descriptor areas are created using the ALLOCATE DESCRIPTOR command, specifying the maximum number of item descriptors that it should contain. For example, to create a descriptor area with ten items:

```
EXEC SQL ALLOCATE DESCRIPTOR desc1 WITH MAX 10;
```

Once a descriptor area is allocated, a DESCRIBE statement is used to populate the item descriptors with type details of the returned columns.

```
EXEC SQL PREPARE s3 FROM :stmt;
EXEC SQL DESCRIBE s3 INTO desc1;
```

The number of item descriptors is found using the GET DESCRIPTOR command specifying COUNT as the required information. To fetch the number of items into a variable called ncols:

```
GET DESCRIPTOR desc1 :ncols = COUNT;
```

Thereafter, other details about each column may be found using the same command with a VALUE clause indicating the column or item number and a list of <host variable> = <identifier> pairs for the required information. To fetch the name, type, length, scale, precision and nullable flag into variables name, type, len, scale, prec and nullable for the item specified in *n*:

```
GET DESCRIPTOR desc1 VALUE :n :name = NAME, :type = TYPE,
                            :len = LENGTH, :scale = SCALE,
                            :prec = PRECISION,
                            :nullable = NULLABLE;
```

Other than the name, which is returned as a string, all of these are returned as integer values. The standard codes for the type are shown in the following table:

CHAR	1
NUMERIC	2
DECIMAL	3
INTEGER	4
SMALLINT	5
FLOAT	6
REAL	7
DOUBLE PRECISION	8
DATETIME	9
INTERVAL	10
VARCHAR	12
BIT	14
BIT VARYING	15

Table 14.2

Any implementation-defined type not defined in the standard returns a negative code. An additional descriptor variable DATETIME_INTERVAL_CODE is used to distinguish between DATE, TIME and TIMESTAMP for DATETIME types, and the possible intervals of an INTERVAL type. Also for intervals, the DATETIME_ INTERVAL_PRECISION variable is used to hold the precision of the leading field. In both cases, PRECISION indicates the optional seconds precision, if applicable.

Given this information, suitable host variables may be allocated. The correspondence between SQL types and those of the host language depends on both the implementation and language. The cursor is then opened as normal but, instead of fetching rows into named variables, the row is fetched into the descriptor area. Within the cursor loop, the program may iterate over the columns checking the null indicator where necessary and fetching the data value from the DATA attribute of the descriptor.

The following code fragment illustrates one method of retrieving data values in a cursor loop. It assumes that suitable data types, including char_data and int_data, have been declared to receive the data, and that two integer arrays, type[] and nullable[], contain the type codes and nullable flags for each column. The constants SQL_CHAR, SQL_INTEGER, and so on, are defined elsewhere to match the type codes. Typically, these are provided in an include file supplied with the database system.

```
EXEC SQL DECLARE csr4 CURSOR FOR s3;
EXEC SQL OPEN csr4 USING :dob;
for ( ; ; ) {
  EXEC SQL FETCH csr4 USING DESCRIPTOR desc1;
  /* process row using the descriptor */
  for ( n = 1; n <= ncols; n++ ) {
    /* if column n is nullable get its indicator */
    if ( nullable[n] == 1 )
      GET DESCRIPTOR desc1 VALUE :n :ind = INDICATOR;
    if ( ind < 0 )
      puts ( " NULL VALUE" );
    else {
      /* get the data value into a suitable variable */
      switch ( type[n] ) {
        case SQL_CHAR:    /* CHAR */
        case SQL_VARCHAR:  /* VARCHAR */
          GET DESCRIPTOR desc1 VALUE :n
                      :char_data = DATA;
          printf ( " %s", char_data );
          break;
        case SQL_INTEGER:  /* INTEGER */
        case SQL_SMALLINT:  /* SMALLINT */
          GET DESCRIPTOR desc1 VALUE :n
```

```
                              :int_data = DATA;
                 printf ( " %d", int_data );
                 break;
                 ... /* and so on for other types */
             }
          }
       }
    }
lab4:
    EXEC SQL CLOSE csr4;
    DEALLOCATE DESCRIPTOR descl;
```

The descriptor area may also be used with SELECT statements that return only a single row and do not need to use a cursor. For insert and update commands, the same PREPARE and DESCRIBE sequence is used, and values are placed into the INDICATOR and DATA descriptor variables using the SET DESCRIPTOR command. For example:

```
SET DESCRIPTOR descl VALUE :n INDICATOR = :ind;
SET DESCRIPTOR descl VALUE :n DATA = :int_data;
```

14.7 Summary

In this chapter we have described and evaluated the principal features of the SQL standard and described the features included in the current version. We have provided extensive descriptions of Dynamic and Embedded SQL as well as a presentation of all the principal features of SQL 2.

Chapter 15

EXTENDED RELATIONAL
DATABASE SYSTEMS

15.1 Introduction

Although network and hierarchical systems are still used for many large-scale mainframe-based transaction processing tasks, relational DBMSs have become widely accepted in almost all traditional database application areas. Indeed, the combination of inexpensive workstation and PC hardware with competitively priced DBMS has enabled a much wider adoption of the database approach.

Marketing and fashion have certainly played their parts, but the success of relational systems owes much to the associated improvements in data independence and in query languages. Declarative, set-based, query languages and the development of query optimization techniques largely freed application programmers from concerns with efficiency and physical storage.

Another major benefit has been the introduction of interpreters for *ad hoc* queries – previously all queries had been performed through compiled programs or report generators. This approach led to the development of increasingly flexible query systems such as Query By Example (QBE), forms-based query interfaces and 4GLs.

The relational approach has not been without its critics. During the 1980s, when the major relational systems were becoming firmly established, there was much debate about how well they supported the theoretical model. Systems were measured by their adherence to Codd's twelve rules of correct relational behaviour [Codd 1985a; 1985b; 1986] and invariably found wanting. When the first SQL standard was drafted, comparisons with other, arguably superior, languages were made and its limitations were highlighted (for example, [Date 1984]).

The late 1980s and early 1990s saw a vigorous debate between the proponents of relational DBMSs and the emerging object-oriented systems. Both were strongly championed as the basis for a new generation of database systems capable of supporting a much wider range of applications than hitherto [Atkinson *et al.* 1989; Manifesto 1990].

Object-oriented systems, discussed in Chapter 16, were developed initially in response to the needs for secure, reliable and persistent storage systems to support applications written in object-oriented programming languages such as C++ and Smalltalk. These systems have been used primarily for specialized applications where there is a clear benefit to be gained from an object-oriented programming approach, and little need for the application-building facilities of a conventional DBMS. Nevertheless, object-oriented concepts have had a major impact on subsequent development of relational systems.

Also, during the later 1980s, conventional database system developers were examining methods of extending the relational model to cater for a wider range of applications. This has led to the development of extended and extensible relational systems that seek to provide much of the functionality offered by object-oriented systems but without abandoning the firm theoretical basis of the relational approach. Indeed, some systems are now being marketed as 'object-relational' DBMSs to indicate this convergence.

In this chapter we review the major limitations of the current generation of relational database systems and examine various ways in which they can be overcome. Many of these problems are being addressed by the major system vendors and the continuing development of the SQL standard.

15.2 Extending the relational DBMS

Most of the limitations of past and current relational systems have been discussed elsewhere in this book. Here we are concerned with methods by which they can be overcome or minimized. They may be summarized as:

- Limitations of the relational model itself. These are mostly concerned with limitations in its capacity to represent some important aspects of data model semantics, such as generalization/specialization.
- Limitations of current implementations of relational DBMS. For example, most systems have a fixed and limited range of data types that is inadequate for the needs of many modern applications. Until quite recently, few systems have had adequate mechanisms for enforcing referential integrity.
- Limitations of set-oriented query languages. For example, the computationally incomplete nature of most query languages such as SQL; the mismatch between record-oriented processing in a conventional programming language and the set-oriented nature of SQL; and the lack of support for navigational access.

15.2.1 *Extending the range of data types*

Like their predecessors, relational DBMSs have evolved primarily to serve the needs of commercial and administrative data processing. The limited range of data types provided by most systems reflects this ancestry. Typically it includes the basic types of integer and floating point numbers, characters and strings, and adds a few others widely used in business applications, such as dates and fixed-precision decimal numbers.

In order to support the increasing range of applications discussed in Chapter 1, database systems need to be able to handle a much wider range of data types. Typical examples include:

- two-and three-dimensional points, lines, polygons, and primitive solids such as cubes, spheres and cylinders for design and manufacturing applications and spatial information systems;
- bitmap images for image processing applications;
- large structured text objects for office information systems and document management systems;
- multimedia video and sound objects for scientific, presentation, conferencing and other advanced information systems.

Each of these types represents an aggregation of other simpler types, but the relational model provides only limited structural support for aggregation. A relation models a class of composite objects formed by the aggregation of simple attributes. Higher-level aggregation in which an entity class is composed of a number of other, possibly composite, classes can only be modelled by relationships. However, such aggregation relationships are not distinguished semantically from any others. This task is left to the application programs.

To satisfy the requirements of modern applications, conventional database systems need to be extended to support the following, either by providing additional built-in types or by allowing programmers to define their own special-purpose types:

- specialized single-valued types;
- simple structured data types composed of a (usually) fixed number of basic component types;
- array and set types;
- complex or nested types in which a single object is composed of other, possibly complex, types;
- large object types such as extensive sections of text or multimedia video and sound clips whose size prevents storage in a single tuple because of the constraints of the underlying page size. In a conventional system these can only be modelled by arbitrary subdivision.

At first sight, many of these extensions might appear to conflict with the fundamental requirement that columns in a relation may only contain atomic values.

It is sufficient, however, for an object to be stored and retrieved as a single 'value'. Recall that Codd's 'Guaranteed Access Rule' simply requires all values to be accessible by a combination of relation name, column name and key value.

There is nothing in the relational model to prevent the use of domain-specific functions from accessing and manipulating information encapsulated within an outwardly atomic object. At some level, each of the standard SQL data types can be regarded as a complex type; an integer has both sign and magnitude, a character string is an ordered sequence of characters and a date has internal day, month and year components. Query languages provide a wide range of functions that may be used to manipulate these types and access their internal components.

Specialized single-valued types

Many simple types can be represented satisfactorily by the normal built-in data types. If necessary, simple integrity constraints may be used to restrict the range of values. Often, the required semantics of the type extend beyond such simple constraints and may conflict with those of a built-in type. Any additional semantics must then be implemented outside the database by applications programs.

For example, grades of employee might be specified as a restricted domain of strings, but grading implies ordering. The alphabetic ordering of grade names is unlikely to reflect the ordering of grades, so this must be implemented in some other way. A typical solution would be to use a separate lookup table of grade names with an ordered primary key, usually an integer. The employee relation would then contain a numeric reference to the grade implemented as a foreign key to the lookup table.

Queries of the form

```
SELECT ... where emp1.grade > emp2.grade ...
```

are then possible, and operations such as 'promotion' can be achieved by simply incrementing or decrementing the grade value. Referential integrity constraints will serve to ensure that the grades stay within the allowable range, but it is less easy to restrict the behaviour of an integer to the more limited semantics of an ordinal type. Queries that need to access employee data including the grade names will require an explicit join between the main table and that used for lookup. In cases where there are several such lookup tables the resulting queries may become excessively complex.

The lookup table solution effectively creates a new composite data type having a numeric and a character component. Queries involving these simple lookup tables can be greatly simplified by hiding the join behind a view, or alternatively, using stored procedures or rules (*see* Chapter 9). These are triggered by operations on what are now virtual columns in the main emp table.

The query language might be extended to allow a further level of 'dot' notation:

```
SELECT emp.grade.order, emp.grade.name from emp where ...
```

or a functional notation:

```
SELECT order(emp.grade), name(emp.grade) from emp where ...
```

Although this approach can simplify queries and make them easier to understand, it does not address the question of restricting the behaviour of the stored types. In this example, the employee's grade name and order are still implemented as character and integer types.

Simple composite types

Composite data types such as complex numbers or spatial coordinates are formed from simple combinations of the basic types. In an EER model these might be represented by compound attributes, reflecting the intention to treat them for many purposes as atomic objects. However, in a conventional DBMS these can only be represented either by a number of separate attributes, or by a single character type.

The SQL 2 standard `date`, `time` and `timestamp` types are built-in composite types. Although entered and retrieved as character strings, they can be manipulated as atomic objects through comparison and other operators. Limited arithmetic capabilities are defined using the `interval` type which can be added to or subtracted from times and dates. Where necessary an application can use function operators to gain access to their component parts representing days, months and years or hours, minutes and seconds.

Unlike these special-purpose types and the more basic built-in data types, the DBMS can have no knowledge of the behaviour of a compound object whether it is defined as a character string or as a group of attributes. The semantics of the type, including all type-specific operations, are external to the database and must be implemented entirely by application programs.

For example, a point in two-dimensional space might be recorded using a pair of numeric attributes for the x and y coordinates. Consider the relation

```
TOWN ( Name, E, N )
```

containing the names of towns and the geographical locations of their centres. The location is expressed as floating point numbers representing distances in kilometres east (E) and north (N) from an arbitrary origin. Most implementations of SQL provide basic mathematical operations such as a square root function, so the distance between a pair of towns could be determined by a statement such as

```
SELECT distance = SQRT((t1.E-t2.E)*(t1.E-t2.E)
                     +(t1.N-t2.N)*(t1.N-t2.N))
FROM town t1, town t2
WHERE t1.name = 'Canterbury' AND t2.name = 'Norwich'
```

Alternatively the application could retrieve the separate coordinate values of each town and perform the calculation itself. In either case, the semantics of distance are entirely external to the database. Such a simple operation may be performed in many different applications, adding to their complexity and with the attendant danger of minor coding errors leading to inconsistent behaviour.

Changes in the semantics of the operation can also lead to problems. A simple example might be a decision to change the units of the returned distance value from, say, kilometres to miles. This would require changes to all instances of the operation in the program source code. Similarly, changing the units of the stored data would require similar changes to the application code if the programs were to continue to present the distances in the same units as before the change.

Carefully controlled application development, libraries of reusable code and the use of source code version control systems would help to reduce the potential for coding and maintenance problems, but it can also be argued that these are tasks that should be under the control of the DBMS.

The presence of type-specific comparison operators for built-in types permits meaningful ordering and indexing within the database. Together with other helper functions, they can enable the query optimizer to substitute inverse (commutator) operators where necessary, to select appropriate join strategies, and to estimate the size of result sets. None of this is possible with externally controlled types with the result that queries are invariably executed less efficiently and a greater volume of data is transferred between database and applications than would be necessary with built-in types.

These problems, along with several others discussed in this chapter, arise from the separation of object state and behaviour between database and applications. Apart from the complexity of applications there are issues of data integrity to be considered. Behaviour that is implemented in applications is not available to users of interactive query systems. In some cases this separation may simply limit the utility of *ad hoc* queries, but in others may cause inconsistencies when query language users are able to bypass constraints that can only be imposed by the application programs.

A partial solution to these problems is to extend the range of built-in types to cover the more common needs. However, we could never hope to satisfy all requirements and a very large type system would inevitably bring with it a large cost in unused complexity and efficiency. A more realistic approach is to provide an extensible type system so that developers can add their own types suited directly to local requirements.

The experimental POSTGRES system [Stonebraker and Rowe 1986] provides both an extensive range of predefined types and an extensible type system. POSTGRES defines three categories of base types:

- Built-in types are those required in the system catalogues. They are hard-wired into the system.
- System types are additional predefined types supplied with the system and are available in each database created within an installation.

- User types are defined by database owners. They are linked into the server at run time and are available only in those databases for which they are defined.

It also provides an additional R-tree access method suitable for use with the predefined (that is, system) 2D spatial types, and some support for user-defined access methods.

Extensible type systems have been introduced in some of the more established commercial relational DBMSs. For example, the optional 'Object Management' extension to INGRES provides a framework for defining new data types that can be linked with the database server [INGRES 1989]. The process involves defining the internal storage structure for the type together with several mandatory functions. These include:

- translation functions between the internal data structure and an external textual representation;
- comparison functions to support equality and inequality tests and define ordering to enable indexing of the new type;
- support functions needed for hashing and generating optimizer statistics;
- any required functions defining the behaviour of the type.

In the spatial coordinate example, additional functions such as distance calculations may be defined. The TOWN relation could then be modified to use a single attribute Location of the new type:

```
TOWN ( Name, Location )
```

The query to find the distance between two towns now becomes

```
SELECT distance ( t1.location, t2.location )
FROM town t1, town t2
WHERE t1.name = 'Canterbury' AND t2.name = 'Norwich'
```

The main problems with extensible type systems are the complexity of the type definition process and the potential for damage to the database by poorly written or inadequately tested code. Coding all of the required functions for a new type is a non-trivial programming task. The compiled code is linked into, and thus becomes part of, the database system.

In POSTGRES, the linkage is dynamic and takes place at run time. This is possible because a multiple server architecture is used with one server for each client process. INGRES uses static linkage with a shared server and so the added types are available to all databases accessed through the enhanced server. With a shared server, errors may lead to corrupted data in any active transaction in any active database, not just those that use the new types.

Although recovery mechanisms may be able to deal with many errors, there remains the possibility that severe errors may cause the server to crash or may interfere with the transaction logging process. Of course, conventional applications may also leave the database in an inconsistent state, but their effects are usually more confined. Extensive testing in a development environment is essential before installation of new data types in a production system.

As the demand for new types increases vendors may choose to provide optional add-on libraries of types grouped by application domain. Developers could then choose to purchase only those types that would enhance their applications. Provided that suitable well-designed and tested libraries are available, this would minimize the potential for failures caused by inadequately tested code.

This approach is taken by Illustra, a commercial derivative of POSTGRES [Illustra 1994]. In addition to an extensible type system the company offers a range of 'DataBlades' tailored to particular problem domains such as 2D and 3D spatial, text handling and image processing. Each library includes the additional data types, related functions and, where appropriate, access methods.

Array types

Several systems now support both array data types. Both POSTGRES and the EXODUS [Carey *et al.* 1988] data language, EXTRA, provides fixed-and variable-length arrays of each base type. Conventional array indexing is supported and all operations defined on the base type are also available on the respective array type. For example, the POSTQUEL statement

```
create department ( name = text, budget = int4[12] )
```

creates a table in which the type of the budget column is an array of twelve integers, representing perhaps a monthly breakdown of the departmental budget. Array elements can be accessed individually:

```
retrieve (department.budget[3])

replace department (budget[6] = 300000)
where department.name = "Computing"
```

Complex (nested) data types

Many classes of object are themselves composed of other objects. In an EER model these may be represented by several entity classes linked together in a hierarchical structure by relationships of the form *HasA* or *Contains*. Within each class, the hierarchy may be further extended by atomic attributes grouped together into compound attributes.

Examples include patient records which contain details of consultations, diagnoses, laboratory tests, periods of hospitalization and other treatment. A hospital can be considered as containing a collection of buildings which in turn contain collections of wards, clinics, laboratories and offices. A medical team contains collections of doctors, nurses and other staff. Doctors and nurses may have collections of qualifications or specializations. All staff may have names and addresses that are modelled as compound attributes.

In a relational model such structures are represented by separate relations for each entity class. Each relation is equally privileged and the compound nature of grouped attributes is typically ignored. There is no means of distinguishing the semantics of containment or use from any other relationship in the schema. The leads to logical and physical storage structures that favour queries on the lower-level component entities rather than on the high-level containing entity.

One approach to dealing with nested objects uses the Non-First Normal Form or NF^2 model. This supports the use of repeating groups of values nested within a relation to an arbitrary depth. Although not widespread, some prototype systems have employed this approach (for example, [Dadam and Linnemann 1989]). Similar capabilities can be provided using set-valued attributes.

Both POSTQUEL and EXTRA support sets of objects, so the value of an attribute can be an arbitrary collection of instances of some type. The following EXTRA statement defines a constructed (composite) type `Department` having two attributes, `name` and `employees`. The first is defined as a variable-length array of characters and the second as a set of references to objects of type `Employee`. It is assumed that this type has already been defined in the schema. Sets of base types, constructed types and reference types are all supported in the EXTRA model [Carey *et al.* 1988].

```
define type Department
(
    name:       char[],
    employees:  { ref Employee }
)


create Departments: { own ref Department }
```

The second statement constructs a persistent set of Department objects. In a conventional relational context, we would say that it creates a relation or table of this type. In EXTRA, however, type definition and object construction are treated separately thus allowing the creation of more than one set of the same type. The words `own ref` mean that the referenced object is owned by the referencing object. This provides cascade delete semantics for the set, so that when the owner is deleted, so too are the referenced objects.

In POSTGRES, type and relation are created together. Whenever a class (relation) is created, an equivalent type is also created. The values of this type are sets of one or more instances of the class. These sets may then appear as an attribute of another class.

```
create course ( code = text, name = text )
create student ( initials = text,
                 name = text, subject = course )
```

The attribute `subject` is of type `course` and refers to one or more instances of the `course` class.

```
append course(code = "T301", name = "Database Technology")
```

Now, given a function `f(code)` which takes a course code as argument and returns an instance of the type `course`, the following is a legal insertion:

```
append student(initials = "A", name = "Jones",
subject = f("T301"))
```

and the query

```
retrieve(student.subject.name)
where student.initials = "A" and student.name = "Jones"
```

would return a set of values including "Database Technology".

Large objects

The file structures employed by most database systems use unspanned records, thus limiting record sizes to a little less than the page size. This prevents storage of large objects such as long sections of text, bitmap images or more complex multimedia objects as single database objects.

There are two common methods for handling such data in a conventional database. The first is to store a reference to an external file containing the object. This provides high access speeds, but leaves the responsibility for managing the object entirely outside of the database. The object is beyond the scope of normal transaction, concurrency and recovery mechanisms with the attendant dangers to the integrity of the stored references should a user or other process update, delete or move the file.

The second method is to divide the object into small sections that can fit within a page. These are then stored in a relation together with an identifier and a tuple sequence number used to retrieve the sections in the correct order for reassembly by the application (Figure 15.1). Typically the relation is stored as a B-tree, keyed on object identifier plus sequence number. Although usually somewhat slower than the external file approach, this method benefits from bringing the data under the control of the database where advantage can be taken of normal transaction semantics, integrity control and recovery mechanisms.

This approach has been adopted by INGRES which provides both text and graphics bitmap types as support mechanisms for its Windows4GL application-building tool. The tables used to store these objects are visible within the database, but the mechanism used to store (fragment) and retrieve (reassemble) stored data are provided only within Windows4GL, and are not accessible by other interfaces.

BLOB TABLE

BlobId	SequenceNo	ByteData
1	1	There are two common methods for handling such data in a
1	2	conventional database. The first is to store a reference to an external file containing the object.
1	3	This provides high access speeds, but leaves the responsibility for managing the object entirely outside the database. The object
1	4	is beyond the scope of normal.
...	...	...

Figure 15.1   Fragmented storage of a large text object as an attribute data in a normal relation.

Many relational systems now provide a generalized BLOB (Binary Large OBject) type which gives limited support for large unstructured objects. In most cases these employ similar methods to those described above, but the mechanism is hidden from the user or application and the object is managed directly by the DBMS as a single atomic unit. Applications need not be concerned with accessing external files or with splitting and reassembling an object.

BLOBs provide a primitive general-purpose mechanism for storing large objects but, because the database has no knowledge of their internal structure or behaviour, retrieval is only possible as an atomic object. This prevents retrieval of, say, a single frame from a video sequence or a rectangular area from within a bitmap image. In both cases the entire object must be transferred to the application for the smaller unit to be extracted. Similarly, the entire object must be passed from application to DBMS as a single object for storage. Knowledge of the object's structure and the operations that can be performed upon it reside entirely in the applications. Clearly this can be very inefficient for applications that frequently access only parts of large objects, need to update parts of an object, or perform operations that depend on the internal structure of the object.

In due course the established systems may support user-defined large object types. Some more recently developed systems already do so. For example, Illustra provides large-object support derived from that of POSTGRES. Here, we briefly describe the implementation of large objects in two experimental systems, POSTGRES and EXODUS. Similar facilities are also provided in Starburst.

POSTGRES provides two types of large object. One is based on external files, while the other, known as 'Inversion Large Objects', employs fragmented storage in a normal relation [Stonebraker and Olson 1993; Olson 1993]. In both cases separate classes of large-object may be defined using a similar approach to that used for small objects. For the programmer defining a new large object type, the data stored in the inversion form may be accessed via C functions that provide a direct analogue to conventional UNIX file I/O operations.

Suitable types for video, sound or image data can be defined together with functions that operate upon them. Unlike the simple BLOB types of other systems the data manager can distinguish between these types, and the defined type-specific operators and functions can be used in POSTQUEL queries. Indexes may be defined on large-object values or functions.

Another approach to fragmented storage that does not enforce a rigid distinction between normal and large objects is used in the EXODUS storage system [Carey *et al.* 1988]. This is a general-purpose storage system capable of managing objects of any size. Object identifiers follow the pattern used in many relational systems such as System R and INGRES, that is, <page_number, slot_number>. Objects that fit within a page are stored at this page/slot address, but for larger objects the address holds a 'large object header'. Normal objects that increase in size beyond the space available on the page are automatically converted to large objects. This involves moving the data to other pages and replacing the original record by a large-object header.

The header is the root of a B-tree index to pages containing large-object data. The header (root) and internal pages of the B-tree contain <count, page_id> pairs, where the count indicates the maximum byte number in the associated sub-tree. Thus the total size of the object is held as the rightmost count element in the root, and the pages containing any part of the object are directly accessible via the index.

15.2.2 Improved representations of data model semantics

The Entity-Relationship model [Chen 1976] has long been the primary conceptual modelling method used in relational database design. Its popularity owes much to the fact that, in its original form, the ER model's concepts can be mapped directly to the relational model. Since its introduction, however, the ER model has been extended by the addition of concepts such as specialization, generalization and compound attributes.

For many years, relational systems provided few mechanisms for adequately enforcing integrity constraints. In most cases this criticism is no longer valid because many commercial systems have implemented mechanisms to support entity, referential and more general integrity constraints. The SQL 2 standard includes specification of primary and foreign keys and associated update and delete behaviour. It also includes a more general assertion mechanism that can be used to test for other integrity violations. An increasing number of systems also now support some form of rule or trigger mechanism that can serve to implement complex constraints and other behaviour (*see* Chapter 9).

Specialization and generalization

Several problems in mapping from an EER logical model to the relational model were mentioned in Chapter 3. The relational model has no mechanism for handling compound attributes and so they are usually ignored when a database is implemented. Specialization and generalization hierarchies can be represented through various configurations of multiple relations. However, as with complex data types, realization of the hierarchy can only be achieved through applications. The special nature of the relationships between participating entity classes is unknown to the DBMS.

One approach to this problem is to provide an inheritance mechanism akin to that of object-oriented languages. For example, POSTGRES relations are referred to as classes following object-oriented terminology. Classes may be defined as derivatives of other classes. For example, the `Person`, `Doctor`, `Patient` generalization hierarchy may be implemented using the following POSTQUEL definitions of classes (relations):

```
create person ( id = integer, name = text, initials = text,
                date_of_birth = abstime, sex = character )

create doctor ( phone_no = text, room = text,
                date_qualified = abstime,
                date_appointed = abstime ) inherits person

create patient ( date_registered = abstime,
                 registered_with = integer ) inherits person
```

Given these definitions, tuples may be added to the doctor and patient classes as follows. Because these both inherit the attributes of person, there is no need to perform separate insertions on the person table.

```
append doctor ( id = 123, name = "Smith", initials = "AA",
                date_of_birth = "18/2/1952", sex = "f",
                phone_no = "7654", room = "21",'
                date_qualified = "18/2/1979",
                date_appointed = "18/2/1989" )

append patient (id = 123, name = "Smith", initials = "AA",
                date_of_birth = "18/2/1952", sex = "f",
                date_registered = "8/12/1993",
                registered_with = 123 )
```

15.2.4 Limitations of set-oriented query languages

One of the most frequent criticisms of SQL and other set-oriented query languages is the so-called impedance mismatch with conventional third generation programming languages. There is no attempt to integrate embedded SQL statements with their host languages and as a result they often follow quite different syntax and scope rules.

SQL returns relations (sets of tuples) as query results. This approach is well suited to *ad hoc* interactive queries, but not to the record-oriented processing style of conventional programming languages. To execute a query that will return more than one tuple, a program using embedded SQL must first declare a cursor for the query. This acts as a pointer to the current tuple and is used with the EXECUTE and FETCH statements to loop over the entire result set one tuple at a time.

Many applications need to deal with collections of related objects that form hierarchies or networks of arbitrary complexity. Examples of hierarchies include the management structure of an organization and, in a manufacturing context, an assembly that comprises many parts which may themselves be assembled from further parts. In both cases the data is structured as a tree of arbitrary depth. A management hierarchy may be indicated by a 'Reports To' relationship between employees. In a relational schema this can be represented by an attribute in the employee relation containing values that identify each person's manager. Thus the relation contains a foreign key to itself.

More complex network structures may be visualized as directed graphs. Examples include data models in a CASE tool, temporal relationships in project management and genealogical relationships between people in genetic or anthropological research. Again, representation in a relational schema is straightforward. In this case an intermediate relation is used to capture the many- to-many relationship.

Locating employees who report directly to any particular manager is straightforward using an SQL query that joins two logical instances of the employee relation:

```
SELECT e2.name
FROM emp e1, emp e2
WHERE e1.empno = e2.reports_to
AND e1.name = 'Jones'
```

as is finding the immediate ancestors of an individual in genealogy:

```
SELECT p2.name
FROM person p1, link l, person p2
WHERE p1.id = l.id1
AND p2.id = l.id2
AND l.type = 'parent'
AND p1.name = 'Henry'
```

However, it is impossible in most query languages to formulate a single query that traverses the hierarchy and returns a complete list of employees for whom a particular manager is ultimately responsible, or a list of indivisible components that make up an assembly. Equally, queries that traverse the more complex network structures, as would be needed to locate all ancestors common to two individuals, are also precluded.

Systems based on the extended relational approach primarily rely on a declarative query language as the main means of data access. For programming purposes, query language statements may be embedded in a host programming language or in a 4GL.

Some systems also provide a programming interface in the form of a function library, thus avoiding the need for a preprocessor. However, the dependence on declarative languages means that few support any form of navigational access to data.

A few systems (such as Starburst [Haas *et al.* 1990]) have implemented extensions to SQL or other query languages that enable recursion by repeatedly executing one query using the results of a second. However, the lack of navigational facilities in most relational systems remains a serious limitation when dealing with the selective traversal of complex nested data structures. This, together with the computationally incomplete nature of most declarative query languages, remains one of the major criticisms of such systems and is one that many object-oriented systems seek to avoid.

15.2.5   Temporal databases

Conventional database systems provide very effective support for shared access to the *current* state of a database. Previous data values are overwritten during an update and deleted records are removed so that they do not persist in the database. There is no means of determining past values other than restoring the database to an earlier state from archived material. Essentially, these systems can only support **snapshot** databases, not **temporal** databases in which access to previous states is equally important. Temporal database systems have extended support for temporal semantics, including methods of automatically associating timestamps with values and query language extensions that support traversal of an object's history.

With the increasing demand for systems to support applications such as CASE tools, design and manufacturing systems has come a need to support both access to historical states and to different versions of objects. Adding a temporal dimension to a conventional two-dimensional relation results in a three-dimensional structure, often referred to as the **time cube** (Figure 15.2). In this view, attributes may have different values at different points along the time dimension. Typically this is represented by attaching timestamps indicating periods of validity either to tuples or to the attributes themselves.

Most systems support **user-defined time** through a suitable built-in timestamp data type [Snodgrass 1987]. Such attributes refer to points in time such as dates of birth and do not result in multiple values through time. Manipulation of attribute values is entirely under user, or application, control and the system typically supports insertion, retrieval, comparison and limited arithmetic operations.

Two other types of time have been identified as being important in temporal data and temporal databases [Snodgrass 1987]. **Transaction time** refers to the period of existence (currency) in the database of a value resulting from insert, update and delete operations by database transactions. Thus the timestamping represents the presence of some particular value from insertion or update to the next update that results in a different value, or its deletion. This differs from **valid time** in which the timestamp indicates the external validity of a recorded fact. Transaction timestamping can be provided transparently by the system, but valid time will normally be managed by applications.

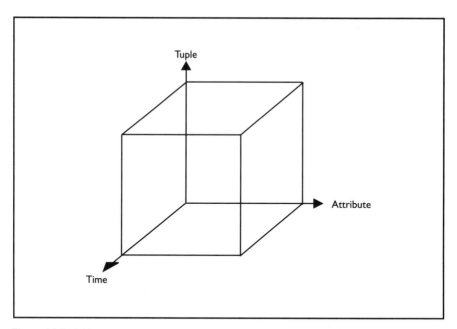

Figure 15.2 Adding a temporal dimension to a relation leads to a three-dimensional 'time cube'.

Perhaps the simplest method of retaining previous data values is tuple timestamping. This uses additional timestamp columns to indicate the start and end points of the period when a tuple is valid (Figure 15.3), in either transaction or valid time. To record transaction time, the start point is set to the current time when a new tuple is inserted and the end point is set to the current time when it is updated or deleted. Instead of updating values in the original tuple, a new tuple is inserted.

patient	condition	tstart	tend
Timms	Angina	2-Jun-94	18-Jun-94
Timms	Confusion	12-Nov-94	22-Nov-94
Waldon	Wound	15-Feb-94	19-Feb-94

Figure 15.3 Tuple timestamping.

This approach benefits from simplicity. Relations remain in 1NF although the primary key must now include one of the timestamps since there may be multiple tuples for any particular object instance. This leads to fragmentation of objects across many tuples and confuses object identity. Because most updates do not affect every non-key attribute in a relation, continued insertion of new tuples leads to redundant storage in the remaining, unchanged, attribute values. This may have a significant impact on both storage requirements and on query performance.

patient	condition
Timms	Angina [2-Jun-94, 18-Jun-94] Confusion [12-Nov-94, 22-Nov-94]
Waldon	Wound [15-Feb-94, 19-Feb-94]

Figure 15.4 Attribute timestamping.

The alternative attribute timestamping approach leads to an NF2 representation involving more complex nested relations (Figure 15.4). Although more difficult to implement it provides a direct representation of time-varying data without fragmenting information across multiple tuples.

Several systems provide some automatic support for transaction time. For example, POSTGRES maintains the history of data values in terms of transaction time using tuple timestamps. The timestamps may be read but not modified by user processes. Their purpose is to support an extension to the query language to support queries of the form 'What was the state of X at time T?' For example,

```
retrieve (p.patient)
from p in patient["10/2/1994"]
where p.condition = "Wound"
```

would retrieve the names of patients with wounds on the specified date. Automated 'vacuuming', the removal of aged tuples to tertiary storage after some defined interval, is also supported.

Proposed extensions to SQL called TSQL2 [Snodgrass *et al.* 1994a; 1994b] provide support for managing transaction and valid time using tuple timestamping. They include table creation statements that specify which time representations are required and, for valid time, a precision or granularity may be specified. Additional predicates provide the means to reference valid and transaction timestamps in queries.

15.2.6 Schema evolution

Changes in usage patterns, existing application requirements and the introduction of new applications may all lead to changes in one or more aspects of the database schema. Performance tuning may involve changes to physical storage structures, partitioning of tables to separate frequently and rarely used columns, or denormalization through the combination of tables to avoid joins. Changing application requirements may lead to changes such as the addition of new columns to a table, splitting or merging of columns, or the introduction or extension of specialization hierarchies.

Tuning is an essential part of the maintenance process throughout the lifetime of a database. Other changes may result from requirements that could not have been foreseen when the database was designed or, indeed, from deficiencies in the original conceptual design or implementation. Whatever their origins, the DBMS should be able to support the changes with a minimum of disruption to existing applications. In the case of high-availability systems, disruption of running applications must also be minimized.

These are areas of ongoing research; results are reported in the major database conferences (for example, VLDB, ACM SIGMOD/PODS, IEEE Data Engineering).

15.3 The EXODUS system

The EXODUS system is best understood as a toolkit for generating database systems; it was developed at the University of Wisconsin. This work has been extensively published in a series of accessible papers and many documents relating to the project are also available from the Wisconsin ftp site. A good summary of the work is given in [Carey *et al.* 1990].

Access to EXODUS facilities is either through the EXTRA data model and EXCESS query language, or through the E programming language [Richardson *et al.* 1993]. E is an extended form of C++ incorporating persistence and implemented on top of the EXODUS storage manager (ESM). More recently, a memory-mapped storage system, QuickStore, has been built on top of ESM but, unlike E, is implemented as a C++ class library, thus needing no additional compiler support for its storage-related facilities [White and DeWitt 1994].

EXODUS has made several important contributions to the development of database systems research:

- It was the first significant prototype to provide comprehensive facilities for constructing domain-specific DBS from generic parts.
- It introduced the term **database implementor (DBI)** to describe the people responsible for building DBS from 'kits'.
- It has been sufficiently designed and implemented to be used as the basis of several other research prototypes.

The EXODUS toolkit consists of:

- a storage manager,
- the E programming language,
- libraries of
    - access method implementations,
    - operator methods,
- a rule-based query optimizer,
- tools for constructing query language optimizers.

A database constructed from these tools (Figure 15.5) comprises the database engine, a schema manager, a query optimizer and parser. The database engine contains three layers: the storage manager, access methods and a set of operator methods which implement the operations of the query language. The operator and access methods may be selected from EXODUS' own libraries or may be written in E by the DBI; the storage manager may also be modified.

Objects are stored as uninterpreted sequences of bytes. Small objects are stored on a single page; objects larger than a page are stored in a B-tree using byte order as the key. Identifiers are structured and contain class information. The storage manager supports buffer management, concurrency control, versioning and recovery.

The EXTRA/EXCESS layer is built from the basic Exodus toolkit.

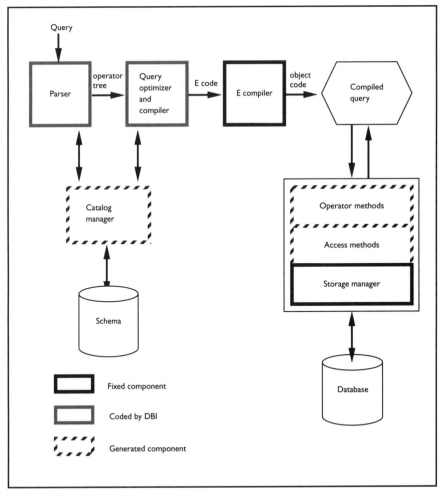

Figure 15.5 EXODUS architecture.

15.4 Summary

This chapter has concentrated on the rapid development of relational systems in the light of the demands of advanced applications and challenges from the object-oriented community. This trend will continue and new features will eventually be incorporated into the international standards. For example, a standard approach to the definition of new data types is expected to be introduced in SQL 3. There will also be an increasing role for toolkits such as that developed by the EXODUS project in the development of more compact systems developed for specialized application areas.

Chapter 16

OBJECT-ORIENTED DATABASE SYSTEMS

16.1 Introduction

In an object-oriented model, all entities are regarded as **objects**. An object has an identity that is independent of its value. It has both **attributes** used to describe its state, and **methods** which operate on the attributes and so implement its behaviour. Similar objects are grouped together to form a class and, individually, are known as instances of the class. The definition of a class includes that of the properties (attributes and methods) applicable to all its members.

In comparison with the relational model, a class definition may be equated with that of a relation, and the instance of an object with a tuple. Attributes perform the same role in both models. There are, however, several important differences. Attributes may be of any type, including user-defined classes; thus a class is potentially a complex nested data structure. Classes have both attributes and methods. Methods provide an interface to the object and are typically used to set, retrieve and otherwise manipulate the attribute values. The ideal practice in an object-oriented environment is to treat attributes as private data with only the methods being visible to objects outside of the class. Thus the only way to interact with an object is through its methods.

This **information hiding** approach ensures that implementation details are hidden from the outside world and only those methods (operations) that are defined for the class may be applied to an object. This separation of visibility is an ideal to which the designer strives. In practice, the programmer may choose to make some attributes directly visible, rather than writing large numbers of trivial functions to get and set their values. In an object-oriented programming language such as C++ the visibility of both attributes and methods is determined by the programmer as private, public or protected. Protected visibility implies that the property is visible to other members of the class and members of derived classes. Private properties may also be made available to members of designated 'friend' classes.

Generalization/specialization (GenSpec) hierarchies are supported through inheritance. Given a generalized class (for example, vehicle) containing attributes and methods appropriate to all vehicles, a derived or specialized class (for example, car) would inherit all of these together with their implementations, and add specialized properties of its own. Where behaviour differs between a class and its superclass, an inherited method may be replaced by a new method of the same name and signature in the derived class. The specialized method is then said to **override** (or **overload**) that of the superclass.

In many object-oriented systems a class may have more than one superclass and thus inherit properties from each. Such multiple inheritance is more flexible than a purely hierarchical single inheritance, but may increase the possibility of name conflicts when properties with the same name are inherited from more than one superclass.

It will be clear from the previous chapter that many of these concepts have influenced the design of extended relational systems. The main difference between the two approaches centres around the role of programming and query languages. The primary motivation behind object-oriented data management systems is the extension of OO programming languages to provide database functionality. This implies a belief in the importance of conventional languages as the main basis for database programming languages. Amongst the major benefits of this approach are that the programmer does not need to work in multiple, often poorly matched, languages. The flexibility of a language such as C++ may also make it possible to choose between navigational and set-oriented data access, thus easing the task of dealing with complex nested objects.

An increasing number of object-oriented systems also support declarative query languages, often based on SQL. In some cases these can be used within programs, usually by passing the query text as a parameter to a query execution function.

16.2 Object-oriented data models

Unlike the relational model, there is no straightforward formal definition of the object-oriented data model. There are many definitions of object-oriented models and a number of sharp disagreements about various features of different models that have been proposed. In this section we outline the principal features of object-oriented data models. This discussion is intended as an overview, not as a comparison of the features in different systems; these issues are well covered in [Cattell 1991a], [Delobel *et al.* 1995] and by overview papers that have been published for a number of systems.

16.2.1 Classes

A **class** is defined as a grouping of objects that share the same structure and behaviour. Every object belongs to a class. A class is defined by a class object. (This is frequently referred to as the **intension** of the class and the instances as the **extension**.) A class object generally:

- acts as a template for instances of the class and provides each instance with a set of attributes, methods and messages (which define the external interface of the class);
- provides a repository for the methods message and attribute definitions of the class;
- records the inheritance lattice for that class.

Some systems allow instances to have variant, or exceptional, properties.

A class object must also belong to a class, usually referred to as its **metaclass**. A metaclass defines the properties of a class object, for example that it should hold certain aggregate information about the class. The class properties inherited from the metaclass are not passed on to the instances of the class.

16.2.2 Types

Types have three principal functions:

- to provide consistent physical representations of values;
- to detect programming errors and help prevent inappropriate operations;
- to provide an implementation-level model of data.

The use of types allows the correctness of many operations to be checked at compile time. This reduces the amount of run-time checking that is needed and therefore improves performance.

A type system comprises:

- a set of elementary types (integer, real, string, and so on) provided by the system;
- a set of type constructors, (tuple, list, set, bag, pointer, array, and so on);
- a type algebra (syntactic constructs for type construction).

Many ODBSs restrict the notion of type to defining the values of a class's attributes and do not allow the type system to provide templates for objects; this is the function of classes.

It is highly desirable that generic functions (for example, sort) are **polymorphic**, that is, usable with a wide variety of types. Otherwise a separate implementation must be written for every combination of input and result types.

16.2.3 Complex and composite objects

Most systems provide constructors for tuple, list, set and a number of others which may include array, bag, pointer, and so on. Some object-oriented database systems give the tuple constructor priority, so that all other types must be defined as belonging to a tuple type. These constructors allow complex objects to be built – here we define a complex object as having complex (for example, set-valued) attributes.

A distinction is sometimes made between complex objects as defined above and **composite objects**, which are objects composed of other objects as well as (possibly complex) values. The relationship between the components of a composite object may be recursive and in some models is distinguished as an **is-part-of** relationship. The assumed semantics of this relationship are that if the root of a composite object is deleted then all its components are also deleted (that is, similar to cascade delete in SQL terminology). The is-part-of relationship usually implies that the participants are exclusive and cannot be part of another composite object.

16.2.4 Encapsulation

The motivation for encapsulation is to preserve the modularity of objects and make an object present a clean external interface. In an ideal object-oriented world the attributes of an object are *all* hidden and the only external interface is provided through a set of **messages** to which an object will respond. A message can be likened to a function call with a distinguished argument, the receiver; the receiver can be regarded as a server for the messages it responds to. The set of messages that an object responds to is called its **behaviour**; messages are the realization of the concept of responsibilities, described in Chapter 4.

The ideal of strict encapsulation has two drawbacks from a database perspective:

- Since very many database operations are simple reads and writes of values the programmer has to provide a large number of trivial methods for each class.
- The overhead of a method invocation for each read or write of a value imposes a substantial performance penalty.

To overcome these problems the majority of systems provide mechanisms to allow attributes to be defined as 'public' and therefore generally accessible, or accessible from a set of other classes which have been defined as 'friends' of a class.

16.2.5 Methods

Objects are manipulated by **methods**, which implement the functionality required to respond to messages. The arguments of a method are usually called its **signature**. In this way an object's internal structure can be modified to meet changing needs and performance requirements without requiring any change to its external interface and without needing any changes to its clients.

Methods may be written in a variety of languages, although C and C++ are the most commonly used in current systems. The biggest problem faced by object-oriented database system (ODBS) designers using a powerful language such as C++ is that methods are executed in privileged environments and there is a danger that an error in a method may cause substantial damage to the whole database. The solutions to this problem are currently based on one of three approaches:

- defining a safe subset of the language and restricting methods to it;
- constructing a safe run-time environment by incorporating substantial run-time checking into the code (with the consequent performance penalty);
- making the safety of methods the programmer's responsibility.

The first alternative appears to have the best long-term future, if sufficiently powerful safe languages can be designed. These problems are similar to those discussed in the previous chapter for user-written functions in extended relational systems.

A transaction or program that requires values from many objects (for example, to determine the average length of stay on a ward) may incur an unacceptably large overhead if the retrieval of every value entails a procedure call. Many systems provide system-defined default methods (get, set) to manipulate values from objects and overcome the problem of invoking a procedure for every retrieval or update of a value. For many database applications the use of these methods provides important performance gains. Systems that support this type of access usually provide it either as part of the default behaviour of every class or require its specific declaration for selected classes. In the first case the programmer can prevent inappropriate access to the values of a class by **overloading** (locally redefining) the methods to produce suitable class-specific behaviour.

16.2.6 *Inheritance*

Inheritance is one of the most important concepts of object-oriented models and is common to all object-oriented data models. A class may be defined as inheriting structure and behaviour from:

- a single superclass, called **single inheritance**, which results in a tree-structured inheritance graph with a single root;
- several superclasses, called **multiple inheritance**, which makes the inheritance graph an acyclic lattice.

Single inheritance is inflexible and frequently results in many artificial classes to represent the semantics of an application adequately and therefore most ODBSs have implemented multiple inheritance.

There are a number of issues which must be addressed by any multiple inheritance scheme because a class may:

- redefine a method or attribute inherited from one of its superclasses,
- inherit conflicting methods or attributes of the same name from different superclasses.

The rules used for resolving conflicts are to use the definition of the method or attribute that is closest in the inheritance lattice (typically the most specialized), unless there is a contrary direction from the user. If there is no clear separation of the conflicting attributes or methods in the inheritance lattice the user is responsible for resolving the conflict.

The redefinition of methods by a subclass is called method **overloading** and it is generally only possible to determine the applicable method code at run time, since the class of the receiver is not known until the message is instantiated (that is, given real parameters).

In most models an object may only be an instance of a single class (that is, be created as an instantiation of a single class object), but is a **member** of each of its superclasses and is capable of responding to the messages of its superclasses.

The notion of **object migration** (sometimes called object evolution), that is, an object of a certain class changing to become an instance of another, is allowed in some systems. An object is allowed to change its structure and behaviour and become an instance of another class while retaining its identity. There are a number of implementation issues in implementing an object evolution mechanism, but from a database perspective there is an additional, more fundamental, issue in deciding what object evolution might mean in the application's UoD.

16.2.7 Schema evolution

Changes to an object's structure are normally made in response to external requirements (for example, enhanced functionality, performance improvement, response to changes in the UoD).

The majority of modern applications must deal with a dynamic world, where changes to the schema are frequently necessary. A successful ODBS must provide facilities to allow changes to the behaviour, structure and implementation of its classes. We need to be able to achieve this without having to:

- exhaustively check the structure of every class in the inheritance lattice whenever there is a change to a method that may be inherited;
- recompile every method that may be affected by a change to the definition of a type or to the attributes of a class.

The changes that are allowed in a system must preserve the structural and behavioural consistency of the database. The types of schema change that may be permitted are described in [Banerjee *et al.* 1987]; these can be summarized:

- Changes to attributes:

- add an attribute,
- drop an attribute,
- change an attribute's name,
- change an attribute's type.
- Changes to methods:
  - add a method,
  - drop a method,
  - change a method's name.
- Changes to the inheritance lattice:
  - add a new inheritance relationship between classes,
  - remove an inheritance relationship,
  - change the overloading of attributed or methods (that is, inherit a different implementation of an overloaded operator).
- Changes to types and classes:
  - add a new type or class,
  - remove a type or class,
  - change the name of a type or class.

When the definition of a class is modified, any new objects created for that class will have the new definition, although a method (or query) may reference objects created with a previous definition. Changes to classes or to methods may cause inconsistencies in method execution.

There are two approaches to dealing with these problems:

- **Immediate change.** Every instance of a class is immediately modified to conform to the new definition and methods are recompiled as necessary so that the structure and behaviour of the system is brought into line with the current schema definition.
- **Deferred change.** Changes to instances are deferred until they are referenced and methods affected by schema changes are recompiled when they are invoked.

A number of issues must be addressed if unwanted run-time exceptions are to be avoided in a deferred change implementation:

- If the modification has been to remove an attribute used by a method, the method should handle the exception gracefully and return an appropriate signal to its sender.
- Methods that access an attribute that has changed its type should be prepared to handle the exception if using the new type might be unsafe.
- Additional attributes do not affect existing methods, but methods need to handle the case of objects that do not possess the new attributes. This is the easiest case to deal with, since the new attributes can be added dynamically and supplied with default or null values.

Many of these can be dealt with by providing a set of suitable migration and exception rules to handle migration from one version to another, on a class-by-class basis, as part of the schema change. In many cases the conversion to a new type can be dealt with as an automatic type conversion operation (for example, mapping between strings of different lengths). Other cases are more difficult and require a rule or procedure for converting between the old and new representations. The usual practice is for the method to detect the exception and pass it to an exception handler that can apply the relevant rules and procedures to convert the object to the new representation before allowing the method to proceed.

Deferred conversion of objects is highly desirable for many applications since it avoids having to perform expensive modifications to objects that are not referenced. The trade-off is that the cost of conversion is incurred at run time, where it may adversely affect performance.

Similar considerations apply to changes to methods. Changes to a method may invalidate the code of other methods. In systems that rely on static checking this can cause many methods to be recompiled, as it is difficult to decide automatically which methods need recompilation as a result of a given change. This problem does not arise where late binding is used; this can avoid many expensive recompilations while an application is being developed and tested.

16.2.8 Object identity

The problem of object identity has already been mentioned in Chapter 3 and in the context of the relational model in Chapter 13. The primary key of a relation is simply an attribute or group of attributes. From one viewpoint this is an example of the elegant simplicity of the model. Unfortunately, like any other attribute, the value of a relational key can be changed, with potentially catastrophic results for the referential integrity of the database.

The problems of keys as data were recognized before commercial relational systems became widely available and a solution that gave primary keys a privileged status formed part of Codd's extended model RM/T [Codd 1979]. Nevertheless, these ideas received little attention in early commercial systems. The schema definition extensions introduced in the SQL 2 standard (see Chapter 14) now enable the database implementor to define update and delete semantics of keys.

The concept of object identity has two distinct roles: as surrogate and as pointer. We will discuss the two roles separately.

Identity as surrogate

The UoD can be regarded as a collection of related entities of interest, which can be aggregated into classes. Attributes describe the properties of interest of the entity class. If the modelling has been done at an appropriate level it follows that a pair of instances of a class which have identical values should be indistinguishable in the model, even if they are physically distinct. For example, several copies of a book in a bookshop are identical (the information required is the description of the book and the number of copies in stock) but for a librarian the distinction between individual copies is important (as a loan must involve a particular instance of a book).

This notion is captured in the relational model by the requirement that every tuple must have a unique key. It is adequate for strong entities, but causes problems for weak, or dependent, entities whose identification is dependent on their relationship with another (strong) entity. In this case the dependent entity is represented in the relational model with a composite key, built from the key of the 'parent' entity and one or more attributes of the dependent entity. Relationships between entities are more generally represented by the use of foreign keys.

Many application areas, such as engineering, design or spatial systems, often involve large numbers of similar objects with no obvious simple key. This leads to compound keys using many attributes or the creation of artificial keys which are difficult to maintain. Even in cases where one attribute appears to be an obvious candidate key, future reorganizations can lead to changes in large numbers of key values. Examples of these problems have been seen in the motor industry when one company is taken over by another. It may take several years for the subsidiary company's part numbers to be replaced by new ones in the form required by its new parent. From this perspective the advantage of object identifiers (OIDs) is that they provide a system-maintained unique value for every entity.

There are differing views on whether identity should be entirely hidden from the application or not and – if it is – on how reference to an existing object should be distinguished from object creation.

There are several advantages in implementing identifiers as logical quantities, often <class identifier, instance identifier> pairs [Kim 1989]:

- A class object can contain information on the location of the code for that class's methods – a method invocation that is not recognized by the class object is not valid for that class. If the class cannot be derived from the identifier a message invocation must first fetch the object to determine its class, before it can find the right method code to execute.
- Indexing on the first part of the identifier will ensure that objects of the same class can be easily stored together.
- A table (frequently hashed) is maintained to map identifiers to memory locations. When an object is moved its entry in this table is changed.

So far we have considered identity from a modelling and logical perspective; the concept of identity is frequently used to express navigational information, that is, the identifier is a pointer. The principal advantage of a pointer is the increased performance of navigational queries, since no lookup and conversion of identifiers to addresses is required. When an object is moved, typically because it outgrows its existing location, a pointer to its new location is left at the old location. References to the object initially access the old location and then follow the pointer to the new location. If the object is moved again, the pointer at the original location is changed to point to the object's current location. O_2 uses this system. This approach can readily be extended to cover distributed systems, although O_2 avoids allocating identifiers to transient objects by allocating temporary identifiers until the transaction commits, at which time permanent identifiers are assigned. This technique also avoids the problem of giving an object an identifier that points to the client workstation on which it was initially created and then making all subsequent accesses of that object fetch the object's current location from there.

The use of physical identifiers is usually associated with ODBSs that are language-based, rather than database-based. The location of an object changes as it is fetched from secondary storage and made available to an application. This necessitates altering the identifier; the operation is known as pointer **swizzling**. The efficiency of the swizzling implementation is an important factor in the performance of many systems that implement physical identifiers.

The problems of this type of solution are essentially those encountered in network database systems. Unless great care is take over the implementation details, recovery, reorganization or movement of the database can become extremely difficult.

Reference and identity

Through the use of surrogates we abrogate to the system the responsibility for maintaining unique identifiers, but this does not remove the problem of maintaining the distinguishability of entities in the model of the UoD. In many cases this is trivial, since the entities being modelled have a natural unique identifier and this can be easily maintained and provides a convenient descriptive identifier. In other cases the distinguishing characteristics of each instance are more complex.

The issue here is whether, for entities without simple natural identifiers, reference by system-supplied identifier is allowed, or reference by description is the only permitted form of access. In the latter case, where the system will not allow an application access to the identifier then, in practice, an application-generated surrogate becomes necessary. This removes one of the principal modelling advantages of identifiers and it becomes difficult to see any expressive advantage of identifiers over foreign keys and referential integrity constraints.

In constructing a database it is frequently the case that much of the required data already exists in a variety of forms and the task is to integrate it, so that disparate values relating to a particular instance are brought together in a structured whole. Assuming we have modelled the entities as complex objects, this is most easily done by altering references to sub-objects. To achieve this without access to the identity of the objects concerned is extremely difficult. We therefore believe that identifiers should be visible to the user (applications programmer).

Increasingly, extended relational systems are making use of inbuilt OIDs to uniquely identify every tuple in the database. These are automatically assigned whenever a new tuple is created. In some cases these are purely internal addressing mechanisms invisible to the user. In others they can be used as reliable and unique system-maintained keys. In many cases, these OIDs are visible to the user when required.

Some early implementations failed to address issues of maintaining such identifiers when exporting and importing data, with the effect that foreign key links were lost when new identifiers were created during an import. This problem is overcome by some more recent systems that provide mechanisms for mapping old identifiers to new OIDs during import, thus retaining relationships while creating new identifiers.

Equality

An object identifier is completely independent of the values taken by the object. This has led to the definition of three forms of equality:

Identity equality. Objects are identical if they have the same identifier, since an identifier only refers to a single object.

Value equality. Two objects are said to be value equal if all their values are equal, but they have different identifiers, for example:

<342459>, PC, Zenith, 486DX, 16Mb, 200Mb
<943761>, PC, Zenith, 486DX, 16Mb, 200Mb

Deep equality. Two objects are said to be deep equal if their values are equal and the values of their object-valued attributes (sub-objects) are also equal, for example:

<342459>, PC, Zenith, 486DX, 16Mb, 200Mb, <938756>
<943761>, PC, Zenith, 486DX, 16Mb, 200Mb, <013821>

and the objects pointed to are:

<938756>, 14, SuperVGA, Sony
<013821>, 14, SuperVGA, Sony

These two instances are not deep equal, because the monitors are only value equal and are not identical.

In another case we might have:

<342459>, PC, Zenith, 486DX, 16Mb, 200Mb, <938756>
<943761>, PC, Zenith, 486DX, 16Mb, 200Mb, <938756>

This means that these two PCs are sharing the same monitor.

These concepts of equality are derived from object-oriented programming. Given that a database is a mapping of some portion of a UoD, the semantics of objects with identical values are not immediately obvious – if we wish to maintain classes as sets it is necessary to specify appropriate integrity constraints, using the mechanisms described in Chapter 9. In a database context we are usually only interested in counting the number of objects whose values are indistinguishable.

16.3 Query languages

One of the major motivations for ODBS has been the desire to merge the capabilities of programming languages and database systems.

Persistent programming languages

There has been active work to provide conventional programming languages with facilities to allow objects to persist between invocations of a program since the late 1970s. The most influential examples of this work include PS-ALGOL [Atkinson *et al.* 1983], its successor Napier88 [Dearle *et al.* 1989] and Galileo [Albano *et al.* 1985]. The most important lessons from these systems are:

- the desirability of making persistence orthogonal to the type system, that is, any type may have persistent values;
- while a value persists, so should its type;
- the transfer of objects to and from secondary storage should be inferred from the operations on the data and not be the responsibility of the programmer[1].

The main emphases of work on persistent programming languages have been to provide an expressive and flexible type system with persistence, and to building sophisticated name spaces (environments).

Database programming languages

Interest in database programming languages (DBPLs) has come from the convergence of persistent programming languages, a desire for integrated languages that seamlessly encompass the scope of database query languages and conventional programming, and database research on providing greater expressiveness in database systems.
The main points are:

- Strong static type checking is important to prevent valuable data being corrupted as a result of programming errors.
- Some type checking must be done dynamically; it must be strong.
- Every type should be allowed to be persistent.
- A consistent set of rules is needed to control binding and name conflicts between independently developed program units.
- Inheritance and polymorphism are good ideas.

---

1 This is separate from the logical issue of making the results of a transaction secure.

- The type and naming systems should allow for a proper distinction to be made between intensional and extensional references.
- The movement and placement of data should be the responsibility of the DBS, not the applications programmers.
- Normal database facilities such as transactions, savepoints, and recovery are needed.

Database programming languages emphasize operations on bulk data and generally provide good facilities for constructing and manipulating collections. They also tend to provide good facilities for content-based retrieval and concurrent multi-user access.

This area is one of active research, with a number of open issues; a list of desirable characteristics for DBPLs is given in [Atkinson and Buneman 1987]. Much of the later work on DBPLs has been reported in a series of workshops starting in 1987 [Bancilhon and Buneman 1990]; the proceedings of subsequent workshops have been published by Morgan Kaufmann.

Object-oriented declarative query languages

Many ODBSs that provide a declarative query language restrict it to retrieving complete objects or a single list of values. The difficulty in supporting projection is that the result of a projection is a new class and the problems of assigning appropriate behaviour to a transient, *ad hoc* class are not easily resolved for the general case.

Many of the issues that concern object-oriented declarative query languages are similar to those identified in the evolution of SQL and its variants; an example is provided in the discussion of OQL later in this chapter.

16.4 Object manipulation issues

The classification of objects according to their independence and sharability provides a useful framework for describing a number of object manipulation issues; following [Dittrich 1990], this gives:

- dependent sharable objects,
- independent sharable objects,
- dependent non-sharable objects,
- independent non-sharable objects.

Adequate query language and implementation mechanisms need to be provided to represent objects of these four categories. The most obvious issues are that:

- sharable objects should be distinguished to prevent their being removed from the system while there are still references to them;

- dependent objects must be removed when they have no more 'parents'.

Deletion

The classification of objects by independence and sharability gives a basis for defining a set of base operations to remove various kinds of object from the system:

- Independent non-sharable objects can be deleted by making a simple request.
- Independent sharable objects should normally be deleted when a request has been made to delete an object and there are no more outstanding references to it.
- A dependent sharable object should only be deleted when there are no more references to it. If it is stored with its first parent it must be moved if that parent is deleted while there are still other parents in existence.
- Non-sharable dependent objects are automatically deleted when their parent is deleted.

Composite objects rely on references to other objects. Attempts to delete referenced objects may be dealt with in a number of possible ways:

- doing nothing, allowing a reference to point to a non-existent object. This may mean (if identifiers are physical) that dereferencing an identifier leads to an object different from that which was expected or to something that can be (wrongly) interpreted as the referenced object;
- posting a null identifier in place of the deleted object, and relying on exception code in the methods to handle the situation gracefully;
- keeping a complete list of backward references and posting a null identifier in every referencing object;
- maintaining a reference count for every shared object and marking the object for deletion – it is only removed if the reference count is zero.

In order to maintain integrity we must ensure that either every object reference must point to an existing object, or the application must deal with dangling references. The first option is obviously more attractive, and is most easily achieved by a reference counter, although this involves extra overhead for reference creation or modification. Schemes that rely on reference counts are most widespread, since they offer a good combination of safety and performance.

Update

The notion of updating a complex object has three separate manifestations. An update of a composite object may:

- change the values of a shared object,
- refer to a different shared object instance,
- create a new object.

The provision of distinct syntax for each of these operations makes the intended semantics clearer and allows compile-time checking; otherwise run-time support is needed if the system is to support these distinctions. The 'do-nothing' option is to rely on the programmer (and subsequent maintainers) to get it right.

The distinction between the different update cases permits a query optimizer to plan more efficiently, since in the first case the shared object must be fetched and locked for update, in the second case the reference must be changed and its validity checked, and in the third case new storage must be allocated and any indexes updated.

16.5 The O₂ system

Current object-oriented database systems vary greatly in their data models, languages and functionality. To illustrate many of the salient points of current database implementations we describe the O_2 system in more detail. A useful summary of several of the main commercial and experimental systems is provided in [Cattell 1991a]. In many respects the EXODUS system, described in the previous chapter, can also be regarded as an example of an object-oriented system and our decision to describe it there serves as an illustration of the convergence between ODBS and extended relational systems.

The O_2 system was built as an example of a complete object-oriented database system, rather than as a research vehicle to investigate particular aspects of ODBS design and implementation. The work was started at Altaïr (founded by INRIA, University of Paris-Sud and IN2) in 1986, the prototype was finished in 1989 and the first commercial version released in early 1991. The system is written in C, using WiSS [Chou *et al.* 1986] as its storage system. Here we present a brief summary of the system; a more extensive summary is given in [Delobel *et al.* 1995] and a full description of various aspects of the system is given in [Bancilhon *et al.* 1991].

Data model

The most important feature of the O_2 data model is the distinction between objects and values. Objects have identity, strict encapsulation, multiple inheritance and classes which serve as instance generators and as repositories for methods. Identifiers are not visible to the application programmer.

Values are either simple (for example, string) or complex (for example, list) and are manipulated through algebraic operations.

Objects in O_2 are composite and may contain both values and identifiers. Classes have a type, methods and a name. The extent of a class is a set of object instances.

Types are constructed recursively from:

- a set of atomic types (integer, float, double, string, char, boolean, bits),
- a set of constructors (tuple, set, list).

The instances of types are values, so they are not encapsulated and are intended as the means to represent non-shared data.

Objects and values can be made persistent by naming them; any object or value referenced by a named object is persistent.

Methods are defined by first declaring their signature and then the method body. The method is stored as a tuple containing its signature, the language it is written in and its body. An application is seen as a tuple containing the identifiers of its methods which are all stored in the database. Late binding and method overloading are supported.

The inheritance mechanism in O_2 relies on subtyping, so that every (possibly refined) attribute in the supertype is present in the subtype.

Applications are written using the CO_2 language, which is an extended version of C. The system contains an interface generator and other tools (debugger and so on) to make a complete ODBS programming environment, the OOPE.

Since the system is designed as a database system, rather than an implementation of persistent C, it also supports a query language, OQL. OQL uses a syntax similar in style to SQL. The main features of the language are:

- A query can return new values, but can only return objects that form part of the database (that is, projection is supported for values in the database).
- Queries can override the encapsulation mechanism.

O_2 uses a hybrid approach to schema change, with a development mode that uses late binding and an execution mode in which dynamic schema changes are disallowed. Execution mode provides static checking and hence better performance than development mode.

Architecture

The functional architecture of the system is shown in Figure 16.1. The shaded portions are only required for development, since all application code is compiled into calls to the lower levels of the system.

The principal functional elements of the O_2 system (summarizing the description in [Delobel *et al.* 1995]) are:

- OOPE – the programming environment;
- Looks – the interface generator;
- the language processor – handles data definition commands and CO_2 compilation;
- the query interpreter – handles OQL query processing and execution by making calls to the schema and object managers;
- the schema manager – maintains method and class data;
- the object manager – consists of several modules: responsible for memory representations of objects (treating values as objects); providing transaction

support, search mechanisms, message sending; distributing objects and messages to client workstations;

- WiSS – the disk manager; responsible for data storage, addressing and disk buffer management.

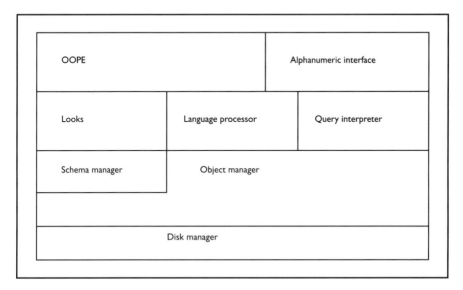

Figure 16.1 O_2 functional architecture (after [Delobel *et al.* 1995]).

16.6 The ODMG-93 standard

A frequent criticism of early object-oriented systems was the lack of any agreed standards. This shortcoming is not surprising in any emerging technology and we should recall that commercial relational systems had been available for almost a decade before the adoption of the first SQL standard. The Object Database Management Group (ODMG) is a consortium of system vendors that was established to address the need for standards [Cattell 1994]. Their aim has been to produce a *de facto* standard and to ensure that it is implemented in their products, rather than working within the framework of national and international standards bodies. This approach has not been without its critics [Kim 1994] (and a rebuttal [ODMG 1994]).

The ODM-93 standard provides a common object model and programming language bindings for an Object Definition Language (ODL), Object Manipulation Language (OML) and Object Query Language (OQL). The current bindings cover C++ and Smalltalk and extend these existing languages to support persistence and other database functionality. The following discussion is based on the C++ bindings, and is intended to give an impression of the ODMG model and languages rather than an exhaustive description (for which, see [Cattell 1994]).

The ODL allows both transient and persistent objects. Transient objects may use any of the language extensions but exist only during the execution of a program. Persistent objects are derived from a class called `Pobject` that supplies all necessary behaviour to support database storage. For example:

```
class Department : public Pobject
{
  public:
      // attributes
         char  *name;
         char  *building;
         Ref<Staff> head;
         Set<Staff> members inverse Staff::dept;
         ...
      // methods
         int num_staff ();
         ...
      // Reference to the class extension
         static Ref<Set<Department>> departments;
  private:
         ...
};
```

This class definition follows standard C++ syntax, but includes additional types `Ref` and `Set`, and a relationship path expressed through an `inverse` clause. A conventional C++ program would use a reference or pointer to address a related object, but these are only suitable for in-memory referencing. The `Ref` type is a form of smart pointer that maintains the reference irrespective of the physical location of the object. Thus the head attribute in the example provides a persistent reference to a Staff object representing the head of the department.

The `members` attribute is defined as a `Set`. This is one of several possible collection types: sets, bags, lists or variable-sized arrays. Whereas the declaration of `head` indicated a unidirectional relationship between `Department` and `Staff` (from the `Department` class), `members` includes an inverse relationship specification. In this case it is a one-to-many relationship represented by a single-valued attribute `dept` in the `Staff` class and the set-valued attribute `members` in `Department`. To complete the definition of this relationship, the `Staff` class would include the following:

```
Ref<Department> dept inverse Department::members;
```

There is an important distinction between relationships with and without an inverse specification. The inverse specification enables the system to maintain the referential integrity of the relationship. In our example, the update and delete behaviour of the members relationship can be handled by the system. However, the head relationship must be enforced by applications.

The final attribute, departments, provides a reference to a set of Department objects that form the extension of the class in the database. This must be initialized at the start of a transaction (*see below*).

The OML C++ binding includes extensions to the language covering creation and deletion of objects, templates for generating collection classes and suitable iterators and additional classes required to manage database and transaction objects. Objects are created using the C++ new operator. For transient objects the syntax is unchanged other than the ability to return a Ref:

```
Ref<Department> tmp_dept = new Department;
```

The new operator is overloaded to accept a reference to a database in which to create a persistent object:

```
Database& theDB;
...
Ref<Department> dept1 = new(theDB) Department;
```

Clustering of stored objects may be requested by using a third form. Here the parameter is a reference to an existing persistent object (Ref<Pobject>) close to which the new object should be stored:

```
Ref<Department> dept2 = new(dept1) Department;
```

Transactions are managed by a Transaction class. This provides methods to start, commit, abort and checkpoint. The latter commits persistent objects but, unlike commit, does not release any locks. The Database class includes methods used to open, close and delete a database. Several other methods allow objects to be manipulated by name. These include assigning names to persistent objects and retrieving an object reference corresponding to a name. For example:

```
database->name(dept1, "Computing");      // (1)
char *nm = database->name(dept1);        // (2)
database->rename(nm, "CompSci");         // (3)
database->lookup(dept, "CompSci");       // (4)
```

(1) associates the name "Computing" with the object referenced by dept1, (2) returns a pointer to the name string associated with the reference dept1 and assigns it to nm, (3) renames the object whose name is passed in the first parameter to that in the second, and (4) finds the persistent object named "CompSci" and places a reference to it in dept.

OQL is a declarative query language closely related to SQL and based on the query language developed for the O_2 DBMS [Bancilhon *et al.* 1991]. When used in a

C++ program, a query statement is passed as the second parameter to the `oql` function. The first parameter is a reference to a persistent object, collection or atomic type, depending on the return type of the query. For example:

```
oql ( sdept, "select d from d in departments");
```

Here, `sdept` is a reference to a set of Departments. Run-time parameters to be substituted into the query text follow the query parameter. Here `bldg` is a pointer to a character string containing a building name:

```
oql ( sdept, "select d from d in departments where \
          d.building = $1s", bldg);
```

Finally, the following fragment shows a simple OML transaction:

```
// start the transaction identified by trans
// and initialize the reference to the class extension
trans->start();
database->lookup(Department::departments, "departments");

// OQL query returning a set of Departments
Set<Department>& sdept;
oql ( sdept, "select d from d in departments where \
                              d.building = \"Main\"");

// construct an iterator for the set of Departments
// and use it to traverse the set, printing the dept name
Ref<Department> d;
Iterator<Person> it = sdept.create_iterator();
while ( it.next(d) )
        cout << d->name << "\n";
it.close();
// commit the transaction
trans.commit();
```

16.7 Summary

We believe that it is still far too early to predict the future degree of success of object-oriented database systems. It is important to remember that we are already at least is years into the commercial development of relational systems and that there are still many potential developments that are still only at the research stage.

Commercial object-oriented systems are still in their infancy. There are, however, already strong moves towards standardization which will help the industry to present a strong challenge to the currently dominant relational systems. The influence of one approach on the other has not been all one way. A critical factor in the development of these systems has been the acceptance of the need for declarative query languages as well as extensions to conventional programming languages. The ODMG has adopted one of the most highly developed object query languages from one of its major members, several of whom already provide some degree of SQL 2 compliance, and has expressed a desire to include an SQL 3 binding at a future date.

Chapter 17

PARALLEL AND DISTRIBUTED DATA MANAGEMENT

17.1 Introduction

The fundamental distinction to be made in multicomputer systems is between client–server and peer-based systems. The first section of this chapter outlines client–server issues from a database perspective. Next we describe the principal design issues and architectures for parallel database servers. The third section describes the more loosely coupled environment of distributed database systems (DDBS), concentrating on conventional distributed applications. In the final section we describe the principal features of federated database systems.

A DDBS is distinguished from a parallel database system by the ability of the DDBS users to run applications at each node (usually called a site); in a parallel database system the nodes are hidden from the user in a 'black box'. The division of material between the sections on distributed and federated database systems is somewhat arbitrary, but the primary focus of the distributed systems section is on systems intended for a single application which is distributed over several sites (for example, a distribution company with several warehouses), whereas the focus of our discussion of federated databases is on multiple systems cooperating to achieve a number of tasks (for example a number of different database systems providing data for a management information application).

17.2 Client–server systems

All modern information systems are based around a client–server model of computing, where the clients make requests of the server. The usual division puts presentation services on the client (typically a workstation) and database management on the server.

Programming is most often done using a host language (for example, C, COBOL) with embedded data manipulation language statements (for example, SQL) which are communicated to the server.

Database applications can be classified according to the granularity of their database accesses:

- Coarse-grained applications have transactions that access large volumes of data (for example, decision support, large scientific applications).
- The transactions of medium-grained applications typically access groups of up to several dozen records (for example, order entry, many conventional commercial applications).
- Fine-grained applications are typically navigational, accessing small portions of linked records (for example, CAx applications).

This classification is a crude characterization of access patterns, since many applications exhibit a variety of granularities of database access.

From a database perspective client–server systems are classified by the amount of database processing (for example, query optimization) and local caching done by the client.

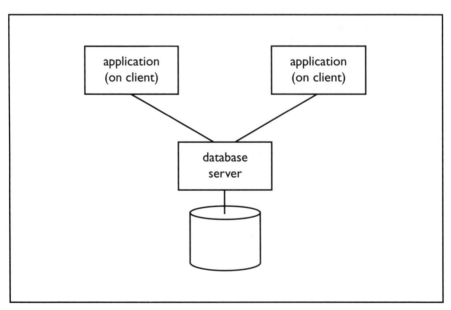

Figure 17.1 Client–server architecture (coarse-grained).

Coarse-grained applications have a few large interactions with the database, but they will benefit from parallel execution of queries on the server. If the query cannot adequately be expressed in the data manipulation language it may be necessary to bring all the potentially useful data back to the client for (sequential) processing. The development of more powerful data manipulation language features (for example, ADTs, procedures, a richer set of operators) and the use of (subsets of) conventional programming language code as methods is improving the ability of database servers to process a wide range of complex queries (*see* Chapters 15 and 16). For these applications the client is mostly concerned with presentation services and the client and database server are connected only by streams of queries and results.

It is often advantageous for a fine-grained application to request a large data transfer from the server to a local cache, for instance CAD and CASE where there are frequently large numbers of references internal to a complex object and very few to other objects. This attempts to minimize the cost of crossing between the database and application, at the cost of maintaining the cache coherency. Since fine-grained operations often have a high locality of reference this approach can give good performance, although if there is poor locality of reference the performance will be extremely poor.

With this architecture there is built-in inter-query parallelism if each client runs on a separate workstation (the normal case). Intra-query parallelism requires parallel client hardware, since the server is functioning as a persistent data store, which simplifies its design. To be effective the client must be able to hold all its frequently accessed data in memory, otherwise thrashing will cause a rapid degradation of performance. It is usually assumed that fine-grained applications are navigational and optimization is left to the programmer.

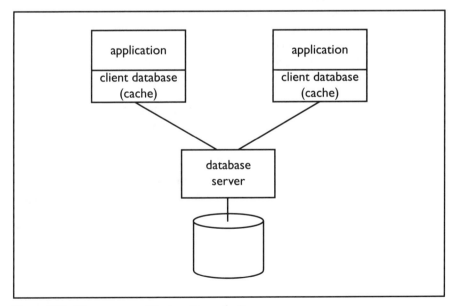

Figure 17.2 Client–server architecture (fine-grained).

The defining characteristic of fine-grained applications that allows them to benefit from a client-resident database cache is that their interactions with the database are frequent, small and the semantics are not readily captured by a declarative specification. Other applications that make many small accesses to the database (for example, debit/credit) can make good use of database procedures, which incorporate several operations in a single database request from the client.

17.3 Parallel database systems

The rapidly increasing use of parallel machines poses a challenge to the designers and implementors of database management systems. We show how parallel systems can be classified and describe the main design choices involved in parallel DBMS.

The use of parallel hardware and software is intended to bring a number of benefits to database management systems. We refer here to nodes of a parallel system; the composition of a node depends on the architecture of the parallel system. The potential benefits of parallelism for database applications are:

- Improved price/performance. Where high performance is essential this can either be achieved by the use of conventional mainframes or by using parallel machines which use standard high production volume components and so are generally cheaper per unit of performance.
- Extensibility. Ideally a parallel system should be incrementally extensible to accommodate increased demand, although in practice there are a number of factors, discussed in the following sections, which conspire against this.
- Availability. Parallel hardware with a suitable replication scheme has fewer single points of failure than conventional uniprocessor machines and makes it easier to design and implement resilient systems. Resilience is critical for the growing number of high-availability ('24 × 7') applications.

There are three metrics that are applicable to measuring the performance benefits of parallelism [DeWitt 1993]: speedup, scaleup and sizeup.

Speedup

Speedup is a measure of the decrease in response time for a given query when more nodes (processors and disks) are used to answer the query, that is, Speedup = Old Time / New Time.

The ideal is a linear speedup, where doubling the number of nodes halves the processing time. A system designed for speedup is intended to perform a given workload in less time as the number of nodes is increased.

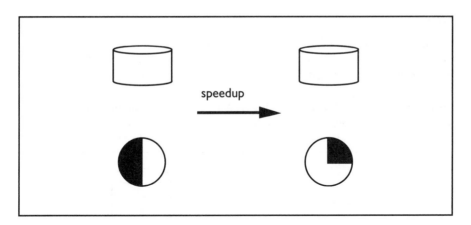

Figure 17.3 Speedup (good: doubling the machine capacity halves the time to perform a task).

Scaleup

Scaleup measures the extent to which the response time can be maintained as the workload and the number of nodes are increased. This measure is most important for applications that have a given window of time in which to complete their operations (for example, the overnight updating of banks' ATM databases). The ideal is for a system to have a constant response time as the workload and number of nodes are increased, that is, a doubling of the workload and of the number of nodes will not result in any increase in response time.

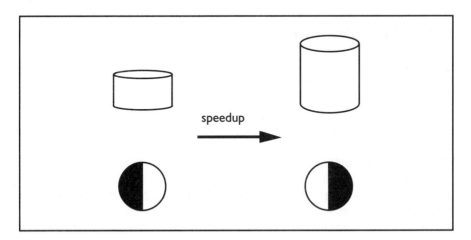

Figure 17.4 Scaleup (good: doubling the machine capacity allows double the work to be done in the same time).

Sizeup

Sizeup is a measure of the extent to which the increase in response time is proportional to the increase in workload for a given hardware configuration. An ideal sizeup is for a doubled workload to result in a doubled response time. Whether a system exhibits good sizeup behaviour depends partly on the workload, since operations such as sorting are $O(N \log N)$ and so will show sublinear sizeup. Others, such as B-tree searches, are $O(N \log N)$ and will therefore show superlinear sizeup.

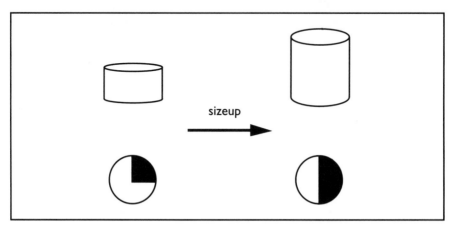

Figure 17.5 Sizeup (good: doubling the size of problem doubles the time).

17.3.1 Data placement

In any parallel database system the data must be spread over the nodes (or disks) of the system. There are two aims:

- Balance the load between nodes (or disks).
- Minimize the data transfers between nodes.

These two aims are incompatible, since the way to eliminate data transfers is to put all the data in the same place, and a random placement of data between nodes is likely to result in an approximately even load distribution. Neither of these extremes is optimal.

The desirable compromise is to place records that are frequently co-referenced on the same node, while ensuring that groups of co-referenced records are evenly distributed between nodes. The optimal size for the groups depends on the range of cost-effective granule sizes for that system and the characteristics of the workload.

Granularity of processes

One of the critical factors in any parallel system is the granularity of the processes. The desirable granularity for any system depends on the size of parallel tasks into which the workload can be partitioned. For database systems the biggest choice is whether to define a query as the unit of granularity (inter-query parallelism) or to distribute a single query over multiple nodes (intra-query parallelism).

A number of successful systems based on inter-query parallelism have been developed, for example, Tandem's NonStop SQL [Tandem 1989]. These systems are simpler to implement than those that exploit intra-query parallelism, but intra-query parallelism can bring substantial benefits in response time for larger queries. In general, the exploitation of inter-query parallelism leads to an increase in throughput (that is, effectively increasing the degree of concurrency by providing more processing capacity).

The successful exploitation of intra-query parallelism depends on achieving the right balance between the performance improvements from dividing the same work between more nodes, which should ideally result in linear improvements, and the costs of using the extra nodes. Three factors interfere with the attainment of linear improvements (particularly speedup):

- **Startup cost.** This is the cost of initiating a process at a node and is a constant. For small queries this may represent a significant fraction of the total execution time of the query.
- **Interference.** Processes are likely to interfere with each other as a result of the need to communicate and coordinate their activities and through competing for resources. Interference is the measure of the slowdown caused by these interactions (*see* Chapter 12).
- **Variance or skew.** This measure expresses the difference in service times between query fragments running on different nodes.

The cost of initiating a process is a fixed overhead and therefore assumes a greater importance in the overall cost as the amount of work done by a process decreases. At some point the benefits of dividing the work between more processes are outweighed by the costs of starting more processes. The point at which this occurs is dependent on the:

- cost of process initiation,
- trade-off of increased response time against decreased throughput.

Processes in a cohort executing fragments of a query are likely to incur some overhead in dealing with other processes for a number of reasons:

- coordination of phases of an operation that is distributed over several nodes (for example, sort);
- exchange of intermediate results (for example, in a parallel join);

- resource contention (for example waiting for communications resources);
- data contention, especially for shared items (for example, metadata).

The cost of interference can quickly limit the speedup that is possible.

Differences in the work done at each node are usually a function of the number of records processed at each. These differences grow in importance as the processing at each node is reduced, so they can form a large part of the total response time if the processes each do very little work.

The trade-offs between the reduction in time from adding more nodes against the overheads of the extra processes mean that, for database work, a medium-grained parallelism is usually appropriate. Medium-grain parallelism is characterized so that each process in a cohort might typically work on the records from one or a small number of pages.

17.3.2 Parallel database architectures

Parallel database systems are classified according to the elements that are shared; a good summary of these issues is provided by [Bergsten *et al.* 1993].

Shared memory systems

In a shared memory system all the processors share the disks and the main memory equally.

The processors generally have their own small cache, whose coherency is maintained by dedicated (currently expensive) hardware mechanisms, usually based on 'bus snooping'. Processor cache sizes currently vary between 64Kb and 4Mb, which is large enough to hold the most frequently accessed data. Processor allocation is usually done automatically by the operating system, so load balancing is easy. Data transfer between processors is done using the shared memory. Inter-query parallelism is simply achieved by adding more processes, although intra-query parallelism is more difficult.

This architecture does not scale well much beyond 20 processors because of the problems of scaling the cache coherency mechanism (bus congestion, propagation of writes, and so on).

Many of the major commercial DBMSs (for example, Oracle, DB2) have been ported to conventional multiprocessor mainframes (for example, IBM 3090, Bull DPS8) and others (for example, INGRES, Sybase, Oracle) have been ported to other multiprocessor systems (for example, Sequent, ICL Goldrush). These systems exploit inter-query parallelism and generally make effective use of the available parallelism.

Prototypes have been developed (for example, XPRES [Stonebraker *et al.* 1988], DBS3 [Bergsten *et al.* 1991]) which explore the use of intra-query parallelism for shared memory architectures.

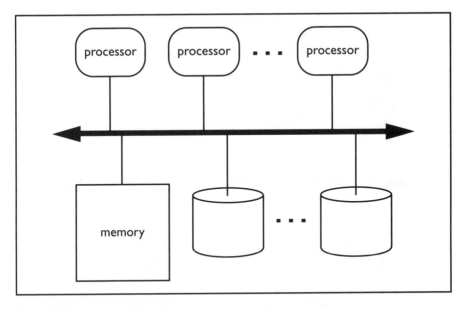

Figure 17.6 Shared memory architecture.

Shared disk systems

The shared disk architecture consists of nodes and a pool of shared disks, all connected by a communications network. Each node comprises one or more processors and memory. Some variants of the architecture have the disks physically attached to some or all of the nodes, but they are logically shared. Because a disk access is approximately 10 times longer than a network transfer the difference between a local and a remote access is small.

The coherence of multiple copies of a page that have been requested by different nodes must be maintained by software which is 10–100 times slower than the hardware mechanisms used in shared memory systems. It is relatively easy to port existing centralized DBMSs to a shared disk architecture, by mapping transactions to single nodes (inter-query parallelism) and developing a suitable coherency mechanism. No significant work has been reported on the development of systems that exploit intra-query parallelism.

This architecture tends to be limited by the volume of traffic on the communications network, since most page transfers use it, or by the cost of the multiple copy coherency mechanism if there are many updates.

Many commercial DBMSs (Oracle, INGRES, Rdb, and so on) have been ported to shared disk machines such as VAXCluster and NCube.

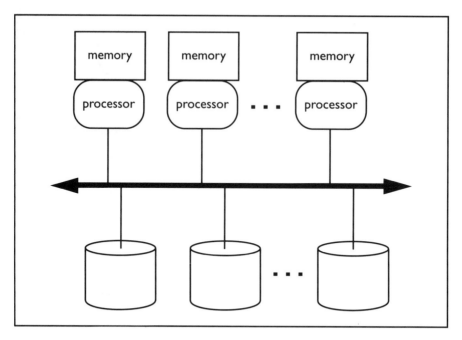

Figure 17.7 Shared disk architecture.

Shared nothing systems

Shared nothing systems consist of nodes linked by a communications network. The nodes each have processor, memory and one or more disks; performance is often enhanced by moving all the communications functions to a specialized processor. The machines can be largely constructed from standard components and the architecture is scalable to thousands of nodes.

The data is allocated to nodes; each node is responsible for the query fragments that use its local data and the transaction code migrates to the relevant nodes. This has two significant consequences:

- every query must be parallelized;
- load balancing is difficult, since the data is statically distributed.

If a node contains a number of frequently accessed data items it may become a bottleneck, degrading the performance of the whole system. Bottlenecks can be overcome either by replicating frequently accessed items and managing them with a suitable coherency protocol, or by reorganizing the database. The first solution poses problems for frequently updated items, as the coherency protocols are based around a Read-One, Write-All discipline, while the second solution is expensive and may cause poor performance in the presence of a cyclically changing workload (for example, with very different query mixes at different times of the day, week or month).

Frequent physical changes to the machine configuration either cause a corresponding number of database reorganizations, or a replication scheme is needed. If every part of the database is replicated on two or more nodes, then the loss of a single node will not affect the availability of the system. Such a scheme must allow for the copies of fragments of the database to be automatically updated when they are reconnected.

The exploitation of shared nothing architecture is heavily reliant on intra-query parallelism, and it is difficult to adapt current commercial systems to a shared nothing machine environment. Nevertheless, these systems can offer very good performance (for example, ICL Goldrush can perform up to 6,000 tps on TPC-B). Tandem NonStop SQL [Tandem 1989], Teradata [Teradata 1985] and ICL Goldrush [ICL 1993] are examples of commercial shared nothing systems.

There has been a great deal of research done on database systems for shared nothing architecture. Some of the more important prototypes include Gamma [DeWitt *et al.* 1990], Bubba [Boral *et al.* 1990] and EDBS [Haworth *et al.* 1990]. The EDS hardware, for which EDBS was targeted, was the prototype for the ICL Goldrush machine.

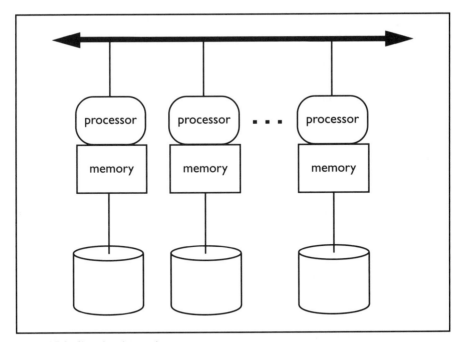

Figure 17.8   Shared nothing architecture.

Hybrid systems

Apart from the basic types of architecture described here there is considerable interest in hybrid architectures, which may have a top-level shared disk architecture and individual nodes which are themselves shared memory systems. This architecture appears to give a good compromise between load balancing and scalability.

17.4 Distributed database systems

In this section we describe the principal issues, developments and products in the area of distributed database systems (DDBS).

A number of definitions of distributed databases are possible; here we restrict ourselves to systems where:

- there is a unified system management,
- a single global schema can be transparently presented to the user,
- the nodes of the system are all treated as peers (even if they have very different processing capabilities).

This largely restricts the focus of the material here to relational systems, as this is the context where most of the work has been done and for which there are prototypes and products available. The issues are similar for other data models, although the provision of transparent distributed navigational facilities presents some interesting challenges.

These properties imply that the underlying system needs facilities to:

1. Perform distributed query optimization;
2. Manage distributed transactions (concurrency control, commit protocol, recovery);
3. Manage data replication (global, external and distribution schemas at least).

The schema maintenance operations require careful engineering, since every transaction needs access to schema tables, although the implementation of any replication scheme without significantly degrading performance can be difficult in a high-update environment.

17.4.1 Homogeneous DDBS

The simplest case of a distributed database is where there are several sites, each running their own applications on the same DBMS. The applications can all see the same schema and run the same transactions they would if they used a centralized DBMS, that is, there is location transparency. The provision of location transparency forms the core of distributed database management systems (DDBMS) development, since it requires all the facilities listed above, that is, global and distribution schemas, distributed query optimization and transaction management.

The use of a single DBMS avoids any problems of mismatched database capabilities between nodes, since the data is all managed within a single framework.

Query processing can be done on the basis that all sites have the same (known) capabilities.

The principal differences between distributed database systems and parallel systems using a shared nothing architecture are:

- **Communications**. A DDBS uses standard, general-purpose links over distances from tens of metres (LAN) to thousands of kilometres (WAN). Parallel systems communication uses specialized links, usually within a single cabinet (although some machines are configured in several cabinets).
- **Autonomy.** Each site in a DDBS has some degree of autonomy and is usually capable of supporting a complete application environment. The nodes in a parallel database system are generally not capable of functioning independently.

Distributed databases are frequently the solution of choice for organizations with naturally distributed operations. The use of smaller machines reduces the system cost and the use of a homogeneous DDBMS should not require any substantial extra management.

17.4.2 Heterogeneous DDBMS

In practice it is common for several existing databases, using different DBMSs, to be linked into a single system.

There are a number of additional problems for query processing because the query processor does not know the query processing capabilities of other sites:

- the costs of operations may vary considerably between sites (for example, depending on the local data organization and indexes);
- some operations may not be available at particular sites (for example, join on a navigational system);
- some DBMSs cannot read the records of others (more likely in systems incorporating DBMSs primarily designed for single-user operation);
- different DBMSs have varying base data types which can cause incompatibilities (for example, the maximum length of a text field, support for BLOBs.).

To deal with these problems the requesting site must either:

- have detailed knowledge of the operation of the remote system, so that it can correctly optimize the query and pass the remote site a fragment which it can execute efficiently, or
- assume that the remote system has only the most rudimentary functionality and simply request all the potentially relevant data, or
- make the programmer do the query decomposition by hand.

INGRES/Star

INGRES/Star, introduced in 1985, was among the first DDBSs. It started as a homogeneous DDBS and acquired the ability to integrate with other vendors' databases. It is probably the most complete heterogeneous DDBS currently available.

In its current form the product uses OpenSQL to communicate requests between different systems. Applications see a consistent view of the global database, so can be run from any node; error and status messages from other systems are interpreted to a consistent format.

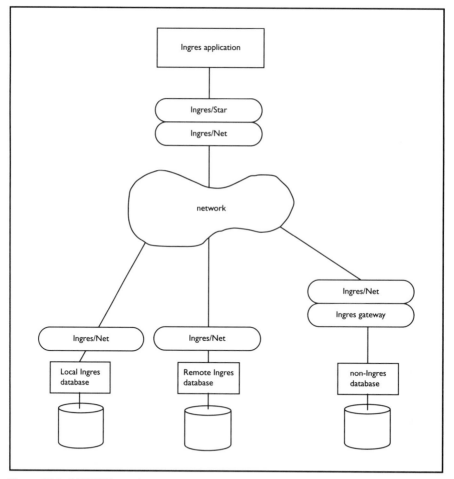

Figure 17.9 INGRES/Star architecture.

INGRES uses a client–server architecture to separate the end-user tools and interfaces from the database server process. INGRES/Net allows a user to use a single remote database as if it were local. Several communications protocols are supported (for example, TCP/IP, LU0).

Access to non-INGRES databases is provided through gateways which present a remote database as if it were an INGRES database, presenting a uniform view and allowing applications to access data transparently (that is, without needing knowledge of the remote system). The gateway mediates between INGRES and the non-INGRES database, using INGRES/Net to provide the communications links.

INGRES/Star provides the ability to access data from several local or remote databases simultaneously, giving an integrated view of a single global schema, although the facilities are limited to those provided by INGRES or which can be emulated by the gateway on the remote machine. Statements can be passed straight through the gateway to a local database to invoke functions unsupported by INGRES/Star. Two-phase commit is supported in the most recent releases of the product.

The distributed schema is created by including the required tables from the local databases. Tables not explicitly declared in the distributed schema remain private to the local database. The query optimizer has sufficient information, provided by INGRES/Net and the gateways, to optimize distributed queries transparently.

Microsoft's ODBC and Access

Microsoft's Open Database Connectivity (ODBC) is a commercial applications programming interface standard which uses OpenSQL, a common subset of SQL, to pass queries between heterogeneous databases. It is certain to be a significant component in the integration of database systems over the next few years, although at the time of writing it is not clear what other standards (if any) will play a significant part in linking small, PC-based, databases into larger corporate database environments and distributed networks of small databases.

The ODBC architecture (Figure 17.10) is based on point-to-point connections between databases, but a database may have several connections. It is usually assumed that a Microsoft product (Access, SQL Server) will form one end of the connection; the other end may be virtually any other SQL compliant database or an xBase (dBase, Clipper, and so on) system. ODBC drivers have been developed by a number of database manufacturers and third-party software vendors.

Since ODBC implementations are RPC libraries they can be layered on top of other RPC products. For example, the INGRES ODBC driver has done this, using INGRES/Net as its substrate and thereby providing access to other systems through the various INGRES Gateway products.

The ODBC driver maintains a list of sites, which comprise node and database names, and provides data translation facilities between the standard types on both systems. In the case of applications hosted on Microsoft Access and using remote databases (which may be at the same or a different node) the connection between the databases is made by specifying the remote site and table names.

Access provides most of the facilities expected of a heterogeneous DBS. A user of an Access database may attach tables from other Access installations, or from databases maintained by dBase, Paradox, INGRES, Oracle, and others. Access keeps an index of primary keys for each attached table which is used in update operations.

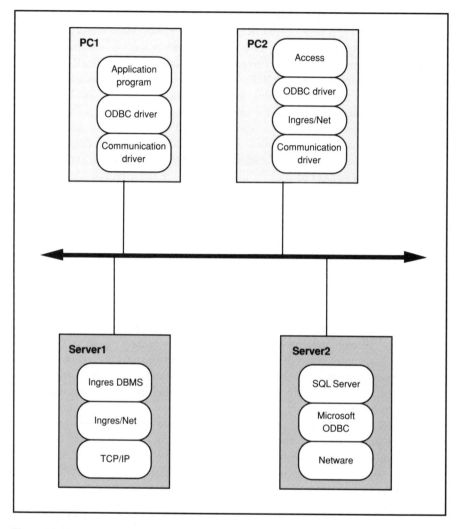

Figure 17.10 Microsoft ODBC architecture.

Distributed retrievals are transparently supported and are specified using OpenSQL either directly or through a forms-based interface. Updates are restricted to a single site, since partitioned tables are not supported and an updatable view must be a simple restriction of a single table. There is an option to pass query language statements straight to another host, allowing supersets of OpenSQL to be used.

The absence of partitioned tables makes transaction management easier; because update statements are confined to a single site, a program that updates tables at several sites is syntactically identical to a series of local updates. It is the programmer's responsibility to check the successful completion of each statement and to initiate suitable transaction control actions.

The ODBC programming interface provides an equivalent to Dynamic SQL through a function library accessible from programs written in C and other languages. SQL statements are submitted as function parameters at run time, rather than being translated by a preprocessor before compilation. The library includes connection management, variable binding and query execution functions.

Connections to heterogeneous systems are aided by support functions that enable the program to determine various capabilities of the remote system (for example, available data types) and to retrieve information from system catalogues. Advanced facilities not covered by the Open SQL specification may be accessed using a pass-through mechanism that submits commands directly to the remote system, untouched by intermediate drivers.

17.4.3 Transaction processing monitors

Transaction processing monitors (TPMs) – the most widely known of which is IBM's CICS – form an important part of the provision of distributed transaction-based services. Transaction processing monitors have been largely neglected in the literature, except for the comprehensive treatment in [Gray and Reuter 1993]. Many definitions and functions have been ascribed to TPMs, although historically they filled the gaps in a particular system that had to be filled to build a transaction-oriented programming facility.

The principal function of a TPM in a distributed environment is to provide a transactional remote procedure call facility; the call interface appears identical to a conventional local call interface. This frees the application from concerns about where particular resources (databases, and so on) are on a network and manages the transaction logic (commit, abort). A TPM may be called directly by an application or by a server needing additional resources (for example, access to a remote database) to complete its work.

The fundamental operations of a TPM are:

1. It receives a request from one of its clients. If this is from an application client it will have no transaction identifier (TrId) and so the TPM will start a transaction. If the request already has a TrId the TPM becomes part of that transaction.
2. The request is validated by the TPM, using whatever authorization and security checks are specified.
3. The TPM creates a server process to fulfil the request. If the system is congested the server creation may be delayed until sufficient resources are available for the server to run efficiently. This is frequently done by having a fixed pool of servers which service requests in order.
4. The server fulfils the request, invoking other servers as necessary; these all become part of the transaction.
5. The TPM server negotiates and coordinates the transaction control with the other servers in the transaction, returning either commit or abort as appropriate.

An application may declare savepoints within the transaction, which allow partial rollback. If a savepoint is declared a transaction can roll back to it and take another course, without losing all its work; the TPM can provide the application with a clean exception-reporting interface. Savepoints in effect provide a single level of nesting for transactions.

These functions give the TPM the overall role in orchestrating and coordinating the transactional activities and resources of a distributed system, including the coordination of recovery and archival storage.

17.5 Federated database systems

A federated database system (FDS) can be defined as a collection of independently managed, heterogeneous database systems that allow partial and controlled sharing of data without affecting existing applications. Most organizations have a hetero-geneous collection of data storage systems that have been built using a variety of data models, software technology and hardware platforms. Increasingly there is a strong imperative for disparate parts of an organization, or a group of organizations, to share data. The proportion of data to be shared and the management and ownership of the data varies. Federated database system concepts provide a framework for addressing these issues and a basis for constructing solutions to them. In many cases the construction of a federated database system involves a large proportion of custom software that provides a uniform interface to the disparate systems of the federation. The essence of an FDS is that there is a collection of local database systems, each of which is (partially) mapped into the federated schema (Figure 17.11).

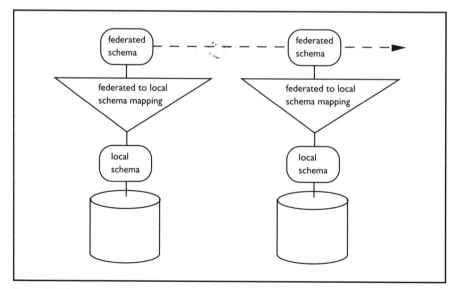

Figure 17.11 Overview of federated database system structure.

The component systems of the FDS may be more or less tightly coupled, merging into what we have classified as DDBS at the more tightly coupled end of the spectrum and into periodic batch data transfers at the other.

17.5.1   Reference architecture

A reference architecture provides the framework for analysing and understanding the architectural options and processes necessary to implement federated database systems [Sheth and Larson 1990]. In this section we provide a summary and overview of the components of a federated database system architecture.

The components of an FDS are:

- data: facts and information managed by a database system;
- database: a structured data store;
- command: a request to retrieve or modify data (issued by a user or a processor);
- processor: a software module that manipulates commands and data;
- schema: a description of data managed by a database management system, consisting of schema objects and their interrelations (for example, entity types and relationship types from an ER model);
- mapping: a function that correlates schema objects in one schema with schema objects in another.

These components allow us to describe a wide variety of systems in a system-independent way, without recourse to implementation-dependent description.

17.5.2   Processor types

Four types of processor can be distinguished: transforming, filtering, constructing and accessing; each type performs specific functions on commands and data.

Transforming processor

A transforming processor, illustrated in Figure 17.12, translates commands or data from one (source) language or format to a different (target) language or format. This type of processor hides differences in data structures and query languages, provided that appropriate mappings can be provided between the source and target languages and structures. Thus, a transforming processor might provide a mapping between data manipulation commands in an object-oriented or navigational language and their SQL equivalents.

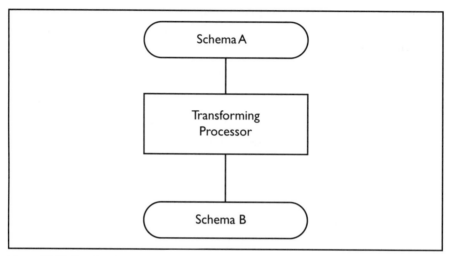

Figure 17.12 Transforming processor.

Filtering processor

A filtering processor (Figure 17.13) constrains the data and commands that can be passed to another processor; it has an associated set of constraints which may either be embedded in the processor or held separately. Filtering processors may be used for functions such as syntactic checking of queries, for enforcing access restrictions on specific data, and so on.

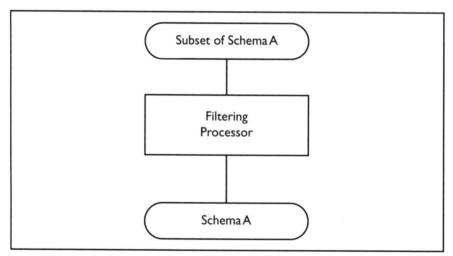

Figure 17.13 Filtering processor.

Constructing processor

A constructing processor (Figure 17.14) partitions or replicates operations submitted by a single processor into operations for a number of other processors and merges data from several other processors into a single stream for consumption by a single processor. A constructing processor provides location, distribution and replication transparency; the tasks it handles may include:

- schema integration,
- query processing,
- global transaction management.

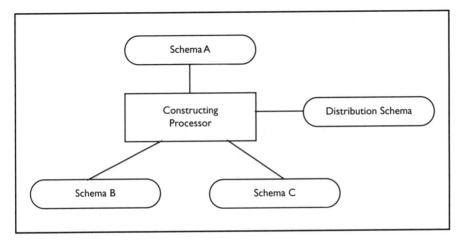

Figure 17.14 Constructing processor.

Accessing processor

An accessing processor accepts commands from other processors and executes them against a database. These operations are carried out at the level of the data manager of a DBMS or an application program that accesses data stored in a conventional file system.

17.5.3   Schema architecture

The schema architecture for a FDBS comprises the following elements:

- **Local Schema**: describes the logical (conceptual) schema of a component DBS; it is expressed in the terms and structures employed by the local DBMS.
- **Component Schema**: is the local schema translated into the common data model of the FDBS. This schema facilitates the specification of multi-

database queries and views in a loosely coupled FDBS and allows any semantics that are missing from the local schema to be added.

The derivation of the component schema from the local schema provides the mappings needed by transforming processors which use them to map commands from the component schemas to the local schemas.

- **Export Schema**: defines the schema objects in the component schema that are accessible to some or all other members of the federation; it is frequently used in conjunction with filtering processors to maintain the autonomy of the local DBS.

- **Federated Schema**: is the union of multiple export schemas that usually contains data distribution information (although this may be held in a separate distribution schema).

- **External Schema**: defines a particular user's view of a subset of the federated schema, which may be large and complex. It is possible for the external schema to have a different data model from the federated schema, in which case a transforming processor is needed to handle the transformation of commands between the external and federated schemas.

Where there is a need for the application to access both federated and local private data the external schema will contain details of the private data.

An important component of these schemas is the mappings which specify the transformations between schema objects at different levels of the schema architecture. These may be stored as part of the schema or may be maintained in an FDBS data dictionary.

The five-level schema architecture described above contains a number of possible redundancies, but is sufficiently elaborate to accommodate a very wide range of possible architectures and component DBMSs, from unstructured files through relational systems of varying capability to object-oriented and deductive database systems. The overall architecture is shown in Figure 17.15 and the application view of a federated database system is illustrated in Figure 17.16.

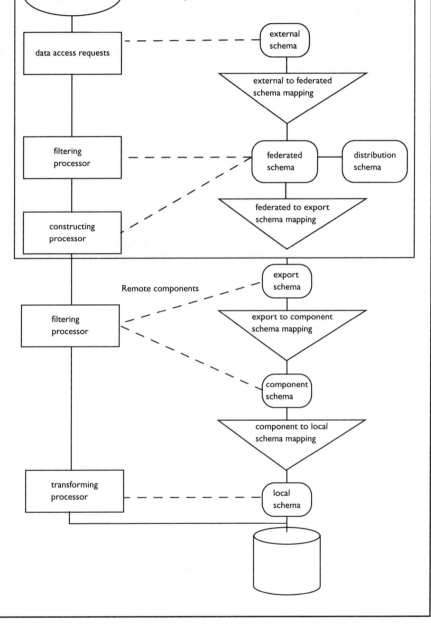

Figure 17.15 Application view of accessing a remote federation member.

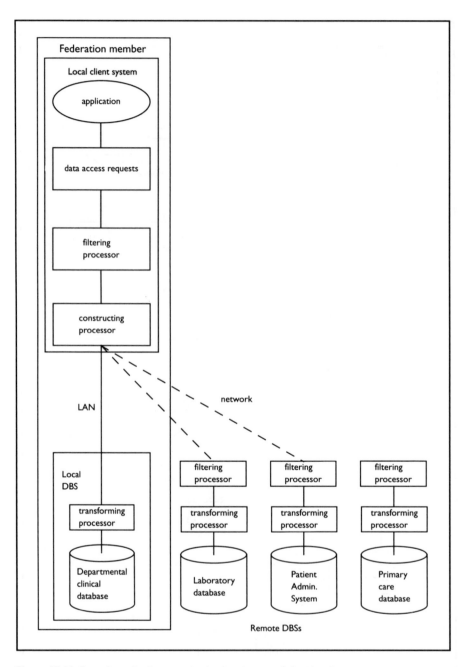

Figure 17.16 Example application accessing local and remote federation data.

17.5.4 Data sharing

We can identify five principal classes of data items of potential interest, illustrated in Figure 17.17 (the heavy circle denotes the extent of the federated schema):

1. Data that is currently shared by (or is common between) all members of the federation.
2. Data that a federation member shares with some (but not all) other members.
3. Data that is currently private but is part of the federated schema. These items are frequently similar to those in 2 above.
4. Data that is currently shared by two or more members.
5. Private data that will continue to be private.

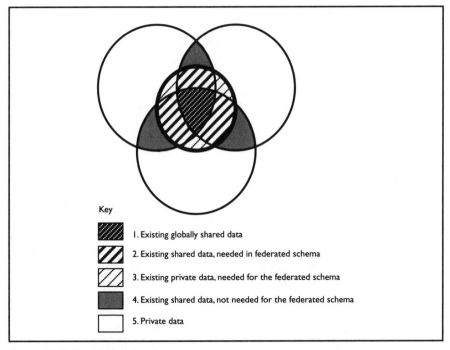

Key

1. Existing globally shared data
2. Existing shared data, needed in federated schema
3. Existing private data, needed for the federated schema
4. Existing shared data, not needed for the federated schema
5. Private data

Figure 17.17 Data sharing classes.

There are a number of problems in constructing a global schema from several existing schemas:

- Identical concepts with different implementations (for example, a doctor's identity might be recorded as a name, a set of initials or a practitioner registration code). Different DBSs will typically have adopted different representations and the federated schema must provide mappings between them.

- Identical names for different concepts (for example, the concept 'name' may be used to refer to a patient, doctor, department, building, drug, and so on).
- Different names for the same concept (for example, patient, client or care subject all refer to people receiving some form of treatment or care).
- Concepts partially implemented on different systems (for example, System A records a patient's health service number, diagnosis and responsible doctor while System B records the patient's name, treatment and ward).

In general these problems are difficult to resolve, usually requiring substantial domain knowledge and needing the involvement of users and domain specialists to resolve. Often the mappings between concepts in different systems are dependent to some extent on the users' perspectives and therefore are liable to be different for different groups of users [Hsiao 1992a]. The difficult problems usually involve differences of semantics, usage and organizational issues rather than issues for which a straightforward technical solution is feasible.

The problems of schema mapping have been the subject of many research efforts, which have increased our understanding of many of the issues involved and produced a number of specific proposals. However, the resolution of the practical integration problems that are likely to be encountered in federated database system construction still relies on cooperation between different groups of users and the system constructors.

17.6 Summary

In this chapter we have described a variety of architectures for distributed database systems spanning a range of integration, from very tightly integrated homogeneous distributed database systems to loosely coupled and independently managed federated database systems. The major issues for these systems are the degree of resilience, the independence of the sites and the homogeneity of the application (that is, are all the sites doing the same thing).

The use of parallel hardware for database systems promises increased performance at a relatively moderate price. The amount of performance improvement, its scalability and the complexity of the database management software form a difficult series of trade-offs and compromises. Our understanding of these trade-offs and ability to construct fully functional parallel database systems has increased considerably in the past few years and the use of parallel systems is increasing significantly.

BIBLIOGRAPHY

[Abdel-Hamid and Madnick 1991]

T. Abdel-Hamid and S. Madnick, *Software Project Dynamics*, Addison-Wesley, 1991

Modern project management text, with an emphasis on the interdependencies between the various activities.

[Agrawal and DeWitt 1985]

R. Agrawal and D.J. DeWitt, 'Integrated Concurrency Control and Recovery Mechanisms: Design and Performance Evaluation', *ACM TODS*, 10, 529–64, 1985

Presents analytic models of a number of concurrency control and recovery strategies.

[Aho *et al.* 1974]

A.V. Aho, J.E. Hopcroft and J.D. Ullman, *The Design and Analysis of Computer Algorithms*, Addison-Wesley, 1974

Classic text on the analysis of algorithms.

[Aho and Ullman 1977]

A.V. Aho and J.D. Ullman, *Principles of Compiler Design*, Addison-Wesley, 1977

The standard (readable) compiler design text.

[Aiken *et al.* 1992]

A. Aiken, J. Widom and J.M. Hellerstein, 'Behaviour of Database Production Rules: Termination, Confluence, and Observable Determinism', *Proc. ACM SIGMOD Int. Conf. on Management of Data,* 59–68, 1992.

Describes methods for determining whether an arbitrary set of production rules will terminate, produce a unique result and produce a unique sequence of observable actions.

[Albano *et al.* 1985]

A. Albano, L. Cardelli and R. Orsini, 'Galileo: A Strongly Typed, Interactive Conceptual Language', *ACM TODS*, 10 (2), 230–60, 1985
Primary paper for an overview and description of the Galileo DBPL, developed at the University of Pisa.

[Alford 1992]

R. Alford, 'Disk Arrays Explained', *Byte*, Vol. 17 (10), 259–66, 1992.
Straightforward description of RAID technology.

[Amdahl 1967]

G. Amdahl, 'Validity of the single processor approach to achieving large scale computing capabilities', *AFIPS Proc. 1967 Spring Joint Computer Conference*, 30, 483–85, 1967.
Classic paper, introducing Amdahl's Law.

[Andres *et al.* 1991]

F. Andres, M. Couprie and Y. Viemont, 'A Multi-Environment Cost Evaluator for Parallel Database Systems', *Proc. 2nd Int. DASFAA*, Japan, 126–35, 1991
Shows current developments in database cost evaluation techniques.

[Anon *et al.* 1985]

Anon *et al.*, 'A Measure of Transaction Processing Power', *Datamation*, 31 (7), 112–18
Proposal for the TP1 benchmark, predecessor of TPC-A. Published anonymously as an attempt to stop the 'benchmark wars' and reduce the number of unsubstantiated and unverifiable claims being made at that time.

[Ashworth and Goodland 1990]

C. Ashworth and M. Goodland, *SSADM: A Practical Approach*, McGraw Hill, London, 1990.
Introduction to SSADM, the UK government-sponsored structured analysis and design method. See also [Weaver 1993].

[Atkinson and Buneman 1987]

M. Atkinson and P. Buneman, 'Types and Persistence in Database Programming Languages', *ACM Computing Surveys*, 19, 105–90, 1987
Comparative early survey of persistent programming languages. There has been much subsequent work in this area.

[Atkinson *et al.* 1983]

M. Atkinson, P. Bailey, W. Cockshott, K. Chisholm and R. Morrison, 'An Approach to Persistent Programming', Computer J., 26 (4), 1983
Description of PS-ALGOL.

[Atkinson *et al.* 1989]   M. Atkinson, F. Bancilhon, D. DeWitt, K. Dittrich, D. Maier and S. Zdonik, 'The Object-Oriented Database System Manifesto', *in* [Kim *et al.* 1989]
Defines the required features of an object–oriented database system. These include the main features of object-oriented programming (encapsulation, inheritance and late binding) and add the conventional database features of persistence, concurrency control, ad hoc queries and recovery mechanisms. User defined types, collections and object identity are also included to address the perceived limitations of conventional DBS. For an alternative view, see [Manifesto 1990].

[Bancilhon *et al.* 1989]   F. Bancilhon, S. Cluet and C. Delobel, 'A Query Language for the O_2 Object-Oriented Database System', *Proc. 2nd Int. Workshop on Database Programming Languages*, 122–38, 1989
Description and comparison of O_2's query language with others.

[Bancilhon *et al.* 1991]   F. Bancilhon, L. Delobel, and P. Kanellakis (eds.), *Building an Object Oriented Database System: The Story of O_2,* Morgan Kaufmann, 1991.
Collection of papers covering all aspects of the development of the O_2 system and related work.

[Bancilhon and Buneman 1990]   F. Bancilhon and P. Buneman (eds.), *Advances in Database Programming Languages*, ACM Press Frontier Series (Addison-Wesley), New York, 1990.
Edited collection of papers from a meeting held in Roscoff, France in 1987 to address the need for coherent database programming languages rather than the multilingual approach required when using embedded query languages. Covers a wide range of language design and implementation issues.

[Bancilhon and Ramakrishnan 1986]   F. Bancilhon and R. Ramakrishnan , 'An Amateur's Introduction to Recursive Query Processing Strategies', *Proc. ACM SIGMOD Int. Conf. on Management of Data,* 16– 52, 1986
Good survey of the main recursive query processing techniques.

[Banerjee *et al.* 1987]   J. Banerjee, W. Kim and H-J Kim, H.F. Forth, 'Semantics and implementation of Schema Evolution in Object-Oriented Databases', *Proc. ACM SIGMOD Int. Conf. on Management of Data*, 311–22, 1987
Account of the types of schema change and rules to ensure consistency for ODBS.

[Batini *et al.* 1992] C. Batini, S. Ceri and S.B. Navathe, *Conceptual Database Design,* Benjamin Cummings, 1992
Integrated transformation-based approach to EER and DFD modelling.

[Beckmann *et al.* 1990] N. Beckmann, H.-P. Kriegel, R. Schneider and B. Seeger, 'The R*-tree: An Efficient and Robust Access Method for Points and Rectangles', *Proc. ACM SIGMOD Int. Conf. on Management of Data,* 322–31, 1990
Description of the R-Tree, an enhanced form of R-Tree, see also [Guttmann 1984] and [Sellis et al. 1987].*

[Bergsten *et al.* 1991] B. Bergsten, M. Couprie and P. Valduriez, 'Prototyping DBS3, a Shared-Memory Parallel Database System', *Proc. PDIS 1991,* 1991

[Bergsten *et al.* 1993] B. Bergsten, M. Couprie and P. Valduriez, 'Overview of Parallel Architectures for Databases', *Computer J.,* 36, 734–40, 1993

[Bernstein *et al.* 1987] P.A. Bernstein, V. Hadzilacos and N. Goodman, *Concurrency Control and Recovery in Database Systems,* Addison-Wesley, 1987
A thorough treatment of conventional locking and logging methods for concurrency control and recovery. They provide good coverage of certification and timestamp schedulers, and recovery strategies for distributed and replicated systems. A chapter is devoted to serializability theory.

[Bernstein and Goodman 1980] P.A. Bernstein and N. Goodman, 'Timestamp-Based Algorithms for Concurrency Control in Distributed Database Systems', *Proc. 6th Int. Conf. on VLDB,* Montreal, 1980
Original proposal for concurrency control using timestamps.

[Bitton *et al.* 1983] D. Bitton, D.J. DeWitt and C. Turbyfill, 'Benchmarking Database Systems: A Systematic Approach', *Proc. 9th Int. Conf. on VLDB,* Florence, 8–19, 1983
Marks the foundation of modern database benchmarking activity.

[Boehm 1986] B. Boehm, 'A Spiral Model of Software Development and Enhancement', *Software Engineering Notes,* 11 (4), 22, 1986.
Original paper describing the spiral model for software development.

[Booch 1994]　　　　　G.Booch, *Object-Oriented Analysis and Design with Applications (2nd ed.)*, Benjamin-Cummings, 1994
Readable exposition of OO system analysis and design. (First edition was 1991.) See [Rumbaugh et al. 1991] for a more evolutionary approach.

[Boral *et al.* 1990]　　H. Boral, W. Alexander, L. Clay, G. Copeland, S. Danforth, M. Franklin, B. Hart, M. Smith and P. Valduriez, 'Prototyping Bubba: A Highly Parallel Database System', *IEEE Trans. on Knowledge and Data Engineering*, 2, 4–24, 1990
An overview of the Bubba project at MCC, an important early parallel DBS with two languages, FAD and LDL. The project explored many important issues in parallel DBS.

[Carey *et al.* 1988]　　M.J. Carey, D.J. DeWitt and S.L. Vandenberg, 'A Data Model and Query Language for EXODUS', *Proc. ACM SIGMOD Int. Conf. on Management of Data,* 1988

[Carey *et al.* 1989]　　M.J. Carey, D. J. DeWitt, J.E. Richardson and E.J. Shekita, 'Storage Management for Objects in EXODUS', *in* [Kim and Lochovsky 1989]

[Carey *et al.* 1990]　　M.J. Carey, D.J. DeWitt, G. Graefe, D.M. Haight, J.E. Richardson, D.T. Schuh, E.J. Shekita and S.L. Vandenberg, 'The EXODUS Extensible DBMS Project: An Overview', *in* [Zdonik and Maier 1990]
A general overview and two papers which give a good summary of the EXODUS system.

[Carey *et al.* 1993]　　M.J. Carey, D.J. DeWitt and J.F. Naughton, 'The OO7 Benchmark', *Proc. ACM SIGMOD Int. Conf. on Management of Data*, 12–21, 1993
Published definition of the OO7 benchmark. A fuller version is available as a Technical Report.

[Cattell 1991a]　　　　R.G.G. Cattell, *Object Data Management: object oriented and extended relational database systems*, Addison-Wesley, 1991.
Contains good outline descriptions of a substantial number of ODBSs.

[Cattell 1991b]　　　　R.G.G. Cattell, 'An Engineering Database Benchmark', *in* [Gray 1991]
Description of the OO1 benchmark. Another version of [Cattell and Skeen 1992].

[Cattell 1994] R.G.G. Cattell (ed.), *The Object Database Standard: ODMG-93*, Morgan Kaufmann, 1994.
Description and definition of proposed standard object definition, manipulation and query languages, including C++ and Smalltalk bindings. Produced by a consortium of object data management system vendors.

[Cattell and Skeen 1992] R.G.G. Cattell and J. Skeen, 'Object Operations Benchmark', *ACM TODS*, 17, 1–32, 1992
Description of the OO1 benchmark, see also [Cattell 1991b].

[Ceri and Widom 1992] S. Ceri and J. Widom, 'Production Rules in Parallel and Distributed Database Environments', *Proc. 18th Int. Conf. on VLDB*, Vancouver, 339–51, 1992
Description of mechanisms to allow rule systems to operate correctly in parallel and distributed DBS. Focus is on active database systems.

[Chamberlin *et al.* 1976] D. Chamberlin *et al.*, 'SEQUEL 2: A Unified Approach to Data Definition, Manipulation and Control', *IBM J. of Research and Development*, 20, 1976
Account of IBM's SEQUEL language, the precursor to SQL.

[Chamberlin *et al.* 1981] D. Chamberlin *et al.*, 'A History and Evaluation of System R', *CACM*, 24 (10), 632
Overview of IBM's System R project, which formed the basis for the development of DB2. See also [Selinger et al. 1979]

[Chen 1976] P. Chen, 'The Entity-Relationship Model: Towards a Unified View of Data', *ACM TODS*, 1 (1), 1976.
Original description of the ER model.

[Chen *et al.* 1994] P.M. Chen, E.K. Lee, G.A. Gibson, R.H. Katz and D.A. Patterson, 'RAID: High-Performance, Reliable Secondary Storage', *ACM Computing. Surveys*, 26, 145–86, 1994
Recent comprehensive survey of RAID technology.

[Chou *et al.* 1986] H. Chou, D. DeWitt, R. Katz and A. Klug, 'Design and Implementation of the Wisconsin Storage System', *Software: Practice and Experience*, 15 (10), 1985
Describes WiSS, used subsequently as the storage manager component of O_2.

[Clifford and Warren 1983] J. Clifford and D.S. Warren, 'Formal Semantics for Time in Databases', *ACM TODS*, 8, 212–54, 1983
Thorough, fairly formal, approach to temporal issues.

[Clifford 1990]   J. Clifford, *Formal Semantics and Pragmatics for Natural Language Querying*, Cambridge Tracts in Theoretical Computer Science 8, CUP, 1990
Formal exposition of a temporal data model based on intensional logic.

[Clocksin and Mellish 1981]   W. Clocksin and C. Mellish, *Programming in Prolog*, Springer-Verlag, Berlin, 1981
Classic introduction to the Prolog programming language.

[Coad and Yourdon 1991a]   P. Coad and E. Yourdon, *Object Oriented Analysis*, Yourdon Press, 1991

[Coad and Yourdon 1991b]   P. Coad and E. Yourdon, *Object Oriented Design*, Yourdon Press, 1991
Coad and Yourdon's approach to OOAD in two volumes. Adopts a practitioner's approach and style. They use their own terms for many techniques better known by other names.

[Codd 1970]   E. Codd, 'A Relational Model of Data for Large Shared Databanks', *CACM*, 13, 377–87, 1970
Paper that first proposed the relational model.

[Codd 1979]   E. Codd, 'Extending the relational database model to capture more meaning', *ACM TODS*, 4 (4), 1979
Reviews the relational model and introduces RM/T. This include several extensions to the original model addressing issues such as identity and generalization.

[Codd 1985a]   E. Codd, 'Is your DBMS really relational?' *Computer World*, October 14th, 1985.

[Codd 1985b]   E. Codd, 'Does your DBMS run by the rules?' *Computer World*, October 21st, 1985.
Popular summaries of Codd's twelve rules for the correct functioning of relational systems.

[Codd 1986]   E. Codd, 'An evaluation scheme for database management systems that are claimed to be relational', *Proc. IEEE CS International Conference on Data Engineering*, Los Angeles, 1986
A more detailed presentation of Codd's twelve rules.

[Comer 1979]   D. Comer, 'The Ubiquitous B-Tree', *ACM Computing Surveys*, 11, 121–37, 1979
Definitive description and nomenclature for B-trees. Describes all the variations.

[Copeland *et al.* 1989] G. Copeland, T. Keller, R. Krishnamurthy and M. Smith, 'The Case for Safe RAM', *Proc. 15th Int. Conf. on VLDB*, Amsterdam, 327–35, 1989
Systematic enumeration of the advantages of stable memory.

[Dadam and Linnemann 1989] P. Dadam and V. Linneman, 'Advanced Information Management (AIM): Advanced Database Technology for Integrated Applications', *IBM Systems Journal*, 28 (4), 1989
Description of a prototype DBS based on Non-First Normal Form relations.

[Date 1984] C. Date, 'A critique of the SQL database language', *ACM SIGMOD Record*, 14 (3), 8–54, 1984
Describes shortcomings in an early form of SQL. Most have been addressed in more recent versions.

[Date 1994] C.J. Date, *Introduction to Database Systems (6th ed.)*, Addison-Wesley, 1994
Latest revision of this textbook; contains a full description of normalization for database design.

[Date and Darwen 1993] C.J. Date and H. Darwen, *A Guide to the SQL Standard*, Addison-Wesley, 1993.
Concise description of the SQL 2 standard.

[Dearle *et al.* 1989] A. Dearle, R. Connor, F. Brown and R. Morrison, 'Napier88 – A Database Programming Language?', *Proc. 2nd Int. Workshop on Database Programming Languages*, 179–95, 1989
Description of Napier88, the successor to PS-Algol.

[DEC 1991] Digital Equipment Corporation, *Building Dependable Systems: The VMS Approach*, Part No AA-PH62A-TE, Digital Equipment Corporation, Maynard, Massachusetts, November 1991
A thorough coverage of reliability issues including operating procedures hardware and software. Describes Digital's approach to building fault-tolerant VAX systems.

[DEC 1993] Digital Equipment Corporation, *DSP3000L Series 3.5-inch Disk Drives: Installation Guide*, Order number EK–RH3CA–IG.A01, June 1993
Specification and installation instructions for a typical small disk drive.

[Delobel *et al.* 1995]   C. Delobel, C. Lecluse and P. Richard, *Databases: From Relational to Object-Oriented Systems*, International Thompson Publishing, 1995
Overview of object-oriented databases, with an emphasis on languages; contains a good summary of O_2.

[DeMarco 1978]   T. DeMarco, *Structured Analysis and System Specification*, Yourdon, New York, 1978
Classic structured systems analysis text; contains a good account of DFDs.

[DeMarco 1982]   T. DeMarco, *Controlling Software Projects*, Addison-Wesley, 1982
Classic text on software project management.

[DeWitt 1993]   D.J. DeWitt, 'The Wisconsin Benchmark: Past, Present and Future', *in* [Gray 1993]
Description of the history, development and current role of this benchmark.

[DeWitt *et al.* 1984]   D.J. DeWitt, R.H. Katz, F. Olken, L.D. Shapiro, M.R. Stonebraker and D. Wood, 'Implementation Techniques for Main Memory Database Systems', *Proc. ACM SIGMOD Int. Conf. on Management of Data,* 1–8, 1984
The first published account of Group Commit.

[DeWitt *et al.* 1990]   D.J. DeWitt, S. Ghandeharizadeh, D. Schneider, A. Bricker, H.I. Hsiao and R. Rasmussen, 'The Gamma Database Machine Project', *IEEE Trans. on Data and Knowledge Engineering*, 2 (1), 44–53, 1990
Overview and summary of the Gamma database machine project at the University of Wisconsin.

[DeWitt and Gerber 1985]   D.J. DeWitt and R. Gerber, 'Multiprocessor Hash-Based Join Algorithms', *Proc. 11th Int. Conf. on VLDB*, Stockholm, 151–64, 1985
Description and analysis of hash-based join algorithms showing their importance and utility for parallel DBS.

[Dittrich 1990]   K. Dittrich, 'Object Oriented Databases: the next miles of the marathon', *Information Systems*, 15 (3), 161–68, 1990
Clear description of ODBS based on sharing/independence and structural/behavioural object orientation.

[Dreger 1989]   B. Dreger, *Function Point Analysis*, Prentice Hall, Englewood Cliffs NJ, 1989
Description of Function Points, probably the most widely used method of software cost estimation.

[Eswaran *et al.* 1976] K. Eswaran, J. Gray, R. Lorie and I. Traiger, 'The notions of consistency and predicate locks in a database system', *CACM*, 19 (11), 624–32, 1976
Original definition of consistency levels for DBS.

[Fagin 1979] R. Fagin, 'Normal Forms and Relational Database Operators', *Proc. ACM SIGMOD Int. Conf. on Management of Data,* 1979
Description of classic normalization theory; introduced 5NF.

[Garcia-Molina and Salem 1987] H. Garcia-Molina and K. Salem, 'Sagas', *Proc. ACM SIGMOD Int. Conf. on Management of Data,* 249–59, 1987
Clear account of long transaction issues.

[Gardarin and Valduriez 1989] G. Gardarin and P. Valduriez, *Relational Databases and Knowledge Bases*, Addison- Wesley, 1989
Contains a useful description of deductive databases and (logic) rule processing.

[Gawlick *et al.* 1989] D. Gawlick, M. Haynie and A. Reuter (eds.), *High Performance Transaction Systems: Proc. 2nd Int. Workshop 1987, LNCS 359,* Springer-Verlag, 1989
Collection of papers describing high performance techniques of the mid-1980s. Contains descriptions of several successful commercial systems. Most subsequent work on high performance systems has concentrated on parallel machines.

[Graefe 1993] G. Graefe, 'Query Evaluation Techniques for Large Databases', *ACM Computing Surveys*, 25, 73–170, 1993
Comprehensive survey of query processing issues.

[Graefe and DeWitt 1987] G. Graefe and D.J. DeWitt, 'The EXODUS Optimizer Generator', *Proc. ACM SIGMOD Int. Conf. on Management of Data,* 160–72 , 1987
Contains the classification of query processing trees.

[Gray 1978] J. Gray, 'Notes on Database Operating Systems', *Operating Systems: An Advanced Course*, LNCS 60, Springer-Verlag
Classic description of the principal issues that are faced in transaction management.

[Gray 1981] J. Gray, 'The Transaction Concept: Virtues and Limitations', *Proc. 7th Int. Conf. on VLDB,* Cannes, 144–54, IEEE, 1981
Clear early description of the concept of a database transaction and related issues.

[Gray 1991]   J. Gray (ed.) *The Benchmark Handbook*, Morgan Kaufmann, 1991

[Gray 1993]   J. Gray (ed.) *The Benchmark Handbook (2nd ed.)*, Morgan Kaufmann, 1993
Essential reading for anybody involved in database benchmarking. Discussion of database benchmarking techniques, history and specifications of a number of important database benchmarks. Updated from the 1991 edition.

[Gray *et al.* 1976]   J. Gray, R.A. Lorie, G.R. Putzolu and I.L. Traiger, 'Granularity of Locks and Consistency in a Shared Data Base', *in* [Nijssen 1976], 365–95
Introduces intention locks and lock escalation.

[Gray and Reuter 1993] J. Gray and A. Reuter, *Transaction Processing: Concepts and Limitations*, Morgan-Kaufmann, 1993
Comprehensive account of transaction processing issues, including much valuable material on transaction processing monitors.

[Guttmann 1984]   A. Guttman, 'R-Trees: A Dynamic Index Structure for Spatial Searching', *Proc. ACM SIGMOD Int. Conf. on Management of Data,* 47–57, 1984
Original description of R-trees. See also [Sellis et al. 1987] and [Beckmann et al. 1990]

[Haas *et al.* 1990]   L. Haas *et al.*, ' Starburst mid-flight: As the dust clears', *IEEE Trans. on Data and Knowledge Engineering*, 2, 143–60, 1990
Overview of the progress and issues facing the Starburst project at IBM.

[Haerder and Reuter 1983] T. Haerder and A. Reuter, 'Principles of Transaction-Oriented Database Recovery', *ACM Computing Surveys*, 15 (4), 287–317, 1983
Gives the basic framework for disk-based recovery strategies.

[Hammer and   M. Hammer and D. McLeod, 'Database Description
McLeod 1981]   with SDM: a Semantic Database Model', *ACM TODS*, 6 (3),1981.
Influential early work on semantic data modelling.

[Hanson 1992]   E. Hanson, 'Rule Condition Testing and Action Execution in Ariel', *Proc. ACM SIGMOD Int. Conf. on Management of Data,* 49–58, May 1992.
Describes rule condition testing and rule execution in the Ariel active DBMS.

[Harel 1987]   D. Harel, 'Statecharts: A Visual Formalism for Complex
                      Systems', *Science of Computer Programming*, 8, 231–74,
                      1987
                      Classic paper giving Harel's definition of statecharts.

[Harel 1992]   D. Harel, *Algorithmics: The Spirit of Computing*,
                      Addison- Wesley, 1992
                      Clear modern treatment of algorithm design and analysis.

[Haworth *et al.* 1990]   G. Haworth, C. Hammer and M. Reeve, 'The European
                      Declarative System, Database and Languages', *IEEE
                      Micro*, 1990, 21–30, 1990
                      Early paper giving an overview of the EDS system.

[Houtsma and Apers 1990] M.A.W. Houtsma and P.M.G. Apers, 'Data and
                      Knowledge Model: A Proposal', in F. Bancilhon and P.
                      Buneman (eds.) *Advances in Database Programming
                      Languages*, ACM Press, New York, 1990
                      *Presents the DK model for deductive and active systems in
                      which knowledge rules/constraints are defined as virtual
                      attributes of entities and relationships.*

[Hsiao 1992a]   D.K. Hsiao, 'Federated Databases and Systems: Part I –
                      A Tutorial on Their Data Sharing', *VLDB Journal*, 1,
                      127–79, 1992

[Hsiao 1992b]   D.K. Hsiao, 'Federated Databases and Systems: Part II–
                      A Tutorial on Their Resource Consolidation', *VLDB
                      Journal*, 2, 285–310, 1992
                      *Two-part tutorial on federated systems. Contains some useful
                      material.*

[Hull and King 1987] R. Hull and R. King, 'Semantic Database Modelling:
                      Survey, Applications and Research Issues', *ACM
                      Computing Surveys*, 19 (3), September 1987
                      Survey of research and development in semantic modelling.

[Hutt 1994]   A.T.F. Hutt (ed.), *Object analysis and design: Description
                      of methods*, Wiley, New York, 1994
                      *Survey and summary description of a large number of OOAD
                      methods.*

[ICL 1993]   ICL, *Goldrush Technical Overview (ref. B93/307)*, ICL
                      Corporate Systems, Manchester, 1993
                      *Goldrush is a parallel shared nothing system developed from the
                      ESPRIT EDS project prototype.*

[Illustra 1994]   *Illustra User's Guide: Server Release 2.1*, Illustra Information Technologies, Inc., Oakland, June 1994
Illustra is a recently introduced commercial system with many extended relational features, with its origins in the POSTGRES project.

[INGRES 1989]   INGRES, *INGRES Object Management Users Guide*, ASK/INGRES Technical Manual 63-9(9)-47301, Release 6.3, November 1989

[INGRES 1991a]   INGRES, *Using INGRES Through Forms and Menus*, ASK/INGRES Technical Manual 64-9(9)-47912, Release 6.4, December 1991

[INGRES 1991b]   INGRES, *INGRES/SQL Reference Manual*, ASK/INGRES Technical Manual 64-9(9)-47101, Release 6.4, December 1991
INGRES is one of the major commercial relational DBMSs.

[ISO 1992]   *ISO,Database Language SQL*, ISO Tech/9075, 1992
The SQL 92 standard. Also published as: The Database Language-SQL, American National Standards Institute, ANSI Document X3.135-1992.

[Jacobson *et al.* 1992]   I.Jacobson, M. Christerson, P. Jonsson and G. Overgaard, *Object-Oriented Software Engineering*, Addison-Wesley, 1992
Description of Use-Case method.

[Jain 1991]   R. Jain, *The Art of Computer Systems Performance Analysis*, John Wiley, New York, 1991
Comprehensive introduction to performance evaluation techniques.

[Kemper and Moerkotte 1990]   A. Kemper and J. Moerkotte, 'Advanced query processing in object bases using access support relations', *Proc. 16th Int. Conf. on VLDB*, Brisbane, 290–301, 1990
An example of the use of ancillary data structures to aid composite object retrieval.

[Kersten and Kwakkel 1993]   M.L. Kersten and F. Kwakkel, 'The Software Testpilot', *Proc. DEXA 93: 4th Inf. Conf. on Database and Expert Systems* Prague, 1993
Example of a modern software tool for configuration and performance evaluation.

[Kiernan *et al.* 1990] J. Kiernan, C. de Maindeville and E. Simon, 'Making Deductive Database a Practical Technology', *Proc. ACM SIGMOD Int. Conf. on Management of Data*, 237–46, 1990
Describes the deductive database language RDL1, see also [*Simon* et al. *1992*].

[Kim and Lochovsky 1989] W. Kim and F. Lochovsky (eds.), *Object Oriented Concepts, Databases and Applications*, ACM Press Frontier Series (Addison-Wesley), 1989
Collection of papers covering research in object-oriented systems, many of which are concerned with object-oriented DBS.

[Kim 1989] W. Kim, 'A model of queries for object-oriented databases', *Proc. 15th Int. Conf. on VLDB*, Amsterdam, 423–32, 1989
Describes a query model for ODBS.

[Kim *et al.* 1989] W. Kim, J-M. Nicolas and S. Nishio (eds.), *First International Conference on Object-Oriented and Deductive Databases*, Kyoto, Japan, 1989
Concentrates on object-oriented and deductive DBS.

[Kim 1994] W. Kim, 'Observations on the ODMG-93 Proposal', *ACM SIGMOD Record*, 23 (1), 4–9, 1994
Critical review of the ODMG-93 work (see also [*ODMG 1994*]).

[Kulkarni 1994] K.G. Kulkarni, 'Object-Oriented Extensions in SQL3: A Status Report', *Proc. ACM SIGMOD Int. Conf. on Management of Data*, 478, 1994
A single page summary of OO features in the SQL3 draft.

[Kumar and Stonebraker 1987] V. Kumar and M. Stonebraker, 'The Effect of Join Selectivities on Optimal Nesting Order', *ACM SIGMOD Record*, 16 (1), 28-41, 1987
Results of a series of experiments to investigate query sensitivity to errors in selectivity estimates.

[Lehman and Lindsay 1989] T. Lehman and B. Lindsay, 'The Starburst Long Field Manager', *Proc. 15th Int. Conf. on VLDB*, Amsterdam, 1989
Description of large object management in Starburst.

[Leutenegger and   S.T. Leutenegger and D. Dias, 'A Modeling Study of the
Dias 1993]   TPC-C Benchmark', *Proc. ACM SIGMOD Int. Conf. on
                        Management of Data*, 22–31, 1993
                        *Analytical model, useful as a source of numbers for TPC-C and
                        approach to analytical modelling.*

[Leveson and Turner 1993] N.G. Leveson and C.S. Turner, 'An Investigation of the
                        Therac-25 Accidents', *Computer*, 26 (7), 18–41, 1993
                        Clear account of the problems and issues.

[Levine *et al.* 1992] J. Levine, T. Mason and D. Brown, *Lex and Yacc*,
                        O'Reilly and Associates, 1992
                        *Description of parsing with the UNIX tools Lex and Yacc; uses
                        SQL as the example language.*

[Litwin 1980]   W. Litwin, 'Linear Hashing: A new tool for file and table
                        addressing', *Proc. 6th Int. Conf. on VLDB*, Montreal,
                        1980
                        *Original linear hashing paper, gives a clear account of the basic
                        algorithms.*

[Lynch *et al.* 1994] N. Lynch, M. Merritt, W. Weihl and A. Fekete, *Atomic
                        Transactions*, Morgan Kaufmann, 1994
                        *Formal treatment of serializability and concurrency, based on
                        I/O automata.*

[Maier 1989]   D. Maier, 'Making Database Systems Fast Enough for
                        CAD Applications', *in* [Kim and Lochovsky 1989],
                        573–82
                        *Discusses the limitations of conventional DBS in CAD
                        applications, enumerates the benefits of an object-oriented
                        approach and outlines several research questions.*

[Manifesto 1990]   The Committee for Advanced DBMS Function, 'Third-
                        Generation Database System Manifesto', *ACM
                        SIGMOD Record*, 19 (3), 31–44, 1990
                        *A proposal giving a broad vision of what the next generation of
                        database systems should be, formulated by a group of experts
                        led by Stonebraker (the Committee for Advanced DBMS
                        Function). Presents an alternative view to that of [Atkinson et
                        al. 1989] in which the next generation of DBS are developed
                        by extending current relational technology.*

[Mayhew and   P.J. Mayhew and P.A. Dearnley, 'Prototyping Classifica-
Dearnley 1987]   tion: An alternative Approach', *Computer J.* 30 (6),
                        481–84, 1987
                        Clear description of the different types of prototyping.

[McCarthy and Dayal 1989]   D.R. McCarthy and U. Dayal, 'The Architecture of an Active Database Management System', *Proc. ACM SIGMOD Int. Conf. on Management of Data*, 215–24, 1989
Describes the specification and implementation of rules in HiPAC.

[Microsoft 1994]   Microsoft, *Microsoft ODBC 2.0 Programmer's Reference and SDK Guide*, Microsoft Press, 1994
Reference manual for the ODBC API.

[Mishra and Eich 1992]   P. Mishra and M.H. Eich, 'Join Processing in Relational Databases', *ACM Computing Surveys*, 24, 63–113, 1992
Good recent survey of join algorithms and their performance characteristics.

[Monarchi and Puhr 1992]   D.E. Monarchi and G.I. Puhr, 'A Research Typology for Object-Oriented Analysis and Design', *CACM*, 35 (9), 35–47, 1992
Contains an analysis and comparison of OOAD methods.

[Mosher 1992]   C. Mosher (ed.), 1992, *The POSTGRES Reference Manual, Version 4*, UCB Technical Report M92/14, Electronics Research Laboratory, University of California at Berkeley, 1992
POSTGRES is an experimental extended relational DBS developed at UCB, see also [Stonebraker and Rowe 1986].

[Newmann 1992]   S. Newmann, 'Multi-Vendor Interoperability Through SQL Access', *Proc. ACM SIGMOD Int. Conf. on Management of Data*, 414, 1992
Single page summary of the work of the SQL Access Group.

[Nievergeldt *et al.* 1984]   J. Nievergeldt, H. Hintenberger and K.C. Sevcik, 'The Grid File: An Adaptable, Symmetric Multi-Key File Structure', *ACM TODS*, 9 (1), 38–71, 1984
Original description of grid files. A clear account of the basics.

[Nijssen 1976]   G.M. Nijssen (ed.), *Modelling in Data Base Management Systems*, Elsevier North-Holland, 1976
Early edited volume containing several historically important papers on modelling.

[Obermarck 1982]   R. Obermarck, 'Distributed Deadlock Detection Algorithms', *ACM TODS*, 7 (2), 187–208, 1982
Description, proof and performance analysis for distributed deadlock detection based on detecting cycles in the waits-for graph.

[ODMG 1994]   ODMG, 'Response to the March 1994 ODMG Commentary', *ACM SIGMOD Record*, 23 (3), 3–7, 1994
Rejoinder to [Kim 1994].

[Olson 1993]   M.A. Olson, 'The design and implementation of the Inversion File System', *Proc. of the Winter USENIX Conference 1993*', San Diego, 1993
Description of one (of two) methods for supporting large objects in POSTGRES, see also [Stonebraker and Olson 1993].

[O'Neil 1986]   P. O'Neil, 'The Escrow Transaction Method', *ACM TODS*, 11, 405–30, 1986
Describes a method for avoiding bottlenecks by allowing 'hot spots' to be updated using a non-blocking protocol. Rollbacks are handled by compensating transactions.

[Orenstein 1986] J. Orenstein, 'Spatial Query Processing in an Object-Oriented Database System', *Proc. ACM SIGMOD Int. Conf. on Management of Data*, 326–36, 1986
Introduces the use of z-order for spatial data storage and indexing.

[Orenstein and Manola 1988] J. Orenstein and F. Manola, 'PROBE Spatial Data Modeling and Query Processing in an Image Database Application', *IEEE Trans. on Software Engineering*, 14 (5), 611-629, 1988
Description of z-order algorithms.

[Patterson *et al.* 1988] D. Patterson, G. Gibson and R. Katz, 'A case for redundant arrays of inexpensive disks (RAID)', *Proc. ACM SIGMOD Int. Conf. on Management of Data*, 109–16, 1988.
Classic definition of RAID architectures.

[Pu 1986]   C. Pu, 'On-the-Fly, Incremental, Consistent Reading of Entire Databases', *Algorithmica*, 1, 271–87, 1986
Original description of black-and-white algorithms.

[Rational 1993] Rational, *Rational Rose Analysis and Design*, (Software package), Rational, Santa Clara, California, 1993
CASE tool for object-oriented design using the Booch method, see also [Booch 1994].

[Reuter 1984]   A. Reuter, 'Performance Analysis of Recovery Techniques', *ACM TODS*, 9, 526–59, 1984
Classic paper describing log-based recovery methods; very informative but not to be tackled lightly. Uses a different terminology from this book.

[Richardson *et al.* 1993] J. Richardson, M. Carey and D. Schuh, ' The Design of the E Programming Language', *ACM TOPLAS,* 15 (3), 1993
Describes the E language, an extended form of C++, used to implement extensions to EXODUS.

[Rubin and Goldberg 1992] K.S. Rubin and A. Goldberg, 'Object Behaviour Analysis', *CACM* , 35 (9), 48–62, 1992
Description of OBA method, with some interesting examples.

[Ruemmler and Wilkes 1994] C. Ruemmler and J. Wilkes, 'An Introduction to Disk Drive Modelling', *IEEE Computer,* 27 (3), 17–28, 1994
Describes techniques for modelling performance of modern small disk drives.

[Rumbaugh *et al.* 1991] J. Rumbaugh, M. Blaha, W. Premerlani, F. Eddy and W. Lorensen, *Object-Oriented Modeling and Design,* Prentice-Hall, Englewood Cliffs NJ, 1991
Important statement of the evolutionary approach to object–oriented analysis and design, c.f. [Booch 1994].

[Sacco and Schkolnick 1986] G.M. Sacco and M. Schkolnick ,'Buffer Management in Relational Database Systems', *ACM TODS,* 11, 473–98, 1986
Description of the main strategies for database buffer management.

[Salem *et al.* 1989] K. Salem, H. Garcia-Molina and R. Alonso, 'Altruistic Locking: A Strategy for Coping with Long Lived Transactions', in [Gawlick *et al.* 1989]
Description of the notion of long-lived transactions that allow shorter transactions to follow, using uncommitted data.

[Salem *et al.* 1994] K. Salem, H. Garcia-Molina and J. Shands, 'Altruistic Locking', ACM TODS, 19 (1), 117–65
Description of altruistic locking, including proof and implementation experiments.

[Salem and Molina 1990] K. Salem and H. Garcia-Molina, 'System M: A Transaction Processing Testbed for Memory-Resident Data', *IEEE Trans. on Data Engineering,* 2 (1), 161–72
Good description of memory-based recovery techniques and performance, particularly black-white checkpointing.

[Samet 1989a] H. Samet, *The Design and Analysis of Spatial Data Structures,* Addison-Wesley, 1989

[Samet 1989b]   H. Samet, *Applications of Spatial Data Structures: Computer Graphics, Image Processing, and GIS*, Addison-Wesley, 1989
                        Two volumes providing a thorough coverage of multi-dimensional data structures and their applications.

[Schneider and   D.A. Schneider and D.J. DeWitt, 'Tradeoffs in Pro-
DeWitt 1990]   cessing Complex Join Queries via Hashing in Multi-processor Database Machines' *Proc 16th Int. Conf. on VLDB*, Brisbane 469–80, 1990

[Schwiderski and   S. Schwiderski and G. Saake, 'Expressing Temporal
Saake 1994]   Behaviour with Extended ECA Rules', *in* D. Bowers (ed.) *Directions in Databases: Proc. of the 12th British National Conference on Databases, BNCOD 12, Guildford, UK*, LNCS 826, Springer Verlag, Berlin, 1994
                        Describes initialized temporal ECA rules (IT-ECA) with conditions expressed as past-directed temporal logic (PTA) formulae.

[Selinger *et al.* 1979]   P. Selinger *et al.*, 'Access path selection in a relational database management system', *Proc. ACM SIGMOD Int. Conf. on Management of Data*, 23–35, 1979
                        Description of the query optimization strategies employed in System R. See also [Chamberlin et al. 1976, 1981].

[Sellis *et al.* 1987]   T. Sellis, N. Roussopoulus and C. Faloutsos, 'The R+-tree: A dynamic index for multi-dimensional objects', *Proc. 13th Int. Conf. on VLDB*, Brighton, 507–18, 1987
                        Description of an R-tree variant, the R+tree. See also [Guttmann 1984] and [Beckmann et al. 1990]

[Serlin 1991]   O. Serlin, 'The History of DebitCredit and the TPC', *in* [Gray 1991]
                        An account of the motivation of the Transaction Processing Council and the specification of the TPC-A and TPC-B benchmarks.

[Sheth and Larson 1990] A.P. Sheth and J.A. Larson, 'Federated Database Systems for Managing Distributed, Heterogeneous, and Autonomous Databases', *ACM Computing Surveys*, 22 (3), 183–236
                        Survey and description of a reference architecture for FDBS.

[Shipman 1981]   D. Shipman, 'The Functional Data Model and the Data Language DAPLEX', *ACM TODS*, 6 (1), 1981.
                        Describes one of the best known examples of a functional data model.

[Simon *et al.* 1992] E. Simon, J. Kiernan and C. de Maindeville, 'Implementing High Level Active Rules on top of a Relational DBMS', *Proc. of the 18th Very Large Data Bases Conference*, Vancouver, 315–26, 1992
Describes extensions to the RDLI (see [Kiernan et al. 1990]) deductive database language to handle active rules.

[Smith and Krabbe 1992] D.J. Smith and J. Krabbe, *Database Tests Using the AS3AP Benchmark*, UEA School of Information Systems Technical Report, SYS92-19, 1992
Description of benchmarking experiences and results, using the AS3AP benchmark.

[Sneath and Sokal 1973] P.H.A. Sneath and R. Sokal, *Numerical Taxonomy*, Freeman, London, 1973
Account of classical quantitative approaches to classification, from a biological perspective.

[Snodgrass, 1987] R. Snodgrass, 'The Temporal Query Language TQUEL', *ACM TODS*, 12, 247–98, 1987
A clear account of temporal database issues, showing how an existing query language can be adapted to incorporate temporal queries.

[Snodgrass and Ahn 1985] R. Snodgrass and I. Ahn, 'A Taxonomy of Time in Databases', *Proc. ACM SIGMOD Int. Conf. on Management of Data*, 236–46, 1985
Discussion of the semantics and representation of time. Covers transaction, valid and user time.

[Snodgrass *et al.* 1994a] R.T. Snodgrass *et al.*, *TSQL2 Language Specification*, published electronically, available via anonymous FTP from ftp.cs.arizona.edu.
Proposal for temporal extensions to SQL. See also ACM SIGMOD Record, March and September 1994.

[Snodgrass *et al.* 1994b] R.T. Snodgrass *et al.*, 'A TSQL2 Tutorial' *ACM SIGMOD Record*, 23 (3), 27–34, September 1994.
Description of a set of SQL extensions to provide temporal capabilities in the query language.

[Stonebraker *et al.* 1976] M. Stonebraker, E. Wong, P. Kreps and G. Held, 'The Design and Implementation of INGRES', *ACM TODS*, 1 (3), 1976
Description of the original INGRES project at Berkeley.

[Stonebraker 1981]
M. Stonebraker, 'Operating System Support for Database Management', *CACM*, 24 (7), 412–18
Critique of several features of the filesystems of UNIX-like operating systems.

[Stonebraker and Rowe 1986]
M. Stonebraker and L. Rowe, 'The Design of POSTGRES', *Proc. ACM SIGMOD Int. Conf. on Management of Data,* 1986
The initial design of POSTGRES, covering the requirements for extensibility, rule support, and so on, while minimising changes to the relational model.

[Stonebraker *et al.* 1987]
M. Stonebraker, E. Hanson and C-H. Hong, 'The Design of the POSTGRES Rules System', *IEEE International Conference on Data Engineering*, 356–74, 1987
Description of the first version of the POSTGRES rules system.

[Stonebraker *et al.* 1988]
M. Stonebraker, R. Katz, D. Patterson and J. Ousterhout, 'The Design of XPRS', *Proc. 14th Int. Conf. on VLDB*, Los Angeles, 318–30, 1988
Description of the XPRS shared-memory parallel database system, built at Berkeley.

[Stonebraker *et al.* 1990a]
M. Stonebraker, L. Rowe and M. Hirohama, 'The Implementation of POSTGRES', *IEEE Transactions on Knowledge and Data Engineering*, 2, 1, March 1990
Reflections on the design and implementation of POSTGRES and the query language POSTQUEL.

[Stonebraker *et al.* 1990b]
M. Stonebraker, A. Jhingran, J. Goh and S. Potamianos, 'On Rules, Procedures, Caching and Views in Data Base Systems', *Proc. ACM SIGMOD Int. Conf. on Management of Data,* 281–90, 1990
Description of the second version of the POSTGRES rules system covering the use of rules to support a wide range of database functions.

[Stonebraker and Olson 1993]
M. Stonebraker and M.A. Olson, 1993, 'Large object support in POSTGRES', *Proc. of the 9th International Conference on Data Engineering*, Vienna, Austria, April 1993
Description of two approaches to supporting large objects in POSTGRES, see also [Olson 1993].

[Tandem 1989]   Tandem Database Group, 'Nonstop SQL: A distributed, high-performance, high-reliability implementation of SQL', *in* [Gawlick *et al.* 1989], 60–104
Description of the Tandem architecture, one of the first commercially successful high performance fault-tolerant systems.

[Tansel *et al.* 1993]   A. Tansel, J. Clifford, S. Gadia, S. Jajodia, A. Segev and R. Snodgrass, *Temporal Databases: Theory, Design and Implementation*, Benjamin-Cummings, Redwood City, California, 1993
Collection of papers providing a thorough coverage of temporal issues.

[Teorey 1993]   T.J. Teorey, *Database Modeling and Design*, Morgan Kaufmann, San Mateo, 1993
Good sections on distributed database design. First edition was 1990.

[Teorey *et al.* 1986]   T.J. Teorey, D. Yang and J.P. Fry, 'A Logical Design Methodology for Relational Databases Using the Extended Entity-Relationship Model', *ACM Computing Surveys*, 18 (2), 197–222, 1986
Definition of the EER model and its use, consolidating several piecemeal extensions to the model in [Chen 1976].

[Teradata 1985]   DBC/1012 Database Computer System manual release 2.0, Teradata Corp., Document No C10-0001-02.

[Tschritzis and Klug 1978] D. Tschritzis and A. Klug (eds.), 'The ANSI/X3/SPARC DBMS Framework: Report of the Study Group on Database Management Systems', *Information Systems*, 3, 1978.
Report of the ANSI committee that drafted the three-level database architecture for relational systems.

[Turbyfill 1988]   C. Turbyfill, *Comparative Benchmarking of Relational Database Systems*, PhD Thesis, Cornell University, January 1988

[Turbyfill *et. al.* 1993] C. Turbyfill, C. Orji and D. Bitton, 'AS3AP – An ANSI Sequel Standard Scaleable and Portable Benchmark for Relational Database Systems', *in* [Gray 1993]
Descriptions of the AS3AP benchmark. The first of these gives the rationale for AS3AP, but the description has been significantly revised and clarified in the second.

[Udell 1993]   J. Udell, 'Start the Presses: CD-ROM Comes to the Desktop', *Byte* 18 (2), 1993, 116–38
Accessible overview of CD-ROM and related technology.

[Ullman 1988]   J.D. Ullman, *Principles of Database and Knowledge-Base Systems*, Volume 1, Computer Science Press, Rockville, Maryland, 1988

[Ullman 1989]   J.D. Ullman, *Principles of Database and Knowledge-Base Systems*, Volume 2, Computer Science Press, Rockville, Maryland, 1989
Comprehensive, formal treatment of data and knowledge-base management issues.

[Ullman 1991]   J.D. Ullman, 'A Comparison of Deductive and Object-Oriented Database Systems', *Proc. DOOD 91,* LNCS 566, 263-277, Springer-Verlag, 1991
Contrasts object-oriented and deductive approaches, arguing for the superiority of the latter.

[Valduriez 1987]   P. Valduriez, 'Join Indices', *ACM TODS*, 12 (2), 218–46, 1987
Description of ancillary data structures to speed up join processing. Also contains a description of storage model concepts.

[Valduriez 1992]   P. Valduriez (ed.), *Parallel Processing and Data Management,* Chapman and Hall, 1992
Collection of papers on issues and progress in parallel databases.

[Valduriez and   P. Valduriez and G. Gardarin,' Join and Semijoin
Gardarin 1984]   Algorithms for a Multiprocessor Database Machine', *ACM TODS*, 9, 133–61, 1984
Description and analysis of parallel join algorithms.

[Vonk 1990]   Vonk R, *Prototyping*, Prentice Hall, 1991
Good prototyping textbook.

[Weaver 1993]   P.L. Weaver, *Practical SSADM 4*, Pitman, London, 1993
A good modern account of the use of SSADM, the UK government-sponsored structured analysis and design method. See also [Ashworth and Goodland 1990].

[Widom and   J. Widom and S.J. Finkelstein, 'Set-oriented Production
Finkelstein 1990]   Rules in Relational Database Systems', *Proc. ACM SIGMOD Int. Conf. on Management of Data,* 259–70, 1990

[Widom *et al.* 1991]   J. Widom, R.J. Cochrane, and B.G. Lindsay, 'Implementing Set-oriented Production Rules as an Extension to Starburst', *Proc. of the 17th International Conference on Very Large Data Bases*, 275–85, Barcelona, 1991
Two papers describing the implementation of rules in Starburst.

[Wiederhold 1987]   G. Wiederhold, *File Organisation for Database Design*, McGraw-Hill, New York, 1987
Extensive coverage of design, implementation and performance of data file structures and access methods.

[Wirfs-Brock *et al.* 1990]   R. Wirfs-Brock, B. Wilkerson and L. Weiner, *Designing Object-Oriented Software*, Prentice Hall, Englewood Cliffs NJ, 1990
Focus on 'responsibility-driven' design.

[White and DeWitt 1994]   S.J. White and D.J. DeWitt, 'QuickStore: A High Performance Memory Mapped Object Store', *Proc. ACM SIGMOD Int. Conf. on Management of Data*, 395–406, 1994
Describes a memory mapped storage system built on top of the EXODUS Storage Manager (for which see [Carey et al. 1989]).

[Wong and Paci 1992]   K-F. Wong and M. Paci, 'Performance Evaluation of an OLTP Application on the EDS Database Server Using a Behavioural Simulation Model', *in* [Valduriez 1992]
Results of some of the simulation work done for the EDS project.

[Zdonik and Maier 1990]   S.B. Zdonik and D. Maier, *Readings in Object-Oriented Database Systems*, Morgan Kaufmann, San Mateo CA, 1990
Good collection of important ODBS papers.

[Zloof 1981]   M. Zloof, 'QBE/OBE: A Language for Office and Business Automation', *IEEE Computer*, 14 (5), 13-22, 1981
Describes the use of a 'form-filling' approach to ad hoc query specification.

INDEX